The
Territories of the
Russian Federation
2002

The
Territories of the Russian Federation
2002

3rd Edition

First published 1999

Third Edition 2002

© **Europa Publications Limited 2002**
11 New Fetter Lane, London, EC4P 4EE, United Kingdom
(A member of the Taylor & Francis Group)

ISBN 1-85743-142-1

ISSN 1465-461X

Imageset by MPG Dataworld and printed by Unwin Brothers Limited, The Gresham
Press, Old Woking, Surrey

Bound by MPG Books Limited, Bodmin, Cornwall

Foreword

The third edition of *The Territories of the Russian Federation* aims to present an insight into an aspect of modern Russia that must be grasped if the country as a whole is to be understood. Not only is it often forgotten that Russia is a federal state, but also that it is still actually emerging as a federal state; the balance of power between the centre and the federal subjects is not yet settled. Since the first edition of this book was published, Vladimir Putin has replaced Russia's first post-Soviet President, Boris Yeltsin, and the long-term consequences of Putin's efforts to consolidate the powers of regional governors and increase central dominance have still to be seen. Moreover, the diverging economic fortunes of the different territories present a further challenge to the structures of the state.

All the themes apparent in the Russian Federation overall are played out in its 89 constituent parts. Issues such as the balance of power between executive and legislative branches of government or the progress of market reforms are alive in the territories as much as in the national capital, Moscow. The shifting tides of personal politics reveal the same conflicting and concurrent flows, of liberalism and conservatism, of socialism and nationalism, and the attempts to balance the need for powerful supporters and the drift towards corruption.

This book is divided into four parts. Part One is an Introduction, with an authoritative article providing a context for regional politics and a description of the place of the territories in the national economy. There is also a Chronology of Russian history and politics, some invaluable statistics and information on the federal administration. The economic data clearly demonstrates the general trends of the economic situation. That time has only consolidated the differences between the regions is often made clear in the text of the Territorial Surveys. This, Part Two, is the heart of the book, with individual chapters on each of the 89 federal units. The geographical and historical background, the current political situation and an economic outline are reinforced by the names and contact details of the main officials in every territory. Each chapter includes a map of the federal unit, and there are, in addition, five maps covering wider geographical areas. A new section, the Select Bibliography of books, appears in Part Three, and the Indexes of Part Four provide an alphabetic listing (including alternative or historical names) of the territories and also group them according to their geographical location within the Federal Okrugs and Economic Areas into which Russia is divided. As a whole, this book aims to furnish a clear and comprehensive introduction to federal Russia's regions, without an understanding of which the world's largest country must remain opaque.

December 2001

Acknowledgements

The editors gratefully acknowledge the co-operation, interest and advice of all who have contributed to this volume. We are also indebted to many organizations within the Russian Federation, such as the territorial administrations that responded to our enquiries, and, particularly, to the State Committee of Statistics. We are very grateful to Eugene Fleury, who prepared the maps included in this book.

The authors of the introductory article, Professor Michael J. Bradshaw of the University of Leicester and Professor Philip Hanson of the University of Birmingham, have undertaken research focusing on the federal territories of Russia, and some of the fruits of their studies of a number of regional economies were published in 2000.

Contents

PART THREE

Select Bibliography

PART FOUR

Indexes

List of Maps

Abbreviations

Acad.	Academician; Academy	Feb.	February
AD	anno domini	Fr	Father
Adm.	Admiral	Fri.	Friday
a/o	avtonomnyi okrug (autonomous okrug)	ft	foot (feet)
AO	Autonomous Oblast	g	gram(s)
AOk	Autonomous Okrug	GDP	gross domestic product
ASSR	Autonomous Soviet Socialist Republic	Gen.	General
		GNP	gross national product
Aug.	August	Gov.	Governor
		Govt	Government
BC	before Christ	GRP	gross regional product
b/d	barrels per day		
Brig.	Brigadier	ha	hectares
		hl	hectolitre(s)
C	Centigrade		
c.	circa	IBRD	International Bank for Reconstruction and Development (World Bank)
Capt.	Captain		
CIS	Commonwealth of Independent States	IMF	International Monetary Fund
cm	centimetre(s)	in (ins)	inch (inches)
CMEA	Council for Mutual Economic Assistance	Inc, Incorp., Incd	Incorporated
Co	Company; County		
Col	Colonel	incl.	including
Commdr	Commander	Is	Islands
Commr	Commissioner		
Corpn	Corporation	Jan.	January
CP	Communist Party	Jr	Junior
CPSU	Communist Party of the Soviet Union		
		kg	kilogram(s)
cu	cubic	KGB	Komitet Gosudarstvennoi Bezopasnosti (Committee for State Security)
Dec.	December		
Dep.	Deputy	km	kilometre(s)
Dr	Doctor	kW	kilowatt(s)
		kWh	kilowatt hours
EBRD	European Bank for Reconstruction and Development	lb	pound(s)
EC	European Community	Lt, Lieut	Lieutenant
EEC	European Economic Community	Ltd	Limited
e.g.	exempli gratia (for example)		
e-mail	electronic mail	m	metre(s)
et al.	et alii (and others)	m.	million
etc.	et cetera	Maj.	Major
EU	European Union	mm	millimetre(s)
excl.	excluding	MWh	megawatt hour(s)
F	Fahrenheit	n.a.	not available
fax	facsimile	nab.	naberezhnaya (embankment, quai)

NATO	North Atlantic Treaty Organization	sel.	seleniyi (settlement)
NMP	net material product	Sept.	September
no.	number	sq	square (in measurements)
Nov.	November	SS	Saints
		SSR	Soviet Socialist Republic
obl.	oblast (region)	St	Saint
Oct.	October	Supt	Superintendent
OECD	Organisation for Economic Co-operation and Development	sv.	svetac (saint)
Ok	Okrug (district)	tel.	telephone
p.	page		
p.a.	per annum (yearly)	UK	United Kingdom
per.	pereulok (lane, alley)	ul.	ulitsa (street)
pl.	ploshchad (square)	UN	United Nations
PLC	Public Limited Company	UNDP	United Nations Development Programme
POB	Post Office Box		
pr.	prospekt (avenue)	UNEP	United Nations Environment Programme
Prof.	Professor		
prov.	provulok (lane)	USSR	Union of Soviet Socialist Republics
q.v.	quod vide (to which refer)		
		VAT	value-added tax
retd	retired	Ven.	Venerable
Rev.	Reverend	viz.	videlicet (namely)
RSFSR	Russian Soviet Federative Socialist Republic	vol.(s)	volume(s)
		yr	year

PART ONE
Introduction

The Territories and the Federation: An Economic Perspective

MICHAEL J. BRADSHAW and PHILIP HANSON

It is customary in Russia to speak of the Russian Federation as consisting of 89 'federal subjects'. To convey something of the reality of Russia's administrative regions, however, one must begin by emphasizing that these are not 89 units of equal status, nor is there comparable information on all of them. The status of one, the Chechen Republic of Ichkeriya (Chechnya), is in dispute, and socio-economic data for the Republic are not reported by the State Committee of Statistics of the Russian Federation (Goskomstat). Of the remaining 88, the 10 autonomous okrugs (AOks) and one autonomous oblast (AO) are, for most purposes, of lesser status than the 20 autonomous republics, 55 oblasts (regions) and krais (provinces) and two federal cities (Moscow and St Petersburg).

Nine of the autonomous okrugs (districts) officially form part of an oblast or krai. The Chukchi AOk, in the far north-east of Russia, facing the US state of Alaska, is an anomaly: it was taken out of Magadan Oblast in July 1992 and left as a free-standing okrug (free-standing, that is, in a purely administrative sense—in every other sense it was collapsing, and the population declined by approximately one-half between 1985 and 1999; its fortunes improved, however, with the election of the oligarch Roman Abramovich as Governor in late 2000). The inappropriately named Jewish Autonomous Oblast, of which only 4.2% of the population was Jewish (according to the 1989 census), was separated from Khabarovsk Krai in 1991. The main point about most of the 11 'lesser autonomies', as they might be called, is that they are remote, underdeveloped and sparsely populated territories of little consequence. A recent analysis by the Russian Ministry of Economy showed these regions to be among the poorest in contemporary Russia. Many of the regional statistics available do not cover them separately. We shall, therefore, in this article refer mainly to the 77 territories with the status of autonomous republic, krai, oblast or federal city. These 77 can, generically, be labelled as 'regions'. Inconveniently, however, among the autonomous okrugs there are exceptions that are of great economic consequence. The most obvious examples are the Khanty Mansii and Yamal-Nenets AOks; these are two isolated, undeveloped and sparsely inhabited districts in Western Siberia, which happen to be floating on oceans of petroleum and natural gas. As might be expected, their local politicians are considerably more assertive than their counterparts in the other lesser autonomies. As a result, the nature of their administrative, electoral and fiscal relations with Tyumen Oblast, of which they form a part, is a matter of ongoing dispute and negotiation. Following the election, in March 2000, of President Vladimir Putin, it was thought that he might simplify the federal structure by abolishing the autonomous okrugs and merging them with the regions to which they were subordinate—this might be welcomed by the poorer autonomous okrugs, which would benefit from greater budgetary support in a larger federal subject; however, rich regions, such as Khanty Mansii and Yamal Nenets, were bound to resist the loss of autonomy. Although by late 2001 rumours continued to persist, no action had been taken.

In May 2000 the territorial–administrative structure was modified. President Putin issued an edict (*ukaz*) establishing another layer of administration: seven federal okrugs covering the whole country and headed by centrally appointed presidential representatives. The creation of these seven okrugs (Central—based in the capital, Moscow, North-Western—based in St Petersburg, Volga—based in Nizhnii Novgorod, Southern—initially named North Caucasus and based in Rostov-on-Don, Urals—based in Yekaterinburg, Siberian—based in Novosibirsk, and Far Eastern—based in Khabarovsk) was part of a package of measures designed to curtail the autonomy of regional leaders. Moreover, the governors and heads of regional parliaments were removed from the upper house of the national legislature, the Federation Council, and in September a new State Council was created to provide a means by which governors could advise the President on regional issues. The presidium of the Council, which consists of the President and one governor from each of the seven Federal Okrugs, rotates every six months. The implications will be considered below.

In the remainder of this essay we shall first describe the evolving status of the Russian federal territories and their relations with the central Government; then review the differences in the economic development levels and production structures they inherited from the Soviet past; next discuss the different economic trajectories that different regions have followed since 1991; then look at the differences in economic conditions among them and their greatly differing investment potential; and, finally, offer some thoughts about the likely longer-term evolution of these enormously different territorial economies.

THE FEDERALIZATION OF RUSSIA

In Soviet times Russia was a nominal federation within a nominal federation that was, in fact, a unitary state. The quaint patchwork of 15 Union Republics (Soviet Socialist Republics—SSRs), some of them sub-divided into autonomous republics and other administrative territories, was managed by the apparatus of the Communist Party of the Soviet Union (CPSU). The Party's officials formed a clear hierarchy, with appointment from above; the territorial divisions were decorative. Part of that decoration consisted in assigning the names of particular national groups to areas historically associated with them. These labels can be grossly misleading. The Jewish AO, as has already been noted, is one such oddity. Located on the Chinese border and containing very few people recorded as Jewish, it was more a message to Soviet Jewry than any sort of homeland. Many other 'ethnic' territories are more in the nature of heritage sites. Thus, Evenks constituted 14.0% of the population of the Evenk AOk, while Khants comprised 0.9% and Mansi 0.5% of the inhabitants of the Khanty-Mansii AOk. Even at the higher level of republics, ethnic Russians are often in the majority in what are nominally ethnic-minority territories: 73.6% in Kareliya (Karelia), 57.7% in Komi, 60.8% in Mordoviya and 58.9% in Udmurt Republic (Udmurtiya), for instance (all 1989 census figures). The results of the census that was due to be held in 2002 were likely to demonstrate a change in the relative importance of the so-called titular nationalities in such regions. In many instances, the actions of republican governments have served to favour the titular group at the expense of others (both Russian and non-Russian), resulting in out-migration by non-titular groups. In addition, the Muslim population of many republics in the Volga-Urals region has continued to register high birth rates relative to the ethnic Russian population.

In general, this Soviet legacy has been preserved in the existing administrative divisions within the Russian Federation. When the USSR disintegrated into 15 states there was some discussion of reshaping Russia's internal administrative boundaries into units of comparable population size, without ethnic labels, but it came to naught. One consequence of this inheritance is that the 77 main territories or regions vary enormously in population size—from just over 203,000 in the Republic of Altai in Western Siberia, to 8.3m. in Moscow City (1999 figures). They also vary enormously in levels of economic development, a matter that will be dealt with in the next section.

Boundaries within independent Russia may have changed very little since the Soviet era, but the formal status of several territories has, however, been amended since 1991. While Russia was still part of the USSR, Boris Yeltsin (Russian leader from 1990 and President in 1991–99), notoriously advised the local leaderships throughout the USSR to 'grab as much sovereignty as you can'. He was engaged in doing just that for the Russian Federation, and the remark no doubt then seemed appropriate. The 1990–91 'parade of sovereignties', however, did not stop at the level of Russia and the other 14 SSRs. Autonomous republics (then known as Autonomous Soviet Socialist Republics—ASSRs) sought to become Union Republics and autonomous okrugs sought to become autonomous republics. At a later stage, in 1992–95, a number of the territorial regions (oblasts and krais) considered declaring themselves to be republics (within Russia), because the powers of republics were, in some ways, greater.

More precisely, it was members of the regions' political élite who initiated such claims. The extent of popular support for autonomist assertiveness varies greatly. In some republics, such as Tatarstan, it is strong, at any rate among ethnic Tatars. In others, a common attitude is that living in an autonomous republic merely means paying more to support a more elaborate and costly government—which is routinely assumed to be corrupt. On the whole, the most assertive republics have been those that are comparatively strong economically, such as Tatarstan and Sakha (Yakutiya).

Chechnya has been the main exception. Although a poor, mountainous region, its inhabitants fought Russian invaders throughout much of the 19th century and in the last decade of the 20th century they saw an opportunity to express their dissatisfaction once more. The first Chechen war (1994–96) ended, effectively, with a retreat by the federal authorities. The second, which commenced in late 1999, led to the central Government securing troubled and uncertain control over Chechen territory north of the guerrillas' mountain strongholds. Official peace negotiations commenced in November 2001, but international pressure on the Russian Government to halt what it presented as its 'anti-terrorism' activity in Chechnya declined substantially after the large-scale attacks on the US cities of New York and Washington, DC, on 11 September, which the US believed to have been co-ordinated by the Islamist fundamentalist, Osama bin Laden, who was resident in Afghanistan. President Putin made much of the fact that both Russia and the USA had recently suffered at the hands of terrorists, in a reference to bombings in Moscow and elsewhere, which had been attributed to Chechen rebels.

Such jostling for autonomy, or even independence, became possible with the collapse of the Communist monopoly on power. The regional élite was often little changed in personnel (one study in the mid-1990s found that about two-thirds of the regional political élite were former members of the Communist-era regional nomenklatura). The chain of command from Moscow, however, had been broken as early as 1988, when Mikhail Gorbachev (the last Soviet leader, 1986–91) introduced the local election of regional leaders, in place of their appointment from above. This opened the way for the local Party chiefs of the old order (or, often, their deputies) to transform their Party positions into post-Communist power.

From the beginning of the post-Communist Russian state, therefore, there was a shifting struggle, between both the regions and the centre, and between the regions themselves, over who was to have power, and at how high a level. It was further complicated by a struggle between different branches of government, notably the executive and legislative branches. Friction over budgets and other matters is a part of everyday political life in any federation and, indeed, in any state with different levels of government. What was exceptional in 1990s Russia was that a new state was being constructed. The rules of the political game were still to be established in 1992, a situation that persisted, to some extent, even at the beginning of the 2000s. So far as the federal territories and the centre are concerned, the bargaining was described by some as a process of 'federalization', the making of a real federation from the smallest of bases. There are other Russians of influence, however, who do not even concede that Russia should be a federation, and who argue for the construction of a unitary state. This view is being re-asserted under the Putin presidency (which effectively started at the beginning of 2000).

In March 1992, three months after Russia's emergence as an independent state, three federal treaties (sometimes known collectively as the Federation Treaty) were signed between the federal leadership, on the one hand, and, on the other, separately, the republics, krais, oblasts and autonomous okrugs. Two republics refused to sign: Tatarstan on the middle Volga and what was then the Chechen-Ingush ASSR in the North Caucasus. (Later Ingushetiya was hived off as a separate republic and the cities of Moscow and St Petersburg were granted the status of federal units.) These treaties set out three areas of competence: those that were exclusively federal, those that were shared and those that were exclusively sub-federal.

The powers of the federal centre were predictable. They included: defence; weapons production; foreign policy; the adoption, amendment and enforcement of federal laws; the establishment of federal legislative, executive and judicial bodies; the determination of internal boundaries; citizenship issues; the operation of the federal budget, the central bank and the money supply; and energy, transport and communications policies. The list of shared powers was long, and the treaties contained little guidance about just how these powers would be distributed. Exclusively sub-national powers were merely whatever was left over. Relations between regional and sub-regional (local) government were left for later legislation and, in many ways, remain legally unclear. For instance, there are no clear rules governing budgetary relations between regions and municipalities or rural districts.

So far as federal–territorial relations were concerned, the federal treaties of March 1992 left three important unresolved problems: the non-participation of two republics; the large and ill-defined area of shared powers; and language that appeared (although contradicted elsewhere in the text) to give republics more control than other regions over natural resources on their territories. These problems were compounded by two other circumstances. There was very little to guarantee that devolved responsibilities would be supported by devolved tax-raising powers— that is, the powers to set tax rates and tax bases. Moreover, the judicial system, in practice, was unsuited to act as an arbiter between the centre and the regions when disagreement over the interpretation of these agreements occurred.

The federal treaties were superseded by the new Russian Constitution approved in late 1993. This specified that where the federal treaties disagreed with the Constitution, the latter had priority. Moreover, the federal Constitution had precedence, in any conflicts, over sub-national constitutions or their equivalent. The new federal Constitution gave the President of the Russian Federation exceptionally strong powers. These were used to ensure that, for the next three years (approximately), regional governors were appointed and subject to dismissal by the President. That, however, did not apply to the republics, where the presidents were, and are, locally elected. It was only in 1996–97 that the executive heads of all the territories became formally answerable to their electorates rather than to the President.

Meanwhile, the Federation negotiated a series of so-called power-sharing treaties with individual territories. This began in February 1994 with Tatarstan, and had extended to more than one-half of the regions by late 1998. At that time the First Deputy Head of the Presidential Administration, Oleg Suysoyuv, spoke publicly of plans to discontinue the practice and, eventually, to reorder uniformly federal–territorial relations. The power-sharing treaties were anomalous, often allowing conflicting provisions in the federal and regional Constitutions simply to co-exist. A number of the treaties also included special arrangements on the retention of larger-than-normal shares of taxes collected within the borders of the territory concerned. This applied to Bashkortostan, Kareliya, Sakha and Tatarstan— all republics and all comparatively strong economically (Sakha, for instance, accounted for almost all Russia's diamond mining). Finally, these budget deals were, typically, not published.

'Asymmetric federalism' would be a generous description of the network of centre–territory relations that emerged. None the less, many observers have concluded that, however shocking the arrangements may seem to constitutional lawyers, they probably helped as interim measures to hold Russia together. For much of the 1990s the centre was weak and divided, with the President and parliament often in conflict and successive governments unable to implement key parts of their agendas (notably in tax collection). Consequently, all the territories, not just the favoured, strong republics, had considerable leeway. In practice, even in 1993–97, regional governors often defied the centre and acted as though they were more beholden to the local élite than to a President who could, in theory, dismiss them. Thus, Yevgenii Nazdratenko, in the Maritime (Primorskii) Krai on the Pacific coast, replaced a Yeltsin-nominated reformer and ran a grossly corrupt regime, while, for a long time, defying the centre's efforts to remove him—he was re-elected in December 1999 with a sizeable majority, largely owing to his ability to discredit the opposition, and his control over the local media.

Until the 1998 Russian financial crisis four developments had tended to stabilize centre–territorial political relations. Firstly, the Russian invasion of Chechnya in December 1994, although ill-managed, costly in human life and unsuccessful in its immediate aim, acted as a deterrent to less determined and less advantageously located secessionists elsewhere. Secondly, the development of the Federation Council as a body representing the territories facilitated accommodation between the centre and the periphery. Thirdly, the eight associations of territories (based on the 11 Economic Areas) had, throughout 1997, begun to emerge as regular channels for informal policy consultation between the central Government and representatives of the regions, and had begun to supplement the Federation Council as an institutionalized communications channel. Finally, the Constitutional Court was beginning to act somewhat more independently and usefully in rulings over conflicts regarding the distribution of powers. The financial crisis undermined some of this progress. It brought to the fore an underlying problem: the centre's dwindling ability to provide economic help to weaker territories and to use economic levers to achieve some consistency in the implementation of economic policy across Russia.

The measures introduced by Putin in May 2000 were designed to reclaim power from the regional governors by strengthening the central Government's control over its federal agencies in the regions and by ensuring regional compliance with federal legislation. Unlike his predecessor, Putin was prepared to move openly and boldly against concentrations of power that limited his own authority. With the advantage of a more compliant parliament and a background in the Security Service, he was prepared to attack determinedly both regional governors and business tycoons. Whereas Yeltsin had relied on negotiations that played region against region, Putin sought directly to limit regional political authority. Putin was assisted in this by the recovery of the Russian economy: the central Government was better resourced and, therefore, better able to fulfil its responsibilities. In the past, the poverty of the federal agencies often meant that they had to turn to regional presidents and governors for financial support, which made them pliable and more sympathetic to regional interests.

Putin's representatives in the seven Federal Okrugs come, for the most part, from a security or military background—in four cases directly from military or security posts. Their role is to oversee and co-ordinate federal administrative work in the regions. They also monitor the legality of the actions of individual governors, and have appointed their own staff to help in this. Although they were not given direct authority over governors of regions or presidents of republics, it was intended that they would be able to assist the federal Government in removing awkward characters from office. In theory, a governor who enacts local legislation that contradicts federal law can now be dismissed. Thus far, the presidential representatives have proved largely ineffective. They lack a clear mandate and the President appears unwilling to give them the necessary political power and financial resources to carry out the tasks that they have set themselves. Each representative faces a distinct set of problems and has approached the job somewhat differently. Some have received a hostile reception. The presidential representative in the Urals, Petr Latyshev, encountered difficulties with the Governor of Sverdlovsk Oblast, Eduard Rossel. The circumstances surrounding the resignation and replacement of Primorskii Governor Nazdratenko, following an extended energy crisis in the region, also proved a major embarrassment for the presidential representative in the Far East, Konstantin Pulikovskii. Pulikovskii (who was, significantly, based in Khabarovsk city, rather than Vladivostok, the capital of Primorskii) was unable to control Nazdratenko, and although the Governor's sudden illness, together with threats from the federal Government, led to his resignation in February 2001 on health grounds, he was subsequently rewarded with a lucrative appointment as the head of the State Fisheries Committee. Although Pulikovskii attempted to bring about the election of his deputy, Gennadii Apanasenko, as Governor, Apanasenko was defeated in a second round of voting, in June, by a local businessman, Sergei Darkin (who was alleged to have connections with Nazdratenko), with 40% of the votes cast; 34% of votes were cast against all candidates. By late 2001 it was probably fair to say that the presidential representatives were engaged in attempts to increase their powers and gain access to additional resources; however, their efforts were being thwarted, not only by the indifference of the regional leaders, many of whom refused to take them seriously, but also by the growing power of federal ministries. Russia is experiencing a re-centralization of power, but it is not necessarily the result of these reforms. Changes in the tax law and a shift in the distribution of revenue between the centre and the regions in favour of the federal authorities mean that the central Government has increasing control over state expenditure.

ECONOMIC DIFFERENTIATION

Russian regional inequality in Soviet times is impossible to assess, chiefly because such data as there were on rouble incomes and outputs concealed differences in availability that, in a geographically huge, shortage economy, were probably very large indeed. It was well-known that the biggest cities had priority in the allocation of consumer goods. Many everyday items that were widely available in Moscow were completely unobtainable in many lesser cities and small towns. Then, as now, barter and subsistence food production were predominant in rural areas, and were poorly accounted for in statistical reporting.

It is, nevertheless, clear that in 1992 the new Russian state had inherited an exceptionally uneven array of regional development levels. Underdeveloped, rural territories had little in common with the very big cities such as Moscow, St Petersburg, Yekaterinburg, Nizhnii Novgorod and Samara. In 1991 both Dagestan and Tyva, for example, had rural populations of more than 50% of the total, while, at the other end of the scale (omitting the far northern districts and cities with regional status), Kemerovo's rural population consisted of only 13% of the total and Samara's 19%. (The Russian average was 26%.) In a country where poverty was concentrated in rural areas, as it was in the USSR, these differences dictated large inequalities in average real incomes across the regions.

Later in the 1990s, as local food-price controls waned and the measurement of regional inequalities became a little less problematic, it was clear that differences in territorial, per-head, real personal incomes were very large indeed. They were also becoming larger over time. In November 1997 the average money income in Moscow city, divided by the cost of the 'subsistence minimum' basket of goods at local prices, was more than eight times the equivalent measure for Tyva. This was substantially greater than the range from poorest to richest region in the European Union (EU), using the EU's second-tier definition of 'region' (in which the average population size happens to be very close to that for Russian regions— 1.9m.). The Moscow–Tyva difference is probably overstated by this measure, because uncounted subsistence food production will play a larger role in Tyva. Nevertheless, even if one guesses at a 'true' ratio of 6:1, the range is still enormous.

A more comprehensive measure of dispersion among regional average real incomes, the co-efficient of variation, shows a clear, rapid increase throughout 1998. In 1992 it was 0.31. In 1998 it was 0.56, although the economic recovery that followed the rouble devaluation of that year seemed to lessen substantially this dispersion, bringing the indicator down to 0.40 by mid-1999. Despite this late amelioration, it is clear that the regions' economic fortunes diverged rapidly from the end of Communist rule. This suggests that there is a large and growing capacity for inter-regional discord under the new economic order. The increasing concentration of state resources within the federal Government in Moscow makes it all the more important for the Government to create a mechanism to redistribute wealth from richer to poorer regions; however, as in every federation, this is a controversial issue.

THE PROCESSES OF CHANGE AND THE ROLE OF THE CENTRE

So far as a territory's economic fortunes are concerned, the fundamental measure must be the standard of living of its inhabitants. The real-income measures that can be made for contemporary Russia are full of problems: neither the data on money incomes nor the data on regional price levels are of good quality, and one cannot assume that these defects produce a bias that is uniform across regions. Regions with particularly large informal economies, such as Kaliningrad, are probably doing better than the official figures suggest; casual observation certainly supports this so far as the Baltic oblast is concerned. Still, the regions that are doing particularly well or particularly badly are probably reasonably well identified by the official statistics. To put these differences in perspective, it should be said that post-communist economic adaptation in Russia as a whole has taken the form of collapse. Measured national income (gross domestic product—GDP) in 1999 was about 57% of the 1989 level. Only one region, Moscow city, has carried all the outward signs of economic success; and even in Moscow large parts of the population have been left behind. However, a small number of other regions have adapted comparatively well; typically, these were territories that began to show real growth in output (gross regional product—GRP) in 1997, well above the marginal improvement of 0.8% recorded for Russian GDP as a whole.

Analyses of inter-regional differences in average real incomes suggest that two kinds of territory fared less badly than the Russian average in the 1990s: those with particularly strong reserves of exploitable petroleum, gas, metals and hydropower (such as Tyumen Oblast in Western Siberia and Irkutsk Oblast in Eastern Siberia); and a handful of regions that contain emerging commercial and financial 'hubs' (Moscow, Nizhnii Novgorod, St Petersburg, Samara and Sverdlovsk). St Petersburg apart, maritime 'gateway' territories, such as Kaliningrad (on the Baltic), Krasnodar (Black Sea) and the Maritime Krai (Pacific), have fared far less well than might have been expected. The reasons for this are not clear, but each has a traditionalist, even xenophobic, leadership. In addition, the Maritime Krai has suffered for reasons common to the Russian Far East as a whole (on which, more below). A study by the Russian economy ministry confirmed this analysis. It suggested that the number of regions enjoying an 'above average' level of economic development increased from 20 in 1998 to 25 in 2000. Of these 25 regions, 17 were characterized as resource-processing, two (Moscow and St Petersburg) as financial–economic centres, and the remainder (including Samara, Moscow Oblast, Belgorod and Tatarstan) as industrial centres. This list reflected the regional consequences, post-1998, of high resource prices, which are of benefit to resource-exporting regions, and a devalued rouble, which increased the costs of imports and provided import-substitution benefits for the major industrial regions.

Those regions where economic adaptation has been more uniformly gloomy are, not to put too fine a point upon it, all the rest. They fall into two main categories: the strongly rural and agricultural regions; and what might be called 'typical Russian regions', mainly industrial, but without the particular attributes that have favoured the emerging hub regions or the industries that have been able to respond to domestic market opportunities post-1998. The former have suffered from a lack of farm restructuring and a massive deterioration in agricultural prices relative to all other prices; the latter have been victims of the lack of competitiveness of Russian industry and have failed to develop new activities on any scale. The natural-resource and the hub regions have in common an engagement with the outside world, either as generators of exports to the West or as magnets for foreign business and for trading in imports, or both. Throughout 1994 the per-head inflow of foreign currency into a region was a statistically significant, positive influence on per-head real incomes. This influence shows up less clearly thereafter, as currency markets within Russia become more integrated, but it probably provides a clue to early adaptation. If so, this is not surprising. The domestic economy was collapsing, but Western demand for Russian energy and materials was growing; also, Russians' appetite for imports was massive, and incomes from the domestic distribution of imports increased rapidly.

The reasons why these particular hub regions have emerged are harder to determine. Econometric studies suggest that small business, the development of which has been generally very weak, has grown rather better in regions with large populations and, therefore, large domestic markets, other things being equal. It also seems the case that those regions that have a positive attitude towards economic reform, in addition to a well-educated population, have the highest level of new-enterprise formation. It appears highly plausible that the development of financial and other services, stunted during the Soviet era, and of new lines of economic activity generally, would be easier in very large cities. In these very large communities a wide range of skills and lines of production are available. This must facilitate the recombining of capital and labour resources into new activities, as well as providing a large market for those activities.

The advantages of being a hub region look more durable than those of being a natural-resource region. Energy and raw-materials reserves become depleted and their prices fluctuate. The slide in petroleum and natural-gas prices in 1996–99 made a difference to the regional rankings. In addition, it is in petroleum, gas, gold, aluminium, and diamonds that the Russian élite is most determined to maintain control of what it views as the serious earners. In many cases it is concerned simply to make private fortunes out of these assets, regardless of the long-term development of the business. Even where it does seem to be concerned with longer-term development, it has, hitherto, resisted any dilution of its control. The usual Russian stance is that Western money and Western technology are welcome, provided no Western control comes with them. Typically, such resistance is aided and abetted by regional political leaders, who usually have stakes in the major local assets or are 'cronies', friends or associates, of those who do. However, some regions have not welcomed the attentions of the central Government's 'oligarchs' and view any source of external control with great suspicion. Thus, it seems clear that Russia's current economic recovery (with GDP growth of 3.5% in 1999, 7.7% in 2000 and 5.1% in the first six months of 2001), will contribute to greater regional differentiation as a relatively small number of regions enjoy sustained economic recovery, while the vast majority of the rest remain depressed. Russia's politicians are increasingly concerned about the development gap between Moscow and the rest of Russia, but outside Moscow there is also a widening gap between the winners in Russia's new economy and the losers from the old economy.

One other factor has been of great importance for the territories of Russia's Far

North and Far East. This is the erosion of the enormous subsidies to transport, energy and food supplies that had supported their development in the Soviet era. Most of that development would not have occurred in a market economy; now that a market economy is being established, these regions have experienced an exceptionally severe decline. One reaction was substantial out-migration from those areas during the 1990s and the Russian Government has been seeking financial assistance from the International Bank for Reconstruction and Development (World Bank) to support further out-migration from the Far North and Far East. However, it is not the case that everybody wants to leave, since these regions are the homelands of indigenous ethnic groups. There is also a large, mainly aged, population who have given their lives to the development of the 'Soviet North' and who, quite literally, have nowhere else to go. The net result is that the economically active are leaving behind a welfare-dependent population in regions that the federal Government is no longer inclined to support, a stark reminder of the human consequences of the collapse of Soviet socialism.

These, then, are (in very crude summary) the factors that lie behind the sharp divergence of regional fortunes. It is doubtful whether differences in policies among regional leaders made much difference to the outcomes during the 1990s. The economic structure inherited from the past, including population size and the presence or absence of major conurbations and natural-resource industries, look to have been far more important. A few regional leaders, such as Boris Nemtsov in Nizhnii Novgorod (1991–97) and Mikhail Prusak in Novgorod, won reputations as serious reformers; but such cases were rare, and even they worked with the grain of their region's inheritance. Governors who were overtly hostile to foreign business activity and economic restructuring, as in Krasnodar and Maritime Krais, were probably capable of making matters worse, but even they were usually at odds with the mayors of their major cities. The latter, like most governors, tended to be pragmatists who saw little personal benefit in making special efforts to block change.

By the end of the Yeltsin era an impasse had been reached. Regional politicians still looked to the centre and lobbied institutions in Moscow, but there was an element of inertia in this. In interviews, regional officials were apt to complain that the centre had become merely a source of trouble. Some regional policy-makers and administrators openly questioned the system of remittances of tax revenue to the centre and transfers back to the federal territories. There may have been little appetite for secession, but there was also little expectation that the central Government would do much to help a region deal with its most pressing problems. Meanwhile, the centre and regions competed to obtain revenue from the same sources (under tax-sharing arrangements), which led both to damagingly high nominal rates of tax and to collusion between regional governments and local businesses to conceal resources from the central budget—a process aided by the use of barter and money surrogates. At the same time, the centre had devolved some major responsibilities for public provision, notably welfare and housing, to sub-national levels, without making available the means to pay for them. It was estimated that in 1998 such 'unfunded mandates' amounted to at least 5% of GDP—an amount that should, in international accounting practice, have been added to the officially reported government deficit.

President Putin has changed things radically. He may not yet have succeeded in resolving the complex issue of centre–regional financial relations, but he is certainly prepared to attempt to tackle it directly. The Audit Chamber claimed that the regions received 60% of tax revenue in 1997, whereas they were to receive just 49% in 2001. This required the cancellation of the stipulation in the budget code that the regions receive at least 50% of tax revenue. In 2002 the regions were expected to receive even less. Thanks to the economic recovery, and the success of the new, flat income-tax rate (of 13%), both of which replenished the coffers of the federal Government, the regions received a smaller proportion of a larger amount of funds. However, if the economy slowed and profits declined, then the regions would begin to come under financial pressure. Already, by late 2001 rich regions, which are the major contributors, and poorer regions, which are more dependent on federal transfers, were claiming that they would be unable to balance their budgets in 2002. By removing the influence of the governors from the federal policy-making process, and by increasing their reliance on funds channelled through the federal Government, President Putin is strengthening central control by stealth. If the Yeltsin era witnessed a shift in centre–regional relations which favoured the regions, the Putin presidency appears to be heralding a reassertion of central influence. By 2001, at least, this had been achieved without open conflict, and most governors remained supportive of the President.

In response to this shift in centre–regional relations, many governors sought to build alliances with large-scale Russian enterprises. A study by the New York-based EastWest Institute has demonstrated that 12 regions in Russia are dominated by just one company. However, the relationship between the particular region and the dominant company varies. In the 2000–01 cycle of gubernatorial elections, large-scale business sought to ensure the election of governors who would promote their interests, as did the federal Government. The most obvious cases where business executives became governors are the Chukchi, Evenk and Taimyr (Dolgan-Nenets) AOks. In other regions there is a close relationship between governor and corporation, for example, between the state-controlled gas monopoly, Gazprom, and Yurii Neyelov in Yamal-Nenets AOk. However, in a number of other regions businesses have supported losing candidates. For example, in the Nenets AOk the petroleum company LUKoil tried, and failed, to oust the incumbent, Vladimir Butov. While governors are happy to receive the tax revenue that may be associated with having a high-placed corporate citizen located in their region, Russian companies can benefit at the same time by securing their own regional bases outside Moscow. By late 2001 the Putin administration was already suspicious of such ties; no doubt they will soon attract the attention of the presidential representatives.

INVESTMENT POTENTIAL

Investment in Russia has declined even faster than output. The country's capital stock has shrunk, although the decline cannot be measured with any confidence. Not surprisingly, while domestic investment has been collapsing, foreign investment has been small. A surge of foreign investment in 1996–97 was dominated by portfolio debt investment, mainly in government treasury bills (GKOs). Foreign portfolio investment in Russia merely rearranged the liabilities.

Foreign direct investment (FDI), however, should have helped to support production capacity. Accurate statistics on FDI are difficult to come by; estimates for the 1990s range from around US $17,000m. to almost $20,000m. by the end of 1999. In its *World Investment Report*, the United Nations Conference on Trade and Development estimated the value of FDI inward stock in Russia at the end of 1998 to be $13,400m., equivalent to 0.3% of global FDI. According to Goskomstat data, by the beginning of 2001 the total amount of foreign investment accumulated in Russia had reached $32,500m., of which $16,100m. was in the form of FDI. Despite its modest total, it is this FDI, establishing or expanding joint ventures and wholly foreign-owned firms, that can channel the flow of investment to different Russian regions. Against a domestic backdrop of plummeting investment levels, FDI, together with the growth of new, small firms, has probably been the major positive influence for economic recovery in Russia. The regional distribution of FDI reflects the perceived economic potential of activities in each region, allowing for the barriers to foreigners gaining significant control in those activities. In turn, FDI influences regional outcomes: it must usually have beneficial effects on a region's output. In practice, FDI has been heavily concentrated in Moscow city, although that dominance is dwindling. During 2000 Moscow city received 33.3% of all FDI in Russia, a decline from its peak level of 76.9% in 1997, but an increase compared to the previous year's level of 23.6%. Such a concentration on the capital city is not unusual for FDI in former communist countries. Some of it was recorded in Moscow only because head offices of large companies are often based there; in so far as the resource inflow goes through that head office to provincial production, the real concentration of FDI resources on the metropolis will be somewhat less. Despite the declining dominance of Moscow, there are still many Russian regions that have received little or no foreign investment. For what the official figures are worth, the 10 leading regions for foreign investment in 1995–2000 received, on average, over 80% of all inward FDI; of this, around one-half went to Moscow city and the rest was distributed in small amounts around an array of regions, which changed from year to year. Moscow Oblast (located around the city), St Petersburg, Tyumen and Samara feature with some regularity and prominence. It is clear, however, that, in a number of second-tier regions, a particular investment project in a particular year can push that region, a little fortuitously, into a leading ranking. A notable exception is Sakhalin Oblast, home to two very large offshore petroleum and gas projects that are being developed under production-sharing agreements. In the period following the financial crisis of 1998 the regional pattern of foreign investment, measured both in terms of capital stock and number of enterprises with foreign involvement, moved away from the resource regions and favoured regions involved in import-substituting manufacturing. It is also noteworthy that, despite their political complexion, the major port regions—St Petersburg/Leningrad, Krasnodar/Rostov and Primorskii, now figure consistently in the top 10. This pattern reflects the impact of rouble devaluation on the cost of imported consumer goods and the failure of the resource sector to capture substantial amounts of investment; the latter is the result of problems in reforming Russia's production-sharing legislation.

Whether the pattern of foreign investment corresponds well to the potential of different Russian territories is not clear. Western investors can be assumed to know what they are doing, but one of the things they are forced to do is to take into account the obstacles placed in their way, often by regional administrations. There are, for instance, a number of natural-resource developments from which, as noted earlier, foreign business has been more or less excluded. There are also some regions, such as Archangel Oblast, where investors have been squeezed out by Russian interests, assisted by the local political élite. Apart from direct investors, a number of research organizations have been evaluating the economies of Russia's territories. These organizations are mainly in Russia itself. Indeed, the compilation of regional ratings is one of the few Russian growth industries. Typically, they consist of rankings of regions by investment potential and/or risk, on the basis of a collection of diverse indicators. Some of the major producers of regional ratings are *Ekspert* magazine, the (unrelated) Expert Institute of the Russian Union of Industrialists and Entrepreneurs, the Federal Fund for the Support of Small Business, Troika Dialog, and BankAustria (commissioning studies from the Institute for Advanced Studies in Vienna, Austria).

The purposes of these rankings are broadly similar: to assess the business climate, attractiveness for investment and risk levels associated with the various federal subjects. Their methods vary, but all perforce operate with official Russian statistics. The indicators used include a core of measures that are used by almost all of the ratings analysts: GRP, population size, per-head incomes (sometimes with adjustment for the still-large differences in regional prices, some without), strength of the regional budget (deficit as a percentage of expenditure, for example), volume of industrial output. Several try to incorporate measures of human capital, such as average years of education of the work-force, or infrastructure indicators, such as the number of telephones per 1,000 inhabitants. The weighting given to different indicators varies and is sometimes far from clear. We have taken three ratings that are very similar in purpose and devised a kind of 'poll of polls'. The three are the ratings of Troika Dialog (August 1997), BankAustria (1998) and *Ekspert* (1998–2000). They differ little in their selection of the most promising 10 territories; they differ rather more in their rankings within the 10, except that Moscow city comes out first in each of them. Combining the three (and assigning a ranking of 11th in the list in question to any region that is omitted from that particular list but does appear in the others), we get the following ranking of 10 (in descending order): Moscow city; St Petersburg; Tyumen Oblast; Sverdlovsk Oblast; Samara Oblast; Nizhnii Novgorod Oblast; Moscow Oblast; Krasnoyarsk Krai; Tatarstan; and Irkutsk Oblast.

This selection displays the mixture of emerging commercial hubs and natural-resource regions described earlier. They form the minority of Russian territories that have adapted less badly than most to the market, and they correspond fairly well to the rankings by inward FDI. However, the changing pattern of investment, away from the dominance of Moscow and the resource regions, and towards the port regions and market-orientated centres, suggests that post-1998 foreign investment is playing a much more constructive role in Russia's economic recovery.

PROSPECTS

Output in Russia declined from 1989 to 1998, with a brief halt in 1997. In 1999 GDP rose by 3.5%, representing the first sign of real recovery for a decade. The Russian Government hopes to attain growth averaging 5% per year in the first decade of the new millennium, although many analysts, including some leading Russian economists, are sceptical about this objective. They regard the massive devaluation of the rouble in 1998 and the unrelated subsequent strengthening of world petroleum prices as generating an upturn that can be sustained only if basic structural reforms arre undertaken. Some continued growth, but at a much slower rate (of, say, 2%–3% per year) seemed more likely, provided that pervasive government intervention hindered the competitive process. However, in 2000 the Russian economy grew by 7.7%, and in the third quarter of 2001 year-on-year growth was 5.7%. Reduced growth had been anticipated, because of the decline in petroleum prices, but a rate of over 5% was a surprise to many. None the less, by late 2001 it was far too early to talk of a sustained recovery. The Government had embarked on an ambitious reform programme, but the weakening petroleum price and global economic downturn threatened to damage Russia's resource-dominated economy. Furthermore, Russia's debt-servicing requirements were growing, which would absorb funds that might otherwise be spent on stimulating the domestic economy.

Whatever the outcome for Russia in the medium term, the fortunes of individual regions will continue to differ enormously. It is possible that the pattern of 1999 will be maintained: that is, regional real income levels may cease to diverge as output recovery is maintained in the hitherto most depressed branches and regions. But sustained convergence of regional living standards may well require a strengthening of market institutions, to facilitate the establishment of new business in low-wage areas and the freer movement of people to high-wage areas.

Putin's evident desire to impose greater central control could help economic change. Regional governments have played a key role in blocking structural change by supporting favoured large enterprises and helping to generate barter and money-surrogate transactions. All other things being equal, the weakening of regional governments should aid economic adjustment. There are, however, two reasons for being cautious about this scenario. Firstly, the power of regional networks of politicians and businessmen may be such that the new federal okrugs and other measures, designed to give the centre more leverage, may turn out, in practice, to make very little difference. Secondly, even if regional power actually is reduced, there is no guarantee that a strengthened national centre will put an end to corrupt and ineffective government. Russia's problem may be not so much that regional government works poorly, but that all levels of government work poorly.

Chronology of Russia

c. 878: Kievan Rus, the first unified state of the Eastern Slavs, was founded, with Kiev (Kyiv) as its capital.

c. 988: Vladimir (Volodymyr) I ('the Great'), ruler of Kievan Rus, converted to Orthodox Christianity.

1237–40: The Russian principalities were invaded and conquered by the Mongol Tatars.

1462–1505: Reign of Ivan III of Muscovy (Moscow), who consolidated the independent Russian domains into a centralized state.

1480: Renunciation of Tatar suzerainty.

1533–84: Reign of Ivan IV ('the Terrible'), who began the eastern expansion of Russian territory.

1547: Ivan IV was crowned 'Tsar of Muscovy and all Russia'.

1552: Subjugation of the Khanate of Kazan.

1556: Subjugation of the Khanate of Astrakhan.

1581: Yermak Timofeyev, an adventurer, led an expedition to Siberia, pioneering Russian expansion beyond the Ural Mountains.

1645: A Russian settlement was established on the Sea of Okhotsk, on the coast of eastern Asia.

1654: Eastern Ukraine came under Russian rule as a result of the Treaty of Pereyaslavl.

1679: Russian pioneers reached the Kamchatka Peninsula and the Pacific Ocean.

1682–1725: Reign of Peter (Petr) I ('the Great'), who established Russia as a European Power, expanded its Empire, and modernized the civil and military institutions of the state.

1703: St Petersburg was founded at the mouth of the River Neva, in north-west Russia.

1721: Peter I, who was declared the 'Tsar of all the Russias', proclaimed the Russian Empire.

1728: The Treaty of Kyakhta with China secured the Russian annexation of Transbaikal.

1762–96: Reign of Catherine (Yekaterina) II ('the Great'—Princess Sophia of Anhaldt-Zerbst), who expanded the Empire in the south, after wars with the Ottoman Turks, and in the west, by the partition of Poland.

1774: As a result of the Treaty of Kuçuk Kainavci with the Turks, Russia gained a port on the Black Sea.

1783: Annexation of the Khanate of Crimea (now in Ukraine).

1801–25: Reign of Alexander (Aleksandr) I.

1809: Finland became a possession of the Russian Crown.

1812: The French under Napoleon I invaded Russia.

1825: Accession of Nicholas (Nikolai) I, despite an unsuccessful coup attempt by a group of young officers known as the 'Decembrists'.

1853–56: The Crimean War was fought, in which the United Kingdom and France aided the Turks against Russia.

1855–81: Reign of Alexander II, who introduced economic and legal reforms.

1859: The conquest of the Caucasus was completed, following the surrender of rebel forces.

1860: Acquisition of provinces on the Sea of Japan from China and the establishment of Vladivostok.

1861: Emancipation of the serfs.

1864: Final defeat of the Circassian peoples and the confirmation of Russian hegemony in the Caucasus.

1867: The North American territory of Alaska was sold to the USA for US $7m.

1875: Acquisition of Sakhalin from Japan in exchange for the Kurile Islands.

1876: Subjugation of the last of the Central Asian khanates.

1881: Accession of Alexander III (upon the assassination of his father), who re-established autocratic principles of government.

1891: Construction of the Trans-Siberian Railway was begun.

1894–1917: Reign of Nicholas II, the last Tsar.

1898: The All-Russian Social Democratic Labour Party (RSDLP), a Marxist party, was founded, five years later dividing into 'Bolsheviks' (led by Lenin—Vladimir Ilych Ulyanov) and 'Mensheviks'.

1905: Russia's defeat in the Russo–Japanese War contributed to unrest, which eventually forced the Tsar to introduce limited political reforms, including the holding of elections to a Duma (parliament).

1912: Lenin formally established a separate party for the Bolsheviks.

1914: Russia entered the First World War against Austria-Hungary, Germany and the Ottoman Empire. St Petersburg was renamed Petrograd.

2 March (New Style: 15 March) 1917: Abdication of Tsar Nicholas II after demonstrations and strikes in Petrograd; a Provisional Government took power.

25 October (7 November) 1917: The Bolsheviks overthrew the Provisional Government; the Russian Soviet Federative Socialist Republic (RSFSR or Russian Federation) was proclaimed.

6 January (19 January) 1918: The Constituent Assembly (elected in November 1917) was dissolved by the Bolsheviks, who were now engaged in a civil war against various anti-Communist leaders (the 'Whites').

14 February (Old Style: 1 February) 1918: First day upon which the Gregorian Calendar took effect in Russia.

3 March 1918: Treaty of Brest-Litovsk: the Bolsheviks ceded large areas of western territory to Germany and recognized the independence of Finland and Ukraine. The capital of Russia was moved to Moscow.

10 July 1918: The first Constitution of the RSFSR was adopted by the Fifth All-Russian Congress of Soviets.

18 July 1918: Tsar Nicholas II and his family were murdered in Yekaterinburg (Sverdlovsk, 1924–91) by Bolshevik troops.

11 November 1918: The Allied Armistice with Germany (which was denied its gains at Brest-Litovsk) ended the First World War.

March 1921: As the civil war ended, the harsh policy of 'War Communism' was replaced by the New Economic Policy (NEP), which allowed peasants and traders some economic freedom.

April 1922: Stalin (Iosif Vissarionovich Dzhugashvili) was elected General Secretary of the Bolshevik Russian Communist Party (RCP).

30 December 1922: The Union of Soviet Socialist Republics (USSR) was formed at the 10th All-Russian (first All-Union) Congress of Soviets by the RSFSR, Belarus, Transcaucasia, Ukraine and the Central Asian states of Khorezm and Bukhara.

21 January 1924: Death of Lenin; Stalin then consolidated his power.

31 January 1924: The first Constitution of the USSR was ratified. The RCP then became the Communist Party of the Soviet Union (CPSU).

1928: The NEP was abandoned; the forced collectivization of agriculture resulted in widespread famine.

5 December 1936: The second Constitution of the USSR (the 'Stalin' Constitution) was adopted—Kazakhstan was detached from the RSFSR, to become one of the 11 constituent Union Republics of the USSR. The decade was also dominated by a number of ruthless political purges.

1939: Following the Treaty of Non-Aggression with Germany (the Nazi–Soviet Pact), Soviet forces invaded eastern Poland and then Finland (the Baltic states and Bessarabia were annexed the following year).

22 June 1941: Germany invaded the USSR.

2 February 1943: German forces surrendered at Stalingrad (now Volgograd), marking the first reverse for the German Army. Soviet forces began to regain territory.

1944: In a consolidation of domestic authority, Stalin ordered a number of mass deportations of populations from the North Caucasus and Crimea. Tannu-Tuva (Tyva), a Russian protectorate from 1914, was formally incorporated into the USSR (as part of the RSFSR).

8 May 1945: The Red Army occupied the German capital, Berlin, and Germany subsequently capitulated; most of Eastern and Central Europe had come under Soviet control.

8 August 1945: The USSR declared war on Japan and occupied Sakhalin and the Kurile Islands.

25 January 1949: The Council for Mutual Economic Assistance (CMEA or Comecon) was established, as an economic alliance between the USSR and its Eastern European allies.

14 July 1949: The USSR exploded its first atomic bomb.

5 March 1953: Death of Stalin; he was replaced by a collective leadership.

September 1953: Nikita Khrushchev was elected First Secretary of the Central Committee of the CPSU.

14 May 1955: The Warsaw Treaty of Friendship, Co-operation and Mutual Assistance was signed by the USSR and its Eastern European satellites, establishing a military alliance known as the Warsaw Treaty Organization (or Warsaw Pact).

4 November 1956: Soviet forces invaded Hungary to overthrow Imre Nagy's reformist Government.

4 October 1957: The USSR placed the first man-made satellite (Sputnik I) in orbit around the earth.

August 1960: Soviet technicians were recalled from the People's Republic of China, as part of the growing dispute between the two Communist countries.

18–28 October 1962: The discovery of Soviet nuclear missiles in Cuba by the USA led to the 'Cuban Missile Crisis'; tension eased when Khrushchev announced the withdrawal of the missiles, following a US blockade of the island.

13–14 October 1964: Khrushchev was deposed and replaced as First Secretary of the CPSU by Leonid Brezhnev.

20–21 August 1968: Soviet and other Warsaw Pact forces invaded Czechoslovakia to overthrow the reformist Government of Alexander Dubček.

May 1972: The US President, Richard Nixon, visited Moscow, thus marking a relaxation in US–Soviet relations, a process which came to be known as *détente*.

16 June 1977: Brezhnev became Chairman of the Presidium of the Supreme Soviet (titular head of state).

7 October 1977: The third Constitution of the USSR was adopted.

24 December 1979: Soviet forces invaded Afghanistan (the last troops were withdrawn in February 1989).

10 November 1982: Death of Leonid Brezhnev; Yurii Andropov succeeded him as Party leader.

9 February 1984: Death of Andropov; Konstantin Chernenko succeeded him as General Secretary.

10 March 1985: Death of Chernenko; he was succeeded as General Secretary of the CPSU by Mikhail Gorbachev.

24 February–6 March 1986: At the 27th Congress of the CPSU, Gorbachev proposed radical economic and political reforms and 'new thinking' in foreign policy; emergence of the policy of *glasnost* (meaning a greater degree of freedom of expression).

26 April 1986: An explosion occurred at a nuclear reactor in Chernobyl (Chornobyl), Ukraine, which resulted in discharges of radioactive material.

October 1986: A summit took place in Reykjavík, Iceland, attended by Gorbachev and the US President, Ronald Reagan, at which the issue of nuclear disarmament was discussed.

January 1987: At a meeting of the CPSU Central Committee, Gorbachev proposed plans for the restructuring (*perestroika*) of the economy.

21 June 1987: At local elections, the CPSU nominated more than one candidate in some constituencies.

21 October 1987: Boris Yeltsin, who had been appointed First Secretary of the Moscow City Party Committee in 1985, resigned from the Politburo of the CPSU.

6 December 1988: With the pace of domestic reform quickening, in a speech at the UN Gorbachev outlined his 'new thinking' on foreign policy.

25 March 1989: Multi-party elections to the newly established legislature, the Congress of People's Deputies, took place.

4 March 1990: Elections took place to the local and republican legislatures of the Russian Federation; reformists made substantial gains in the larger cities (elections elsewhere in the USSR produced overtly nationalist majorities in the Baltic republics and Moldova).

15 March 1990: The all-Union legislature approved the establishment of the post of President of the USSR and elected Mikhail Gorbachev to that office.

29 May 1990: Boris Yeltsin was elected as Chairman of the Supreme Soviet of the Russian Federation. Two weeks later, with a background of increasing restiveness in a number of other Union Republics, Congress adopted a declaration of sovereignty within the USSR.

3 September 1990: Boris Yeltsin announced a 500-day programme of economic reform.

17 March 1991: In an all-Union referendum on the issue of the future state of the USSR, some 75% of participants approved Gorbachev's concept of a 'renewed federation' (several Union Republics did not participate).

12 June 1991: Yeltsin was elected President of the Russian Federation in direct elections, with Aleksandr Rutskoi, a former general in the Afghan war, as Vice-President. Residents of Leningrad (as it had been known since 1924) voted to change the city's name back to St Petersburg.

1 July 1991: The USSR, together with the other member countries of the Warsaw Pact, signed a protocol that formalized the dissolution of the alliance.

18–21 August 1991: An attempted *coup d'état* was frustrated by popular and institutional opposition, with Yeltsin prominent in the successful campaign to reinstate Gorbachev.

6 September 1991: The newly formed State Council, which comprised the supreme officials of the Union Republics, recognized the independence of Estonia, Latvia and Lithuania.

8 December 1991: The leaders of the Russian Federation, Belarus and Ukraine resolved to form a Commonwealth of Independent States (CIS) to replace the USSR—the so-called Minsk Agreement.

21 December 1991: At a meeting in Almaty, Kazakhstan, the leaders of 11 former Union Republics of the USSR signed a protocol on the formation of the new CIS.

25 December 1991: Mikhail Gorbachev formally resigned as President of the USSR, thereby confirming the effective dissolution of the Union.

2 January 1992: A radical economic reform programme was introduced in Russia.

31 March 1992: President Yeltsin and the leaders of the country's administrative units signed three documents together known as the Federation Treaty; representatives from the Chechen-Ingush ASSR and Tatarstan did not participate.

June 1992: Yeltsin appointed Yegor Gaidar, an economist and supporter of radical market reform, as acting Prime Minister. Ingushetiya was recognized as a federal republic separate from Chechnya.

9 December 1992: The Russian legislature rejected Gaidar as Prime Minister; Viktor Chernomyrdin was subsequently appointed instead.

25 April 1993: In a referendum organized by President Yeltsin, in order to resolve the increasing conflict between the executive and the legislature, 57.4% of the electorate endorsed the President and 70.6% voted in favour of early parliamentary elections.

24 July 1993: In an attempt to control inflation in Russia, all rouble notes printed between 1961 and 1992 were withdrawn from circulation and replaced with new ones; this effectively ended the old Soviet 'rouble zone'.

31 August 1993: A majority of territorial leaders approved President Yeltsin's proposal for the establishment of a Federation Council, which convened in mid-September.

21 September 1993: Yeltsin issued a decree On Gradual Constitutional Reform (Decree 1,400), which suspended the powers of the legislature with immediate effect. The defiance of the legislators, and Vice-President Rutskoi, eventually provoked a state of emergency to be declared in Moscow on 3 October.

4 October 1993: The White House, the seat of the legislature, was shelled by government forces and severely damaged by fire; the leaders of the parliamentary revolt surrendered.

12 December 1993: A proposed new Constitution was approved by 58.4% of participating voters in a referendum. On the same day elections to the State Duma, the lower house of a new Federal Assembly (the upper house was provided by the Federation Council) were held.

11 October 1994: The rouble collapsed, losing almost one-quarter of its value against the US dollar.

11 December 1994: Following the collapse of peace negotiations earlier in the month, Yeltsin ordered the invasion of Chechnya (which had ambitions to secede) by some 40,000 federal ground troops, who met with bitter resistance.

30 July 1995: Opposition to the continuing war in Chechnya prompted a military accord on the gradual disarmament of the Chechen rebels, in return for the partial withdrawal of federal troops from Chechnya; it remained in effect until October.

17 December 1995: At the general election the Communist Party of the Russian Federation (CPRF) achieved the greatest success, winning 22.7% of the votes cast; the radical nationalist Liberal Democratic Party of Russia (LDPR) won 11.2%, Our Home is Russia (a centre-right electoral bloc headed by Chernomyrdin) 10.1% and the liberal Yabloko 6.9%.

16 June 1996: Eleven candidates contested the presidential election; Yeltsin secured the greatest number of votes (35%), followed by the leader of the CPRF, Gennadii Zyuganov (32%); retired Lt-Gen. Aleksandr Lebed won an unexpectedly high level of support, with 15% of the votes cast, and was later appointed to the Government.

3 July 1996: Amid increasing speculation about his health, Boris Yeltsin won the second round of voting in the presidential election, with 53.8% of the votes cast.

Yeltsin was inaugurated as the first democratically elected President of post-Soviet Russia on 9 August.

31 August 1996: Lebed, who only survived in government until October, negotiated a cease-fire with the Chechen rebels; the so-called Khasavyurt Accords included postponing resolution of the issue of sovereignty until 2001.

17 January 1998: A reallocation of cabinet portfolios indicated a further erosion of reformist influence in government, to the satisfaction of a critical parliament.

27 March 1998: Following the dismissal, four days earlier, of Chernomyrdin and his Government, Sergei Kiriyenko, a reformist, but hitherto not a prominent minister, was nominated as premier. Kiriyenko was confirmed as Prime Minister by the State Duma on 24 April, having been rejected twice earlier in the month.

17 August 1998: Following an escalating financial crisis, and in a complete reversal of its monetary policies, the Government announced a series of emergency measures, which included the effective devaluation of the rouble.

23 August 1998: President Yeltsin dismissed Kiriyenko's administration and reappointed Chernomyrdin premier.

11 September 1998: Following the State Duma's second conclusive rejection of Chernomyrdin's nomination as Prime Minister, a compromise candidate, the foreign minister, Yevgenii Primakov, was confirmed as premier.

5 November 1998: The Constitutional Court ruled that Boris Yeltsin was ineligible to stand for a third presidential term.

24 March 1999: Russia condemned NATO airstrikes against Yugoslav targets, initiated in response to the repression of ethnic Albanians in the Serbian province of Kosovo and Metohija, and suspended relations with the Organization. The former Prime Minister and Russia's special envoy to the Balkans conflict, Chernomyrdin, helped to negotiate a peace settlement in June.

12 May 1999: The dismissal of Primakov and his Government was effected by Yeltsin, who cited their failure to improve the economic situation, and appointed Sergei Stepashin, hitherto First Deputy Prime Minister and Minister of the Interior, as acting premier; he was approved by the State Duma one week later.

7 August 1999: Armed Chechen guerrillas invaded neighbouring Dagestan and seized control of two villages. Federal troops retaliated and claimed, by the end of the month, to have quelled the rebel action.

9 August 1999: In an unforeseen move, Prime Minister Sergei Stepashin was dismissed by Yeltsin, and replaced by Vladimir Putin, hitherto the Secretary of the Security Council and head of the Federal Security Service (FSB).

23 September 1999: Russia initiated airstrikes against Chechnya, officially in retaliation for a number of bomb explosions in Moscow, which had been attributed to Chechen rebel extremists. A full-scale invasion of Chechnya was initiated at the beginning of November, and in December commenced a ground offensive against the Republic's capital, Groznyi (Dzhokhar).

19 December 1999: In elections to the State Duma the CPRF secured the most seats, with 113. Unity (Yedinstvo), formed by 31 leaders of Russia's regions, obtained 72 seats, and the Fatherland—All Russia bloc obtained 67. The Union of Rightist Forces, led by Sergei Kiriyenko, obtained 29 seats, Yabloko took 21, and the Zhirinovskii bloc won 17. The participation rate was 62%; the Chechen constituency remained vacant, owing to the continuing conflict.

31 December 1999: President Yeltsin unexpectedly resigned; he was succeeded, in an acting capacity, by Vladimir Putin.

26 March 2000: Fourteen candidates contested the presidential election. Putin achieved a clear victory in the first round, with 52.9% of the votes cast. He was inaugurated on 7 May, and subsequently formed a new Government, headed by the former First Deputy Prime Minister, Mikhail Kasyanov.

5 May 2000: Putin decreed that, henceforth, Chechnya was to come under direct federal, rather than direct presidential, rule.

13 May 2000: The President issued a decree dividing Russia's 89 constituent regions and republics between seven federal districts. Each district was to come under the control of a presidential envoy, who was to oversee local regions' compliance with federal legislation and receive funding from the federal authorities, in order to prevent local governors from acting in contravention of central policy. Of the new presidential envoys, who were appointed a few days later, only two were civilians, the rest being senior officers of the security services or the military.

31 May 2000: Three pieces of legislation, proposed by Putin to extend presidential powers and curtail those of the regional governors, were passed by the State Duma. The first proposed that regional governors should lose their seats in the Federation Council, and be replaced by representatives elected from regional legislatures; following its ratification by the Federation Council in July, all existing Council members were to be replaced by the beginning of 2002. The second bill accorded the President the right to dismiss regional governors, and the third allowed governors to remove from office elected officials who were subordinate to them.

20 August 2000: Tsar Nicholas II and his family were canonized by the Patriarch of the Russian Orthodox Church, Aleksei II.

October 2000: Relations with the Taliban authorities in Afghanistan were strained, following the arrest of a number of Afghan citizens for alleged violations of Russia's borders. The Taliban accused Russia of supporting the Afghan opposition and of military activity hostile to Afghanistan in neighbouring states. Russia claimed that Afghanistan was training and harbouring alleged Islamist terrorists.

23 November 2000: The State Council, a body comprising the President and territorial governors and formed as part of the ongoing reform of the Federation Council, convened for the first time.

22 January 2001: Putin signed a decree transferring control of operations in Chechnya from the defence ministry to the FSB.

1 September 2001: Following condemnation by the Minister of Defence, Sergei Ivanov, of the reported appointment of the Islamist extremist, Osama bin Laden, as Commander-in-Chief of the defence forces of the Taliban leadership in Afghanistan, the military districts of Russia were reformed; the former Volga and Urals regions were combined in a new, strengthened Trans-Volga region, in response to the perceived heightened security threat from the Central Asian region.

18 November 2001: Official direct negotiations on a political settlement for Chechnya finally commenced, two years after the renewed conflict had been initiated, following the federal Government's decision to set aside its demand that the Chechen rebels first surrender their weapons.

Statistics

MAJOR DEMOGRAPHIC AND ECONOMIC INDICATORS

	Area ('000 sq km)	Population at 1 Jan. 1999 ('000)	Population density, 1999 (per sq km)	Average annual change in population, 1994–98 (%)	Life expectancy at birth, 1998
Autonomous Republics					
Adygeya	7.6	449	59.1	0.0	69.04
Altai	92.6	203	2.2	0.6	64.14
Bashkortostan . .	143.6	4,110	28.6	0.3	67.88
Buryatiya	351.3	1,038	3.0	-0.2	65.27
Chechnya . . .	n.a.	781	n.a.	-6.2	n.a.
Chuvashiya . . .	18.3	1,362	74.4	0.0	68.85
Dagestan	50.3	2,120	42.1	1.7	70.14
Ingushetiya . . .	n.a.	317	n.a.	9.1	71.91
Kabardino-Balkariya. .	12.5	786	62.9	0.2	68.89
Kalmykiya . . .	75.9	316	4.2	-0.3	66.36
Karachayevo-Cherkessiya	14.1	434	30.7	0.1	69.38
Kareliya . . .	172.4	771	4.5	-0.5	65.70
Khakasiya . . .	61.9	581	9.4	0.0	63.69
Komi	415.9	1,151	2.8	-1.3	66.37
Marii-El . . .	23.2	761	32.8	-0.1	67.03
Mordoviya . . .	26.2	937	35.8	-0.5	68.79
North Osetiya . .	8.0	663	82.8	0.4	68.00
Sakha (Yakutiya) . .	3,103.2	1,001	0.3	-1.6	64.95
Tatarstan . . .	67.8	3,784	55.6	0.2	68.77
Tyva	170.5	311	1.8	0.3	58.25
Udmurtiya . . .	42.1	1,633	38.8	-0.1	67.61
Krais					
Altai	169.1	2,665	15.8	-0.2	67.73
Khabarovsk. . .	788.6	1,523	1.9	-0.9	64.75
Krasnodar . . .	76.0	5,010	65.9	0.5	67.68
Krasnoyarsk[1] . .	2,339.0	3,076	-0.5	-0.4	63.92
Maritime (Primorskii)	165.9	2,194	13.2	-0.8	65.68
Stavropol . . .	66.5	2,660	40.0	0.6	68.46

[1] Figures for Krasnoyarsk Krai include Evenk and Taimyr AOks.

Gross regional product, 1997 ('000m. old roubles)	GRP per head, 1997 ('000 old roubles)	Official rate of un- employment, 1998 (%)	Inflation rate, 1998 (%)*	Foreign investment, 1998 (US $m.)	
2,554.0	5,673.0	3.0	168	0.6	. . . Adygeya
1,476.9	7,304.0	6.0	182	0.0†	. . . . Altai
64,557.3	15,731.0	4.4	179	67.3	. . Bashkortostan
11,541.3	11,010.6	3.7	164	13.0	. . . Buryatiya
n.a.	n.a.	n.a.	n.a.	n.a.	. . . Chechnya
11,573.5	8,511.8	3.6	168	11.6	. . . Chuvashiya
9,164.8	4,397.5	5.9	178	0.5	. . . Dagestan
955.5	3,072.3	n.a.	173	n.a.	. . . Ingushetiya
5,440.8	6,877.0	3.2	168	2.8	. Kabardino-Balkariya
1,788.8	5,635.8	8.1	169	1.6†	. . . Kalmykiya
2,747.5	6,297.3	1.4	173	3.1	Karachayevo-Cherkessiya
10,067.6	12,932.4	7.4	180	5.1	. . . .Kareliya
8,032.4	13,740.0	5.2	182	2.3	. . . Khakasiya
27,176.8	23,285.7	7.4	170	218.1	. . . . Komi
6,221.1	8,143.8	3.0	180	0.4	. . . .Marii-El
9,331.2	9,848.3	4.9	174	11.6	. . . Mordoviya
3,405.6	5,127.4	3.8	174	n.a.	. . North Osetiya
29,960.1	29,678.1	2.6	155	196.7	. Sakha (Yakutiya)
67,160.3	17,813.5	2.8	176	684.1	. . . Tatarstan
1,803.8	5,814.9	3.5	154	n.a.	. . . . Tyva
22,114.3	13,513.1	7.1	165	7.9	. . . Udmurtiya
22,052.2	8,243.2	3.8	171	6.0	. . . . Altai
31,380.6	20,227.0	5.3	164	40.1	. . . Khabarovsk
48,949.8	9,650.0	1.5	175	320.1	. . . Krasnodar
65,481.9	21,208.0	4.9	160	7.6	. . Krasnoyarsk[1]
30,545.5	13,720.9	3.8	170	46.1	Maritime (Primorskii)
25,688.6	9,589.1	1.5	171	67.3	. . . Stavropol

* Percentage change in the Consumer Price Index, Dec.–Dec.
† 1995 figure.

MAJOR DEMOGRAPHIC AND ECONOMIC INDICATORS (continued)

	Area ('000 sq km)	Population at 1 Jan. 1999 ('000)	Population density, 1999 (per sq km)	Average annual change in population, 1994–98 (%)	Life expectancy at birth, 1998
Oblasts					
Amur	363.7	1,008	2.8	-0.8	65.24
Archangel[2]	587.4	1,478	2.5	-0.9	66.09
Astrakhan	44.1	1,020	23.1	0.2	66.35
Belgorod	27.1	1,490	55.0	0.7	69.27
Bryansk	34.9	1,451	41.6	-0.2	66.70
Chelyabinsk	87.9	3,678	41.8	0.0	67.50
Chita	412.5	1,266[3]	2.9[3]	-0.6[3]	64.79[3]
Irkutsk[4]	767.9	2,758	3.6	-0.3	64.19
Ivanovo	21.8	1,232	56.5	-0.7	65.82
Kaliningrad	15.1	951	63.0	0.8	65.66
Kaluga	29.9	1,088	36.4	0.0	66.35
Kamchatka[5]	472.3	396	0.8	-2.4	64.68
Kemerovo	95.5	3,002	31.4	-0.5	64.61
Kirov (Vyatka) . . .	120.8	1,603	13.3	-0.6	67.51
Kostroma	60.1	787	13.1	-0.4	65.92
Kurgan	71.0	1,102	15.5	-0.2	67.06
Kursk	29.8	1,324	44.4	-0.2	67.17
Leningrad[6]	84.5	1,674	19.8	0.2	66.37
Lipetsk	24.1	1,245	51.7	0.0	68.08
Magadan	461.4	246	0.5	-4.8	66.63
Moscow[7]	46.0	6,501	141.3	-0.3	66.99
Murmansk	144.9	1,018	7.0	-1.7	68.85
Nizhnii Novgorod . .	76.9	3,688	48.0	-0.3	67.15
Novgorod	55.3	734	13.3	-0.3	65.02
Novosibirsk	178.2	2,748	15.4	0.0	67.77
Omsk	139.7	2,180	15.6	0.1	68.17
Orel	24.7	903	36.5	-0.2	67.87
Orenburg	124.0	2,226	17.9	0.2	66.79
Penza	43.2	1,542	35.7	-0.3	68.26
Perm[8]	160.6	2,970	18.5	-0.4	66.13
Pskov	55.3	811	14.7	-0.6	64.17
Rostov	100.8	4,368	43.3	-0.1	67.58
Ryazan	39.6	1,298	32.8	-0.6	66.87
Sakhalin	87.1	609	7.0	-2.8	64.20
Samara	53.6	3,305	61.7	0.2	67.31
Saratov	100.2	2,719	27.1	-0.1	67.55
Smolensk	49.8	1,143	22.9	-0.3	65.70
Sverdlovsk	194.8	4,631	23.8	-0.3	66.41
Tambov	34.3	1,284	37.4	-0.5	67.55
Tomsk	316.9	1,072	3.4	0.0	66.46
Tula	25.7	1,763	68.6	-0.7	65.88
Tver	84.1	1,614	19.2	-0.4	65.19
Tyumen[9]	1,435.2	3,244	2.3	0.6	67.76
Ulyanovsk	37.3	1,472	39.5	0.0	68.35
Vladimir	29.0	1,618	55.8	-0.3	66.65
Volgograd	113.9	2,693	23.6	0.2	67.63
Vologda	145.7	1,328	9.1	-0.4	66.69
Voronezh	52.4	2,472	47.28	-0.2	68.66
Yaroslavl	36.4	1,425	39.2	-0.5	67.21

[2] Including Nenets AOk; [3] including Aga-Buryat AOk; [4] including Ust-Orda Buryat AOk;
[5] including Koryak AOk; [6] excluding St Petersburg; [7] excluding Moscow city;
[8] including Komi-Permyak AOk; [9] including Khanty-Mansii and Yamal-Nenets AOks.

Gross regional product, 1997 ('000m. old roubles)	GRP per head, 1997 ('000 old roubles)	Official rate of un-employment, 1998 (%)	Inflation rate, 1998 (%)*	Foreign investment, 1998 (US $m.)				
15,664.7	15,248.4	3.3	171	0.4	.	.	.	. Amur
19,245.2	12,831.8	8.1	172	22.8	.	.	. Archangel[2]
11,223.1	10,900.4	4.7	171	7.6	.	.	. Astrakhan
18,154.3	12,254.0	1.8	168	156.1	.	.	. Belgorod
12,336.6	8,395.1	5.5	175	0.6	.	.	. Bryansk
51,467.1	13,987.1	2.2	189	59.1	.	.	. Chelyabinsk
12,737.8[3]	9,938.2[3]	4.8[3]	166[3]	12.5[3]	.	.	. . Chita
56,083.1	20,173.8	3.1	172	135.2	.	.	. Irkutsk[4]
8,847.0	7,071.9	6.1	176	0.1	.	.	. Ivanovo
8,466.1	9,022.3	3.4	203	39.4	.	.	. Kaliningrad
10,919.0	9,972.6	2.3	174	65.5	.	.	. Kaluga
8,146.4	20,360.8	5.6	162	42.9	.	.	. Kamchatka[5]
48,778.6	16,083.1	2.9	170	8.1	.	.	. Kemerovo
17,369.0	10,733.5	6.0	163	0.1	.	.	Kirov (Vyatka)
8,835.4	11,056.7	3.6	172	1.9	.	.	Kostroma
9,088.3	8,215.8	3.6	174	0.9	.	.	. Kurgan
15,404.4	11,499.3	1.9	172	13.9	.	.	. Kursk
19,456.2	11,580.4	5.3	166	190.7	.	.	. Leningrad[6]
15,736.9	12,604.7	1.2	161	14.8	.	.	. Lipetsk
6,402.4	25,774.5	5.4	154	53.7	.	.	. Magadan
97,419.5	14,824.1	3.2	183	708.7	.	.	. Moscow[7]
19,017.9	18,561.3	8.1	179	9.6	.	.	. Murmansk
52,943.7	14,293.7	2.5	200	149.7	.	Nizhnii Novgorod
7,728.5	10,460.8	4.0	172	44.5	.	.	. Novgorod
39,072.6	14,220.1	1.8	171	186.2	.	.	. Novosibirsk
33,787.1	15,526.5	2.1	172	452.2	.	.	. . Omsk
8,889.7	9,779.7	1.7	168	33.0	.	.	. . .Orel
30,594.0	13,729.8	1.0	179	130.0	.	.	. Orenburg
12,951.2	8,345.4	4.2	176	93.4	.	.	. . Penza
51,331.4	17,223.1	1.5	184	42.7	.	.	. Perm[8]
6,956.4	8,445.3	5.7	169	3.7	.	.	. . Pskov
35,062.0	7,947.1	1.5	179	16.8	.	.	. Rostov
14,404.6	10,981.6	2.4	179	4.9	.	.	. Ryazan
13,368.8	21,335.5	7.0	174	136.1	.	.	. Sakhalin
72,603.4	21,953.2	4.6	183	192.9	.	.	. Samara
31,767.6	11,654.8	1.7	184	37.3	.	.	. Saratov
12,029.8	10,352.7	1.1	177	26.6	.	.	. Smolensk
73,923.2	15,853.5	3.0	195	120.7	.	.	. Sverdlovsk
9,434.4	7,272.3	4.9	170	0.1	.	.	. Tambov
21,299.9	19,836.0	4.6	175	97.0	.	.	. Tomsk
16,577.1	9,244.4	1.9	169	31.5	.	.	. .Tula
16,213.1	9,896.9	1.7	171	4.9	.	.	. Tver
209,198.0	65,460.3	3.8	165	182.3	.	.	. .Tyumen[9]
16,564.6	11,141.1	2.6	163	0.2	.	.	. Ulyanovsk
15,265.0	9,342.7	5.9	172	198.9	.	.	. .Vladimir
32,296.3	12,026.3	1.4	172	82.6	.	.	. Volgograd
20,802.9	15,508.3	3.8	164	7.9	.	.	. . Vologda
25,737.4	10,326.8	2.0	174	4.0	.	.	. Voronezh
21,093.4	14,659.4	3.0	173	23.0	.	.	. Yaroslavl

* Percentage change in the Consumer Price Index, Dec.–Dec.

MAJOR DEMOGRAPHIC AND ECONOMIC INDICATORS (continued)

	Area ('000 sq km)	Population at 1 Jan. 1999 ('000)	Population density, 1999 (per sq km)	Average annual change in population, 1994–98 (%)	Life expectancy at birth, 1998
Federal Cities					
Moscow City . . .	1.0	8,300	8,300.0	-0.4	68.46
St Petersburg . . .	0.6	4,700	7,833.3	-0.6	69.33
Autonomous Oblast					
Jewish (Birobidzhan) .	36.0	201	5.2	-1.4	64.90
Autonomous Okrugs					
Aga-Buryat	19.0	79	4.3	-0.1	66.31
Chukchi	737.7	83	0.1	-7.5	64.95
Evenk	767.6	19	0.0	-3.4	60.75
Khanty-Mansii . . .	523.1	1,384	2.6	0.8	68.44
Komi-Permyak . . .	32.9	151	4.6	-1.0	64.57
Koryak	301.5	31	0.1	-3.2	59.81
Nenets	176.7	46	0.3	-1.8	65.79
Taimyr (Dolgan-Nenets)	862.1	44	0.1	-2.4	65.29
Ust-Orda Buryat . .	22.4	143	6.4	0.2	65.02
Yamal-Nenets . . .	750.3	507	0.7	1.2	69.68
Russian Federation. .	17,075.4	146,693	8.6	-0.2	67.02

Source: mainly Goskomstat, *The Regions of Russia*, 2 vols (in Russian). Moscow, 1999.

Gross regional product, 1997 ('000m. old roubles)	GRP per head, 1997 ('000 old roubles)	Official rate of un-employment, 1998 (%)	Inflation rate, 1998 (%)*	Foreign investment, 1998 (US \$m.)	
320,084.8	37,073.0	1.0	210	5,860.0	. . Moscow City
75,783.5	15,908.5	1.7	178	413.3	. . St Petersburg
1,300.1	6,302.2	1.9	166	n.a.	.Jewish (Birobidzhan)
n.a.	n.a.	9.3	177	n.a.	. . . Aga-Buryat
2,388.8	28,745.4	5.7	152	n.a.	. . . .Chukchi
n.a.	n.a.	6.1	125	n.a.	. . . . Evenk
n.a.	n.a.	4.4	165	106.6	. . Khanty-Mansii
n.a.	n.a.	3.8	157	n.a.	. . Komi-Permyak
n.a.	n.a.	9.7	130	7.1	. . . Koryak
n.a.	n.a.	9.6	161	2.6	. . . . Nenets
n.a.	n.a.	6.8	150	n.a.	Taimyr (Dolgan-Nenets)
n.a.	n.a.	3.6	157	n.a.	. . Ust-Orda Buryat
n.a.	n.a.	4.5	160	28.2	. . Yamal-Nenets
2,521,941.5	17,120.7	n.a.	184	11,773.0	. **Russian Federation**

* Percentage change in the Consumer Price Index, Dec.–Dec.

RUSSIAN CURRENCY AND EXCHANGE RATES

Monetary Units

    100 kopeks = 1 Russian rouble (rubl or ruble).

Sterling, Dollar and Euro Equivalents (28 September 2001)

    £1 = 43.21 roubles;
    US $1 = 29.39 roubles;
    €1 = 26.84 roubles;
    1,000 roubles = £23.14 = $34.03 = €37.26.

Average Exchange Rates (roubles per US dollar)

1998	9.7051
1999	24.6199
2000	28.1292

On 1 January 1998 the new rouble, equivalent to 1,000 of the former units, was introduced. Figures in this book are expressed in terms of new roubles unless otherwise indicated.

RUSSIAN INFLATION

The annual increase in consumer prices in the Russian Federation as a whole, according to official figures, for the year to December was:

1998	84.4%
1999	36.5%
2000	20.2%

 For the same years the International Monetary Fund cites average annual inflation rates of 27.7% in 1998, 85.7% in 1999 and 20.8% in 2000.

The Government of the Russian Federation

(December 2001)

According to the Constitution of December 1993, the Russian Federation is a democratic, federative, multi-ethnic republic, in which state power is divided between the executive, the legislature and the judiciary, which are independent of one another. The President of the Russian Federation is Head of State and Commander-in-Chief of the Armed Forces. The President, who wields considerable executive authority, is elected for a term of four years by universal direct suffrage. The President appoints the Chairman (Prime Minister) of the Government, but the cabinet must be approved by the legislature. Supreme legislative power is vested in a bicameral Federal Assembly.

There are 89 members (federal territorial units) of the Russian Federation. The recognized territories consist of 21 autonomous republics, six krais (provinces), 49 oblasts (regions), two cities of federal status, one autonomous oblast and 10 autonomous okrugs (districts). Largely based on the old Soviet divisions, their status as constituent members of the Federation began to be regularized by the so-called Federation Treaty of 31 March 1992. These three documents provided for a union of 20 republics (16 of which had been Autonomous Soviet Socialist Republics—ASSRs under the old regime, and four of which were autonomous oblasts), six krais and one autonomous oblast. The 10 autonomous okrugs remained under the jurisdiction of the krai or oblast within which they were located (a situation which largely continued thereafter) but, as federal units, were raised to the same status as oblasts and krais. A further republic, Ingushetiya, was acknowledged in June 1992. Moscow and St Petersburg subsequently assumed the status of federal cities.

Under the terms of the 1992 treaties, republics were granted far wider-reaching powers than the other federal units, specifically over the use of natural resources and land. They consequently represent autonomous states within the Russian Federation, as opposed to being merely administrative units of a unitary state. The exact delimitation of powers remained controversial and, often, modified by bilateral treaty between a territory and the central authorities. This process began in 1995 with treaties with seven republics and one oblast, but by the end of 1998 more than one-half of all the territories had signed such agreements. In March 1996 the precise terms of the delimitation of jurisdiction and powers between federal and regional authorities was decreed; no treaty could change the status of a federal unit, threaten the territorial integrity of the Russian Federation or violate the terms of the federal Constitution.

Autonomous republics, autonomous okrugs and the autonomous oblast are ethnically defined, while krais and oblasts are defined on territorial grounds. One of Vladimir Putin's earliest actions after his election as federal President in March 2000 was to group the federal subjects into seven large 'federal okrugs' (see the index of territories by okrug in Part Four). These seven districts, broadly similar to the organizational units of the Federation's Armed Forces in existence at that time, are the Central Federal Okrug (based in the capital, Moscow), the North-Western Federal Okrug (St Petersburg), the Southern (initially named North Caucasus) Federal Okrug (Rostov-on-Don), the Volga Federal Okrug (Nizhnii Novgorod), the Urals Federal Okrug (Yekaterinburg), the Siberian Federal Okrug (Novosibirsk) and the Far Eastern Federal Okrug (Khabarovsk). Additionally, each of the federal units is grouped into one of 11 economic areas (see the index of territories by area in Part Four). These are the Central Economic Area, the Central Chernozem (Black Earth) Economic Area, the Eastern Siberian Economic Area, the Far Eastern (sometimes known as the Pacific) Economic Area, the North Caucasus Economic Area, the North-Western Economic Area, the Northern Economic Area, the Urals Economic Area, the Volga Economic Area, the Volga-Vyatka Economic Area and the Western Siberian Economic Area.

Of the 89 members of the Russian Federation, the 21 republics are each administered by a president and/or prime minister. The remaining federal units are governed by a local administration, the head (governor) of which is the highest official in the territory, and a representative assembly (usually known as a soviet or duma). Governors are able to veto regional legislation, although their vetoes may be overridden by a two-thirds parliamentary majority. The federal legislature, which created the post of governor in August 1991, intended that the official be elected by popular vote. The federal President, Boris Yeltsin, however, secured an agreement that the governors be appointed. In many regions conflict subsequently arose between the executive and legislative bodies, as the presidential appointees encountered much resistance from the Communist-dominated assemblies. In those cases where a vote of 'no confidence' was passed in the governor, elections were permitted. (This occurred in seven oblasts and one krai in December 1992.) Following President Yeltsin's dissolution of the Russian legislature in September 1993, and parliament's violent resistance, it was announced that all heads of local administrations would, henceforth, be appointed and dismissed by presidential decree. In response to increasing pressure, however, this ruling was relaxed in December 1995, when gubernatorial elections were held in one krai and 11 oblasts. By the late 1990s elected governors had become the norm in all federal subjects.

Presidential Representative in the Central Federal Okrug: GEORGII SERGEYE-VICH POLTAVCHENKO; internet www.cfo-regions.ru.

Presidential Representative in the North-Western Federal Okrug: VIKTOR VASILYEVICH CHERKESOV; internet www.strana.ru/northwest.

Presidential Representative in the Southern Federal Okrug: Col-Gen. VIKTOR GERMANOVICH KAZANTSOV; internet polpred-ug.donpac.ru.

Presidential Representative in the Volga Federal Okrug: SERGEI VLADILENO-VICH KIRIYENKO; internet www.pfo.ru.

Presidential Representative in the Urals Federal Okrug: PETR MIKHAILOVICH LATYSHEV; internet www.uralfo.ru.

Presidential Representative in the Siberian Federal Okrug: LEONID VADIMO-VICH DRACHEVSKII; internet www.sfo.nsk.su.

Presidential Representative in the Far Eastern Federal Okrug: Col-Gen. KON-STANTIN BORISOVICH PULIKOVSKII; internet www.strana.ru/fareast.

Head of State

President of the Russian Federation: VLADIMIR V. PUTIN (elected President 26 March 2000; assumed office 7 May).

PRESIDENTIAL ADMINISTRATION

Office of the President: 103073 Moscow, Kremlin; tel. (095) 925-35-81; fax (095) 206-51-73; e-mail president@gov.ru; internet president.kremlin.ru.

The Government

Chairman (Prime Minister): MIKHAIL M. KASYANOV.

Deputy Chairman and Minister of Industry, Science and Technology: ILYA I. KLEBANOV.

Deputy Chairman and Minister of Agriculture and Foodstuffs: ALEKSEI V. GORDEYEV.

Deputy Chairman and Minister of Finance: ALEKSEI L. KUDRIN.

Deputy Chairmen: VIKTOR B. KHRISTENKO, VALENTINA I. MATVIYENKO.

Minister for Antimonopoly Policy and Support for Entrepreneurship: ILYA A. YUZHANOV.

Minister of Civil Defence, Emergencies and Clean-up Operations: Lt-Gen. SERGEI K. SHOIGU.

Minister of Communications and Information Technology: LEONID D. REYMAN.

Minister of Culture: MIKHAIL YE. SHVYDKOI.

Minister of Defence: SERGEI B. IVANOV.

Minister of Economic Development and Trade: GERMAN O. GREF.

Minister of Education and Vocational Training: VLADIMIR M. FILIPPOV.

Minister of Energy: IGOR KH. YUSUFOV.

Minister of Foreign Affairs: IGOR S. IVANOV.

Minister of Health: YURII L. SHEVCHENKO.

Minister of Internal Affairs: BORIS V. GRYZLOV.

Minister of Justice: YURII YA. CHAIKA.

Minister of Labour and Social Development: ALEKSANDR P. POCHINOK.

Minister of Natural Resources: VITALII G. ARTYUKHOV.

Minister of Nuclear Energy: ALEKSANDR YU. RUMYANTSEV.

Minister of the Press, Broadcasting and Mass Media: MIKHAIL YU. LESIN.

Minister of Railways: NIKOLAI YE. AKSENENKO.

Minister of State Property: FARIT R. GAZIZULLIN.

Minister of Transport: SERGEI O. FRANK.

Minister of Taxes and Levies: GENNADII I. BUKAYEV.

Head of the Presidential Administration and Minister Without Portfolio: IGOR I. SHUVALOV.

Ministers without Portfolio: VLADIMIR V. YELAGIN, VLADIMIR ZORIN.

MINISTRIES

Office of the Government: 103274 Moscow, Krasnopresnenskaya nab. 2; tel. (095) 925-35-81; fax (095) 205-42-19.

Ministry of Agriculture and Foodstuffs: 107139 Moscow, Orlikov per. 1/11; tel. (095) 207-83-62; fax (095) 207-80-00; e-mail info@aris.ru; internet www.aris.ru.

Ministry for Antimonopoly Policy and Support for Entrepreneurship: 123995 Moscow, ul. Sadovaya-Kudrinskaya 11; tel. (095) 252-76-53; fax (095) 254-75-21; e-mail info@maprus.ru; internet www.maprus.ru.

Ministry of Civil Defence, Emergencies and Clean-up Operations: 103012 Moscow, Teatralnyi proyezd 3; tel. (095) 926-39-01; fax (095) 924-19-46; e-mail pressa@emercom.gov.ru; internet www.emercom.gov.ru.

Ministry of Communications and Information Technology: 103375 Moscow, ul. Tverskaya 7; tel. (095) 292-71-44; fax (095) 292-74-55; internet www.minsvyaz.ru.

Ministry of Culture: 103074 Moscow, Kitaigorodskii proyezd 7; tel. (095) 925-11-95; fax (095) 928-17-91; e-mail root@mincult.isf.ru; internet www.mincult.isf.ru.

Ministry of Defence: 101000 Moscow, ul. Myasnitskaya 37; tel. (095) 293-38-54.

Ministry of Economic Development and Trade: 125993 Moscow, POB A-47, ul. Tverskaya-Yamskaya 1/3; tel. (095) 200-03-53; e-mail presscenter@economy.gov.ru; internet www.economy.gov.ru.

Ministry of Education and Vocational Training: 113833 Moscow, ul. Lyusinov-skaya 51; tel. (095) 237-76-75; fax (095) 237-83-81; e-mail mail@ministry.ru; internet www.ed.gov.ru.

Ministry of Energy: 103074 Moscow, Kitaigorodskii proyezd 7/191; tel. (095) 220-42-88; fax (095) 220-56-56; e-mail abs@cdu.oilnet.ru; internet www.mte.gov.ru.

Ministry of Finance: 103097 Moscow, ul. Ilinka 9; tel. (095) 298-91-01; fax (095) 925-08-89; internet www.minfin.ru.

Ministry of Foreign Affairs: 121200 Moscow, Smolenskaya-Sennaya pl. 32/34; tel. (095) 244-16-06; fax (095) 230-21-30; e-mail ministry@mid.ru; internet www.mid.ru.

Ministry of Health: 101431 Moscow, Rakhmanivskii per. 3; tel. (095) 927-28-48; fax (095) 928-58-15; e-mail minzdrav@cnt.ru; internet www.minzdrav-rf.ru.

Ministry of Industry, Science and Technology: 125889 Moscow, POB A-47, Miusskaya pl. 3; tel. (095) 229-11-92; fax (095) 229-55-49; e-mail info@mpnt.gov.ru; internet www.minprom.ru.

Ministry of Internal Affairs: 117049 Moscow, ul. Zhitnaya 16; tel. (095) 239-74-26; fax (095) 293-59-98; e-mail uimvd@mvdinform.ru; internet www.mvdinform.ru.

Ministry of Justice: 109830 Moscow, ul. Vorontsovo Pole 4A; tel. (095) 206-05-54; fax 916-29-03; internet www.scli.ru.

Ministry of Labour and Social Development: 103706 Moscow, Birzhevaya pl. 1; tel. (095) 928-06-83; fax (095) 230-24-07; e-mail press_mt@zanas.ru; internet www.mintrud.ru.

Ministry of Natural Resources: 123812 Moscow, ul. B. Gruzinskaya 4/6; tel. (095) 254-48-00; fax (095) 254-43-10; e-mail admin@mnr.gov.ru; internet www.mnr.gov.ru.

Ministry of Nuclear Energy: 101000 Moscow, ul. B. Ordynka 24/26; tel. (095) 239-45-45; fax (095) 230-24-20; e-mail info@minatom.ru; internet www.minatom.ru.

Ministry of the Press, Broadcasting and Mass Media: 101409 Moscow, POB 4, Strastnoi bul. 5; tel. (095) 229-68-93; fax (095) 200-22-81; internet www.mptr.ru.

Ministry of Railways: Moscow, ul. Novobasmannaya 2; tel. (095) 262-10-02; e-mail info@mps.ru; internet www.mps.ru.

Ministry of State Property: 103685 Moscow, Nikolskii per. 9; tel. (095) 298-75-62; fax (095) 206-11-19; e-mail mgi1@ftcenter.ru; internet www.mgi.ru.

Ministry of Taxes and Levies: 103381 Moscow, ul. Neglinnaya 23; tel. (095) 200-38-48; fax (095) 200-11-78; e-mail mns@nalog.ru; internet www.nalog.ru/.

Ministry of Transport: 101433 Moscow, ul. Sadovaya-Samotechnaya 10; tel. (095) 200-08-09; fax (095) 200-33-56; e-mail mcc@morflot.ru; internet www.mintrans.ru.

Federal Assembly

The Federal Assembly of the Russian Federation is a bicameral national parliament. Its upper chamber, the Federation Council, comprises 178 members, two appointed from each of the federal units, representing the executive and legislative branches of power in each territory. The lower chamber is the State Duma, with 450 deputies elected for a four-year term (the last general election was held on 19 December 1999).

Chairman of the Federation Council: SERGEI MIRONOV; 103426 Moscow, ul. B. Dmitrovka 26; tel. (095) 203-90-74; fax (095) 203-46-17; e-mail post_sf@gov.ru; internet www.council.gov.ru.

Chairman of the State Duma: GENNADII N. SELEZNEV; 103265 Moscow, Okhotnyi ryad 1; tel. (095) 292-83-10; fax (095) 292-94-64; internet www.duma.ru.

PART TWO
Territorial Surveys

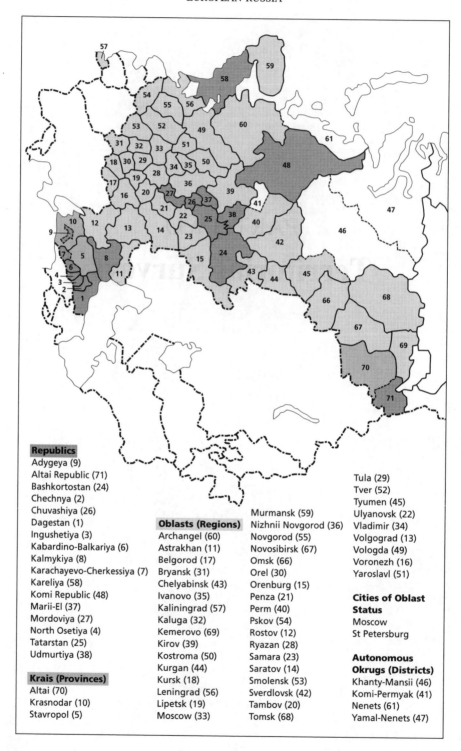

Republics
Adygeya (9)
Altai Republic (71)
Bashkortostan (24)
Chechnya (2)
Chuvashiya (26)
Dagestan (1)
Ingushetiya (3)
Kabardino-Balkariya (6)
Kalmykiya (8)
Karachayevo-Cherkessiya (7)
Kareliya (58)
Komi Republic (48)
Marii-El (37)
Mordoviya (27)
North Osetiya (4)
Tatarstan (25)
Udmurtiya (38)

Krais (Provinces)
Altai (70)
Krasnodar (10)
Stavropol (5)

Oblasts (Regions)
Archangel (60)
Astrakhan (11)
Belgorod (17)
Bryansk (31)
Chelyabinsk (43)
Ivanovo (35)
Kaliningrad (57)
Kaluga (32)
Kemerovo (69)
Kirov (39)
Kostroma (50)
Kurgan (44)
Kursk (18)
Leningrad (56)
Lipetsk (19)
Moscow (33)

Murmansk (59)
Nizhnii Novgorod (36)
Novgorod (55)
Novosibirsk (67)
Omsk (66)
Orel (30)
Orenburg (15)
Penza (21)
Perm (40)
Pskov (54)
Rostov (12)
Ryazan (28)
Samara (23)
Saratov (14)
Smolensk (53)
Sverdlovsk (42)
Tambov (20)
Tomsk (68)

Tula (29)
Tver (52)
Tyumen (45)
Ulyanovsk (22)
Vladimir (34)
Volgograd (13)
Vologda (49)
Voronezh (16)
Yaroslavl (51)

Cities of Oblast Status
Moscow
St Petersburg

Autonomous Okrugs (Districts)
Khanty-Mansii (46)
Komi-Permyak (41)
Nenets (61)
Yamal-Nenets (47)

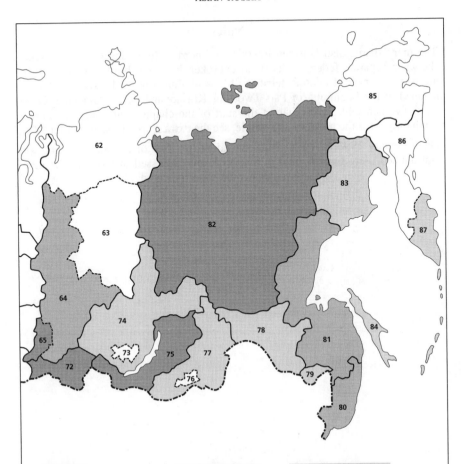

Republics
Buryatiya (75)
Khakasiya (65)
Tyva (72)
Republic of Sakha (82)
(Yakutiya)

Krais (Provinces)
Khabarovsk (81)
Krasnoyarsk (64)
Maritime (Primorskii) (80)

Oblasts (Regions)
Amur (78)
Chita (77)
Irkutsk (74)
Kamchatka (87)
Magadan (83)
Sakhalin (84)

Autonomous Oblast
Jewish Autonomous Oblast (79)

**Autonomous
Okrugs (Districts)**
Aga-Buryat (76)
Chukchi (85)
Evenk (63)
Koryak (86)
Taimyr (Dolgan-Nenets) (62)
Ust-Orda Buryat (73)

Notes

The maps distinguish between international borders (dots and dashes), borders between separate federal units (bold unbroken line) and borders of units that are formally part of another territory. Maps of European and Asian Russia are included at the beginning of Part Two. For Krasnoyarsk Krai, Archangel Oblast and Tyumen Oblast, the map at the start of the chapter illustrates the 'core' region only—for the territory as a whole, see the extra maps at the end of Part Two.

On 1 January 1998 a new rouble, equivalent to 1,000 of the former units, was introduced. Any figures cited in this book are expressed in terms of the new rouble, unless otherwise indicated.

AUTONOMOUS REPUBLICS

Republic of Adygeya

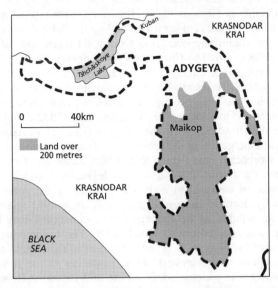

The Republic of Adygeya (Adygheya) is situated in the foothills of the Greater Caucasus, in the basin of the Kuban river. It lies within Krasnodar Krai, of which it forms a part (the city of Krasnodar itself faces territory in north-western Adygeya across the Kuban). The Republic is in the North Caucasus Economic Area and the Southern Federal Okrug. The Black Sea resort of Sochi lies some 40 km (25 miles) to the south of Adygeya, itself land-locked. The territory of the Republic, of which some two-fifths is forested, is characterized by open grassland, fertile soil and numerous rivers. The Republic has an area of 7,600 sq km (2,930 sq miles) and is comprised of seven administrative districts and two cities. At 1 January 1999 it was estimated to have 449,300 inhabitants, of whom 53.9% were urban. The population density per sq km in 1999 was 59.1. In 1989, according to the census, of the total republican population some 68% were ethnic Russian and 22% Adyges (otherwise known as Lower Circassians or Kiakhs). Of the Adyge population, an estimated 95% speak the national tongue, Adyge—part of the Abkhazo-Adyge group of Caucasian languages—as their native language, although some 82% are also fluent in Russian. The dominant religion in the Republic, owing to the preponderance of Russian inhabitants, is Orthodox Christianity, but the traditional religion of the Adyges is Islam. The administrative centre of Adygeya is at Maikop, which had a total of 166,700 inhabitants at 1 January 1999. Its other major city is Adygeysk, which had only 12,400 inhabitants.

History

The Adyges were traditionally renowned for their unrivalled horsemanship and marksmanship. They emerged as a distinct ethnic group among the Circassians in the 13th century, when they inhabited much of the area between the Don river and the Caucasus, and the Black Sea and the Stavropol plateau. They were conquered by the Mongol Empire in the 13th century. In the 1550s the Adyges entered into an alliance with the Russian Empire, as protection against the Tatar Khanate of Crimea and against Turkic groups such as the Karachais, the Kumyks and the Nogais, which had retreated into the Caucasus from the Mongol forces of Temujin (Chinghiz or Ghengis Khan). Russian settlers subsequently moved into the Don and Kuban regions, causing unrest among the Adyges and other Circassian peoples, many of whom supported the Ottoman Empire against Russia in the Crimean War of 1853–56. The Circassians were finally defeated by the Russians in 1864. Most were forced either to emigrate or to move to the plains that were under Russian control. A Kuban-Black Sea Soviet Republic was established in 1918, but the region was soon occupied by anti-Communist forces ('Whites'). The Adygeya Autonomous Oblast was established on 27 July 1922. From 24 August 1922 until 13 August 1928 it was known as the Adygeya (Circassian) Autonomous Oblast.

Following the emergence of the policy of *glasnost* (openness) in the USSR, under Mikhail Gorbachev, the Adyge-Khase Movement was formed. This group, which demanded the formation of a national legislative council or khase, began to raise the issues of nationalism and independence in the Autonomous Oblast. Adygeya officially declared its sovereignty on 28 June 1991 and was recognized as an autonomous republic at the signing of the Federation Treaty in March 1992. Its Constitution was adopted on 10 March 1995. The Communists remained the most popular party (winning 41% of the votes cast in the Republic at the Russian State Duma elections of December), while suspicion of the reformists and the federal Government was widespread. From the mid-1990s the Republic developed close links with the other Circassian Republics (Kabardino-Balkariya and Kara-chayevo-Cherkessiya). In May 1998, at the second session of an interparliamentary council, a programme was adopted on the co-ordination of legislative, economic, environmental and legal activities. The Adyge President, Aslan Aliyevich Dzhar-imov, was among those instrumental in forming the parliamentary bloc 'All Russia' in 1999.

Economy

Agriculture is, traditionally, the principal economic activity of Adygeya. In 1997 the territory's gross regional product was 2,554,000m. old roubles, or 5,673,000 old roubles per head. The territory's major industrial centres are at the cities of Maikop and Kamennomostskii. There are 148 km of railway track on its territory and 1,509 km of paved roads.

Agricultural production consists mainly of grain, sunflowers, sugar beets, tobacco and vegetables, cucurbit (gourds and melons) cultivation and viniculture. The Republic produced over 17% of the Federation's output of grape wine in the first half of 2000. The entire sector employed some 15.4% of the working population in 1998. The decline in overall agricultural production in the Republic slowed during the mid-1990s, although animal husbandry decreased to less than one-half of its 1991 level by 1998. Owing to the growth in prices of resources and fodder and the restriction of credits, some 300 farmers ceased activity between 1992 and

1996. The value of agricultural output in 1998 was 996m. roubles. There is some extraction of natural gas. In industry, food processing is particularly important, accounting for over one-half of industrial production. Timber processing, mechanical engineering and metal working are also significant. Adygeya also lies along the route of the 'Blue Stream' pipeline, which was to deliver gas to Turkey, and planned petroleum pipelines from the Transcaucasus and Dagestan to the Black Sea ports of Novorossiisk and Tuapse. Some 17.0% of the working population were engaged in industry in 1998. Industrial production declined during the early 1990s, but began to stabilize during the second half of the decade, amounting to 1,018m. roubles in 1998. In 1998 the trade of the Republic amounted to a value of US $13.7m. (significantly less than its value in the mid-1990s), of which $10.1m. were imports and $3.6m. exports. Its main trading partners, in the mid-1990s, in terms of exports, were Belarus, France, Kazakhstan, Poland, Turkey and Ukraine. Exports consisted mainly of food products, machine-tools and petroleum and chemical products.

In 1998 the economically active population in Adygeya amounted to 150,200, of whom 4,500 were registered as unemployed. The average monthly wage was 532.3 roubles. In 1998 there was a budgetary deficit of 13m. roubles. There was relatively little foreign investment in the Republic: in 1998 it amounted to just $648,000. At 1 January 1999 there were 2,203 small businesses registered on its territory.

Directory

President: ASLAN ALIYEVICH DZHARIMOV; respublika Adygeya, 352700 Maikop, ul. Zhukovskaya 22; tel. (87722) 2-19-00; fax (87722) 2-59-58.

Premier: MUKHARBII KHADZHIRETOVICH TKHARKAKHOV; respublika Adygeya, 352700 Maikop, ul. Zhukovskaya 22; tel. (87722) 2-22-22.

Chairman of the Khase (State Council): YEVGENII IVANOVICH SALOV; respublika Adygeya, 352700 Maikop; tel. (87722) 2-19-02.

Permanent Representative in Moscow: RUSLAN YUNUSOVICH GUSARUK; tel. (095) 291-00-69.

Head of Maikop City Administration: MIKHAIL NIKOLAYEVICH CHERNICHENKO; respublika Adygeya, 352700 Maikop, ul. Krasnooktyabrskaya 21; tel. (87722) 2-17-08; internet www.maykop.ru.

Republic of Altai

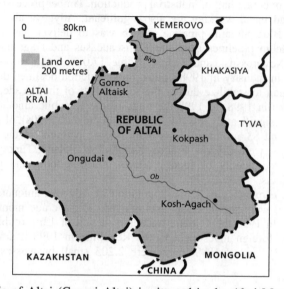

The Republic of Altai (Gornyi Altai) is situated in the Altai Mountains, in the basin of the Ob river. The Republic forms the eastern part of the Altai Krai and belongs to the Western Siberian Economic Area and the Siberian Federal Okrug. It has international borders with Kazakhstan in the south-west, a short border with the People's Republic of China to the south, and with Mongolia to the south-east. Kemerovo Oblast lies to the north, the Republics of Khakasiya and Tyva to the east. The Republic is mountainous (Belukha, at 4,506 m or 14,783 feet, is the highest peak in Siberia) and heavily forested (about one-quarter of its territory). Its major rivers are the Katyn and the Biya and it has one lake, Teletskoye. It contains one of Russia's major national parks, Altai State National Park, covering an area of some 9,000 sq km. The Republic occupies 92,600 sq km (35,750 sq miles) and comprises 10 administrative districts and one city. Its climate is continental, with short summers and long, cold winters. At 1 January 1999 it was estimated to have a population of 203,100 and a population density, therefore, of only 2.2 per sq km. Of its inhabitants, 25.0% resided in urban areas at this time. The census of 1989 put the number of Russians at some 60% of the total and of ethnic Altai at 31%. Some 5.6% of the population were Kazakh, 0.9% Ukrainian and 0.4% German at this time. The Altai people can be divided into two distinct groups: the Northern Altai, or Chernnevye Tatars, consisting of the Tubalars, the Chelkans or Leberdin and the Kumandins; and the Southern Altai, comprising the Altai Kizhi, the Telengit, the Telesy and the Teleut. The language spoken by both groups is from the Turkish branch of the Uralo-Altaic family: that of the Northern Altais is from the Old Uigur group, while the language of the Southern Altais is close to the Kyrgyz language and is part of the Kipchak group. Over 84% of Altais speak one or other language as their native tongue, and some 62% of the Altai population is fluent in Russian. Although the traditional religion of the Altai was animist, many were converted to Christianity, so the dominant religion in the

Republic is Russian Orthodoxy. The Republic's administrative centre is at Gorno-Altaisk, which had an estimated population of 50,600 at 1 January 1999.

History

From the 11th century the Altai peoples inhabited Dzungaria (Sungaria—now mainly in the north-west of the People's Republic of China). The region was under Mongol control until 1389, when it was conquered by the Tatar forces of Tamerlane (Tamberlane or Timur 'the Lame'); it subsequently became a Kalmyk confederation. In the first half of the 18th century many Altais moved westwards, invading Kazakh territory and progressing almost as far as the Urals. In 1758, however, most of Dzungaria was incorporated into Xinjiang (Sinkiang), a province of the Chinese Empire. China embarked on a war aimed at exterminating the Altai peoples. Only a few thousand survived, finding refuge in the Altai Mountains. In the 19th century Russia began to assert its control over the region and the Altai territory was finally annexed in 1866. In the early 1900s Burkhanism or White Faith, a strong nationalist religious movement, emerged. The movement was led by Oirot Khan, who claimed to be a descendant of Chinghiz (Genghis) Khan and promised to liberate the Altais from Russian control. However, in February 1918 it was a secular nationalist leader, B. I. Anuchin, who convened a Constituent Congress of the High Altai and demanded the establishment of an Oirot Republic—to include the Altai, the Khakassians and the Tyvans. In partial recognition of such demands, on 1 July 1922 the Soviet Government established an Oirot Autonomous Oblast in Altai Krai. Nationalist feeling remained strong in the region, however, and in 1933 many members of the local Communist Party were purged. On 7 January 1948 the region was renamed the Gorno-Altai Autonomous Oblast, in an effort to suppress nationalist sentiment.

In the late 1980s nationalism re-emerged in response to Mikhail Gorbachev's policy of *glasnost* (openness). Renamed Altai, the region became an autonomous republic at the signing of the Russian Federation Treaty in March 1992, having adopted its State Sovereignty Declaration on 25 October 1990. A resolution adopted on 14 October 1993 provided for the establishment of a State Assembly (El Kurultai), which comprised 27 deputies and represented the highest body of power in the Republic. Following the blockade by public-sector workers of the State Assembly in mid-1998, in protest at payment arrears, the legislature obtained federal transfers of 100m. roubles. The Altai Republic was one of only four subjects of the Russian Federation to award the Communist candidate, Yevgenii Zyuganov, a higher proportion of the votes than Vladimir Putin in the presidential election of 26 March 2000. In June the Russian Constitutional Court demanded that several articles of the Altai Republic's Constitution be amended in order to conform to the fundamental laws of the Russian Federation. Several amendments to this end were approved by the republican parliament in February 2001, including the removal of a provision that had forbidden persons of the same nationality from simultaneously occupying the posts of chairman of the republican government and parliamentary speaker. Following an inconclusive first round of voting in the election to the post of chairman of the government held in the Republic on 16 December, the incumbent, and Agrarian Party of Russia leader Mikhail Lapshin were to contest a second round.

Economy

The Republic of Altai is predominantly an agricultural region. Its gross regional product amounted to 1,476,900m. old roubles in 1997, or 7,304,200 old roubles per head. The main industrial centre in the Republic is at its capital, Gorno-Altaisk. Owing to its mountainous terrain, it contains just 2,636 km (1,638 miles) of paved roads, of which 572 km comprise a section of the major Novorossiisk–Biisk–Tashanta highway. There are no railways or airports. In March 1996 the Russian Government allocated some 1,800m. old roubles to alleviate the effects in the Republic of the nuclear tests conducted at Semipalatinsk (Kazakhstan) between 1949 and 1962.

Agriculture in the Republic of Altai, which employed 25.4% of the working population in 1997, consists mainly of livestock breeding (largely horses, deer, sheep and goats, amounting to 60% of agricultural activity), bee-keeping, grain production and hunting. The export of the antlers of Siberian maral and sika deer, primarily to South-East Asia, is an important source of convertible ('hard') currency to the Republic. The total value of agricultural output in 1998 was 764.5m. roubles. The Republic's mountainous terrain often prevents the easy extraction or transport of minerals, but there are important reserves of manganese, iron, silver, lead and wolfram (tungsten), as well as timber. Stone, lime, salt, sandstone, gold, mercury and non-ferrous metals are also produced. There are food-processing, light, chemical, metal-working and machine-tool industries, as well as factories assembling tractors, automobiles, radios, televisions, engines, boilers and electrical appliances. Industry employed just 7.3% of the working population in 1998, while the value of industrial production amounted to 131,000m. roubles. In that year the value of the Republic's exports was US $24.3m., while its imports were equivalent to around $83.4m.

In 1998 a total of 73,600 of the Republic's inhabitants were economically active, of whom 4,400 were registered unemployed. The average monthly wage in that year was 565.0 roubles. The territory suffered severe financial difficulties in the late 1990s. Teachers took industrial action to protest against continued wage arrears throughout 1999, which, even at the end of that year, stood at an average of 9.4 months and amounted to over 60m. roubles. A budgetary surplus of 44m. roubles was achieved in 1998; at the beginning of the following year there were approximately 800 small businesses operating in the Republic.

Directory

Chairman of the Government: SEMEN IVANOVICH ZUBAKIN; respublika Altai, 659700 Gorno-Altaisk, ul. Kirova 16; tel. (38822) 2-26-30; e-mail gornyaltay@ mtu-net.ru internet www.mtu-net.ru/gornyaltay.

Chairman of the El Kurultai (State Assembly): DANIIL IVANOVICH TABAYEV; respublika Altai, 659700 Gorno-Altaisk, ul. Erkemena Palkina 1; tel. (38822) 2-26-18; fax (38822) 2-27-61.

Permanent Representative in Moscow: SERGEI DEMIDOVICH KONCHAKOVSKY; 10375 Moscow, ul. Malaya Dmitrovka 3, kom. 221; tel. (095) 299-50-87; fax (095) 299-81-97.

Head of Gorno-Altaisk City Administration: VIKTOR ALEKSANDROVICH OBLOGIN; respublika Altai, 659700 Gorno-Altaisk, pr. Kommunisticheskii 18; tel. (38822) 2-07-31.

Republic of Bashkortostan

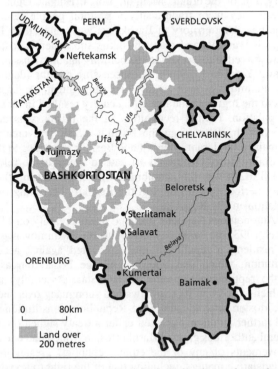

The Republic of Bashkortostan (Bashkiriya) is situated on the slopes of the Southern Urals. It forms part of the Urals Economic Area and the Volga Federal Okrug. Orenburg Oblast lies to the south and south-west of Bashkortostan, the Republics of Tatarstan and Udmurtiya lie to the north and north-west, respectively. There are borders with Perm and Sverdlovsk Oblasts to the north and Chelyabinsk to the east. The north of the Republic (more than one-third of its land area) is forested, while the southern part is steppe. The Republic occupies an area of 143,600 sq km (55,440 sq miles) and comprises 54 administrative districts and 20 cities. At 1 January 1999 Bashkortostan had an estimated population of 4,110,300, some 65.0% of which inhabited urban areas, and a population density of 28.6 per sq km. The most numerous ethnic group was Russian (39% in 1989, according to census figures). Tatars made up 28% of the population, while Bashkirs only constituted 22%. Of the ethnic Bashkir inhabitants, some 72% spoke Bashkir as their native tongue. Bashkir is a Kipchak language closely related to that spoken by the Tatars. There are two distinct Bashkir dialects: Kuvakan is spoken in the north of the Republic, while Yurmatin (Yurmatyn) is current in the south. The majority of Bashkirs and Tatars are Sunni Muslims of the Hanafi school, although some Bashkirs, the Nagaibak (Noghaibaq or Nogaibak) were converted to Orthodox Christianity. The Republic's administrative centre is at Ufa, which had an estimated population of 1,086,600 at 1 January 1999. Its other major cities, with populations in excess of 100,000, are Sterlitamak, Salabat, Neftekamsk and Oktyabrskii.

History

The Bashkirs were thought to have originated as a distinct ethnic group during the 16th century, out of the Tatar, Mongol, Volga, Bulgar, Oguz, Pecheneg and Kipchak peoples. They were traditionally a pastoral people renowned for their bee-keeping abilities. The territory of Bashkiriya was annexed by Russia in 1557, during the reign of Ivan IV, and many Bashkirs subsequently lost their land and wealth and were forced into servitude. Rebellions against Russian control, most notably by Salavat Yulai in 1773, were unsuccessful, and the identity and survival of the Bashkir community came under increasing threat. A large migration of ethnic Russians to the region in the late 19th century resulted in their outnumbering the Bashkir population. Formal recognition of the Bashkirs as an ethnic group occurred on 23 March 1919, when the Bashkir ASSR was created. The Soviet Government remained intolerant of unrest and Bashkir resistance to the collectivization policy of Stalin (Iosif Dzhugashvili) caused many to be relocated to other regions in the USSR. It was this, combined with losses during the civil wars of the revolutionary period, that resulted in the Bashkirs becoming outnumbered by the Tatar population in the Republic.

The Bashkir Autonomous Republic declared its sovereignty on 11 October 1990. On 12 December 1993, the same day that Murtaza Rakhimov was elected to the new post of President, a republican majority voted against acceptance of the Russian Constitution, which was approved in the Federation as a whole. On 24 December the republican Supreme Soviet (State Assembly) adopted a new Constitution, which stated that its own laws had supremacy over federal laws. The name of Bashkortostan was adopted. The Republic's constitutional position was regularized and further autonomy granted under a treaty signed on 3 August 1994. By this, the federal authorities granted Bashkortostan, which had one of the strongest sovereignty movements of any of the ethnic republics, greater independence in economic and legislative matters, including that of the right to levy taxes. A further bilateral treaty was signed in 1995. Bashkortostan enjoyed close relations with the Republic of Tatarstan: on 28 August 1997 the Presidents of the two territories signed a treaty on co-operation. The Republic's administration was traditionally centralized and conservative but keen to attract foreign investment. A presidential election, held on 14 June 1998, returned the incumbent, Rakhimov, to office, with 73% of the votes cast, his candidacy having been endorsed publicly by the Russian President, Boris Yeltsin. In January 1999 the premier, Rim Bakiyev, retired, to be replaced by his first deputy, Rafael Baidevletov. In the federal parliamentary elections of December 1999, the candidates of Rakhimov's favoured grouping, Fatherland—All Russia, were successful in the Republic; prior to the election Rakhimov was rebuked by the federal Prime Minister, Vladimir Putin, for blocking the transmission of two television channels opposed to the grouping. Commentators also observed the absence of any opposition press in Bashkortostan, and the removal from electoral lists of most of Rakhimov's opponents, owing to alleged electoral violations. In the federal presidential election of 26 March 2000, Bashkortostan returned 62% of votes in favour of Vladimir Putin, well above the national average, reflecting Rakhimov's support for Putin during the election campaign. None the less, two months later Putin ordered that Bashkortostan's Constitution be altered to conform with Russia's basic law. A new republican Constitution was introduced in November; although several articles continued to contradict federal norms, the presidential representative to the Volga Federal Okrug, Sergei Kiriyenko, expressed satisfaction with the revised document. In January 2001 one of the most significant contradictions, the statement that republican legislation should take precedence over federal law, was rescinded, and several powers formerly attributed to the republican prime minister were transferred to the republican president. In March Rakhimov was appointed by President Putin to serve on the presidium of the State Council; in this position he established himself as a leading critic of proposed reforms that sought to increase the powers of the federal authorities. Also in 2001, Rakhimov announced his support for the merger of Fatherland—All Russia with the Yedistvo (Unity) party, in order to encourage the development of a two- or three-party system that he believed was symptomatic of mature democracies.

Economy

Bashkortostan's economy is dominated by its fuel and energy and agro-industrial complexes. The Republic is one of Russia's key petroleum-producing areas and the centre of its petroleum-refining industry. It produced 4% of Russia's total petroleum output in the first six months of 2000 and accounted for around 15% of its petroleum refining. However, the quantity of petroleum both produced and refined in the Republic declined significantly during the 1990s. In 1997 the territory's gross regional product stood at 64,557,300m. old roubles, or 15,731,100 old roubles per head. Its major industrial centres are at Ufa (at which the Republic's petroleum refineries are based), Sterlitamak, Salavat and Ishimbai. In 1997 there were 1,475 km of railways on its territory and 21,517 km of paved roads. Aviakompaniya BAL (Bashkirskiye Avialiniya—Bashkir Air Lines) operates air services between Ufa and major centres within Russia and elsewhere within the Commonwealth of Independent States from the Republic's international airport.

Bashkortostan's agricultural production, the value of which amounted to 10,662.3m. roubles in 1998, ranks among the highest in the Russian Federation. Its main agricultural activities are grain, sugar-beet, sunflower and vegetable production, animal husbandry, poultry farming and bee-keeping. Some 16.7% of the Republic's work-force were employed in agriculture in 1998. As well as its petroleum resources (of which the deposits amount to 400m. metric tons), Bashkortostan contains deposits of natural gas (55m. tons), brown coal—lignite (250m. tons), iron ore, copper, gold (with reserves amounting to 32 tons in 1997, sufficient for 19 years of production), zinc, aluminium, chromium, salt (2,270m. tons), manganese, gypsum and limestone. The Republic's other industries include processing of agricultural and forestry products, mechanical engineering, metal working, metallurgy, production of mining and petroleum-exploration equipment, automobiles, geophysical instruments, cables and electrical equipment and building materials. In 1998 industry employed 25.2% of the Republic's working population. Total industrial output was worth 46,038m. roubles in that year. In the same year the Republic's external trade totalled US $1,600m.: exports exceeded imports by around 400% and largely comprised petroleum products and petrochemical goods. Bashkortostan's principal trading partner is Germany.

In 1998 the economically active population in the Republic amounted to 1,665,900, of which 72,600 (4.4%) were unemployed. The average monthly wage at that time was 655.5 roubles. There was a budgetary deficit of 296m. roubles in that year. Foreign investment in the Republic in 1998 amounted to some US $67.31m. In March 1998 the republican premier, Rim Bakiyev, signed an agreement on a two-year loan arranged by Moscow Narodnyi Bank and HSBC

Markets (United Kingdom) to be used in its petrochemicals and hydrocarbons industry. At 1 January 1999 there were 14,200 small businesses registered on the Republic's territory.

Directory

President: MURTAZA GUBAIDULLOVICH RAKHIMOV; respublika Bashkortostan, 450101 Ufa, ul. Tukayeva 46; tel. (3472) 50-27-24; fax (3472) 50-02-81; e-mail aprb_webmaster@kmrb.bashnet.ru; internet president.bashkortostan.ru.

Prime Minister: RAFAEL IBRAGIMOVICH BAIDAVLETOV; respublika Bashkortostan, 450101 Ufa, ul. Tukayeva 46; tel. (3472) 50-24-01; fax (3472) 50-57-47; e-mail info@bashkortostan.ru.

Chairman of the State Assembly: KONSTANTIN BORISOVICH TOLKACHEV; respublika Bashkortostan, 450101 Ufa, ul. Tukayeva 46; tel. (3472) 50-19-15; fax (3472) 50-17-52.

Permanent Representative in Moscow: IREK YUMBAYEVICH ABLAYEV; 103045 Moscow, ul. Sretensky Bulvar 9/2; tel. (095) 208-26-79; fax (095) 208-39-25.

Head of Ufa City Administration (Mayor): RAUF SAMIGULLOVICH NUGU-MANOV; respublika Bashkortostan, 450098 Ufa, pr. Oktyabrya 120; tel. (3472) 21-28-16; fax (3472) 33-18-73; e-mail major@cityadmin.ufanet.ru; internet www.misufa.ru.

Republic of Buryatiya

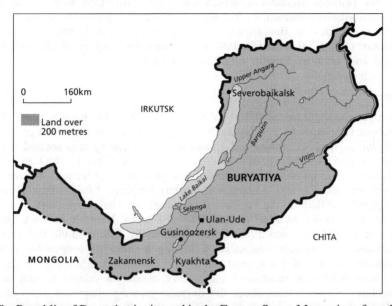

The Republic of Buryatiya is situated in the Eastern Sayan Mountains of southern Siberia and forms part of the Eastern Siberian Economic Area and the Siberian Federal Okrug. It lies mainly in the Transbaikal region to the east of Lake Baikal, although it also extends westwards along the international boundary with Mongolia in the south, to create a short border with the Russian federal territory of Tyva in the extreme south-west. Irkutsk Oblast lies to the north and west, and Chita Oblast to the east. Buryatiya's rivers mainly drain into Lake Baikal, the largest being the Selenga, the Barguzin and the upper Angara, but some, such as the Vitim, flow northwards into the Siberian plains. The Republic's one lake, Baikal, forms part of the western border of the Republic. Baikal is the oldest and deepest lake in the world, possessing over 80% of Russia's freshwater resources and 20% of the world's total. Considered holy by the Buryats, until the 1950s it was famed for the purity of its waters and the uniqueness of the ecosystem it sustained. Intensive industrialization along its shores threatened Baikal's environment, and only in the 1990s were serious efforts made to safeguard the lake. Some 70% of Buryatiya's territory, including its low mountains, is forested, while its valleys are open steppe. The Republic's territory covers 351,300 sq km (135,640 sq miles) and comprises a total of 21 administrative districts and six cities. Temperatures in the Republic fall as low as −50°C in winter, which is protracted but sees little snow, and can reach up to 40°C in summer. Buryatiya is sparsely populated: it had an estimated population of 1,038,200 at 1 January 1999 and a population density of 3.0 per sq km. Around 59.6% of the population inhabited urban areas at that time. At the 1989 census, some 70% of the inhabitants were ethnic Russians and 24% Buryats. The industrial areas of the Republic are mainly inhabited by ethnic Russians. The Buryats are a native Siberian people of Mongol descent. The majority of those inhabiting the Republic are Transbaikal Buryats, as distinct from the Irkutsk Buryats, who live west of Lake Baikal. The Buryats' native tongue is a Mongol dialect. Some Buryats are Orthodox Christians, but others still practise Lamaism (Tibetan Buddhism), which has been syncretized with the region's traditional animistic shamanism. The Khambo Lama, the spiritual leader of Russia's Buddhists, resides in Buryatiya's capital, Ulan-Ude, which had an estimated population of 370,700 in January 1999 and is paired, for the purpose of commercial, cultural and social exchanges, with Taipei in Taiwan.

History

Buryatiya was regarded as strategically important from the earliest years of the Muscovite Russian state, as it lay on the Mongol border. Russian influence reached the region in the 17th century and Transbaikal was formally incorporated into the Russian Empire by the Treaties of Nerchinsk and Kyakhta in 1689 and 1728, respectively. The latter agreement ended a dispute over the territory between the Russian and the Chinese Manzhou (Manchu) Empires. Many ethnic Russians subsequently settled in the region, often inhabiting land confiscated from the Buryats, many of whom were 'russified'. Other Buryats, however, strove to protect their culture, and there was a resurgence of nationalist feeling in the 19th century. Jamtsarano, a prominent nationalist, following a series of congresses in 1905 demanding Buryat self-government and the use of the Buryat language in schools, led a movement that recognized the affinity of Buryat culture to that of the Mongolians. Russia's fears about the Buryats' growing allegiance to its eastern neighbour were allayed, however, after a formal treaty signed with Japan in 1912 recognized Outer Mongolia (Mongolia) as a Russian sphere of influence.

With the dissolution of the Far Eastern Republic (based at Chita), a Buryat-Mongol ASSR was established on 30 May 1923. In the early 1930s, following Stalin—Iosif Dzhugashvili's policy of collectivization, many Buryats fled the country or were found guilty of treason and executed. In 1937 the Soviet Government considerably reduced the territory of the Republic, transferring the eastern section to Chita Oblast and a westerly region to Irkutsk Oblast. Furthermore, the Buryat language's Mongolian script was replaced with a Cyrillic one. In 1958 the Buryat-Mongol ASSR was renamed the Buryat ASSR, amid suspicions of increasing co-operation between the Mongolian People's Republic (Mongolia) and the People's Republic of China. The territory declared its sovereignty on 10 October 1990, and was renamed the Republic of Buryatiya in 1992. On 30 December a draft constitution was published. It was adopted by the legislature, the Supreme Soviet, on 4 March 1994. The Constitution provided for Buryatiya as a sovereign, democratic, law-governed state within the Russian Federation. It established an executive presidency, a post first held by the then-Chairman of the Supreme Soviet, Leonid Potapov, and redesignated the elected legislature as the People's Khural. A bilateral treaty on a division of powers was signed with the Federation Government in 1995. On 21 June 1998 presidential and legislative elections were held in the Republic: Potapov was re-elected President, with 63.25% of the votes cast. In October 2000 the People's Khural approved several amendments to Buryatiya's Constitution in order that it conform more closely with federal norms. However, the Khural rejected the implementation of several proposed amendments required by federal legislation, including, notably, the abolition of the requirement that presidential candidates know both state languages, Russian and Buryat. However, the People's

Khural proposed that a special commission be created in order to establish mechanisms for the future co-ordination of regional and federal legislation.

Economy

In 1997 Buryatiya's gross regional product amounted to 11,541,300m. old roubles, equivalent to 11,010,600 old roubles per head. Its major industrial centre is at Ulan-Ude, which is on the route of the Trans-Siberian Railway.

The Republic's agriculture, which employed around 11.3% of the work-force in 1998, consists mainly of animal husbandry (livestock and fur-animal breeding), grain production and hunting. Total agricultural production in 1998 was worth 2,633m. roubles. The Republic is rich in mineral resources, including gold, uranium, coal, wolfram (tungsten), molybdenum, brown coal, graphite and apatites. Its main gold-mining enterprise, Buryatzoloto, operates two mines near Lake Baikal. In 1997 the company's largest shareholder was High River Gold, of Canada, which owned a 23% stake. In 1996 its reserves were estimated at 3.2m. troy ounces (almost 100 metric tons). Apart from ore mining and the extraction of minerals, its main industries are mechanical engineering, metal working, timber production and wood-working. The Republic is also a major producer of electrical energy. The industrial sector employed 19.4% of the Republic's work-force in 1998, and its total output in that year was of a value of 5,330m. roubles. The services sector with the most potential is tourism, owing to the attractions of Lake Baikal.

The territory's economically active population totalled 370,300 in 1998, of which 13,600 were officially registered as unemployed. The average monthly wage in the Republic was 601.4 roubles. In 1998 there was a budgetary surplus of 36m. roubles. Continuing deficits had earlier exacerbated the problem of the late payment of wages, a phenomenon common throughout Russia in the 1990s, but increasingly provoking labour unrest (for example, in the education sector in December 1998). Foreign trade in 1999 comprised US $92.6m. in exports and $19.4m. in imports; the Republic has over 50 trading partners, and over one-half of its international trade was with the People's Republic of China in that year. Foreign investment in Buryatiya amounted to $13.04m. in 1998, major investors being China, Ireland and Austria. At 1 January 1999 there were 5,200 small businesses registered in the Republic.

Directory

President and Chairman of the Government: LEONID VASILIYEVICH POTAPOV; respublika Buryatiya, 670001 Ulan-Ude, ul. Lenina 54; tel. (3012) 21-51-86; fax (3012) 21-02-51; internet www.buryatia.ru.

Chairman of the People's Khural: MIKHAIL INNOKENTIYEVICH SEMENOV; tel. (3012) 21-51-86; fax (3012) 21-02-51.

Permanent Representative in Moscow: INNOKENTY NIKOLAYEVICH YEGOROV; tel. (095) 286-30-83.

Head of Ulan-Ude City Administration (Mayor): GENNADII ARKHIPOVICH AYDAYEV; respublika Buryatiya, 670000 Ulan-Ude, ul. Lenina 54; tel. (3012) 21-57-05; fax (3012) 26-32-44; internet www.ulan-ude.ru.

Chechen Republic of Ichkeriya (Chechnya)

The territory of Chechnya is located on the northern slopes of the Caucasus. It forms part of the North Caucasus Economic Area and the Southern Federal Okrug. To the east, Chechnya abuts into the Republic of Dagestan. Stavropol Krai lies to the north-west and the Republics of North Osetiya—Alaniya (Ossetia) and Ingushetiya to the west. There is an international boundary with Georgia (South Osetiya) to the south-west. The exact delimitation of the western boundary remained uncertain in 2001, awaiting final agreement between Chechnya and Ingushetiya on the division of the territory of the former Chechen-Ingush ASSR. The region consists of lowlands along the principal waterway, the River Terek, and around the capital, Groznyi (also known as Dzhokhar Ghala), in the north; mixed fields, pastures and forests in the Chechen plain; and high mountains and glaciers in the south. The former Chechen-Ingush ASSR had an area of some 19,300 sq km (7,450 sq miles), most of which was allotted to the Chechens. At 1 January 1999 the Republic had an estimated population of 780,500, of which 32.8% inhabited urban areas. The Chechens, who refer to themselves as Nokchi, are closely related to the Ingush (both of whom are known collectively as Vainakhs). They are Sunni Muslims, and their language is one of the Nakh dialects of the Caucasian linguistic family. Founded as Groznyi in 1818, the capital had a population of 405,000 in 1989, but an estimated 182,700 inhabitants in 1995. The Republic's other major towns are Urus-Martan, Gudermes (the oldest town in the territory, founded in the mid-18th century), Shali and Argun.

History

In the 18th century the Russian, Ottoman and Persian (Iranian) Empires fought for control of the Caucasus region. The Chechens violently resisted the Russian forces with the uprising of Sheikh Mansur in 1785 and throughout the Caucasian War of 1817–64. Chechnya was finally conquered by Russia in 1858 after the resistance led by Imam Shamil ended. Many Chechens were exiled to the Ottoman Empire in 1865. Subsequently, ethnic Russians began to settle in the lowlands, particularly after petroleum reserves were discovered around Groznyi in 1893. Upon the dissolution of the Mountain (Gorskaya) People's Soviet Republic in 1922, Chechen and Ingush Autonomous Oblasts were established; they merged in 1934 and became the Chechen-Ingush Autonomous Soviet Socialist Republic (ASSR) two years later. This was dissolved in 1944, when both peoples were deported en masse to Central Asia and Siberia in retaliation for various uprisings and their alleged collaboration with Germany in the Second World War. On 9 January 1957 the ASSR was reconstituted, but with limited provisions made for the restoration of property to the dispossessed Chechens (and Ingush). Furthermore, the territory's Russian inhabitants had seized control of its flourishing petroleum industry, and its mosques, destroyed in 1944, were not restored.

During 1991 an All-National Congress of the Chechen People seized effective power in the Chechen-Ingush ASSR and agreed the division of the territory with Ingush leaders. Exact borders were to be decided by future negotiation, but by far the largest proportion of the territory was to constitute a 'Chechen Republic' (Chechnya). Elections to the presidency of this new polity, which claimed independence from Russia, were held on 27 October, and were won by Gen. Dzhokhar Dudayev. The Chechen Republic under Dudayev, although unrecognized internationally, continued to insist on its independence. In 1993 the territory refused to participate in the Russian general election and rejected the new federal Constitution. Dudayev's policies provoked the Chechen opposition into violent conflict from August 1994. In December federal Russian troops entered Chechnya and, by January 1995, had taken control of the city, including the presidential palace. Fierce resistance by Chechen rebels continued throughout the Republic and spread to neighbouring regions. In an effort to end hostilities, the federal President, Boris Yeltsin, signed an accord with the Chechen premier granting the Republic special status, including its own consulate and foreign-trade missions. A peace agreement was not signed, however, until late May 1996, one month after the death of Dudayev in a Russian missile attack. (Dudayev was succeeded by Zemlikhan Yandarbiyev.) The truce immediately showed signs of strain, and ended following Yeltsin's re-election to the Russian presidency in July. One month later Chechen rebel forces led a successful assault on Groznyi, prompting the negotiation of a cease-fire by Lt-Gen. Aleksandr Lebed (newly appointed Secretary of the federal Security Council). This agreement, the Khasavyurt Accords, was signed in Dagestan on 31 August. At the beginning of September a proposed peace settlement incorporated a moratorium on discussion of Chechnya's status for five years, until 31 December 2001. An agreement on the withdrawal of the last Russian troops by January 1997 was signed in late November 1996, signalling the end of a war that had claimed between 60,000 and 100,000 lives. A formal Treaty of Peace and Principles of Relations was signed on 12 May 1997 and ratified by the Chechen Parliament the following day.

On 1 January 1997 a presidential election was held in the Republic, at which Khalid 'Aslan' Maskhadov, former Chechen rebel chief of staff, gained 64.8% of the votes cast, defeating another rebel leader, Shamil Basayev. On 25 March 1998 the republican Parliament officially renamed the capital Dzhokhar Ghala, after the late Gen. Dudayev, and changed the territory's name to the Chechen Republic of Ichkeriya. The main issues to dominate politics were the increasing lawlessness in the Republic and the growth of Islamist groupings. During 1998 two particularly dramatic incidents drew attention to the disorderly state of Chechen society: Valentin Vlasov, the federal presidential representative in Chechnya, was kidnapped in May and held for six months; later in the year international attention was focused on the Republic following the capture and murder of four engineers from the United Kingdom and New Zealand. With political opposition to Maskhadov led by other former warlords and organized crime powerful in the territory, violence was constantly imminent. By the end of the year the President was also challenged by a 'Commanders' Council' (on which Basayev had joined Salman Raduyev and Khunkar-Pasha Israpilov) and his own Vice-President, Vakha Arsanov. The capital was no longer secure for the Government and Maskhadov was mainly based on the outskirts of the city, in the old military base of Khankala.

The resurgence of Chechen nationalism in the 1990s was accompanied by a renaissance for Islam. Even after the 1996 peace agreements the territory's leadership remained committed to complete independence from Russia, reinforcing this intent with the 1997 decision to introduce Islamic law (*shari'a*—in contravention of federal norms) and religious education. Hostilities between armed groupings in Gudermes in July 1998 resulted in the outlawing of Wahhabis in Chechnya. ('Wahhabis' was a term applied to strict Sunni Muslims, but was, erroneously, interchangeable with 'fundamentalists' and loosely applied to any opposition groups with a religious agenda.) The process of transition to an Islamist state was also fraught with difficulties and engendered instability. In January 1999 Maskhadov declared that *shari'a* would be introduced over a three-year period, supervised by an Islamic council or *shura*. The composition of such a body remained a potent source of dispute, initially between the Government and the Commanders' Council.

In August 1999 militant Chechen Islamist factions associated with Basayev launched a series of attacks on Dagestan. The incursions continued, and a series of bomb explosions, officially attributed to Chechen separatists, killed almost 300 people across Russia in August–September, prompting the redeployment of federal armed forces in the Republic from late September; the recently inaugurated premier, Vladimir Putin, presented the campaign as necessary to quell incipient terrorism. In late 1999 the federal regime declined requests from Maskhadov for the negotiation of a settlement, stating that it recognized only the Moscow-based State Council of the Chechen Republic, which had been formed in October by former members of the republican legislature.

In early February 2000 federal forces took control of Groznyi and proceeded to destroy much of the city, after the federal Government issued a controversial ultimatum in December 1999, which warned civilians to leave the Chechen capital immediately, or face death; many republican and federal administrative bodies were relocated to Gudermes. However, Maskhadov stated that the rebels' withdrawal from Groznyi was tactical, and the federal army's victory remained largely symbolic. In early May 2000 Putin, by this time the elected President of the Russian Federation, decreed that Chechnya would, henceforth, be ruled federally. Former Mufti Akhmad Kadyrov was inaugurated as administrative leader (President) of the Republic on 20 June. Kadyrov, a former ally of Maskhadov, was directly responsible to Putin and to the presidential representative to the new Southern Federal Okrug, Col-Gen. Viktor Kazantsev.

In 2000 Maskhadov's authority over the Chechen rebels was believed to be growing, as the Islamist politics of Basayev, and Khattab, another commander, thought to originate from Saudi Arabia and reputedly a supporter of Afghanistan-based Islamist dissident Osama bin Laden, reportedly failed to gain widespread popular support. In September the elected speaker of the Chechen Parliament, Ruslan Alikhadzhiyev, who had been imprisoned in Moscow for three months, died; Chechen rebels imputed the death to torture. In the following month it was announced that all Chechen ministries and government departments were to be relocated from Gudermes to Groznyi, to take effect from November. In January 2001 Putin signed a decree transferring control of operations in Chechnya from the Ministry of Defence to the Federal Security Service (FSB). The majority of troops in the region were to be withdrawn, leaving a 15,000-strong infantry division and 7,000 interior ministry troops. The FSB was to strengthen its presence in Chechnya, however, in order to combat insurgency. The local administration in Chechnya was restructured to allow it greater autonomy, and Stanislav Ilyasov, a former Governor of Stavropol Krai, was appointed as Chechen premier.

Despite claims that the military phase of the 'anti-terrorist operation' had ended, guerrilla attacks showed no sign of abating, and although, in February 2001, official figures put the number of Russian dead at 2,955, according to Chechen estimates federal losses were between 24,000 and 27,000. Meanwhile, concern escalated among international human-rights organizations about reportedly widespread detention, torture and extortion by federal troops and, in particular, the discovery of a mass grave, containing severely mutilated corpses, prompted outrage. In late August Kadyrov criticized the federal defence forces for abusing the human rights of civilians while conducting so-called 'cleansing' operations, in which entire towns or areas were searched for rebels. Although hostilities in Chechnya intensified in mid-September, as rebels staged a co-ordinated series of attacks in Gudermes and Argun, on the outskirts of Groznyi, proposals for a political solution to the conflict arose, particularly following the declaration by the USA of a 'war against terrorism', after large-scale attacks against that country, on 11 September, were attributed to bin Laden's al-Qa'ida (Base) organization. In late September Putin urged rebels to 'halt all contacts with international terrorists' (the Russian Government presented evidence, which purported to link Chechen rebel elements with bin Laden) and to establish contact with the federal authorities, citing a 72-hour period during which arms could be surrendered without charge; however, only a negligible quantity of weapons was surrendered during the amnesty. None the less, on 18 November the first official, direct negotiations to take place since the renewal of hostilities in 1999 commenced in Moscow, between Col-Gen. Viktor Kazantsev and Akhmed Zakayev, a representative of Maskhadov. Meanwhile, the trial of the Chechen field commander, Salman Raduyev, who was charged with murder, kidnap and terrorism, opened in Makhachkala, Dagestan, in mid-November 2001.

Economy

Prior to armed hostilities in the region in 1994–95 Groznyi was the principal industrial centre in Chechnya. The Republic's agriculture consisted mainly of horticulture, production of grain and sugar beets and animal husbandry. Its main industrial activities were production of petroleum and petrochemicals, petroleum refining, power engineering, manufacture of machinery and the processing of forestry and agricultural products. Conflict in 1994–96, and again from 1999, seriously damaged the economic infrastructure and disrupted both agricultural and industrial activity. At April 1998 around four-fifths of the Republic's population were unemployed, and the 1998 budget showed a deficit of 68m. roubles. In 2001 the federal Government was implementing an economic and social reconstruction programme, which aimed to put in place conditions to permit the repatriation of some 110,000 refugees by the end of the year. However, future developments depended on greater stability in the territory, certainly as foreign investment was likely to remain low while lawlessness was commonplace. Another asset that could be sabotaged by, or displaced because of, violence was one of Russia's major petroleum pipelines that crossed Chechnya (transit fees from Caspian hydrocarbons could be a major source of revenue in the 21st century). In mid-1999 the Chechen section of a petroleum pipeline from Baku, Azerbaijan, to Novorossiisk, was closed, owing to the lack of security in the region. However, attempts were being made to restore industry in the Republic, and a sugar refinery and a brickworks were in operation there in 2001.

Directory

President and Head of the Republic: KHALID ('ASLAN') ALIYEVICH MASKHADOV.

Governor and Head of the Administration: AKHMED haji KADYROV.

Prime Minister: STANISLAV ILYASOV.

Chairman of the Parliament: (vacant).

Chairman of the Supreme Shari'a Court: BEKKHAN NUSUKHANOV.

Regional Representation in Moscow: tel. (095) 241-03-59; fax (095) 241-73-80; Head of Representation ADLAN MAGOMADOV.

Head of Dzhokhar Ghala City Administration (Mayor): BISLAN GANTAMIROV; tel. (8712) 22-01-42.

Chuvash Republic (Chuvashiya)

The Chuvash Republic is situated in the north-west of European Russia. It forms part of the Volga-Vyatka Economic Area and the Volga Federal Okrug. It lies on the Eastern European Plain on the middle reaches of the Volga. Ulyanovsk Oblast neighbours it to the south, the Republic of Mordoviya to the south-west, Nizhnii Novgorod Oblast to the west and the Republics of Marii-El and Tatarstan to the north and the east, respectively. The Republic's major rivers are the Volga and the Sura, and one-third of its territory is covered by forest. It occupies 18,300 sq km (7,070 sq miles) and comprises 21 administrative districts and nine cities. The territory measures 190 km (118 miles) from south to north and 160 km from west to east. At 1 January 1999 the Republic had an estimated total population of 1,361,800 and a relatively high population density of 74.4 per sq km. Some 61.1% of the population lived in towns. In contrast to the native peoples in the majority of autonomous republics, the Chuvash outnumber ethnic Russians in Chuvashiya: in the census of 1989, 67.8% of inhabitants were Chuvash and 26.7% Russian. In addition, 2.7% of the population were Tatar and 1.4% Mordovian. The native tongue of the Republic is Chuvash, which has its origins in the Bulgar group of the Western Hunnic group of Turkic languages and is related to ancient Bulgar and Khazar. It is spoken as a first language by an estimated 76.5% of Chuvash. The dominant religions in Chuvashiya are Islam and Orthodox Christianity. Chuvashiya's capital is at Cheboksary (Shupashkar—with an estimated population of 458,500 in 1999). Its other major town is Novocheboksarsk, with an estimated 124,700 inhabitants.

History

The Chuvash, traditionally a semi-nomadic people, were conquered by the Mongol-Tatars in the 13th century. Their territory subsequently became part of the dominion of the Golden Horde and many were converted to Islam. From the late 1430s the Chuvash were ruled by the Kazan Khanate. In 1551 Chuvashiya became a part of the Russian Empire and Kazan itself was subjugated by Ivan IV in 1552. The Chuvash nation had been formed by the end of the 15th century, with a syncretized culture of Suvar-Bulgar and Finno-Ugric components. Despite intense Christianization and russification on the part of the Russian state, the Chuvash acquired their own national and cultural identity. The Chuvash capital was founded at Cheboksary in 1551, at the site of a settlement first mentioned in Russian chronicles in 1469. The construction of other towns and forts, intended to encourage migration into the area, followed. After the Revolutions in Russia in 1917 the Chuvash people made vociferous demands for autonomy to the Soviet Government. A Chuvash Autonomous Oblast was established on 24 June 1920, which was upgraded to the status of an ASSR on 21 April 1925.

Chuvash nationalism re-emerged in the early 1990s: the Chuvash ASSR declared its sovereignty on 27 October 1990. It adopted the name of the Chuvash Republic in March 1992. In December 1993 the Republic voted against acceptance of the federal Constitution. In January 1995 the Chuvash President, Nikolai Fedorov, organized a meeting of republican heads, which urged a greater degree of decentralization. In May 1996 the Chuvash Government signed a treaty with the Russian President, Boris Yeltsin, on the delimitation of powers. It granted the Republic greater freedom to determine policy in political, economic and social areas. Elections to the 87-seat State Council were held on 13 July 1998, with further elections for the 23 unfilled seats on 1 November. Compliant voting habits, however, did not mean a passive population—particularly during 1998, the territory experienced a notable volume of litigation, encouraged by the media, over arrears in pension payments and the lack of discounts on utility bills for veterans (in accordance with federal law). Wage arrears continued to rank among the most serious in the Russian Federation into 2000. In October 2001 the Chairman of the republican Council of Ministers, Enver Ablyakimov, resigned; Fedorov appointed himself to the position, announcing that combining the roles of republican president and prime minister would increase the Government's accountability. According to preliminary results, Fedorov was re-elected, with some 41% of the votes, in the presidential election held in Chuvashiya on 16 December.

Economy

The Republic's gross regional product in 1997 amounted to 11,573,500m. old roubles, equivalent to 8,511,800 old roubles per head. Chuvashiya's major industrial centres are at Cheboksary, Novocheboksarsk, Kanash, Alatyr and Shumerlya.

Its agriculture, which employed 18.4% of the work-force in 1998, consists mainly of grain, potato, vegetable, hop, hemp and makhorka-tobacco production, horticulture and animal husbandry. The value of total agricultural output in that year amounted to 3,526m. roubles. The Republic contains deposits of peat, sand, limestone and dolomite. Its main industries are mechanical engineering, metal working, electricity generation, production of chemicals, light industry, woodworking, manufacture of building materials and food processing. The industrial sector employed 25.3% of the working population in 1998 and generated 8,148m.

roubles in income. Chuvashiya's major trading partners are the People's Republic of China, Finland, Germany, Italy, the Netherlands, Poland, Ukraine and the USA.

The economically active population in Chuvashiya amounted to 553,700 in 1998, of which 19,900 (3.6%) were unemployed, well under one-half the number unemployed in 1995. The average monthly wage in the territory was 428 roubles. There was a budgetary surplus in that year of 38m. roubles. The federal authorities announced at the beginning of 1999 that Chuvashiya was among those territories that would receive increased assistance for the year ahead. Foreign investment in 1998 was worth US $11.55m. At 1 January 1999 there were 4,200 small businesses operating in Chuvashiya.

Directory

President and Chairman of the Council of Ministers: NIKOLAI VASILIYEVICH FEDOROV; respublika Chuvashiya, 428004 Cheboksary, pl. Respubliki 1, Dom Pravitelstva; tel. (8352) 62-46-87; fax (095) 973-22-38; e-mail president@cap.ru; internet www.cap.ru.

Chairman of the State Council (Parliament): NIKOLAI IVANOVICH IVANOV; respublika Chuvashiya, 428004 Cheboksary, pl. Respubliki 1, Dom Pravitelstva; tel. (8352) 62-22-72; e-mail gs@chuvashia.com.

Plenipotentiary Representative in Moscow: GENNADII SEMENOVICH FEDOROV; 109017 Moscow, ul. Bolshaya Ordynka 46, stroyenie 1; tel. (095) 953-21-59.

Head of Cheboksary City Administration: ANATOLII ALEKSANDROVICH IGUMNOV; respublika Chuvashiya, 428004 Cheboksary, ul. K. Marksa 36; tel. (8352) 22-35-76; e-mail gcheb@chuvashia.com; internet www.cheboksary.chuvashia.com.

Republic of Dagestan

The Republic of Dagestan (Daghestan) is situated in the North Caucasus on the Caspian Sea. Dagestan forms part of the North Caucasus Economic Area and the Southern Federal Okrug. It has international borders with Azerbaijan to the south and Georgia to the south-west. The Republic of Chechnya and Stavropol Krai lie to the west and the Republic of Kalmykiya to the north. Its largest rivers are the Terek, the Sulak and the Samur. It occupies an area of 50,300 sq km (19,420 sq miles) and measures some 400 km (250 miles) from south to north. Its Caspian Sea coastline, to the east, is 530 km long. The north of the Republic is flat, while in the south are the foothills and peaks of the Greater Caucasus. The Republic's lowest-lying area is the Caspian lowlands, at 28 m (92 feet) below sea level, while its highest peak is over 4,000 m high. Dagestan is made up of 41 administrative districts and 10 cities. The climate in its mountainous areas is continental and dry, while in coastal areas it is subtropical with strong winds. Dagestan is the third-most populated republic of the Russian Federation, with an estimated population of 2,120,100 at 1 January 1999, some 41.0% of whom inhabited urban areas. Its population density was 42.1 per sq km at that time. In 1989, according to the census, some 27.5% of the population of Dagestan were Avars, 15.6% Dargins, 12.9% Kumyks, 11.3% Lezgis, 5.1% Laks, 4.3% Tabasarans, 1.6% Nogais, 0.8% Rutuls, 0.8% Aguls and 0.3% Tsakhurs, while ethnic Russians formed the fifth-largest nationality, with 9.2%. Dagestan's capital is at Makhachkala, which had an estimated 332,200 inhabitants in 1999. The city lies on the Caspian Sea and is the Republic's main port. Other major cities are Derbent, Khasavyurt, Kaspiisk and Buinaksk.

History

Dagestan formally came under Russian rule in 1723, when the various Muslim khanates on its territory were annexed from Persia (now Iran). The Dagestani peoples conducted a series of rebellions against Russian control, including the Murid Uprising, which lasted from 1828 to 1859, before Russian control could be established. A Dagestan ASSR was established on 20 January 1920.

The Republic of Dagestan acceded to the Federation Treaty in March 1992 and officially declared its sovereignty in May 1993. The Republic voted against the new Russian Constitution in December and adopted its own on 26 July 1994. On 21 March 1996 the powers of the Dagestani State Council, the supreme executive body, were prolonged by a further two years. When this extra term had elapsed, the republican legislature convened as a Constituent Assembly and, on 26 June 1998, confirmed Magomedali Magomedov as the Chairman of the State Council. Parliamentary elections, for a new People's Assembly, were held on 7 March 1999, at the same time as a referendum to decide whether to institute an executive presidency in Dagestan; the proposal was rejected for a third time. The republican Government was widely regarded as the federal Government's closest ally, and the most active supporter of Russian territorial integrity, among the North Caucasian republics. Consequently, it was a focus of opprobrium for rebel groups from neighbouring Chechnya, which sought to destabilize the regime or initiate political unity between the two republics. Wider inter-ethnic tensions in the North Caucasus area further destabilized the republic, although until the mid-1990s it was felt that the continuing dominance of the Communist Party had largely prevented ethnic concerns rising to the fore among the extremely diverse ethnic communities of Dagestan itself. In the second half of the decade, however, particularly strong demands for greater autonomy came from the Lezgin and Avar communities, ethnic groups represented on both sides of the Azerbaijani–Dagestani border. A constitutional change of March 1998, which permitted Magomedov to serve a second term, also removed the nationality requirements for senior republican positions; this was thought to further unsettle the fragile balance of power between the different ethnic groups in the republic.

In January 1996 Chechen rebels seized some 2,000 hostages in the town of Kizlyar, and fighting ensued between Chechen groups and Russian federal troops at Pervomaiskoye. (The trial of the Chechen field commander, Salman Raduyev, who was accused of co-ordinating the incident, commenced in November 2001.) Between the two wars in Chechnya (November 1994–August 1996, and from September 1999), insurgency and hostage-taking took place in Dagestan and, indeed, formed a major factor in the federal Government's decision to recommence armed conflict in Chechnya. In 1998 alone, over 100 hostages were reported in the republic, with the actual figure considered to be probably twice that number. At that time political unrest in the republic was led by Nadirshakh Khachilayev, the leader of the republican parliamentary faction, Union of Russian Muslims, and the brother of the head of the ethnic Lak community in Dagestan. On 21 May 1998 a group of 200–300 fighters belonging to that party occupied a government building in Makhachkala; simultaneously, 2,000 demonstrators gathered in the main city square to demand the resignation of the republican Government. The arrest of the two brothers in September prompted threats of further civil unrest. Fears of increasing religious fundamentalism in the region were heightened in 1999. In August 'Wahhabis', members of an ascetic Sunni Muslim sect, seized several villages in Buinaksk district as 'a separate Islamic territory', while later in the same month a self-styled 'Islamic Parliament of Dagestan' was established under Siradjin Ramazanov; this Parliament was defended by an armed guard and called for a *jihad* or holy war in the North Caucasus. Although the captured villages were returned to federal control, incursions by Chechen guerrillas became more common, with Chechen Islamists, believed to be linked to the rebel commander Shamil Basayev, seeking to form a single Islamist state. A dissident campaign continued in Dagestan once armed conflict had returned to Chechnya; in September an explosion in Buinaksk, outside accommodation used by Russian troops, killed about 60 people; a larger bomb nearby was defused. Conversely, in August 2000 a Wahhabi group from Dagestan was thought to be responsible for ambushing and killing an élite unit of Russian paratroopers in Chechnya five months earlier. In mid-2001 a number of explosions in Dagestan, some of which targeted infrastructure, including a gas pipeline and railway line, were attributed to dissident groups linked to Chechen separatists. The republican Minister of National Policy, Information and Foreign Affairs, Magomedsalikh Gusayev, escaped an assassination attempt in Makhachkala in early June.

Economy

In 1997 gross regional product in the Republic of Dagestan amounted to 9,164,800m. old roubles, or 4,397,500 old roubles per head—one of the lowest figures among the federal units. The economic situation in the Republic suffered greatly from the wars in Chechnya, mainly as a result of the transport blockade, the energy shortage and the influx of refugees. The Republic's major industrial centres are at Makhachkala, Derbent, Kaspiisk, Izberbash, Khasavyurt, Kizlyar, Kizilyurt and Buinaksk. There are fishing and trading ports in Makhachkala. It is a major junction for trading routes by rail, land and sea. The major railway line between Rostov-on-Don and Baku, Azerbaijan, runs across the territory, as does the federal Caucasus highway and the petroleum pipeline between Groznyi (Dzhokhar) and Baku. There is an airport some 15 km from Makhachkala. In September 1997 the federal Government announced that a new section of the petroleum pipeline from Baku would traverse the southern part of Dagestan, rather than run through Chechnya. The construction of the section was expected to take up to two years. However, the section was closed indefinitely in June 1999, following an explosion, caused by insurgents.

Owing to its mountainous terrain, Dagestan's economy is largely based on animal husbandry, particularly sheep-breeding. Its agriculture also consists of grain production, viniculture, horticulture and fishing. The agricultural sector employed around 29.1% of the Republic's work-force in 1998 (while just 11.2% worked in industry) and total output in that year amounted to a value of 1,592m. roubles. Its main industries are petroleum and natural-gas production, electricity generation, mechanical engineering, metal working, food processing, light industry and handicrafts (especially chiselling and carpet-making). Industrial production in 1998 was worth 1,761m. roubles. The Republic's large defence-sector enterprises, such as the Dagdizel Caspian Plant, the Mogomed Gadzhiyev Plant, Aviagregat and the Dagestan Plant of Electrothermal Equipment, were operating below capacity by the mid-1990s.

Dagestan's economically active population comprised 697,600 inhabitants in 1998. Some 41,100 of these were registered unemployed; the remainder earned an average monthly wage of 364.2 roubles. There was a budgetary surplus of 424m. roubles. Foreign investment in the territory was minimal (amounting to just US \$53,000 in 1998), owing to its proximity to Chechnya and its own incidences of insurgency and unrest during the 1990s. In August 1999 the federal Government approved funds of 100m. roubles in reconstruction assistance and a further 12m. roubles to aid displaced persons.

Directory

Chairman of the State Council (Head of the Republic): MAGOMEDALI MAGOME-DOVICH MAGOMEDOV; respublika Dagestan, 367000 Makhachkala, pl. Lenina 1; tel. (8722) 67-30-59.

Chairman of the Government: KHIZRI ISAYEVICH SHIKHSAIDOV; respublika Dagestan, 367000 Makhachkala, pl. Lenina; tel. (8722) 67-20-17.

Chairman of the People's Assembly: MUKHU GIMBATOVICH ALIYEV.

Permanent Representative in Moscow: Gadzhi MAGOMED KADIYEVICH GAMZAYEV; tel. (095) 916-15-36.

Head of Makhachkala City Administration: SAID DZHAPAROVICH AMIROV; respublika Dagestan, 367025 Makhachkala, pl. Lenina 2; tel. (8722) 67-21-57; internet www.makhachkala.dgu.ru.

Republic of Ingushetiya

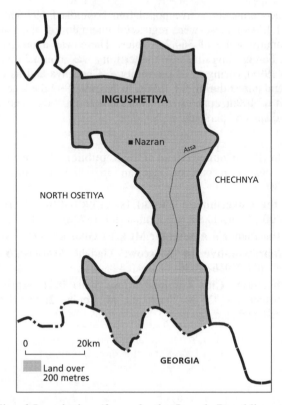

The Republic of Ingushetiya (formerly the Ingush Republic and prior to that part of the Chechen-Ingush ASSR) is situated on the northern slopes of the Greater Caucasus, in the centre of the Northern Caucasus mountain ridge. It forms part of the North Caucasus Economic Area and the Southern Federal Okrug. The Republic of Chechnya borders Ingushetiya on its eastern and northern sides and the Republic of North Osetiya—Alaniya (Ossetia) lies to the west. In the southern mountains there is an international border with Georgia. The Terek, which forms part of the northern border of Ingushetiya, the Assa and the Sunzha are the territory's main rivers. The Republic is extremely mountainous, with some peaks over 3,000 m high. The territory of the Republic occupies about 3,600 sq km (1,400 sq miles) and comprises four administrative districts. The border with Chechnya is not exactly determined, and the Ingushetians are also in dispute with the Osetians. At 1 January 1999 Ingushetiya had an estimated population of 317,000. Its population density was, therefore, 88.1 per sq km. There were thought to be around 35,000 displaced persons from the Prigorodnyi raion of North Osetiya—Alaniya in the republic. The number of refugees from Chechnya has fluctuated with the conflict; estimated figures in October 1999, in the early stages of the 'Second Chechen War', were in the region of 155,000, but one year later the establishment of large-scale refugee camps in the Republic brought the total to around 210,000. In September 2000 the United Nations announced that it was to open a refugee camp in the Republic. The Ingush are a Muslim people closely related to the Chechens (collectively they are known as Vainakhs). They are indigenous to the Caucausus Mountains and have been known historically as Galgai, Lamur, Mountaineers and Kist. With the Chechens, the Ingush are the only people of the North Caucasus to have had no aristocracy. Like the Chechen language, their native tongue is a dialect of the Nakh group of the Caucasian language family. Ingushetiya's administrative centre is at Magas, a new city, opened officially in October 1998, which was named after the medieval Alanic capital believed to have been situated thereabouts. Initially the city consisted solely of a gold-domed presidential palace and government buildings. The former capital of Nazran, approximately 15 miles from Magas, remained the largest city in the Republic, with an estimated population of 77,000 at January 1999. Its other principal cities are Malchobek (35,900) and Karabulak (18,800).

History

The Ingush are descended from the western Nakh people, whose different reaction to Russian colonization of the Caucasus region in the 1860s distinguished them from their eastern counterparts (subsequently known as the Chechens). The Chechens resisted the invaders violently and were driven into the mountains, while the Ingush reacted more passively and settled on the plains. Despite this, the Ingush suffered badly under Soviet rule. In 1920 their territory was temporarily integrated into the Mountain (Gorskaya) People's Republic, but became the Ingush Autonomous Oblast on 7 July 1924. In 1934 the region was joined to the Chechen-Ingush Autonomous Oblast, which was upgraded to the status of a Republic in 1936. At this time, many leading Ingush intellectuals were purged and the Ingush literary language banned. In February 1944 the entire Ingush population (74,000, according to the 1939 census) was deported to Soviet Central Asia, owing to their alleged collaboration with Nazi Germany. Their territory was subsequently handed over to the Osetians. On their return after rehabilitation in 1957 they were forced to purchase their property from Osetian settlers.

Their treatment at the hands of the Government encouraged anti-Russian sentiment among the Ingush and they began to seek more autonomy and independence from their Chechen neighbours (who had also been deported). With the ascendancy in the ASSR of the All-National Congress of the Chechen People in 1991, a *de facto* separation was achieved. In June 1992 the Supreme Soviet of the Russian Federation formalized Ingushetiya's existence as an autonomous republic within the Russian Federation. The exact borders within the former ASSR were not delineated, but the Ingush dominated the western territories. In addition, the new Republic claimed the eastern regions of North Osetiya and part of the Osetian capital, Vladikavkaz. The city had been a shared capital until the 1930s. The raion of Prigorodnyi, with a majority of Ingush inhabitants, was at the centre of the dispute. (A federal law passed in April 1991 established the right for deported peoples to repossess their territory.) Armed hostilities between the two Republics ensued between October 1992 and the signature of a peace agreement in 1994, although subsequent relations between the Republics remained strained, particularly over the issue of the return and resettlement of refugees; protests at the failure of regional and federal government to facilitate rehabilitation arrangements continued in 2001. The successful implementation of a settlement between Ingushetiya and North Osetiya, signed in March, according to which the Ingush could return to their former homes in Prigorodnyi and Vladikavkaz, was inhibited by logistical difficulties and protests by Osetiyans. In common with other republics in the North Caucasus, Ingushetiya was troubled by incidents of violence and hostage-taking from the mid-1990s.

On 27 February 1994, alongside simultaneous parliamentary and presidential elections in the Republic, 97% of the electorate voted in favour of a draft republican constitution, which took immediate effect. The population of Ingushetiya remained generally supportive of the regime of the federal President, but strongly opposed the war in Chechnya. This apparent inconsistency was reflected in the outcome of the federal presidential election of 26 March 2000; despite his leading role in recommencing armed hostilities in Chechnya, Ingushetiya awarded Vladimir Putin the largest proportion of the votes (85.4%) cast for any candidate in any federal subject. At the republican presidential election, held on 1 March 1998, Ruslan Aushev was re-elected. Against a background of continuing extremist violence in the Republic, Aushev declared his intention to pursue a policy of further stabilization in the Caucasus. His popular mandate, however, emboldened him to seek to amend federal law to conform more closely with what he termed 'national traditions', but which could also be described as a variety of *shari'a*, or Islamic law. Following a declaration by President Boris Yeltsin that a planned referendum, which sought, in particular, to pardon those charged with crimes such as revenge killings, was unconstitutional, in February 1999 Aushev signed a power-sharing agreement with the Minister of Internal Affairs, Sergei Stepashin, and the Secretary of the Security Council, Nikolai Bordyuzha. In July 1999 Aushev issued a decree, permitting men up to four wives, in breach of the Russian Federation's family code. Aushev was critical of the federal Government's actions in Chechnya, stating in June 2001 that the conflict in the Republic could not be resolved by the use of military force; in 2000 Aushev had been stripped of the rank of lieutenant-general by President Putin, and sources suggested this was in response to his criticism of federal policy in Chechnya.

Economy

In 1997 gross regional product in the Republic totalled 955,500m. old roubles, or just 3,072,300 old roubles per head. Essentially agricultural, Ingushetiya had hoped to benefit from the transit of Caspian hydrocarbons from the beginning of the 21st century, although continuing instability in neighbouring Chechnya and Dagestan appeared to reduce its prospects in the short term.

In the early 1990s Ingushetiya's economy was largely agricultural (the sector employed 19.9% of the Republic's work-force in 1998, one-third less than just three years previously), its primary activity being cattle-breeding. The serious decline in agricultural production led to intervention by the republican Government; unprofitable collective farms were converted into private enterprises and joint-stock companies. By 1 January 1997 there were over 1,000 private farms and 20 joint-stock companies in the Republic. In 1998 the value of its agricultural output was 331m. roubles. Ingushetiya's industry, which employs just 9.7% of the working population, consists of chemical production, petroleum refining and light industry. Total industrial production amounted to a value of 195m. roubles in 1998. During the mid-1990s the services sector had also made a contribution to the economy, with the local economy receiving substantial benefits from registration fees paid by companies operating in the so-called 'offshore' tax haven (*ofshornaya zona*) that was in operation between 1994 and 1997. The resources of this zone accounted for some 70% of the Republic's capital investments, but it was terminated following criticism by the International Monetary Fund. A total of 88 enterprises and projects came into being between 1995 and 1996, and a further 165 between 1997 and 1998.

In 1998 the average monthly wage in the Republic was 332.2 roubles. The regional budget showed a surplus of 58m. roubles in that year. At the end of 1996 the republican President, Aushev, signed an agreement with the President of the major petroleum company, LUKoil, which provided the company with favourable rates of taxation in return for investing some US $5,000m. in a variety of technical and construction projects. LUKoil was also a participant in the construction of the Caspian pipeline running through the territory. In 1998 foreign trade with Ingushetiya amounted to $52.5m. in exports and some $459.5m. in imports.

Directory

President: RUSLAN SULTANOVICH AUSHEV; respublika Ingushetiya, 366720 Magas; tel. and fax (87322) 334-20-39; e-mail murad@ingushetia.ru; internet www.ingushetia.ru.

Chairman of the Government (Prime Minister): AKHMET ISAYEVICH MALSAGOV; respublika Ingushetiya, 366720 Nazran, pr. I. Bazorkina; tel. (87322) 2-56-80.

Chairman of the People's Assembly: RUSLAN SULTANOVICH PLIYEV; tel. (87322) 2-61-81.

Permanent Representative in Moscow: KHAMZAT MAGOMEDOVICH BELKHAROYEV; tel. (095) 912-92-75.

Head of Magas City Administration: ILEZ MAKSHARIPOVICH MIZIYEV; tel. (87322) 6-10-81.

Kabardino-Balkar Republic (Kabardino-Balkariya)

The Kabardino-Balkar Republic (Kabardino-Balkar ASSR prior to March 1992) is situated on the northern slopes of the Greater Caucasus and on the Kabardin Flatlands. It forms part of the North Caucasus Economic Area and the Southern Federal Okrug. The Republic of North Osetiya—Alaniya (Ossetia) lies to the east and there is an international border with Georgia in the south-west. The rest of the territory's border is with Stavropol Krai, with the Republic of Karachayevo-Cherkessiya to the west. Kabardino-Balkariya's major rivers are the Terek, the Malka and the Baskan. The territory of the Republic occupies an area of 12,500 sq km (4,800 sq miles), of which one-half is mountainous. The highest peak in Europe, twin-peaked Elbrus, at a height of 5,642 m (18,517 feet), is situated in Kabardino-Balkariya. The Republic consists of nine administrative districts and seven cities. At 1 January 1999 the estimated population of the Republic was 786,300 (57.3% of which lived in urban areas) and its population density was 62.9 per sq km, one of the highest in the Russian Federation. Figures from the census of 1989 indicate that at that time some 48.2% of inhabitants were Kabardins, 9.4% were Balkars and 32.0% were Russian. Both the Kabardins and the Balkars are Sunni Muslims. The Kabardins' native language belongs to the Abkhazo-Adyge group of Caucasian languages. The Balkars speak a language closely related to Karachai, part of the Kipchak group of the Turkic branch of the Uralo-Altaic family. Both peoples almost exclusively speak their native tongue as a first language, but many are fluent in the official language, Russian. The capital of the Republic is at Nalchik (formerly Petrovsk-Port), which had an estimated population of 230,800 at 1 January 1999. Its other major city, Prokhladnyi, had around 59,600 inhabitants at that time.

History

The Turkic Kabardins, a Muslim people of the North Caucasus, are believed to be descended from the Adyges. They settled on the banks of the Terek river, mixed with the local Alan people, and became a distinct ethnic group in the 15th century. The Kabardins were converted to Islam by the Tatar Khanate of Crimea in the early 16th century, but in 1561 appealed to Tsar Ivan IV for protection against Tatar rule. The Ottoman Turks and the Persians (Iranians) also had interests in the region and in 1739 Kabardiya was established as a neutral state between the Ottoman and Russian Empires. In 1774, however, the region once again became Russian territory under the terms of the Treaty of Kuçuk Kainavci. Although the Kabardins were never openly hostile to the Russian authorities, in the 1860s many of them migrated to the Ottoman Empire. The Balkars were pastoral nomads until the mid-18th century, when they were forced by threats from marauding tribes to retreat further into the Northern Caucasus Mountains and settle there as farmers and livestock breeders. They were converted to Islam by Crimean Tatars, followed by the Nogais from the Kuban basin, although their faith retained strong elements of their animist traditions. Balkariya came under Russian control in 1827, when it was dominated by the Kabardins. Many ethnic Russians migrated to the region during the 19th century. In 1921 Balkar District was created as part of the Mountain (Gorskaya) People's Republic (which also included present-day Chechnya, Ingush-etiya, Karachayevo-Cherkessiya and North Osetiya), but was integrated into the Kabardino-Balkar Autonomous Province the following year. The Kabardino-Balkar ASSR was established on 5 December 1936. In 1943 the Balkars were deported to Kazakhstan and Central Asia and the Balkar administrative district within the Republic was disbanded. The Balkars were not recognized as a people until 1956, when they were allowed to return to the Caucasus region.

Thus, although greatly outnumbered by Kabardins and Russians, the Balkars had developed a strong sense of ethnic identity. In 1991 they joined the Assembly of Turkic Peoples and on 18 November the first congress of the National Council of the Balkar People declared the sovereignty of Balkariya and the formation of a 'Republic of Balkariya' within the Russian Federation. Kabardino-Balkariya declared its sovereignty on 31 December 1991, and signed a bilateral treaty with the federal authorities during 1995. The Republic also developed links with its neighbours: on 21 February 1996 its President, Valerii Kokov, declared that Kabardino-Balkariya would not abide by the Commonwealth of Independent States' decision to impose sanctions on Abkhazia (Georgia), as that would run counter to a treaty between the two polities. In May 1998, at the second session of an interparliamentary council with the Republics of Adygeya and Karachayevo-Cherkessiya, a programme was adopted on the co-ordination of legislative, eco-nomic, environmental and legal activities.

Kabardino-Balkariya has an executive presidency and a bicameral Legislative Assembly or Parliament, consisting of an upper chamber known as the Soviet of the Republic and a lower chamber known as the Soviet of Representatives. The old nomenklatura class remained firmly in control, although their allegiance was divided between the federal Government and the Communist Party. The republican leadership took a pragmatic approach to reform and encouraged foreign investment. A new republican Constitution was adopted in July 2001, which prevented the Republic from existing independently of the Russian Federation. In August it was reported that an attempt to stage a *coup d'état* in the Republic, and in neighbouring Karachayevo-Cherkessiya, had been prevented, and that the alleged leader of the plot, Khysyr Sallagarov, had been arrested, along with his accomplices.

Economy

Gross regional product in Kabardino-Balkariya amounted to 5,440,800m. old roubles in 1997, equivalent to 6,876,600 old roubles per head. The Republic's main industrial centres are at Nalchik, Tyrnyauz and Prokhladnyi. Prokhladnyi is an important junction on the North Caucasus Railway. There is an international airport at Nalchik, from which there are regular flights to the Middle East, as well as to other cities within the Russian Federation.

Karbardino-Balkariya's main agricultural products are maize and sunflowers. Animal husbandry, horticulture and viniculture are also important. In 1998 around 13.0% of the Republic's work-force was engaged in the agricultural sector, the output of which was worth a total of 2,505m. roubles. By 1997 there were over 600 private agricultural enterprises in the Republic, covering some 5,500 ha. Like the rest of the North Caucasus region, the Republic is rich in minerals, with reserves of petroleum, natural gas, gold, iron ore, garnet, talc and barytes. It is a net importer of electricity, producing less than one-10th of its requirement. The Republic's main industries, which employed some 21.4% of the work-force in 1998, are mechanical engineering, metal working, non-ferrous metallurgy, food processing and light industry, manufacture of building materials and the production and processing of tungsten-molybdenum ores. Total industrial output in 1998 was worth 2,415m. roubles. Most of the Republic's exports (of which raw materials comprise some 70%) are to Finland, Germany, the Netherlands, Turkey and the USA. Some four-fifths of its imports are from Europe.

The economically active population in Kabardino-Balkariya in 1998 totalled 243,800, of which 7,900 (3.2%) were registered unemployed. The previous year those in employment were earning an average of 544,800 old roubles per month. There was a budgetary deficit of 46m. roubles in 1998. Foreign investment in the Republic in that year amounted to US $2.78m. At 1 January 1999 there was a total of 2,300 small businesses in operation.

Directory

President: VALERII MUKHAMEDOVICH KOKOV; respublika Kabardino-Balkariya, 360028 Nalchik, pr. Lenina 27; tel. (86622) 2-20-64.

Vice-President: GENNADII SERGEYEVICH GUBIN; respublika Kabardino-Balkariya, 360028 Nalchik, pr. Lenina 27; tel. (86622) 2-21-62.

Prime Minister: KHUSEIN DZHABRAILOVICH CHECHENOV; respublika Kabardino-Balkariya, 360028 Nalchik, pr. Lenina 27; tel. (86622) 2-21-26.

Chairman of the Soviet of the Republic of the Legislative Assembly (Parliament): ZAURBI AKHMEDOVICH NAKHUSHEV; respublika Kabardino-Balkariya, Nalchik, pr. Lenina 55, Dom Parliamenta; tel. (86622) 7-13-74.

Chairman of the Soviet of Representatives in the Legislative Assembly: ILYAS BORISOVICH BECHELOV; respublika Kabardino-Balkariya, Nalchik, pr. Lenina 55, Dom Parliamenta; tel. (86622) 7-33-04.

Permanent Representative in Moscow: MUKHAMED MAYEVICH SHOGENOV; tel. (095) 271-18-52.

Head of Nalchik City Administration: (vacant); respublika Kabardino-Balkariya, Nalchik, ul. Sovetskaya 70; tel. (86622) 2-20-04.

Republic of Kalmykiya

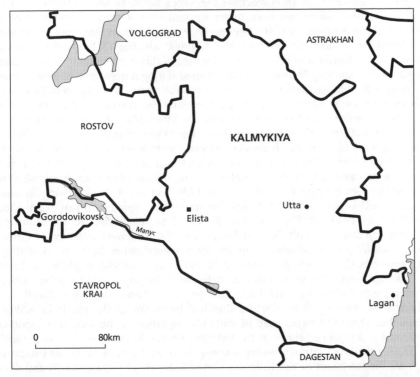

The Republic of Kalmykiya (known as the Republic of Kalmykiya-Khalmg Tangch from February 1992 until February 1996) is situated in the north-western part of the Caspian Sea lowlands. It forms part of the Volga Economic Area and the Southern Federal Okrug. The south-eastern part of the Republic lies on the Caspian Sea. It has a southern border with the Republic of Dagestan and a south-western border with Stavropol Krai, while Rostov, Volgograd and Astrakhan Oblasts lie to the west, north-west and north-east, respectively. The Republic occupies an area of 75,900 sq km (29,300 sq miles), one-half of which is desert, and comprises 13 administrative districts and three cities. At 1 January 1999 it had an estimated population of 316,100, of which 40.3% lived in urban areas, and a population density of 4.2 per sq km. In 1989, according to the census, some 45.4% of the total population were Kalmyks and 37.7% Russians. Unusually for Europe, the dominant religion among the Kalmyks is Lamaism (Tibetan Buddhism). Their native language is from the Mongol division of the Uralo-Altaic family and is spoken as a first language by some 90% of the indigenous population. The capital of Kalmykiya is at Elista, which had an estimated 101,600 inhabitants at 1 January 1999.

History

The Kalmyks (also known as the Kalmuks, Kalmucks, and Khalmgs) originated in Eastern Turkestan (Central Asia—Dzungaria or Sungaria, mostly now part of

75

the province of Xinjiang, People's Republic of China) and were a semi-nomadic Mongol-speaking people. Displaced by the Han Chinese, some 100,000 Kalmyks migrated westwards, in 1608 reaching the Volga basin, an area between the Don and Ural rivers, which had been under Russian control since the subjugation of the Astrakhan Khanate in 1556. The region, extending from Stavropol in the west to Astrakhan in the east, became the Kalmyk Khanate (Kalmykiya), but was dissolved by Russia in 1771. By this time the Kalmyk community was severely depleted, the majority having been slaughtered during a mass migration eastwards to protect the Oirots from persecution by the Chinese. Those that remained were dispersed: some settled along the Ural, Terek and Kuma rivers, some were moved to Siberia, while others became Don Cossacks. Many ethnic Russians and Germans invited by Catherine (Yekaterina) II (the 'Great') settled in Kalmykiya during the 18th century. In 1806 the Kalmyks' pasture lands were greatly reduced by the tsarist Government, forcing many to abandon their nomadic lifestyle and find work as fishermen and salt miners. A Kalmyk Autonomous Oblast was established by the Soviet Government on 4 November 1920 and the Kalmyks living in other regions of Russia were resettled there. Its status was upgraded to that of an ASSR in 1935. In 1943 the Republic was dissolved as retribution for the Kalmyks' alleged collaboration with German forces. The Kalmyks were deported to Central Asia, where they lived until their *de facto* rehabilitation in 1956. A Kalmyk Autonomous Oblast was reconstituted in 1957 and an ASSR in 1958. However, in the late 1990s territorial disputes between Kalmykiya and Astrakhan Oblast over a particularly fertile area known as the 'Black Lands' have resurfaced, with Kalmykiya claiming three districts that had been part of the pre-1943 Kalmyk Republic. These territories were of particular significance, because they stood on the route of a pipeline being constructed from Tengiz, Kazakhstan, to Novorossiisk.

During the late 1980s a growing Kalmyk nationalist movement began protesting against the treatment of the Kalmyks under Stalin (Iosif Dzhugashvili) and demanding local control of the region's mineral resources. A declaration of sovereignty by the Republic was adopted on 18 October 1990. On 28 December 1993 the Kalmyks were formally rehabilitated by the Russian President. On 11 March 1994 the President of Kalmykiya, Kirsan Ilyumzhinov, abrogated the republican Constitution and decreed that from 25 March only the Russian basic law would be valid in the Republic. However, a new republican Constitution, known as the Steppe Legislation, was adopted on 5 April 1994. The loyalty of the republican political establishment to the Federation was demonstrated by the high level of support for Our Home is Russia in the general election of December 1995. However, during the mid-1990s it became clear that Ilyumzhinov, who suspended all local councils and suppressed political parties and publications critical of his regime, was adopting a 'cult of personality' and an increasingly autocratic style of government and economic control in Kalmykiya.

In 1995 Ilyumzhinov was the sole, unopposed candidate in the presidential election, in contravention of federal legislation. There was little serious challenge to his rule in the second half of the decade, although he attracted an increasing degree of controversy. On 16 February 1998 he issued a decree abolishing the republican Government, in order to reduce public spending and bureaucracy. Of particular concern, however, was the arrest of one of the President's former aides in connection with the alleged murder, on 6 June, of Larisa Yudina, editor of the sole opposition newspaper (printed by necessity outside the republic, in Volgograd).

The controversy surrounding Yudina's death added to outside interest in the 1998 Chess Olympiad, held in September in Elista. The event, promoted by Ilyumzhinov (head of the International Chess Federation—FIDE), was allegedly funded by government money intended for social security and investment in agriculture and industry. There were repeated reports of financial irregularities on the part of the republican authorities—the federal legislature instructed the Audit Chamber to investigate the legitimacy of federal budget spending in 1996–98. Subsequently, Ilyumzhinov became regarded as one of the founders of the pro-Government Unity (Yedinstvo) bloc prior to the federal parliamentary election of December 1999.

Economy

The Republic's gross regional product amounted to 1,788,800m. old roubles, or 5,635,800 old roubles per head in 1997. Kalmykiya is primarily an agricultural territory. In the 1990s much of its agricultural land suffered from desertification, a consequence of its irresponsible exploitation by the Soviet authorities during the 1950s, when the fragile black topsoil on the steppe was ploughed up or grazed all year round by sheep and cattle. Between 1991 and 1999, moreover, the number of sheep in the Republic decreased by 80% and, with the exception of 1997, agricultural output declined sharply in real terms throughout the 1990s. Kalmykiya's major industrial centres are at Elista and Kaspiisk. The Republic is intersected by the Astrakhan–Kizlyar railway line and is noted for the relatively low proportion of paved roads (65% in 1998). The Republic has serious problems with its water supply, with a deficit of fresh water affecting almost all regions.

Kalmykiya's agriculture consists mainly of grain production and animal husbandry. The sector employed 26.6% of the Republic's work-force and generated 447m. roubles in 1998. Its industry, which engaged just 8.8% of the working population at that time, consists mainly of mechanical engineering, metal working, manufacture of building materials, food and timber processing and the production of petroleum and natural gas. In 1998 industrial output was equivalent to 619m. roubles. The Republic has major hydrocarbons reserves, the more efficient exploitation of which was named a primary objective of Aleksandr Dordzhdeyev, the premier appointed in August 1999, who aimed to increase petroleum output in the Republic to between 1.5m. and 2m. metric tons each year. In 1995 Kalmykiya extracted an estimated 500,000 tons of crude petroleum, which was exported to neighbouring regions in return for manufactured goods. In August Kalmykiya began negotiations with several foreign countries to build a petroleum refinery in Elista with an annual capacity of 500,000 tons of petroleum products. The Oman Oil Company and LUKoil (a Russian company) showed interest in exploiting the Republic's petroleum and natural-gas deposits, as part of a wider programme of exploitation across the Northern Caspian region. In September 2000 discussions began on the establishment of a Kalmyk-Belarusian joint venture to extract and process crude petroleum. Despite its potential, Kalmykiya is a net importer of energy. The construction and services sectors benefited from preparations for, and the hosting of, the Chess Olympiad in Elista in September 1998.

The economically active population in the Republic amounted to 116,700 in 1998, of which 9,500 (8.1%) were registered as unemployed. The average monthly wage at this time was 430.8 roubles and there was a budgetary surplus of 18m. roubles. Indeed, from 1996 Kalmykiya was declared a 'donor' region (one of only 13 such in the Federation during 1998), although at the beginning of 1999 the

77

federal Government objected to the republican authorities' failure to hand over certain revenues in full, apparently to fund its programme of social assistance. In 1995 there was some US $1.64m.-worth of foreign investment in the Republic (more recent figures were unavailable). By the beginning of 1999 the Republic had 1,300 small businesses, almost one-half of which were involved in catering and trade.

Directory

President: KIRSAN NIKOLAYEVICH ILYUMZHINOV; respublika Kalmykiya, 358000 Elista, pl. Lenina, Dom Pravitelstva; tel. (84722) 6-13-88; fax (84722) 6-28-80; internet kirsan.kalmykia.ru.

Chairman of the Government: RAFAEL ALEKSANDROVICH METRIKIN; respublika Kalmykiya, 358000 Elista, pl. Lenina, Dom Pravitelstva; tel. (84722) 6-11-23; internet www.kalmyk.ru.

Chairman of the People's Khural (Parliament): KONSTANTIN NIKOLAYEVICH MAKSIMOV; respublika Kalmykiya, 358000 Elista, pl. Lenina, Dom Pravitelstva; tel. (84722) 5-27-35.

Permanent Representative in Moscow: ALEKSEI MARATOVICH ORLOV, 121170 Moscow, ul. Poklonnaia 12/2; tel. (095) 249-87-30; fax (095) 249-87-11; e-mail kalmykia@data.ru; internet www.kalmykembassy.ru.

Head of Elista City Administration (Mayor and Representative of the President): VYACHESLAV MIKHAILOVICH SHAMAYEV; respublika Kalmykiya, 358000 Elista, pl. Lenina; tel. (84722) 5-35-81; fax (84722) 2-55-35.

Republic of Karachayevo-Cherkessiya

The Republic of Karachayevo-Cherkessiya (formerly an Autonomous Oblast) is situated on the northern slopes of the Greater Caucasus. It forms part of Stavropol Krai, the North Caucasus Economic Area and the Southern Federal Okrug. Krasnodar Krai borders it to the north-west, Stavropol Krai proper to the north-east and the Republic of Kabardino-Balkariya to the east. There is an international boundary with Georgia (mainly with Abkhazia) to the south. Its major river is the Kuban. The total area of the Republic occupies some 14,100 sq km (5,440 sq miles). The territory measures 140 km (87 miles) from north to south and 160 km from west to east. Karachayevo-Cherkessiya consists of eight administrative districts and four cities. It had an estimated population of 433,500 at 1 January 1999 (of which 44.3% inhabited urban areas) and a population density of 30.7 per sq km. The capital city, Cherkass, had an estimated population of 121,400 at that time. Figures from the 1989 census showed that the Karachai accounted for 31.2% of the Republic's population, the Cherkess (Circassians) for 9.7% and ethnic Russians for 42.4%. Both the Karachai and the Cherkess are Sunni Muslims of the Hanafi school. The Cherkess speak a language close to Kabardin, from the Abkhazo-Adyge group of Caucasian languages, while the Karachais' native tongue, from the Kipchak group, is the same as that of the Balkars. The other cities in the Republic are Ust-Dzheguta (with an estimated 31,500 inhabitants at 1 January 1999) and Karachayevsk (15,100).

History

The Karachais, a transhumant group descended from Kipchak tribes, were driven into the highlands of the North Caucasus by marauding Mongol tribes in the 13th century. Their territory was annexed by the Russian Empire in 1828, although, like their neighbouring North Caucasian peoples, they continued to resist Russian rule throughout the 19th century. In the 1860s and 1870s many Karachais migrated to the Ottoman Empire to escape oppression by the tsarist regime. Many of the Cherkess, a Circassian people descended from the Adyges who inhabited the region between the lower Don and Kuban rivers, also fled across the Russo-Turkish border at this time. They had come under Russian control in the 1550s, having sought protection from the Crimean Tatars and some Turkic tribes, including the Karachais. Relations between the Cherkess and Russia deteriorated as many Russians began to settle in Cherkess territory. Following the Treaty of Adrianople in 1829, by which the Ottomans abandoned their claim to the Caucasus region, a series of rebellions by the Circassians and reprisals by the Russian authorities occurred. In 1864 Russia completed its conquest of the region and many Cherkess fled.

The Cherkess Autonomous Oblast was established in 1928 and was subsequently merged with the Karachai Autonomous Oblast to form the Karachayevo-Cherkess Autonomous Oblast. This represented part of Stalin—Iosif Dzhugashvili's policy of 'divide and conquer', by which administrative units were formed from ethnically unrelated groups (the same applied to the Kabardino-Balkar ASSR). The Karachai were among the peoples Stalin deported during the Second World War (they were moved to Central Asia in late 1943), but the Cherkess remained in the region, which was renamed the Cherkess Autonomous Oblast, until the Karachai were rehabilitated and permitted to return in 1957. Ethnic separatism in the territory, which was upgraded to republican status under the terms of the 1992 Federation Treaty, was relatively minimal, in comparison with other Caucasian republics. On 6 March 1996 a new constitutional system was adopted in the Republic, based on the results of a referendum on a republican presidency. The Republic had already, in the previous year, agreed on a division of responsibilities by treaty with the Russian Federation. The Communists remained the predominant party, winning 40% of the republican vote in federal parliamentary elections at the end of 1995. In May 1998, at the second session of an interparliamentary council with the Republics of Adygeya and Kabardino-Balkariya, a programme was adopted on the co-ordination of the Republics' legislative, economic, environmental and legal activities. In September 1998 enabling legislation providing for direct elections to the republican presidency was enacted. However, the Republic's first presidential election provoked violence and ethnic unrest, when a second round of voting, in May 1999, reversed the positions achieved by the 'run-off' candidates, Stanislav Derev, an ethnic Cherkess (who secured 40% of the votes in the first round and 12% in the second), and Gen. Vladimir Semonov, an ethnic Karachai and a former Commander-in-Chief of the Russian Ground Troops (who secured 18% of the votes in the first round and 85% in the second). Pending consideration by the republican Supreme Court, federal President Boris Yeltsin appointed Valentin Vlasov as acting President; Semonov was confirmed as the winning candidate in August and sworn in on 14 September. Derev's supporters continued to protest against the decision, and in mid-September a congress of the Republic's Cherkess and Abazin groups voted to pursue reintegration into the former Cherkess Autonomous oblast in neighbouring Stavropol Krai. The Republic also contained sympathizers of the secessionist regime of fellow Circassians in Abkhazia, Georgia. In August 2001 it was reported that an attempt to stage a *coup d'etat* in the Republic, and in neighbouring Kabardino-Balkariya, had been prevented, and that the alleged leader of the plot, Khysyr Sallagarov, and his accomplices, had been arrested. Strong concern was subsequently expressed in the Republic at the rising levels of crime, which included the murder of both police officers and politicians.

Economy

In 1997 gross regional product in Karachayevo-Cherkessiya totalled 2,747,500m. old roubles, or 6,297,300 old roubles per head. The predominant sector within the economy, in terms of volume of output and number of employees, is industry. The Republic's major industrial centres are at Cherkessk, Karachayevsk and Zelenchukskaya. It contains 51 km of railway track and 1,890 km of paved roads, including the Stavropol–Sukhumi (Georgia) highway.

Karachayevo-Cherkessiya's agriculture, which employed some 19.3% of the working population in 1998, consists mainly of animal husbandry. At 1 January 1999 there were some 133,000 cattle, 11,700 pigs and 362,800 sheep and goats in the Republic. The production of grain, sunflower seeds, sugar beets and vegetables is also important. Total agricultural production in 1998 amounted to a value of 1,523m. roubles. The Republic's main industries are petrochemicals, chemicals, mechanical engineering and metal working. Light industry, the manufacture of building materials, timber processing and coal production are also important. In 1998 industry's total output was equivalent to 1,254m. roubles, and it employed around 23.0% of the work-force.

In 1998 the economically active population in the Republic amounted to 132,700 of its inhabitants, although 1,900 of these were registered unemployed. The average wage was 442.4 roubles per month. There was a budgetary deficit, amounting to 6m. roubles. In 1998 foreign investment in the Republic amounted to US $3.07m., and international trade was minimal in comparison with other areas in the Federation. Exports amounted to $7.9m., imports to $16.5m. At 1 January 1999 there were 2,300 small businesses registered in the Republic.

Directory

President and Head of the Republic: VLADIMIR MAGOMEDOVICH SEMENOV; respublika Karachayevo-Cherkessiya, 369000 Cherkessk, ul. Lenina, Dom Pravitelstva; tel. (87822) 5-88-37; fax (87822) 5-29-80.

Chairman of the Government: ALIK KARDANOV.

Chairman of the People's Assembly: ZHANIBEK YUNUSOVICH SUYUNOV.

Permanent Representative in Moscow: GENNADII BORISOVICH LOPATIN; tel. (095) 959-55-15.

Head of Cherkessk City Administration (Mayor): STANISLAV EDUARDOVICH DEREV; respublika Karachayevo-Cherkessiya, 357100 Cherkessk, pr. Lenina 54A; tel. (87822) 5-37-23; fax (87822) 5-78-43.

Republic of Kareliya

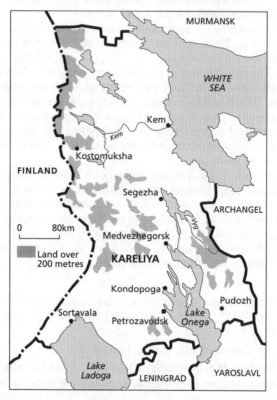

The Republic of Kareliya (Karelia) is situated in the north-west of the country, on the edge of the Eastern European Plain. The Republic forms part of the Northern Economic Area and the North-Western Federal Okrug. It is bordered by Finland to the west. The White Sea lies to the north-east, Murmansk Oblast to the north and Vologda and Archangel Oblasts to the south. It contains some 83,000 km (51,540 miles) of waterways, including its major rivers, the Kem and the Vyg, and its numerous lakes (the Ladoga, Ladozhskoye, and the Onega, Onezhskoye, being the largest and second-largest lakes in Europe). A canal system 225 km long, the Belomorkanal, connects the Karelian port of Belomorsk to St Petersburg. One-half of its territory is forested and much of the area on the White Sea coast is marshland. It lies, on average, 300 m–400 m above sea level. Kareliya measures some 600 km south–north and 400 km west–east and occupies an area of 172,400 sq km (66,560 sq miles). It comprises 16 administrative districts and 13 cities. At 1 January 1999 it had an estimated population of 771,100, of whom some 73.9% inhabited urban areas, and a population density of 4.5 per sq km. In 1989 some 10.0% of the population were Karelians (Finnish—also known as Karjala or Karyala, Korela and Karyalainen) and 73.6% Russians. The dominant religion among Karelians, and in the Republic as a whole, is Orthodox Christianity. The Karelian language consists of three dialects of Finnish (Livvi, Karjala and Lyydiki), which are all strongly influenced by Russian. In 1989, however, more than one-half of the Karelian population spoke Russian as their first language. The capital of Kareliya is at Petrozavodsk, with an estimated population of 282,600 at 1 January 1999. Other major cities are Kondopoga (36,600) and Segezha (34,500).

History

Kareliya was an independent, Finnish-dominated state in medieval times. In the 16th century the area came under Swedish hegemony, before being annexed by Russia in 1721. A Karelian Labour Commune was formed on 8 June 1920 and became an autonomous republic in July 1923. A Karelo-Finnish SSR, including territory annexed from Finland, was created in 1940 as a Union Republic of the USSR. However, part of its territory was ceded to the Russian Federation in 1946 and Kareliya subsequently resumed its status of an ASSR within the Russian Federation. The Republic declared sovereignty on 9 August 1990. It was renamed on 13 November 1991 as the Republic of Kareliya. Its Constitution was adopted on 20 January 1994. On 17 April elections took place to a new bicameral legislature, the Legislative Assembly (consisting of a Chamber of the Republic and a Chamber of Representatives). The premier, who was vested with a quasi-presidential status as the republican head, Viktor Stepanov, was prominent in urging greater decentralization. On 17 May 1998 Stepanov was narrowly defeated in the second round of direct elections to the premiership by the former Mayor of Petrozavodsk, Sergei Katanandov.

Economy

The economy of Kareliya is largely based on its timber industry. In 1997 its gross regional product was 10,066,600m. old roubles, equivalent to 12,932,400 old roubles per head. Its major industrial centres include those at Petrozavodsk, Sortavala and Kem. In the first quarter of 2000, Kareliya produced over 50% of the paper bags, over 30% of newsprint, and over 22% of all paper in the Russian Federation. In the mid-1990s Russia's first commercial railway was constructed on the territory of Kareliya. The Republic is at an important strategic point on Russia's roadways, linking the industrially developed regions of Russia with the major northern port of Murmansk. Its main port is at Petrozavodsk.

Kareliya's agriculture, which employed just 4.1% of the work-force in 1998, consists mainly of animal husbandry, fur farming and fishing. Total production within the sector was equivalent to 1,060m. roubles. The Republic has important mineral reserves, and ranks among the leading producers of rosin and turpentine in the Russian Federation. An important agreement with the city of Moscow, which had need for construction materials, promised an increase in natural-stone production from some 3,000 cu m in 1998 to 20,000 cu m by 2002. Its main industries, apart from the processing of forestry products, are mechanical engineering, metallurgy and the extraction of iron ore and muscovite (mica). Industry engaged some 25.5% of the Republic's labour force in 1998, while total output within the sector was worth 8,195,000m. old roubles. The Republic's major enterprise, Segezhabumprom, is one of the world's largest pulp and paper manufacturers. In July 1997 the Swedish group, AssiDoman, purchased a controlling stake in the company. However, various legal, environmental and bureaucratic problems led the group to withdraw its involvement in February 1998. The enterprise was subsequently re-organized as a joint-stock company in 1999. It was also suggested that new duties on forestry products, introduced in December 1999, would threaten the fulfilment of existing contracts with Western customers.

The economically active population in 1998 amounted to 311,600, of whom 23,200 were unemployed. The average monthly wage in the Republic was a considerable 1,052.4 roubles. The republican budget showed a deficit of 72m. roubles in 1998. Foreign investment in Kareliya at that time amounted to US $5.14m. There were some 400 foreign joint enterprises in Kareliya in 1997, of which more than one-half had Finnish partners. In 1998 exports from the Republic were worth almost four times as much as imports and total external trade amounted to $573.9m. At 1 January 1999 there were some 3,900 small businesses operating in the Republic.

Directory

Chairman of the Government (Head of the Republic): SERGEI LEONIDOVICH KATANANDOV; respublika Kareliya, 185028 Petrozavodsk, pr. Lenina 19; tel. (8142) 76-41-41; fax (8142) 77-41-48; internet www.gov.karelia.ru.

Legislative Assembly: respublika Kareliya, 185610 Petrozavodsk, ul. Kuibysheva 5; tel. and fax (8142) 78-28-27; e-mail root@parl.karelia.ru; internet www.gov .karelia.ru/LA.

Chairman of the Chamber of the Republic: VLADIMIR VASILIYEVICH SHIL-NIKOV.

Chairman of the Chamber of Representatives: NIKOLAI IVANOVICH LEVIN.

Permanent Representative in Moscow: ANATOLII ARKADIYEVICH MARKOV; tel. (095) 207-87-24.

Head of Petrozavodsk City Administration: ANDREI YURIYEVICH DEMIN; respublika Kareliya, 185620 Petrozavodsk, pr. Lenina 2; tel. and fax (8142) 78-49-47; e-mail mayor@ptz.ru; internet admpetrozavodsk.karelia.ru.

Republic of Khakasiya

The Republic of Khakasiya is situated in the western area of the Minusinsk hollow, on the left bank of the River Yenisei, which flows northwards towards, ultimately, the Arctic Ocean. In the heart of Eurasia, it lies on the eastern slopes of the Kuznetsk Alatau and the northern slopes of the Western Sayan Mountains. It lies within Krasnoyarsk Krai and is part of the Eastern Siberian Economic Area and the Siberian Federal Okrug. The Republic of Tyva lies to the south-east and the Republic of Altai to the south-west. To the west is Kemerovo Oblast, while Krasnoyarsk Krai proper is beyond its northern and eastern frontiers. Its major rivers are the Yenisei and the Abakan. Khakasiya occupies 61,900 sq km (23,900 sq miles) and comprises eight administrative regions and five cities. At 1 January 1999 it had an estimated population of 581,400 and a population density, therefore, of 9.4 per sq km. In 1989 ethnic Khakassians were found to number 11.1% of the population, compared to 79.5% Russians. However, at this time over 76% of the Khakass spoke the national language, primarily derived from the Uigur group of Eastern Hunnic languages of the Turkic family, as their native tongue. Khakasiya's capital is at Abakan, with an estimated 169,700 inhabitants in 1999. Other major cities are Chernogorsk (79,300) and Sayanogorsk (55,800).

History
The Khakassians were traditionally known as the Minusinsk (Minusa), the Turki, the Yenisei Tatars or the Abakan Tatars. They were semi-nomadic hunters, fishermen

85

and livestock-breeders. Khakasiya was a powerful state in Siberia, owing to its trading links with Central Asia and the Chinese Empire. Russian settlers began to arrive in the region in the 17th century and their presence was perceived as valuable protection against Mongol invasion. The annexation of Khakassian territory by the Russians was eventually completed during the reign of Peter (Petr) I ('the Great'), with the construction of a fort on the River Abakan. The Russians subsequently imposed heavy taxes, seized the best land and imposed Orthodox Christianity on the Khakassians. After the construction of the Trans-Siberian Railway in the 1890s the Khakassians were heavily outnumbered. Following the Revolution in Russia the Khakass National Okrug was established in 1923, which became the Khakass Autonomous Oblast on 20 October 1930, as part of Krasnoyarsk Krai. In 1992 it was upgraded to the status of an Autonomous Republic under the terms of the Federation Treaty, having declared its sovereignty on 3 July 1991.

The Communist Party remained the most popular political grouping in the Republic in the early 1990s, and the nationalist ideas of Vladimir Zhirinovskii also enjoyed significant support. On 25 May 1995 the Republic adopted its Constitution. Aleksei Lebed, an independent candidate and younger brother of the politician and former general, Aleksandr Lebed (Governor of Krasnoyarsk Krai from May 1998), was elected to the presidency of the Republic in December 1996, when elections were also held for a new republican legislature. A former representative of the Republic in the State Duma, Lebed had based his electoral campaign on the issues of administrative, budgetary, social and economic reform. There were reports in mid-1998 that the Khakasiya Government was considering reunion with Krasnoyarsk Krai and withholding transfers to the federal budget, but neither came to pass once Aleksei Lebed's Government convinced the federal authorities to increase financial transfers to the Republic for 1999. Lebed was re-elected as Chairman of the Government, receiving 72% of the votes cast, in December 2000.

Economy

Khakasiya's gross regional product amounted to 8,032,400m. old roubles in 1997, or 13,740,000 old roubles per head. The Republic's industrial output amounted to a value of 6,024m. roubles in 1998, when the industrial sector employed 24.1% of the work-force. Khakasiya's major industrial centres are at Abakan, Sorsk, Sayanogorsk, Chernogorsk and Balyksa. A major element of industrial activity was the processing of natural resources. In 1997 Khakasiya was estimated to have reserves of 36,000m. metric tons of coal and 1,500m. tons of iron ore. Other mineral reserves included molybdenum, lead, zinc, barytes, aluminium and clay. There was also the potential for extraction of petroleum and natural gas. The Republic's main industries are forestry (it contained some 2.8m. ha of forests and had an estimated 170m. cu m in timber reserves in 1997), ore mining, light manufacturing, mechanical engineering, non-ferrous metallurgy and the processing of agricultural products.

The Republic's agriculture, which employed around 8.8% of the working population in 1998, consists mainly of grain production and animal husbandry. Total agricultural production in 1998 was worth 1,011m. roubles.

The Republic's economically active population numbered 227,900 in 1998, of whom 11,900 were registered unemployed. The average monthly wage stood at 655.3 roubles. The republican budget for 1998 showed a deficit of 66m. roubles.

Foreign investment in Khakasiya has been minimal. Throughout the 1990s the highest level recorded was US \$2.29m. in 1996. At 1 January 1999 there were 900 small businesses registered in the Republic.

Directory

Chairman of the Government: ALEKSEI IVANOVICH LEBED; respublika Khakasiya, 655019 Abakan, pr. Lenina 67; tel. (39022) 9-91-02; fax (39022) 6-50-96; e-mail pressa@khakasnet.ru; internet www.gov.khakassia.ru.

Chairman of the Supreme Council: VLADIMIR NIKOLAYEVICH SHTYGASHEV; tel. (39022) 6-74-00.

Permanent Representative in Moscow: SERGEI BORISOVICH GRUZDEV; tel. (095) 203-83-45.

Head of Abakan City Administration: NIKOLAI GENRIKHOVICH BULAKIN; respublika Khakasiya, 662600 Abakan, ul. Shchetinkina 10A/6 a/ya 6; tel. and fax (39022) 6-31-31; internet www.abakan.ru/meria/index.php.

Republic of Komi

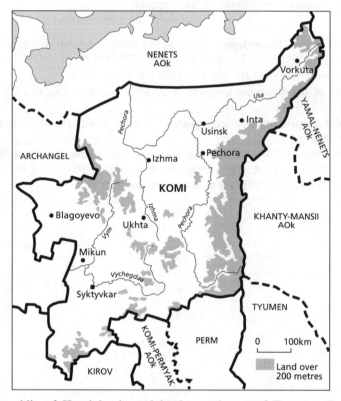

The Republic of Komi is situated in the north-east of European Russia. Its northern border lies some 50 km within the Arctic Circle. It forms part of the Northern Economic Area and the North-Western Federal Okrug. Mountains of the Northern, Circumpolar and Polar Urals occupy the eastern part of the Republic. Its major rivers are the Pechora, the Vychegda and the Mezen. Komi is bordered to the west by Archangel Oblast, to the north by the Nenetsk Autonomous Oblast, and to the east by the Tyumen Oblast. To the south it has borders with Kirov Oblast, Perm Oblast and Sverdlovsk Oblast. Some 90% of its territory is taiga (forested marshland), while the extreme north-east of the Republic lies within the Arctic tundra zone. The Republic occupies an area of 415,900 sq km (160,580 sq miles). It comprises 12 administrative districts and 10 cities and had an estimated population of 1,151,400 at 1 January 1999, and a population density, therefore, of 2.8 per sq km. Of these, some 23.3% of the Republic's inhabitants were Komis and 57.7% were ethnic Russians. The predominant religion in the region is Orthodox Christianity, although among the Komi this faith is combined with strong animist traditions. Their language, spoken as a native tongue by some 74% of the Komi population, belongs to the Finnic branch of the Uralo-Altaic family. Komi's capital is at Syktyvkar (known as Ust-Sysolsk before 1930), which had an estimated population of 230,500 in 1999. The Republic's other major cities are Ukhta (102,100), Vorkuta (92,900) and Pechora (60,900).

History

The Komi (known historically as the Zyryans or the Permyaks) are descended from inhabitants of the river basins of the Volga, the Kama, the Pechora and the Vychegda. From the 12th century Russian settlers began to inhabit territory along the Vychegda, and later the Vym, rivers. The Vym subsequently acquired a strategic significance as the main route along which Russian colonists advanced to Siberia and Ust-Sysolsk (now Syktyvar), the territory's oldest city, was founded in 1586. The number of Slavs increased after the territory was annexed by Russia in 1478. The region soon acquired importance as the centre of mining and metallurgy, following the discovery of copper and silver ores in 1491 by a search party sent by Ivan III. In 1697 petroleum was discovered in the territory; the first refinery was built by F. Pryadunov in 1745. The Komi were renowned as shrewd commercial traders and exploited important trade routes between Archangel and Siberia, via the Vyatka-Kama basin. Trade in fish, furs and game animals developed in the 17th century, while coal, timber, iron ore and paper became significant in the years prior to the Russian Revolution. The Komi Autonomous Oblast was established on 22 August 1921 and became an ASSR in 1931.

The Komi Republic declared its sovereignty on 30 August 1990. A new republican Constitution was adopted on 17 February 1994, establishing a quasi-presidential premier at the head of government and a State Council as the legislature; the territory became known as the Republic of Komi. In March 1996 the republican and federal Governments signed a power-sharing treaty, which included agreements on foreign relations, energy, education, natural resources and employment. In mid-1998 the republican Government came under pressure from local miners, who were owed more than 400m. roubles in wage arrears, and in November the Government retained federal revenues in order to pay pensioners. The Republic repudiated its declaration of sovereignty in September 2001, following a ruling of the federal Supreme Court, which stated that over one-half of the provision's declarations were in contravention of federal law. The republican presidential election, held on 16 December, was won by Vladimir Torlopov, hitherto Chairman of the Republic's State Council.

Economy

The Republic of Komi is Russia's second-largest fuel and energy base. Apart from a wealth of natural resources, it is strategically placed close to many of Russia's major industrial centres and has a well-developed transport network. It also contains Europe's largest area of virgin forest—approximately one-third of its massive forest stock (amounting to 2,800m. cu m) has never been cut. In the 1990s Komi had a high ranking within the Federation in terms of gross domestic product per head and it possessed a wealth of natural resources. However, in order to fulfil its economic potential the Republic needed to improve its export performance and diversify its economy into higher value-added activities. In 1997 gross regional product in the Republic amounted to 27,176,800m. old roubles. This was equivalent to 23,285,700 old roubles per head—one of the highest figures in Russia. Komi's major industrial centres are at Syktyvkar, Ukhta and Sosnogorsk.

Komi's agriculture, which employed 4.5% of the work-force, consists mainly of animal husbandry, especially reindeer-breeding. Total production within the sector amounted to a value of 1,733m. roubles in 1998. Ore-mining was developing in the mid-1990s: the Republic contained the country's largest reserves of bauxite, titanium, manganese and chromium ore. It also accounted for around one-half of northern Europe's petroleum stock and one-third of its natural-gas reserves. Total output from industry, which was based on the processing of forestry products, the production of coal and the production and processing of petroleum and natural gas, was worth 17,709m. roubles in 1998. Foreign trade was encouraged, with, for example, an agreement being reached with Iran in December 1998.

In 1998 the economically active population numbered 494,600, of whom 36,600 were unemployed. The average monthly wage in the Republic was relatively high, at 1,155.8 roubles. There was a budgetary deficit of some 852m. roubles in 1998. Foreign investment in Komi was substantial during the late 1990s, amounting to US $218.13m. in 1998 alone. In the mid-1990s a number of joint ventures were established in Komi, with investment from France, the United Kingdom and the USA. These included Komi Arctic Oil, Sever TEK and Northern Lights. In 1998 exports from the Republic amounted to $580.5m., compared with $136.5m. of imports. At 1 January 1999 there were 4,700 small businesses in operation.

Directory

Chairman of the Government (Head of the Republic): VLADIMIR ALEKSANDROVICH TORLOPOV; respublika Komi, 167010 Syktyvkar, ul. Kommunisticheskaya 9; tel. (8212) 28-51-05; fax (8212) 28-52-52; internet www.rkomi.ru.

Chairman of the State Council: (vacant); respublika Komi, 167010 Syktyvkar, ul. Kommunisticheskaya 9; tel. (8212) 28-55-28.

Permanent Representative in Moscow: NIKOLAI NIKOLAYEVICH KOCHURIN; Moscow, Novyi Arbat 21; tel. (095) 291-47-03.

Head of Syktyvkar City Administration: YEVGENII NIKOLAYEVICH BORISOV; respublika Komi, 167000 Syktyvkar, ul. Babushkina 22; tel. (8212) 42-41-20.

Republic of Marii-El

The Republic of Marii-El is situated in the east of the Eastern European Plain in the middle reaches of the River Volga. It forms part of the Volga-Vyatka Economic Area and the Volga Federal Okrug. Tatarstan and Chuvashiya neighbour it to the south-east and to the south, respectively. Nizhnii Novgorod Oblast lies to the west and Kirov Oblast to the north and north-east. Its major rivers are the Volga and the Vetluga and about one-half of its territory is forested. Marii-El measures 150 km (over 90 miles) from south to north and 275 km from west to east. It occupies an area of 23,200 sq km (9,000 sq miles) and consists of 14 administrative districts and four cities. At 1 January 1999 the estimated population was 761,200 and the population density approximately 32.8 per sq km. In 1989 some 43.3% of the Republic's inhabitants were Maris (also known as Cheremiss) and 47.5% ethnic Russians. Orthodox Christianity is the predominant religion in Marii-El, although many Maris have remained faithful to aspects of their traditional animistic religion. Their native language belongs to the Finnic branch of the Uralo-Altaic family. The capital of the Republic is at Ioshkar-Ola, with an estimated population of 249,800 at 1 January 1999. The Republic's other major cities are Volzhsk (61,800) and Kozmodemyansk (24,500).

History

The Mari emerged as a distinct ethnic group in the sixth century. In the eighth century they came under the influence of the Khazar empire, but from the mid-ninth to the mid-12th century they were ruled by the Volga Bulgars. In the 1230s Mari territory was conquered by the Mongol Tatars and remained under the control of the Khazar Khanate until its annexation by Russia in 1552. Nationalist feeling on the part of the Maris did not become evident until the 1870s, when a religious movement, the Kugu Sorta (Great Candle), attacked the authority of the Orthodox Church in the region. A Mari Autonomous Oblast was established in 1920. On 5 December 1936 the territory became the Mari ASSR.

The Republic declared its sovereignty on 22 October 1990. A presidential election was held on 14 December 1991. In December 1993 elections were held to a new

300-seat parliament, the State Assembly, which was dominated by the Communist Party and members of the old nomenklatura. The new legislature adopted the republican Constitution in June 1995, when the territory became known as the Republic of Marii-El. Republican legislative elections in October 1996 saw 18 of the 67 seats won by mayors and executive branch officials, despite this being in breach of federal law; consequently the Russian Supreme Court ruled these elections illegal on 23 October. A power-sharing agreement between the Republic and the federal Government was signed in May 1998. At parliamentary elections held in the Republic in October 2000, left-wing and Communist candidates again secured the highest proportion of the votes cast. At gubernatorial elections in December the incumbent, Vyacheslav Kislitsyn, was defeated by Leonid Markelov, an executive in a state insurance company, who represented the nationalist Liberal Democratic Party of Vladimir Zhirinovskii.

Economy

In 1997 the Republic's gross regional product amounted to 6,221,100m. roubles, equivalent to 8,143,800 roubles per head. Its major industrial centres are at Ioshkar-Ola and Volzhsk.

Marii-El's agriculture, which in 1998 employed 16.6% of the work-force, consists mainly of animal husbandry and flax and grain production. Total agricultural output in 1998 was worth 2,325m. roubles. The Republic's main industries are mechanical engineering, metal working, light industry and the processing of forestry products. The total value of production within the industrial sector (which employed 22.4% of the work-force) was 4,166m. roubles in 1998. Marii-El is a net importer of energy: in July 1998 Yedinaya Electricheskaya Sistema, the state-owned power grid, imposed energy rationing on the Republic, owing to an accumulation of debts for electricity supplied. In 1998 the value of trade in the Republic amounted to just US $45.6m. (of which exports were worth $27.1m. and imports $18.5m.). Exports primarily comprised raw materials (peat), machine parts and medical supplies. Its major trading partners were Belarus, Finland, France, Germany, Ireland, Italy, Kazakhstan, the Netherlands, Ukraine, the United Kingdom and the USA.

In 1998 the economically active population in the Republic numbered 313,700, of whom 9,300 (3.0%) were officially unemployed: those in employment earned an average of only 420.8 roubles per month. There was a budgetary surplus in 1998, of 75m. roubles. Foreign investment in Marii-El was minimal, amounting to $380,000 in 1998. The situation in the Republic prompted the federal Government to offer increased aid for 1999. At 1 January 1999 there was a total of 2,800 small businesses registered in the Republic.

Directory

President and Head of the Government: LEONID IGOREVICH MARKELOV; respublika Marii-El, 424001 Ioshkar-Ola, Leninskii pr. 29; tel. (8362) 64-15-25; fax (8362) 64-19-21; internet gov.mari.ru.

First Deputy Head of the Government: SERGEI GRIGORIYEVICH ZHILIN; tel. (8362) 55-68-33.

Chairman of the State Assembly: MIKHAIL MIKHAILOVICH ZHUKOV; respublika Marii-El, 424001 Ioshkar-Ola, Lenina pr. 29; tel. (8362) 55-68-12.

Permanent Representative in Moscow: VIKTOR PETROVICH RASSONOV; tel. (095) 291-48-38.

Head of Ioshkar-Ola City Administration (Mayor): VENIAMIN VASILIYEVICH KOZLOV; respublika Marii-El, 424001 Ioshkar-Ola, Leninskii pr. 27; tel. (8362) 55-64-01; fax (8362) 55-64-22; internet capital.mari-el.ru:8101.

Republic of Mordoviya

The Republic of Mordoviya is situated in the Eastern European Plain, in the Volga river basin. The north-west of the Republic occupies a section of the Oka-Don plain and the south-east lies in the Volga Area Highlands (Privolzhskaya Vozvyshennost). The region forms part of the Volga-Vyatka Economic Area and the Volga Federal Okrug. The Republic of Chuvashiya lies to the north-east of Mordoviya. The neighbouring oblasts are Ulyanovsk to the east, Penza to the south, Ryazan to the west and Nizhnii Novgorod to the north. The major rivers in Mordoviya are the Moksha, the Sura and the Insar; one-quarter of its land area is forested. The territory of Mordoviya straddles the two major natural regions in Russia, forest and steppe, and occupies an area of 26,200 sq km (10,110 sq miles). The Republic consists of 22 administrative districts and seven cities. Its climate is continental, but with unpredictable levels of precipitation. At 1 January 1999 the Republic had a population of 937,100 (of whom 59.6% inhabited urban areas) and a population density, therefore, of approximately 35.8 per sq km. In 1989 some 32.5% of the total population were Mordovians and 60.8% Russians. The majority of Mordovians inhabited the agricultural regions of the west and north-east. The capital, Saransk, is a major rail junction and the Moscow–Samara highway passes through the south-west of the Republic. The dominant religion amongst the Republic's inhabitants is Orthodox Christianity. The native tongue of the Mordovians belongs to the Finnic group of the Uralo-Altaic family, although this is spoken as a first language by less than two-thirds of the ethnic group. Mordoviya's capital is at Saransk, which lies on the River Insar and had an estimated population of 317,000 at 1 January 1999. The Republic's second-largest city is Ruzayevka (50,800 inhabitants).

History

The Mordovians (Mordvinians) first appear in historical records of the sixth century, when they inhabited the area between the Oka and the middle Volga rivers. Their territory's capital was, possibly, on the site of Nizhnii Novgorod, before it was conquered by the Russians in 1172. In the late 12th and early 13th centuries a feudal society began to form in Mordoviya. One of its most famous fiefdoms was Purgasov Volost, headed by Prince Purgas, which was recorded in the Russian chronicles. The Mordovians came under the control of the Mongols and Tatars between the 13th and the 15th centuries and, at the fall of the Khanate of Kazan in 1552, they were voluntarily incorporated into the Russian state. Many thousands of Mordovians fled Russian rule in the late 16th and early 17th centuries to settle in the Ural Mountains and in southern Siberia, while those that remained were outnumbered by ethnic Russian settlers. The region was predominantly agricultural until the completion of the Moscow–Kazan railway in the 1890s, when it became more commercial and its industry developed.

Mordovians became increasingly assimilated into Russian life from the end of the 19th century, although in 1919 a Mordovian section was established in the People's Commissariat for Nationalities. The Mordovian Autonomous Okrug was created in 1928, and this was upgraded to the Mordovian Autonomous Oblast on 10 January 1930. The territory acquired republican status on 20 December 1934. It declared its sovereignty on 8 December 1990. A politically conservative region, the territory was only renamed the Republic of Mordoviya (dispensing with the words Soviet and Socialist from the title) in January 1994. Its Constitution was adopted on 21 September 1995, establishing an executive presidency and a State Assembly as the legislature. In February 1998 President Merkushkin was re-elected, with 96.6% of votes cast, owing to a legislative device that disqualified all opponents other than the director of a local pasta factory, who had frequently announced his support for Merkushkin's policies. Merkushkin had also increased his popularity by paying pension and salary arrears in the months preceding the election.

Economy

In 1997 the gross regional product of Mordoviya was 9,331,200m. old roubles, or 9,848,300 old roubles per head. Industry is the dominant sector of the economy, with output amounting to a value of 6,147m. roubles in 1998. The territory's major industrial centres are at Saransk and Ruzayevka.

The principal crops in Mordoviya are grain, sugar beets, potatoes and vegetables. Animal husbandry (especially cattle) and bee-keeping are also important. Agriculture employed 15.5% of the working population in 1998, while total agricultural production was worth 3,104m. roubles. Its main industries are mechanical engineering and metal working. There is also some light industry, production of chemicals and construction materials, and food processing. Total employment in industry was equal to 25.2% of the Republic's work-force. Mordoviya is the centre of the Russian lighting-equipment industry and contains the Rossiiskii Svet (Russian Light) association. In December 1995 the federal Government approved a programme for the economic and social development of Mordoviya, to be implemented in 1996–2000 at a cost of around US $10,000m. The programme was to include 60 investment projects to assist the re-equipping and development of the high-technology sectors of Mordoviya's industry, the conversion of defence plants to civilian purposes, as well as to improve the efficiency of its agro-industrial complex. Merkushkin established close links and trading relationships with Moscow City under Yurii Luzhkov; the capital purchased over one-half of the Republic's output.

In 1998 the economically active population was 393,400, although 19,200 of those were registered unemployed. The average monthly wage in the Republic was 566 roubles and there was a budgetary deficit of 195m. roubles. In 1998 foreign investment in the Republic amounted to US $11.55m. At 1 January 1999 there were some 2,200 small businesses in the Republic.

Directory

President: NIKOLAI IVANOVICH MERKUSHKIN; respublika Mordoviya, 430002 Saransk, ul. Sovetskaya 35; tel. and fax (8342) 17-45-26; e-mail radm@whrm .moris.ru; internet whrm.moris.ru.

Chairman of the Government (Prime Minister): VLADIMIR DMITRIYEVICH VOLKOV; respublika Mordoviya, 430002 Saransk, ul. Sovetskaya 35; tel. (8342) 32-74-69; fax (8342) 17-36-28; e-mail pred@whrm.moris.ru.

Chairman of the State Assembly: VALERII ALEKSEYEVICH KECHKIN; respublika Mordoviya, 430002 Saransk, ul. Sovetskaya 26; tel. and fax (8342) 17-04-95; e-mail gsprot@whrm.moris.ru.

Permanent Representative in Moscow: VIKTOR IVANOVICH CHINDYASKIN; tel. (095) 219-40-49.

Head of Saransk City Administration: IVAN YAKOVLEVICH NENYUKOV; respublika Mordoviya, 430002 Saransk, ul. Sovetskaya 34; tel. (8342) 17-64-16; fax (8342) 17-67-70; e-mail saransk@moris.ru.

Republic of North Osetiya—Alaniya

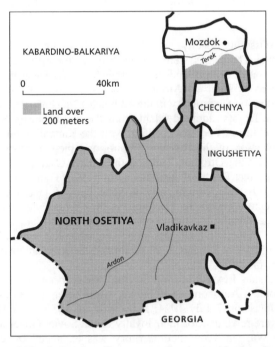

The Republic of North Osetiya (Severnaya Osetiya), Alaniya, is situated on the northern slopes of the Greater Caucasus and forms part of the North Caucasus Economic Area and the Southern Federal Okrug. Of the other federal subjects, Kabardino-Balkariya lies to the west, Stavropol Krai to the north and Ingushetiya to the east. There is an international boundary with Georgia (South Osetiya or Ossetia) in the south. Its major river is the Terek. In the north of the Republic are the steppelands of the Mozdok and Osetian Plains, while further south in the foothills are mixed pasture and beechwood forest (about one-fifth of the territory of the Republic is forested). Narrow river valleys lie in the southernmost, mountainous region. The territory of North Osetiya covers a total of 8,000 sq km (3,090 sq miles) and comprises eight administrative districts and six cities. It had an estimated population of 662,700 at 1 January 1999, some 68.6% of which inhabited urban areas. The population density was 82.8 per sq km. In 1989 some 53.0% of the population were Osetians and 29.9% ethnic Russians, although around one-quarter of Russians were thought to have left North Osetiya between 1989 and 1999, largely owing to the decline of the military-industrial complex in the Republic, which had been their major employer. The Osetians speak an Indo-European language of the Persian (Iranian) group. In January 1999 an estimated 309,100 of the region's inhabitants lived in the capital, Vladikavkaz (Ordzhonikidze 1932–90), situated in the east of the Republic. At the end of 1999 there were approximately 37,000 registered refugees from the armed hostilities between South Osetian and Georgian government forces, although around 1,500 others had returned to Georgia from 1997, as conditions there improved and the economy of North Osetiya deteriorated further. By the end of 1999 about 35,000 Ingush had been displaced from the Prigorodnyi raion of North Osetiya, most of whom were living in Ingushetiya.

History

The Osetians (Ossetins, Oselty) are descended from the Alans, a tribe of the Samartian people. The Alans were driven into the foothills of the Caucasus by the Huns in the fourth century and their descendants (Ossetes) were forced further into the mountains by Tatar and Mongol invaders. Although the Osetians had been converted to Orthodox Christianity in the 12th and 13th centuries by the Georgians, a sub-group, the Digors, adopted Islam from the neighbouring Kabardins in the 17th and 18th centuries. Perpetual conflict with the Kabardins forced the Osetians to seek the protection of the Russian Empire, and their territory was eventually ceded to Russia by the Ottoman Turks at the Treaty of Kuçuk Kainavci in 1774 and confirmed by the Treaty of Iaşi (Jassy) in 1792. (Transcaucasian Osetiya, or South Osetiya—Ossetia, subsequently became part of Georgia.) The Russians fostered good relations with the Osetians, as they represented the only Christian group among the hostile Muslim peoples of the North Caucasus. Furthermore, both ends of the strategic Darial pass were situated in the region. The completion of the Georgian Military Road in 1799 facilitated the Russian conquest of Georgia (Kartli-Kakheti) in 1801.

After the Russian Revolution and having briefly been part of the Mountain (Gorskaya) People's Autonomous Republic, North Osetiya was established as an Autonomous Oblast on 7 July 1924. It became an ASSR on 5 December 1936. The Osetians were rewarded for their loyalty to the Soviet Government during the Second World War: in 1944 their territory was expanded by the inclusion of former Ingush territories to the east and of part of Stavropol Krai to the north. Furthermore, for 10 years the capital, renamed Ordzhonikidze in 1932, was known as Dzaudzikau, the Osetian pronunciation of Vladikavkaz. The Digors, however, were deported to Central Asia, along with other Muslim peoples, in 1944.

The Republic declared sovereignty in mid-1990. From 1991 there was considerable debate about some form of unification with South Osetiya. This resulted in armed hostilities between the South Osetians and Georgian troops, during which thousands of refugees fled to North Osetiya. Meanwhile, the Republic's administration refused to recognize claims by the Ingush to the territory they were deprived of in 1944 (the Prigorodnyi raion), which led to the onset of violence in October 1992 and the imposition of a state of emergency in the affected areas (see Ingushetiya, above). Despite a peace settlement in 1994, the region remained unstable. Under the terms of its Constitution, adopted on 7 December 1994, the Republic's name reverted to Alaniya. A power-sharing agreement was signed with the federal authorities the following year. The territory was a redoubt of the Communist Party, as proved by federal parliamentary elections of 1995 and 1999, republican parliamentary elections in 1999 and the Russian presidential election of 1996; however, in the presidential election of 26 March 2000 Vladimir Putin defeated his Communist opponent, Gennadii Zyuganov, in this region, as well as overall. In January 1998 Aleksandr Dzasokhov, a former member of the Communist Party of the Soviet Union Politburo, and a subsequent member of the State Duma and the Chairman of the Russian delegation to the Parliamentary Assembly of the Council of Europe, was elected the President of North Osetiya—Alaniya, with

75% of the votes cast, in comparison with the 15% cast in favour of the incumbent. His election was initially welcomed by the President of Ingushetiya, Ruslan Aushev, who had despatched several thousand displaced eligible voters from that Republic. However, relations between the two Republics remained strained, and Aushev subsequently suggested that the administration of the Prigorodnyi raion be appointed by the Government of Ingushetiya. In September a border incident, in which six people were killed and 70 temporary dwellings set on fire, increased tensions between the republics. On 30 July 1999 Aushev announced the suspension of all negotiations with North Osetiya and proposed that direct federal rule be imposed on Prigorodnyi, owing to an influx of Osetian Ingush into Ingushetiya; in March 2000, however, Vladimir Putin rejected the proposal as unconstitutional. Instability in North Osetiya, as elsewhere in the North Caucasus, increased during 1999, as insurgency became increasingly widespread. A bomb exploded in Vladikavkaz on 19 March, killing 42, and three further bombs exploded in military residences on 17 May. In March 2001 three simultaneous explosions, which killed over 20, were attributed to Chechen separatists.

Economy

In 1997 gross regional product in North Osetiya—Alaniya totalled 3,405,600m. old roubles, equivalent to 5,127,400 old roubles per head. Its major industrial centres are at Vladikavkaz, Mozdok and Beslan. It contains 144 km of railway track, including a section of the North Caucasus Railway, and the only direct road route from Russia to the Transcaucasus. There is an international airport at Vladikavkaz.

Agriculture in North Osetiya, which employed 9.0% of the labour force in 1998, consists mainly of vegetable and grain production, horticulture, viniculture and animal husbandry. The rate of reform in agriculture during the 1990s was slow. Agricultural production in 1998 amounted to a value of 1,298m. roubles. In the same year industrial output was worth 1,435m. roubles and the sector employed 17.9% of the working population. The Republic's main industries are radio electronics (until the 1990s largely used for defence purposes), non-ferrous metallurgy, mechanical engineering, wood-working, light industry, chemicals, glass-making and food processing. There are also five hydroelectric power-stations, with an average capacity of around 80 MWh. By the mid-1990s some 70% of industrial production within the defence sector had been converted to civilian use.

The economically active population totalled 213,600 in 1998, of whom 8,100 (3.8%) were unemployed. Those in employment earned an average wage of 663.8 roubles per month. The republican budget in that year showed a surplus of 41m. roubles. Foreign investment remained deterred by the instability endemic to much of the North Caucasus region. In 1998 export trade amounted to US $85.6m., and imports to $56.2m. At 1 January 1999 there was a total of 1,700 small businesses in operation on North Osetiyan territory.

Directory

President of the Republic: ALEKSANDR SERGEYEVICH DZASOKHOV; respublika Severnaya Osetiya, 362038 Vladikavkaz, pl. Svobody 1, Dom Sovetov; tel. (8672) 53-35-24.

Chairman of the Government: KAZBEK KARGINOV (acting); respublika Severnaya Osetiya, 362038 Vladikavkaz, pl. Svobody 1, Dom Sovetov; tel. (8672) 53-35-56.

Chairman of the Parliament: TAIMURAZ DZAMBEKOVICH MAMSUROV; respublika Severnaya Osetiya, 362038 Vladikavkaz, pl. Svobody1, Dom Sovetov; tel. (8672) 53-35-53.

Permanent Representative in Moscow: ERIK RUSLANOVICH BUGULOV; tel. (095) 916-21-47.

Head of Vladikavkaz City Administration (Mayor): MIKHAIL MIKHAILOVICH SHATALOV; respublika Severnaya Osetiya, 362040 Vladikavkaz, pl. Shtyba 1; fax (8672) 75-34-35.

Republic of Sakha (Yakutiya)

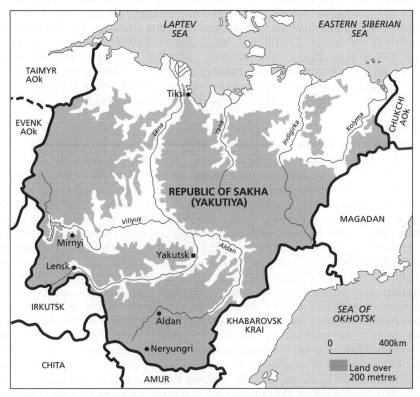

The Republic of Sakha (Yakutiya) is situated in eastern Siberia on the Laptev and Eastern Siberian Seas. Some two-fifths of the Republic's territory lies within the Arctic Circle. It forms part of the Far Eastern Economic Area and the Far Eastern Federal Okrug. To the west it borders Krasnoyarsk Krai (the Taimyr and Evenk AOks), while Irkutsk and Chita Oblasts lie in the south-west, Amur Oblast to the south and Khabarovsk Krai and Magadan Oblast in the south-east. In the north-eastern corner of the territory there is a border with the Chukchi AOk. Its main river is the Lena, which drains into the Laptev Sea via a large swampy delta; other important rivers are the Lena's tributaries, the Aldan, the Viliyuy, the Olenek, the Yana, the Indigirka and the Kolyma. Apart from the Central Yakut Plain, the region's territory is mountainous and four-fifths is taiga (forested marshland). Yakutiya is the largest federal unit in Russia, occupying an area of 3,103,200 sq km (1,198,150 sq miles), making it larger than Kazakhstan, itself the second-largest country, after Russia, in Europe or the former USSR. It consists of 33 administrative districts and 11 cities. Its climate, owing to its size, is varied: temperatures in January can be as low as −48°C in some northern areas, while in more temperate regions in July they are around 18°C. At 1 January 1999 the Republic had an estimated population of just 1,000,700 and a population density, therefore, of 0.3 per sq km. Some 64.2% of the population inhabited urban areas at this time. In the late 1990s there was a continuous outflow of population from the Republic. During the 1990s the extent of paved roads in the Republic increased twofold to some 7,071 km (4,394 miles). In 1989 33.4% of the total population were the indigenous Yakuts (who represent the largest ethnic group in Siberia, apart from Russians) and 50.3% Russians. Orthodox Christianity is the dominant religion in the region. The Yakuts' native tongue, spoken as a first language by over 93% of the indigenous population, is part of the North-Eastern branch of the Turkic family, although it is considerably influenced by Mongolian. The capital is at Yakutsk, which had an estimated population of 196,500 at 1 January 1999. The Republic's other major cities are Neryungri (75,100) and Mirnyi (36,700).

History

The Yakuts (Iakuts), also known as the Sakha (Saka), were historically known as the Tungus, Jekos and the Urangkhai Sakha. They are believed to be descended from various peoples from the Lake Baikal area, Turkish tribes from the steppe and the Altai Mountains, and indigenous Siberian peoples, including the Evenks. They were traditionally a semi-nomadic people, with those in the north of the region occupied with hunting, fishing and reindeer-breeding, while those in the south were pastoralists who bred horses and cattle and were also skilled blacksmiths. Their territory, briefly united by the toion (chief), Tygyn, came under Russian rule in the 1620s and a fur tax was introduced. This led to violent opposition from the Yakuts between 1634 and 1642, although all rebellions were crushed. Increasing numbers of Russians began to settle in the region as Yakutiya became a link between eastern and western Siberia. The completion of the mail route also increased the Russian population, as did the construction of camps for political opponents to the tsars and the discovery of gold in 1846. The territory became commercialized after the construction of the Trans-Siberian Railway in the 1880s and 1890s and the development of commercial shipping on the River Lena. The economic resources of the territory enabled the Yakut to secure a measure of autonomy as an ASSR in 1922 (its first leader was the Yakut poet, Platon Oyunskii). Collectivization and the purges of the 1930s greatly reduced the Yakut population during the Soviet era, and the region was rapidly industrialized, largely involving the extraction of gold, coal and timber.

Nationalist feeling, which first found voice in Yakutiya in 1906 with the founding of the Yakut Union, but was subsequently suppressed, re-emerged during the period of *glasnost* (openness) in the late 1980s. Cultural, ecological and economic concerns led to the proclamation of a Yakut-Sakha SSR on 27 April 1990. The Yakut Republic was officially declared by the Supreme Soviet on 15 August 1991, which demanded local control over the Republic's reserves of gold, diamonds, timber, coal, petroleum and tin. On 22 December elections for an executive presidency were held, and were won by the former Chairman of the Supreme Soviet, Mikhail Nikolayev. The Republic was renamed the Republic of Sakha in March 1992 and a new Constitution was promulgated on 27 April. On 12 October 1993 the Supreme Soviet dissolved itself and set elections to a 60-seat bicameral legislature for 12 December. On 26 January 1994 the new parliament (previously the Legislative State Assembly) named itself the State Assembly; it consisted of an upper Chamber of the Republic and a lower Chamber of Representatives. Although Communist support was relatively high in Sakha, the federal Government's willingness to concede a significant degree of local control over natural resources ensured that it too enjoyed some confidence. Local officials also proved concerned to address the problems of the minority indigenous peoples or 'small-numbered nations'. Native languages were designated official in certain areas and attempts to protect traditional lifestyles even involved the restoration of land. Thus, a Yeven-Bytantai Okrug was established on traditional Yeven territory in the mid-1990s. In June 1997 the Republic was honoured at a UN special session on the environment held in New York, the USA, for its commitment to preserving its natural heritage (around one-quarter of its territory had been set aside as protected areas). Meanwhile, in December 1996 Nikolayev was re-elected President by an overwhelming majority and continued his efforts to win greater autonomy from the centre, including the maintenance (in breach of federal law) of gold and hard-currency reserves, and, from August 1998, a ban on the sale of gold outside the republican government. A power-sharing agreement with the federal Government in June 1995 was followed, in March 1998, by a framework agreement on co-operation for five years, which provided for collaboration on a series of mining and energy projects. In May 2001 over 5,000 people were adversely affected by particularly severe flooding in the Republic. In December the federal Audit Chamber announced that an investigation was to take place into the alleged misspending by the republican Government of funds allocated for restoration work. In the same month Nikolayev withdrew his candidacy from the gubernatorial election scheduled to take place on 23 December, and urged voters to transfer their support to Vyacheslav Shtyrov, the President of the local diamond-producing joint-stock company, Almazy Rossii-Sakha—Alrosa. The federal Government had been attempting to prevent Nikolayev from standing for a third term of office.

Economy

Owing to the Republic's wealth of mineral reserves, its gross regional product in 1997 was 29,960,100m. old roubles, equivalent to 29,678,100 old roubles per head, the second-highest figure in the Russian Federation after the city of Moscow. The Republic's major industrial centres are at Yakutsk, Mirnyi, Neryungra, Aldan and Lensk. Its main port is Tiksi.

Yakutiya's agriculture, in which 9.9% of the working population was engaged in 1998, consists mainly of animal husbandry (livestock- and reindeer-breeding), hunting and fishing. Grain and vegetable production tends to be on a small scale. Total agricultural output in 1998 was worth 2,338m. roubles (compared to a figure of 24,511m. roubles for the industrial sector). Yakutiya's industrial sector employed 14.9% of its working population in 1998: its main industries are ore mining (gold— Sakha produced approximately 25% of the Russian Federation's output in the first half of the 1990s, diamonds—of which Sakha is the second-largest producer and exporter in the world, tin, muscovite—mica, antimony and coal), manufacture of building materials, processing of timber and agricultural products, and natural-gas production. Both industrial output and foreign trade in Yakutiya increased throughout the 1990s. In September 1997, following a decree passed by federal President Boris Yeltsin, Alrosa signed a preliminary one-year trade accord with the South African diamond producer, De Beers. The accord was subsequently extended until 2001, and De Beers was to purchase US $550m. worth of raw diamonds during this period. Alrosa also diversified its operations into polishing and selling its gems. A new, five-year agreement was signed with De Beers in December 2001. In January 1999 the President of Sakha, Mikhail Nikolayev, approved a five-year programme to upgrade the Republic's telecommunications infrastructure.

The social situation in Yakutiya from the mid-1990s was typical of the northern regions of the Russian Federation. Growth in the cost of goods and services was compounded by a weak economic structure, poorly developed social services and inappropriate conditions for people to grow their own food. In 1999, in terms of a 'consumer basket', the Republic was one of the most expensive regions in the country. Unemployment, however, was relatively low: the official figure for 1998 was 12,700 out of an economically active population of 481,000 (2.6%). The average monthly wage in that year was 1,663.2 roubles (considerably higher than the national average, but offset by the high cost of living). During the late 1990s the Republic maintained consistently large budgetary deficits; in 1998 the deficit amounted to 2,238m. roubles. Export trade in 1998 amounted to some US $748.8m., compared with imports of $87.7m. Foreign investment in Sakha (Yakutiya) in 1998 amounted to some $196.65m. At 1 January 1999 there were 4,300 small businesses registered on its territory.

Directory

President: MIKHAIL YEFIMOVICH NIKOLAYEV; respublika Sakha, 677012 Yakutsk, ul. Kirova 11; tel. (4112) 43-50-50; fax (4112) 24-06-24; internet www .sakha.gov.ru.

Vice-President: SPARTAK STEPANOVICH BORISOV; respublika Sakha, 677000 Yakutsk, ul. Kirova 11.

Chairman of the Government: VASILII MIKHAILOVICH VLASOV; respublika Sakha, 677000 Yakutsk, ul. Kirova 11; tel. (4112) 43-55-55.

State Assembly (Il Tumen): respublika Sakha, 677000 Yakutsk, ul. Kirova 11.

  Chairman of the Chamber of the Republic: VASILII VASILIYEVICH FILIPPOV; tel. (4112) 43-53-04.

  Chairman of the Chamber of Representatives: NIKOLAI IVANOVICH SOLOMOV; tel. (4112) 43-52-03.

Permanent Representative in Moscow: KLIMENT YEGOROVICH IVANOV; tel. (095) 923-10-97.

Head of Yakutsk City Administration (Mayor): ILYA FILIPPOVICH MIKHALCHUK; respublika Sakha, 677000 Yakutsk, ul. Kirova 11; tel. (4112) 42-30-20; fax (4112) 42-48-80; e-mail erb@yacc.yakutia.su.

Republic of Tatarstan

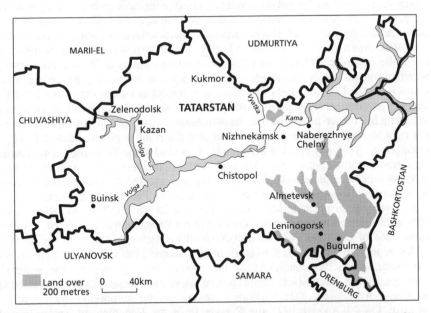

The Republic of Tatarstan is situated in the east of European Russia and forms part of the Volga Economic Area and the Volga Federal Okrug. It neighbours several other Republics: Bashkortostan to the east; Udmurtiya to the north; Marii-El to the north-west; and Chuvashiya to the west. The regions of Ulyanovsk, Samara and Orenburg lie to the south, that of Kirov to the north. Its major rivers are the Volga and the Kama and one-fifth of its total territory, of 67,836 sq km (26,260 sq miles), is forested. It measures 290 km (180 miles) from south to north and 460 km from west to east. The Republic is divided into 43 administrative districts and 19 cities. At 1 January 1999 it had an estimated population of 3,784,000 and, therefore, a population density of 55.6 per sq km. In 1989 some 48.5% of the total population were Tatars and 43.3% Russians. Tatarstan's capital is Kazan, which lies on the River Volga and had an estimated population of 1,091,500 in 1999. Other major cities include Naberezhnye Chelny (formerly Brezhnev—523,100), Nizhnekamsk (223,700), Almetevsk (141,900) and Zeleno-dolsk (101,500).

History

After the dissolution of the Mongol Empire the region became the Khanate of Kazan, the territory of the Golden Horde. It was conquered by Russia in 1552. Some of the Muslim Tatars succumbed to Russian pressures to convert to Orthodox Christianity (the Staro-Kryashens still exist, using Tatar as their spoken and liturgical tongue), but most did not. A modernist school of thought in Islam, Jadidism, originated among the Volga Tatars, who attained an exceptionally high cultural level in the 19th-century Russian Empire. A Tatar ASSR was established on 27 May 1920.

105

On 31 August 1990 the Chairman of the republican Supreme Soviet, Mintimer Shamiyev (elected President of the Republic in 1991), declared Tatarstan a sovereign republic. As President, Shamiyev continued to strive for the Republic's independence from the Federation Government, and a combination of harmony and tension between the regional and federal regimes characterized post-Soviet politics in Tatarstan. Apart from secessionist Chechnya, Tatarstan was the only republic to reject the Federation Treaty, adopting its own Constitution on 6 November 1992, which provided for a presidential republic with a legislative, bicameral State Council. On 15 February 1994 Shamiyev won important concessions from Russia's central Government by signing a treaty that ceded extensive powers to Tatarstan, including full ownership rights over its petroleum reserves and industrial companies, the right to retain most of its tax revenue and the right to pursue its own foreign-trade policy. This was the first agreement of its kind in the Federation and, despite significant contradictions and weaknesses, it became a model for other federal subjects seeking to determine their relations with the federal centre. The division of responsibilities was confirmed by treaty with the Federation in 1995.

In a republican presidential election, held on 24 March 1996, in which some 76% of the electorate participated, the incumbent President was re-elected, winning some 93% of the votes cast. Shamiyev owed his victory, in part, to the success of his economic policy: his Government had adapted the reforms of *perestroika* (restructuring) to the conditions of the region, thereby averting the negative consequences of excessively rapid privatization and social upheaval. Tatarstan became a model for other territories seeking greater autonomy and economic security. On 28 August 1997 the Presidents of the Republics of Tatarstan and Bashkortostan signed a treaty on co-operation at the second World Congress of Tatars, held in Kazan. The Congress adopted a resolution praising the development of Tatarstan into a 'new kind of sovereign state'. During 1999 Shamiyev was one of the regional governors most active in the creation of the new All Russia political bloc. Republican parliamentary by-elections that March gave the President's supporters a clear majority in the legislature. The moderate nationalism adopted by the regime was reflected in a decision, to be implemented over 10 years from August 2000, to revert to the use of the Latin (as opposed to the Cyrillic) script for the Tatar language. The previous year, Tatar authorities had suspended conscription to the Russian army following a number of deaths of Tatar draftees in Dagestan, also reflecting Shamiyev's previously stated support for Chechen President Khalid 'Aslan' Maskhadov. In 2000 federal President Vladimir Putin had offered Shamiyev the post of presidential envoy to the new Volga Federal Okrug, which he declined, amid constitutional uncertainty regarding the legitimacy of Shamiyev's intention to contest a third term of office as Governor. Although an initial decision to bring forward the gubernatorial election to December 2000 was subsequently rescinded, Shamiyev was permitted to compete in the election when it was held, as originally scheduled, on 25 March 2001. He gained some 80% of the votes cast, to become the first Governor of any federal subject in the Russian Federation to have been elected three times to that post. In May the Russian Supreme Court declared that some 42 articles of the Republic's Constitution were at variance with federal law. Despite federal government demands that these inconsistencies be removed, in July Shamiyev signed an agreement with the Presidential Representative to the Volga Federal Okrug, Sergei Kiriyenko, which permitted the continued operation of various practices that contradicted federal practice; in particular, a highly centralized system of local governance was to be retained in Tatarstan.

Economy

In 1997 the Republic's gross regional product stood at 67,160,300m. old roubles, or 17,813,500 old roubles per head. The territory is one of the most developed economic regions of the Russian Federation and has vast agricultural and industrial potential. Its main industrial centres are Kazan, Naberezhnye Chelny, Zelenodolsk, Nizhnekamsk, Almetyevsk, Chistopol and Bugulma. Kazan is the most important port on the Volga and a junction in national rail, road and air transport systems. Russia's second primary petroleum export pipeline to Europe starts in Almetyevsk.

Tatarstan's agriculture, in which some 13.0% of the work-force were engaged in 1998, consists mainly of grain production, animal husbandry, horticulture and bee-keeping. Total output in this sector amounted to a value of 10,752m. roubles in 1998. Mineral natural resources are more important—in early 1998 the Republic was ranked 18th in the world in terms of its hydrocarbons reserves. The region is an important industrial centre (industry accounts for 24.9% of its working population): its capital, Kazan, and the neighbouring towns of Zelendolsk and Vasilyevo are centres for light industry, the manufacture of petrochemicals and building materials, and mechanical engineering. The automobile and petroleum industries are major employers in the region. Kazanorgsintez, a petrochemicals giant, is the largest polyethylene producer in Russia. Industries connected with the extraction, processing and use of petroleum represent around one-half of the Republic's total industrial production, which was worth 59,568m. roubles in 1998. By the mid-1990s Tatarstan was also attracting foreign investors. For example, the US automobile company, General Motors, signed a contract to manufacture 50,000 automobiles per year at the Yelabuga plant, which later became the centre of a zone offering special tax incentives. In April 1996 a programme, drafted with French and US assistance, which envisaged the transformation of Tatarstan's economy from a military to a socially orientated system, was adopted by the Council of Ministers. France also granted US $215m. credit for the reconstruction of Kazan's international airport and the development of the agricultural-tool industry. In 1996 an International Centre for Investment Assistance was created, with offices in five countries. Foreign investment in the Republic during 1998 amounted to some $684m., with over 230 companies attracting foreign capital from Finland, Germany, the Netherlands, Poland, Turkey, the United Kingdom and the USA. In November 1998 some anxiety was caused when Tatarstan defaulted on a debt to a Western bank, although the republican authorities blamed the general economic crisis in Russia.

The economically active population in the Republic amounted to 1,597,000 in 1998, of whom 45,000 (2.8%) were unemployed. The average monthly wage at that time was 747.5 roubles. The 1998 budget saw a deficit of 923m. roubles. By the beginning of 1997 over 1,000 large and medium-sized enterprises in Tatarstan had been privatized; at 1 January 1999 some 102,000 people were employed in some 15,600 small businesses. Tatarstan also fared well in terms of trade; the value of exports amounted to US $1,230.5m. in 1998 and imports to $436.6m.

Directory

President: MINTIMER SHARIPOVICH SHAIMIYEV; respublika Tatarstan, 420014 Kazan, Kreml; tel. (8432) 92-74-66; fax (8432) 92-70-88; e-mail secretariat@ tatar.ru; internet www.tatar.ru.

Prime Minister: RUSTAM NURGALIYEVICH MINNIKHANOV; respublika Tatarstan, 420060 Kazan, pl. Svobody 1; tel. (8432) 32-79-03; fax (8432) 36-28-24.

Chairman of the State Council: FARID KHAIRULLOVICH MUKHAMETSHIN; respublika Tatarstan, 420060 Kazan, pl. Svobody 1; tel. (8432) 64-15-00.

Permanent Representative of the Republic of Tatarstan in the Russian Federation: NAZIF MUZAGIDANOVICH MIRIKHANOV; tel. (095) 915-05-02.

Head of Kazan City Administration: KAMIL SHAMILYEVICH ISKHAKOV; respublika Tatarstan, 420014 Kazan, ul. Kremlevskaya 1; tel. (8432) 92-38-38; fax (8432) 92-76-72; e-mail kanc@kazan.gov.tatarstan.ru; internet www.kazan.org.ru.

Republic of Tyva

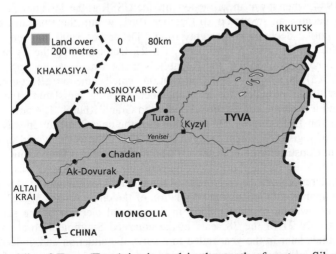

The Republic of Tyva (Tuva) is situated in the south of eastern Siberia in the Sayan Mountains. It forms part of the Eastern Siberian Economic Area and the Siberian Federal Okrug. Tyva has an international border with Mongolia to the south. The Republic of Altai lies to the west, Khakasiya is in the north-west and the rest of Krasnoyarsk Krai in the north, Irkutsk Oblast lies to the north-east and the Republic of Buryatiya forms part of the eastern border. Its major river is the Yenisei, which rises in the Eastern Sayan mountain range. The territory of the Republic consists of a series of high mountain valleys. One-half of its area is forested. The Republic has numerous waterways, including over 12,000 rivers and 8,400 freshwater lakes. Tyva occupies 170,500 sq km (65,830 sq miles) and consists of 16 administrative districts and five cities. At 1 January 1999 it had an estimated population of 310,700 and a population density of only 1.8 per sq km. Some 47.8% of the population lived in urban areas at this time. In 1989 some 64.3% of inhabitants were Tyvans (Tuvinians) and 32.0% Russians. Lamaism (Tibetan Buddhism) is the predominant religion in the Republic. The Tyvan language belongs to the Old Uigur group of the Turkic branch of the Uralo-Altaic linguistic family. The capital of Tyva is at Kyzyl, which had an estimated population of 98,700 at 1 January 1999.

History

The Tyvans (known at various times as Soyons, Soyots and Uriankhais) emerged as an identifiable ethnic group in the early 18th century. The territory of what is now Tyva was occupied in turn between the sixth and the ninth centuries by the Turkish Khanate, the Chinese, the Uigurs and the Yenisei Kyrgyz. The Mongols controlled the region from 1207 to 1368. In the second half of the 17th century the Dzungarians (Sungarians) seized the area from the Altyn Khans. In 1758 the Manzhous (Manchus) annexed Dzungaria and the territory thus became part of the Chinese Empire. Russian influence dates from the Treaty of Peking (Beijing) of 1860, after which trade links were developed and a number of Russians settled there. One year after the Chinese Revolution of 1911 Tyva declared its independence.

109

In 1914, however, Russia established a protectorate over the territory, which became the Tannu-Tuva People's Republic. This was a nominally independent state until October 1944, when it was incorporated into the USSR as the Tuvinian Autonomous Oblast. It became an ASSR on 10 October 1961, within the Russian Federation.

The Republic declared sovereignty on 11 December 1990 and renamed itself the Republic of Tuva in August 1991. On 21 October 1993 the Tyvan (Tuvin) Supreme Soviet resolved that the Republic's name was Tyva (as opposed to the russified Tuva) and adopted a new Constitution, which came into effect immediately. The Constitution provided for a 32-member working legislature, the Supreme Khural, and a supreme constitutional body, the Grand Khural. The new parliament was elected on 12 December. On the same day, the new Constitution was approved by 62.2% of registered voters in Tyva. Only 32.7%, however, voted in favour of the Russian Constitution. The victory of a nationalist Liberal Democratic candidate, Aleksandr Kashin, in the April 1998 mayoral elections in Kyzyl was, perhaps, a sign of intolerance with the reformism of the federal Government (certainly among the predominantly ethnic Russian population of the city). Apathy was also a likely cause, as a low rate of participation in the general election of the same month meant that only 21 of the 38 seats in the enlarged Supreme Khural were filled. Further rounds later in the year failed to resolve the situation and, indeed, for two months in 1998–99 the parliament was rendered inquorate by the death of a deputy. The following year the Grand Khural was obliged to make 26 amendments to the republican Constitution, in order to comply with the All-Russian Constitution. A new Constitution, which removed Tyva's right to self-determination and to secede from the Federation, was approved by referendum in May 2001.

Economy

Tyva's economy is largely agriculture-based. In 1997 its gross regional product stood at 1,803,800m. old roubles, or 5,814,900 old roubles per head. The Republic's main industrial centres are at Kyzyl and Ak-Dovurak. There are road and rail links with other regions, although the distance from Kyzyl to the nearest railway station is over 400 km (250 miles).

The Republic's agriculture, which employed 17.9% of the work-force in 1998, consists mainly of animal husbandry, although forestry and hunting are also important. Total agricultural production in 1998 amounted to a value of 546m. roubles. At 1 January 1999 there were some 670,400 sheep and goats, 140,100 cattle and 19,200 pigs in the Republic. Gold extraction was developed from the mid-1990s: in 1996 it amounted to almost one metric ton. Its main industries were ore mining (asbestos, coal, cobalt and mercury), production of electricity, the processing of agricultural and forestry products, light manufacturing, manufacture of building materials and metal working. Industry in 1998 employed 8.4% of the working population and total production within the sector was worth just 392m. roubles. However, in the late 1990s the Republic was one of the areas of the Russian Federation worst affected by wage arrears and most dependent on federal transfers. In September 2000 the federal Government arranged to pay wage arrears amounting to 216.7m. roubles in Tyva, in addition to providing for improvements to educational and medical services in the Republic.

The economically active population of Tyva in 1998 totalled 107,500, of whom 3,800 were unemployed. The average monthly wage in the Republic at this time was only 491 roubles, while the 1998 budget showed a surplus of 24m. roubles.

At 1 January 1999 there was a total of 600 small businesses registered in the Republic.

Directory

President: SHERIG-OOL DIZIZHIKOVICH OORZHAK; respublika Tyva, 667000 Kyzyl, ul. Chulduma 18, Dom Pravitelstva; tel. (39422) 1-12-77; fax (39422) 3-74-59; e-mail tuva@tuva.ru; internet www.tuva.ru/tuva.

Vice-President: ALEKSEI ALEKSANDROVICH MELNIKOV; tel. (39422) 3-63-20.

Chairman of the Supreme Khural: SHOLBAN VALERIYEVICH KARA-OOL; respublika Tyva, 667000 Kyzyl, ul. Lenina 32; tel. (39422) 3-73-25.

Permanent Representative in Moscow: ORLAN OORZHAKOVICH CHOLBENEI; tel. (095) 236-48-01.

Head of Kyzyl City Administration (Mayor): ALEKSANDR YURIYEVICH KASHIN; respublika Tyva, 667000 Kyzyl, ul. Lenina 32; tel. (39422) 3-50-55.

Udmurt Republic (Udmurtiya)

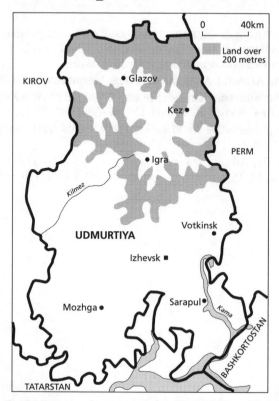

The Udmurt Republic occupies part of the Upper Kama Highlands. It forms part of the Urals Economic Area and the Volga Federal Okrug. Tatarstan lies to the south, Bashkortostan to the south-east, Perm to the east and Kirov to the north and west. Its major river is the Kama, dominating the southern and eastern borderlands, while the Vyatka skirts the territory in the west. About one-half of its territory is forested. Its total area covers some 42,100 sq km (16,250 sq miles). The Republic consists of 25 administrative districts and six cities. At 1 January 1999 Udmurtiya had an estimated population of 1,632,600, of which some 69.5% inhabited urban areas. The population density in the Republic at this time was 38.8 per sq km. In 1989 some 30.9% of the total population were Udmurts and 58.9% ethnic Russians. The dominant religion in the Republic is Orthodox Christianity. The 1989 census showed that some 70% of Udmurts spoke their native tongue, from the Permian group of the Finnic branch of the Uralo-Altaic family, as their first language. The capital of Udmurtiya is at Izhevsk (known as Ustinov for much of the Soviet period), which had an estimated population of 654,900 in 1999. Other major towns in the region are Glazov (106,300), Sarapul (106,200) and Votkinsk (102,300).

History

The first appearance of the Votyaks (the former name for Udmurts) as a distinct ethnic group occurred in the sixth century. The territories inhabited by Votyaks were conquered by the Khazars in the eighth century, although Khazar influence gave way to that of the Volga Bulgars in the mid-ninth century. In the 13th century the Mongol Tatars occupied the region, but were gradually displaced by the Russians from the mid-15th century. By 1558 all Votyaks were under Russian rule. A Votyak Autonomous Oblast was established on 4 November 1920. On 1 January 1932 it was renamed the Udmurt Autonomous Oblast, which became an ASSR on 28 December 1934.

The Republic declared sovereignty on 21 September 1990, although a new republican Constitution was not adopted until 7 December 1994. According to this basic law, the Chairman of the legislature, the State Council, remained head of the Republic, and a premier chaired the Government. In 1996 the Udmurt parliament was accused of having virtually eliminated local government in the Republic, in contravention of federal law. Measures to introduce a presidential system of regional government in Udmurtiya, in common with most other Republics within the Russian Federation, were endorsed by a referendum held on 26 March 2000. In June the Udmurt State Council adopted a number of draft laws transferring the Republic to presidential rule. Aleksandr Volkov, hitherto the parliamentary speaker, was elected President on 15 October. The Republic's Prime Minister, Nikolai Ganza, who was supported by the Unity movement, was the third-placed candidate; he resigned three days later.

Economy

The Republic's gross regional product in 1997 amounted to 22,114,300m. old roubles, equivalent to 13,513,100 old roubles per head. Udmurtiya possesses significant hydrocarbons reserves and is an important arms-producing region. Its major industrial centres are at Izhevsk, Sarapul and Glazov. Its main river-ports are at Sarapul and Kambarka. In 1998 there were 778 km of railway track on its territory. In the same year there were 5,064 km of paved roads and 178 km of navigable waterways. Twelve major gas pipelines and two petroleum pipelines pass through the Udmurt Republic.

Udmurtiya's agriculture employed 11.8% of the working population in 1998 and consists mainly of livestock breeding, grain production and flax growing. Total agricultural production in 1998 was worth 3,935m. roubles. There are substantial reserves of coal and of petroleum (prospected resources are estimated at 379,543m. metric tons), which in the late 1990s the Republic hoped to exploit with the aid of foreign investment. In 1998 some 28.5% of its working population was engaged in industry. The main industries in Udmurtiya, apart from the manufacture of weapons, are mechanical engineering (in the first half of 2000 the Republic produced some 89% of all the motor cycles manufactured in Russia), metal working, metallurgy, processing of forestry and agricultural products, petroleum production, glass-making, light manufacturing and the production of peat. Total industrial output in 1998 amounted to a value of 16,385m. roubles. External trade in Udmurtiya in 1998 amounted to US $495.4m., of which $458.8m. was with partners outside the CIS. Exports largely comprised metallurgical products, engines and machinery and rifles. In the late 1990s the Republic had particularly active trade links with Germany.

In 1998 the economically active population amounted to 700,800. Some 50,100 (7.1%) of these were registered unemployed; those in employment earned an average of 827 roubles. The budget in 1998 showed a deficit of 229m. roubles.

There was US $7.90m. of foreign investment in the Republic in that year. At 1 January 1999 there were approximately 7,100 small businesses registered in the Republic. In the mid-1990s the disposal of chemical weapons on the territory of Udmurtiya was proving to be a serious social and ecological problem—the Republic was thought to contain around one-quarter of Russia's entire arsenal of such weapons. In January 2000 Italy agreed to contribute $8.3m. to the Russian Federation for the destruction of stockpiled chemical weapons in Udmurtiya.

Directory

President: ALEKSANDR ALEKSANDROVICH VOLKOV; respublika Udmurtiya, 426074 Izhevsk, pl. 50 let Oktyabrya 15; tel. (3412) 75-48-01; fax (3412) 25-50-17; e-mail president@udmurt.ru.

Chairman of the Government: YURII STEPANOVICH PITKEYVICH; respublika Udmurtiya, 426007 Izhevsk, ul. Pushkinskaya. 214, Dom Pravitelstva; tel. (3412) 25-45-67; fax (3412) 25-50-17; e-mail premier@udmurt.ru.

Permanent Representative in Moscow: ANDREI VLADIMIROVICH SAKOVICH; tel. (095) 203-53-52.

Head of Izhevsk City Administration (Mayor): ANATOLII IVANOVICH SALTYKOV; respublika Udmurtiya, 426070 Izhevsk, ul. Pushkinskaya 276; tel. (3412) 22-38-62; fax (3412) 22-84-94; e-mail izhersk@izh.ru; internet www.izh.ru.

KRAIS (PROVINCES)

Altai Krai

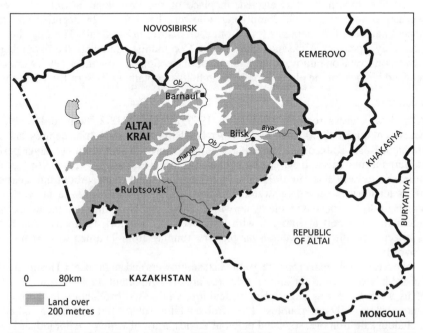

Most of Altai Krai lies within the Western Siberian Plain. Part of the Western Siberian Economic Area and the Siberian Federal Okrug, it has international boundaries to the south with Kazakhstan, the People's Republic of China and Mongolia. To the north lie the federal subjects of Novosibirsk Oblast, Kemerovo Oblast and the Republic of Khakasiya (formally part of Krasnoyarsk Krai) and the Republic of Tyva lies beyond the eastern border. The eastern part of the Krai is constituted as the Republic of Altai (see above—formerly the Gorno-Altai Autonomous Oblast). Its major river is the Ob, which has numerous tributaries (there are altogether some 17,000 rivers within the territory). It has one main lake, the Teletskoye, although there are a total of 13,000 lakes, one-half of which are fresh water. About one-third of its total area is forested. In the east of the Krai are mountains, in the west steppe. Excluding the Altai Republic, the Krai occupies an area of 169,100 sq km (65,290 sq miles). It is divided into 60 administrative districts and 12 cities, as well as the autonomous republic. It had an estimated population of 2,664,800 at 1 January 1999, of whom 58.3% lived in urban areas. Its population density at this time was 15.8 per sq km. In 1996 ethnic Russians comprised an estimated 90.3% of the population, Germans 4.8%, Ukrainians 2.4% and Altais just 0.1%. The Krai's administrative centre is at Barnaul, which had an estimated population of 583,000 at 1 January 1999. Other major cities are Biisk (224,800) and Rubtsovsk (163,900).

History

The territory of Altai Krai was annexed by Russia in 1738. The region was heavily industrialized during the Soviet period, particularly in the years 1926–40. Altai Krai was formed on 28 September 1937. On 13 March 1994, in accordance with a federal presidential decree of October 1993, a new provincial legislature, the Legislative Assembly, was elected, in place of the Provincial Soviet. The new legislature was bicameral, comprising a lower chamber of 25 deputies and an upper chamber of 73 deputies (one from each district in the Krai). The Legislative Assembly speaker, Aleksandr Surikov, a Communist, defeated the incumbent Governor, Lev Korshunov, in the gubernatorial election of November 1996. Surikov retained his post in the election of 26 March 2000, obtaining 77% of the votes cast.

Economy

Altai Krai's gross regional product in 1997 totalled 22,052,200m. old roubles, equivalent to 8,243,200 old roubles per head. Its main industrial centres are at Barnaul, Biisk, Rubtsovsk, Novoaltaisk and Slavgorod. There are major river-ports at Barnaul and Biisk. It has well-developed transport networks—1,803 km (1,067 miles) of railway lines in 1998 and 14,267 km of paved roads. About one-quarter of its territory is served by water transport, which operates along a network of some 1,000 km of navigable waterways. There are five airports, including an international airport at Barnaul, with a service to Düsseldorf, Germany. The Krai is bisected by the main natural-gas pipeline running from Tyumen to Barnaul via Novosibirsk.

The Krai's principal crops are grain, flax, sunflowers and sugar beets. Horticulture, animal husbandry and fur-animal breeding are also important. In 1998 some 21.2% of its work-force was engaged in agriculture, while total production in the sector amounted to 7,994m. roubles. The Krai contains substantial mineral resources, including salt, iron ore, soda and precious stones, most of which are not industrially exploited. Its main industries are mechanical engineering (including tractor manufacturing, primarily by the Rubtsovsk tractor plant), metallurgy, chemicals and petrochemicals, the manufacture of building materials, ore mining (complex ores, gold, mercury, salt), food processing (the Krai's agro-industrial complex is one of the largest in the country), textiles and light manufacturing. Barnaul contains one of the largest textile enterprises in Russia, producing cotton fibre and yarn for cloth. Industry employed 20.4% of the population in 1998 and total production in the sector amounted to a value of 14,810m. roubles.

In 1998 the economically active population in Altai Krai totalled 1,050,200, of whom 39,600 were unemployed. The average monthly wage at that time was 503.8 roubles, while the local budget showed a surplus of 93m. roubles in 1998. There was US $5.976m. of foreign investment in the territory in 1998. Leading foreign trading partners included the People's Republic of China, Germany, Italy, Kazakhstan and Uzbekistan. At 1 January 1999 there were 10,800 small businesses registered in the Krai.

Directory

Head of the Provincial Administration (Governor): ALEKSANDR ALEKSANDRO-VICH SURIKOV; Altaiskii krai, 656035 Barnaul, pr. Lenina 59; tel. (3852) 35-69-35; e-mail glava@alregn.ru.

Chairman of the People's Deputies' Council: ALEKSANDR GRIGORIYEVICH NAZARCHUK; tel. (3852) 22-86-61; fax (3852) 22-85-42.

Head of the Provincial Representation in Moscow: TIMUR SURENOVICH BABLU-MYAN; tel. (095) 951-01-57.

Head of Barnaul City Administration (Golova): VLADIMIR NIKOLAYEVICH BAVARIN; Altaiskii krai, 656035 Barnaul, pr. Lenina 18; tel. (3852) 23-65-41.

Khabarovsk Krai

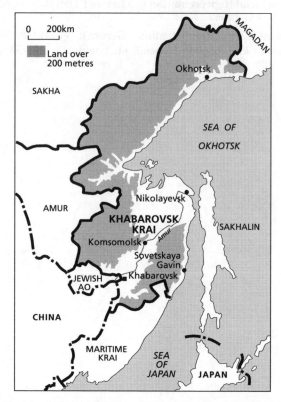

Khabarovsk Krai is situated in the Far East on the Sea of Okhotsk and the Tatar Strait. The region forms part of the Far Eastern Economic Area and the Far Eastern Federal Okrug. Maritime Krai lies to the south, the Jewish Autonomous Oblast (Birobidzhan—part of the Krai until 1991) is to the south-west, Amur Oblast lies to the west, the Republic of Sakha (Yakutiya) to the north-west and, in the north of the province, Magadan Oblast lies to the east. The island of Sakhalin (part of Sakhalin Oblast) lies offshore to the east, across the Tatar Strait. There is a short international border with the People's Republic of China in the south-west. Its main river is the Amur, which rises near the Russo-Chinese border and flows into the Tatar Strait at the town of Nikolayevsk-on-Amur (Nikolayevsk-na-Amure). More than one-half of the Krai's total area of 788,600 sq km (304,400 sq miles) is forested and almost three-quarters comprises mountains or plateaux. The territory, one of the largest in the Federation, measures 1,780 km (1,105 miles) south to north and 7,000 km west to east. Its coastline is 2,500 km long. It is divided into 17 administrative districts and seven cities. The climate is monsoon-like in character, with hot, humid summers. Annual average precipitation in mountain areas can be as much as 1,000 mm (40 inches), while in the north it averages 500 mm. The total population in Khabarovsk Krai at 1 January 1999 was an estimated 1,523,300, of whom a large proportion (80.7%) lived in urban areas. The population density of the Krai was 1.9 per sq km. Khabarovsk Krai's administrative centre is at Khabarovsk, which had an estimated population of 611,200 in 1999. Other major cities are Komsomolsk-on-Amur (296,000), Amursk (54,300) and Nikolayevsk-on-Amur (32,700).

History

Khabarovsk city was established as a military outpost in 1858. It was named after Yerofei Khabarov, a Cossack who in 1650 led an expedition to the junction of the Amur and Ussuri rivers, the approximate location of Khabarovsk. The region prospered significantly with the construction of the Trans-Siberian Railway, which reached Khabarovsk in 1905. The Krai was formally created on 20 September 1938. The area was industrialized in 1946–80. Following the dissolution of the Provincial Soviet in late 1993, elections to a new legislative body, the Duma, were held in the Krai on 6 March 1994. In April 1996 the Russian President, Boris Yeltsin, and the head of the provincial administration, Viktor Ishayev, signed an agreement on the division of powers between the provincial and federal governments. Ishayev also headed the Association of Economic Interaction, 'Far East—Transbaikal', which sought to promote a coherent programme of economic development across the Russian Far East. Ishayev was re-elected as Governor on 10 December 2000, gaining 88% of the votes cast.

Economy

The Krai's principal land use is forestry. In 1997 its gross regional product totalled 31,380,600m. old roubles, or 20,227,300 old roubles per head. Its main industrial centres are at Khabarovsk, Komsomolsk-on-Amur, Sovetskaya Gavan, Nikolayevsk-on-Amur and Amursk. Its principal ports are Vanino (the port of Sovetskaya Gavan), Okhotsk and Nikolayevsk-on-Amur. It is traversed by two major railways, the Trans-Siberian and the Far Eastern (Baikal–Amur). A ferry service runs between the Krai and Sakhalin Oblast. The Krai is the most important Far Eastern territory in terms of its national and international air services, which connect Moscow and other European cities with Japan.

Agriculture, which employed just 3.0% of the working population in 1998 and generated 3,023m. roubles, consists mainly of grain production, animal husbandry, bee-keeping, fishing and hunting. Hunting is practised on about 97.5% of the Krai's territory. In August 1997 the federal Government approved a programme to rescue the Siberian tiger (435 of which inhabited the forests of Khabarovsk and Maritime Krais) from extinction at the hands of poachers. Its main industries are mechanical engineering, metal working, ferrous metallurgy, the processing of forestry products, extraction of coal (1.9m. metric tons of which were mined in 1999), ores and non-ferrous metals, shipbuilding (including oil rigs) and petroleum refining. Some 19.4% of the territory's work-force was engaged in industry in 1998. Total industrial output in that year amounted to a value of 15,517m. roubles. In the 1990s the territory began to develop its trade links with 'Pacific Rim' nations apart from Japan (with which it had a long trading history), such as Canada, the People's Republic of China, the Democratic People's Republic of Korea (North Korea) and the Republic of Korea (South Korea), Australia, New Zealand, Singapore and the USA. Its exports largely consisted of raw materials (timber, petroleum products, fish and metals).

Khabarovsk Krai's economically active population was 653,200 in 1998, of whom 34,300 were registered as unemployed. Its overall unemployment rate was 5.25% in 1998, but in certain parts of the territory the figure was much higher. A lack of funds to convert former military enterprises to civilian production in Amursk and Komsomolsk-on-Amur, and the liquidation of the only steel mill in the Russian Far East and a major paper and pulp producer counterbalanced the effects of considerable foreign investment and trade. In 1998 the average monthly wage was some 1,024.3 roubles. The provincial administration achieved a budgetary deficit in that year, of 674m. roubles. Total foreign investment amounted to US $40.1m. According to the regional foreign investment promotion agency, in January 2000 731 joint ventures were registered in the territory. At 1 January 1999 there were 8,000 small businesses in operation.

Directory

Head of the Provincial Administration (Governor): VIKTOR IVANOVICH ISHAYEV; Khabarovskii krai, 680000 Khabarovsk, ul. Karla Marksa 56; tel. (4212) 33-55-40; fax (4212) 33-87-56; internet www.adm.khv.ru.

Chairman of the Provincial Legislative Duma: YURII ONOPRIYENKO; Khabarovskii krai, 680002 Khabarovsk, ul. Muravyeva-Amurskogo 19; e-mail serge@duma.khv.ru; internet www.duma.khv.ru.

Principal Representative in Moscow: ANDREI BORISOVICH CHIRKIN; tel. (095) 203-41-28.

Head of Khabarovsk City Administration (Mayor): ALEKSANDR NIKOLAYEVICH SOKOLOV; Khabarovskii krai, 680000 Khabarovsk, ul. Karla Marksa 66; tel. (4212) 23-58-67; fax (4212) 33-53-46; internet www.khabarovsk.kht.ru.

Krasnodar Krai

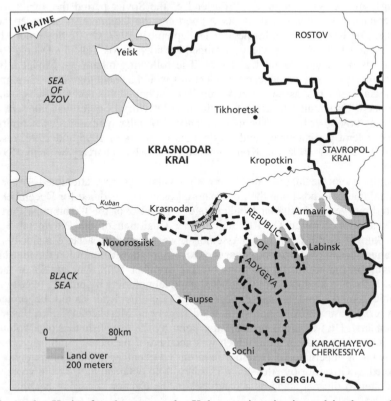

Krasnodar Krai, often known as the Kuban region, is situated in the south of European Russia, in the north-western region of the Greater Caucasus and Kuban-Azov lowlands. The Krai forms part of the North Caucasus Economic Area and the Southern Federal Okrug. It has a short international border with Georgia in the south, while Karachayevo-Cherkessiya and the rest of Stavropol Krai lie to the east and Rostov Oblast to the north-east. The Krai's territory includes and encloses the Republic of Adygeya. The Krai lies on the Black Sea (on the shores of which is sited the famous resort town of Sochi) in the south-west and on the Sea of Azov in the north-west. The narrow Kerch Gulf, in places only 10 km (six miles) wide, separates the western tip of the province from the Crimean Peninsula (Ukraine). Its major river is the Kuban. The territory of Krasnodar Krai, excluding Adygeya, covers 76,000 sq km (29,340 sq miles) and measures 372 km south to north and 380 km west to east. The region is divided into 38 administrative districts and 26 cities. It had an estimated population of 5,009,900 at 1 January 1999. Its population density at this time was 65.9 per sq km, a considerably higher figure than the national average. Krasnodar, the Krai's administrative centre, had an estimated population of 642,200.

History
Krasnodar city (known as Yekaterinodar until 1920) was founded as a military base in 1793, during the campaign of Catherine (Yekaterina) II ('the Great') to

win control of the Black Sea region for the Russian Empire, which was eventually achieved in 1796. Dominated by the 'Whites' in the civil wars that followed the collapse of the tsarist regime, by the end of the Soviet period the area's innate conservatism was confirmed by its support for the Communists in independent Russia. The Krai had been formed on 13 September 1937. On 22 September 1993 the Krasnodar Provincial Soviet condemned President Boris Yeltsin's Decree 1,400, which dissolved the federal legislature. The following month the Soviet refused to dissolve itself, but announced that elections would be held to a new, 32-member, provincial legislative assembly in March 1994, although this poll was subsequently postponed. Communist leadership of the new Provincial Soviet was not seriously challenged by other forces. The general tenor of popular sympathies was confirmed by the federal parliamentary and presidential elections of 1995 and 1996, respectively. In January 1996 the Krai signed a power-sharing treaty with the federal authorities.

During 1996 the incumbent Governor, Nikolai Yegorov, attempted to use the regional courts to postpone the gubernatorial election scheduled for December. He failed, however, and Nikolai Kondratenko, a member of the Communist Party of the Russian Federation (KPRF) and former Chairman of the Provincial Soviet (later known as the Legislative Assembly), was elected by a large majority. The Communists and other supporters of the Governor retained control of the legislative assembly in the provincial elections of 22 November 1998, winning 37 of the 50 seats. Kondratenko consistently attracted national notoriety by making overtly anti-Semitic remarks and promoting the notion that the Krai should be protected from an 'invasion of foreigners' (defined largely as Meshketian Turks, Jews and Armenians). He was aided in this latter point by the establishment of a voluntary Cossack militia in the region, which was accused of persecuting minority groups. Following a gubernatorial election, held on 3 December 2000, Kondratenko was replaced as Governor by Aleksandr Tkachev, who obtained 82% of the votes cast. Kondratenko did not stand as a candidate in the election, citing ill-health.

Economy

In 1997 gross regional product in Krasnodar Krai amounted to 48,949,800m. old roubles, or 9,650,000 old roubles per head. Krasnodar is one of the Krai's main industrial centres, as are Armavir, Novorossiisk, Kropotkin, Tikhoretsk and Yeisk. Novorossiisk, Tuapse, Yeisk, Temryuk and Port Kavkaz are important sea-ports. In 1998 the Krai had 10,208 km (6,433 miles) of paved roads and 2,174 km of railway track.

The Krai's principal crops are grain, sugar beets, rice, tobacco, essential-oil plants, tea and hemp. Horticulture, viniculture and animal husbandry are also important. Agricultural output was worth 13,811m. roubles in 1998, when some 19.7% of the working population was engaged in agriculture. There are important reserves of petroleum and natural gas in Krasnodar Krai. In 1996 around 1.7m. metric tons of petroleum were extracted, while 4.3m. tons were refined on the Krai's territory. Its main industries are food processing (which comprised around two-fifths of industry in the mid-1990s), electricity generation, chemical and light manufacturing, mechanical engineering, metal working and timber processing. Total production in the sector (which employed 15.1% of the territory's population in 1998) amounted to a value of 21,920m. roubles. The tourism sector is also important: the Kuban region's climate, scenery and mineral and mud springs attracted around 6m. visitors annually in the mid-1990s, when some 400,000 people were employed in tourism. The Krai contains the resort towns of Sochi, Anapa, Tuapse and Gelendbaz. In 1997 there were over 50 commercial banks operating in Krasnodar Krai. The transportation and refinery of Caspian Sea hydrocarbons reserves (particularly in Novorossiisk, the terminus of a major petroleum pipeline from Baku, Azerbaijan) brought economic benefits to the region in the late 1990s, and unemployment declined by over 20% between 1996 and 1998, to stand at 28,700 (1.5%) in the latter year.

In 1998 the economically active population numbered 1,882,900. The average monthly wage was 666.1 roubles. There was a budgetary deficit in 1998 of 144m. roubles. Foreign investment in 1998 amounted to US $320.08m., 20 times as much as it had been one year previously. International trade in 1998 amounted to $1,133.5m., almost equally divided between imports and exports. At 1 January 1999 there were 24,500 small businesses in operation in the Krai.

Directory

Head of the Provincial Administration: ALEKSANDR TKACHEV; Krasnodarskii krai, 350014 Krasnodar, ul. Krasnaya 35; tel. (8612) 62-57-16; fax (8612) 68-45-38.

Chairman of the Legislative Assembly: VLADIMIR ANDREYEVICH BEKETOV; tel. (8612) 52-50-07; fax (8612) 52-88-80.

Provincial Representation in Moscow: tel. (095) 917-35-82.

Head of Krasnodar City Administration (Mayor): NIKOLAI VASILYEVICH PRIZ; Krasnodarskii krai, 350014 Krasnodar, ul. Krasnaya 122; tel. (8612) 55-43-48; fax (8612) 55-01-56; e-mail post@krd.ru; internet www.krd.ru.

Krasnoyarsk Krai

Krasnoyarsk Krai occupies the central part of Siberia and extends from the Arctic Ocean coast in the north to the western Sayan Mountains in the south. The Krai forms part of the Eastern Siberian Economic Area and the Siberian Federal Okrug. It is bordered by the Republic of Sakha (Yakutiya) and Irkutsk Oblast to the east and the Republic of Tyva to the south. Khakasiya, an autonomous republic which is, formally, part of the Krai, gives it a border with the Republic of Altai in the south-west. Otherwise, to the west lie the regions of Kemerovo and Tomsk, as well as Tyumen Oblast's Khanty-Mansii and Yamal-Nenets AOks. Its major river is the Yenisei, one of the longest in Russia, measuring 4,102 km (2,549 miles). Most of its area is covered by taiga (forested marshland). The Krai, including its two autonomous okrugs (Evenk and Taimyr or Dolgan-Nenets), covers a total area of 2,339,000 sq km (902,850 sq miles), the second-largest federal unit in Russia, or 710,000 sq km (274,133 sq miles) when they are excluded. Krasnoyarsk Krai measures almost 3,000 km from south to north. In the Krai proper there are 42 administrative districts and 22 cities. The Krai lies within three climatic zones—arctic, sub-arctic and continental. It had an estimated total population of 3,075,600 at 1 January 1999 and a population density of 1.3 per sq km. Some 74.3% of the population inhabited urban areas at that time. The Krai's administrative centre is at Krasnoyarsk, which had an estimated population of 877,600 at 1 January 1999.

Other major cities include Norilsk (151,600), Achinsk (122,800), Kansk (108,100) and Zheleznogorsk (94,600).

History

The city of Krasnoyarsk was founded in 1628 by Cossack forces as an ostrog (military transit camp) during the period of Russian expansion across Siberia (1582–1639). The region gained importance after the discovery of gold, and with the construction of the Trans-Siberian Railway. The Krai was formed on 7 December 1934. During the Soviet era the region was closed to foreigners, owing to its nuclear-reactor and defence establishments.

A gubernatorial election in December 1992 was won by Valerii Zubov (the incumbent, a supporter of President Boris Yeltsin), and elections to a new parliament, the Legislative Assembly, were held on 6 March 1994. The dominance of the old nomenklatura in the Krai was indicated by the high level of support for the Communists (mainly in the countryside), but also by the mainly urban support for pro-Yeltsin and reformist parties, which tended to be represented by respected members of the old establishment. During the mid-1990s, however, Zubov's regime, though enlightened, proved to be increasingly ineffectual—in 1997 the provincial administration collected less than one-half of the taxes it was owed and had one of the worst records on wage arrears in the country. This largely contributed to the victory in the 1998 gubernatorial elections of Aleksandr Lebed, who was perceived by many as a suitably strong leader capable of defending the interests of the territory against the federal Government. Lebed, who allegedly had strong support for his campaign from powerful industrial figures in the Krai, defeated Zubov in the second round of elections, held on 17 May, with 57.3% of the votes cast, compared to Zubov's 38.2%. He remained a controversial figure, mainly in national politics, but his popular rhetoric would be tested by provincial government.

Economy

Krasnoyarsk Krai is potentially one of Russia's richest regions, containing vast deposits of minerals, gold and petroleum. It also has serious economic problems, many of them typical of northern regions. In 1997 its gross regional product (including the autonomous okrugs) amounted to 65,481,900m. old roubles, equivalent to 21,208,000 old roubles per head. The Krai's major industrial centres are at Krasnoyarsk, Norilsk, Achinsk, Kansk and Minusinsk.

The principal crops are grain, flax, and hemp. Animal husbandry, fur farming and hunting are also important. The agricultural sector employed just 7.6% of the working population in 1998. Total output within the sector was worth 8,475m. roubles. At the beginning of 1999 the provincial assembly considered the state of farming to be critical, reported no sign of a revival of industry and expressed concern at the continued deterioration in living standards. The Krai's main industries are non-ferrous metallurgy, mechanical engineering, metal working, ore mining (particularly bauxite, for aluminium), chemicals, forestry, light manufacturing and food processing. Industry employed 26.1% of the Krai's work-force in 1998. The combined industrial output of Krasnoyarsk Krai and its two autonomous okrugs amounted to a value of 60,908m. roubles. The Krai contains the world's second-largest aluminium smelter, Krasnoyarsk Aluminium, which in 1998 was 20%-owned by the British-based company, Trans-World.

In 1998 the territory's economically active population totalled 1,371,100. The number of registered unemployed for the entire province was 66,700 (4.9%) at that time, a figure that had increased rapidly during the 1990s. The average monthly wage in the Krai was some 1,033.6 roubles, while the local budget, which included the two autonomous okrugs, showed a deficit of some 510m. roubles. Foreign investment was somewhat sporadic, and totalled US $7.6m. in 1998. In that year export trade amounted to $2,953.3m. and imports to $207.5m. At the beginning of 1999 there were 12,800 small businesses in Krasnoyarsk Krai, and by 1996 93.2% of small businesses were privately owned.

Directory

Head of the Provincial Administration (Governor): ALEKSANDR IVANOVICH LEBED; Kranoyarskii krai, 660009 Krasnoyarsk, pr. Mira 110; tel. (3912) 22-22-63; fax (3912) 22-11-78; internet www.alebed.org.

Chairman of the Legislative Assembly: ALEKSANDR VIKTOROVICH USS; Krasnoyarskii krai, 660009 Krasnoyarsk, pr. Mira 110; tel. (3912) 23-28-10.

Provincial Representation in Moscow: tel. (095) 284-85-79.

Head of Krasnoyarsk City Administration (Mayor): PETR IVANOVICH PIM-ASHKOV; Krasnoyarskii krai, 660049 Krasnoyarsk, ul. Karla Marksa 93; tel. (3912) 22-22-31; fax (3912) 22-25-12; e-mail webmaster@admkrsk.ru; internet www.admkrsk.ru.

Maritime (Primorskii) Krai

Maritime (Primorskii) Krai (Primorye) is situated in the extreme south-east of the country on the Tatar Strait and the Sea of Japan. The province is part of the Far Eastern Economic Area and the Far Eastern Federal Okrug. Its only border with another federal subject is with Khabarovsk Krai to the north. There is an international border with the People's Republic of China to the west and a short border with the Democratic People's Republic of Korea (North Korea) in the south-west. Its major river is the Ussuri. The territory occupies 165,900 sq km (64,060 sq miles), more than two-thirds of which is forested. It is divided into 25 administrative districts and 12 cities. At 1 January 1999 the total number of inhabitants in the territory was estimated at 2,194,200 and the population density was, therefore, 13.2 per sq km. Of this total, some 78.3% lived in urban areas. Maritime Krai's administrative centre is at Vladivostok, which had an estimated 610,300 inhabitants. Other major cities are Nakhodka (159,600), Ussuriisk (formerly Voroshilov—157,600), Arsenev (67,300) and Artem (66,900).

History

The territories of the Maritime Krai were recognized as Chinese possessions by Russia in the Treaty of Nerchinsk in 1687. They became part of the Russian Empire in 1860, however, being ceded by China under the terms of the Treaty of Peking (Beijing), and the port of Vladivostok was founded. Along with other Transbaikal and Pacific regions of the former Russian Empire, the territory was part of the Far Eastern Republic until its 1922 reintegration into Russia under Soviet rule. Maritime Krai was created on 20 October 1938.

The territory declared itself a republic in mid-1993, but was not recognized as such by the federal authorities. On 28 October 1993 the provincial Governor disbanded the Soviet as it had failed to muster a quorum. Elections for a Governor of the territory were set for 7 October 1994, but were cancelled by presidential decree, after alleged improprieties by the incumbent, Yevgenii Nazdratenko, during his election campaign. Nazdratenko was elected, however, on 17 December 1995, having won some 76% of the votes cast and was re-elected by a similar majority on 20 December 1999. His populist and nationalistic style of government, development of a 'cult of personality', and control of the local media reinforced his position.

The Governor's disputes with the central Government, particularly with President Boris Yeltsin's reformist chief of staff, Anatolii Chubais, continued after his election—in October 1996 Chubais publicly blamed Nazdratenko for the serious energy crisis in the region, citing his failure to introduce market reforms. In 1997 a long-standing feud between Nazdratenko and the liberal Mayor of Vladivostok, Viktor Cherepkov, resulted in the latter's resignation in November (although he remained in office for a further 13 months). Throughout that year, the Governor's uncompromising demands for subsidies and his outspoken attacks over border issues against the Chinese Government had further alienated him from the federal Government. On 9 July 1998 an agreement 'on measures to improve finances' was signed, which rescheduled the repayment of wages and federal debts. However, a state of emergency was declared in December following heating shortages in Vladivostok. Controversy over the mayoral election in Vladivostok continued, with the poll of September 1998 being deemed invalid and a new contest scheduled for 17 January 1999. Meanwhile, Cherepkov was ousted from office (although he resisted this move) and declared that he would stand for re-election. However, legal moves further delayed a mayoral contest until after a city duma had introduced a local charter—Vladivostok remained the only city in Russia not to have such a charter or a legislative assembly. On 17 January a duma was duly elected, although the provincial authorities challenged the results, which were overwhelmingly in favour of Cherepkov and his supporters, leading to further elections on 18 June. Vladivostok residents remained unrepresented on the City Administration throughout 1998 and 1999, because of persistently low participation rates at elections; by June 1999 18 rounds of elections had been cancelled or, when held, had failed to establish the necessary quorum. However, the June election succeeded in electing a new Mayor, Yurii Kopylov, who had previously been a supporter and deputy of his rival, Cherepkov, but who, by the time of the election, had switched sides to support Nazdratenko. An ongoing energy crisis in the region, owing to non-payment of bills, finally forced the resignation of Nazdratenko (officially on health grounds), in February 2001, following reports that President Vladimir Putin had accused the Governor of incompetence. In gubernatorial elections held in May–June, Sergei Darkin, a local businessman, was elected Governor in the second round of voting, with some 40% of the votes cast, defeating Gennadii Apanasenko, the deputy presidential representative to the region, who secured 24% of the votes; the rate of voter participation was just 36%. Cherepkov, who had taken second place in the first round of voting, behind Darkin, was barred from standing as a candidate in the second round of the elections by the regional court, which cited irregularities in his campaign. Following his exclusion from the electoral process, Cherepkov encouraged his supporters to vote against all candidates, and 34% of voters did so. Regional legislative elections, held in December, were declared invalid, owing to an insufficient rate of voter participation; residents in Vladivostok, Nakhodka and Ussuriisk failed to elect a single candidate.

Economy

Maritime Krai's gross regional product totalled 30,545,500m. old roubles in 1997, equivalent to 13,720,900 old roubles per head. Its major industrial centres are at Vladivostok, the terminus of the Trans-Siberian Railway, Ussuriisk, Nakhodka, Dalnegorsk, Lesozavodsk, Dalnorechensk and Partizansk. The Krai's most important ports are at Vladivostok, Nakhodka and Vostochnyi (formerly Vrangel). Vessels based in these ports comprise around four-fifths of maritime transport services in the Far East. Maritime Krai has rail links with Khabarovsk Krai and, hence, other regions, as well as international transport links with North Korea and the Republic of Korea (South Korea).

Its agriculture, which employed just 5.5% of the labour force in 1998, consists mainly of grain and soya production, animal husbandry, fur farming, bee-keeping and fishing. Total agricultural output in 1998 amounted to a value of 2,438m. roubles. Illicit agricultural activities were also thought to include the cultivation of marijuana, an illegal drug, particularly in the Khankai district. Serious pollution of the Krai's gulfs and bays (which some estimated to contain over 800,000 metric tons of metallic waste) was combated from September 1997 by a number of projects undertaken with financial assistance from the USA and Norway. The Krai contains some 1,200m. metric tons of coal reserves. The hydroelectric-energy potential of the region's rivers is estimated at 25,000m. kWh, while timber reserves are estimated at 1,500m.–1,800m. cu m. Its main industries are fuel and energy production, non-ferrous metallurgy, ore mining, the processing of fish and forestry products, mechanical engineering and ship repairs, metal working and chemicals. Total industrial production was worth 19,019m. roubles in 1998, when the sector employed 21.2% of the working population. Energy production in the Krai was hindered from the mid-1990s by political mismanagement. Dalenergo, its electricity-generation monopoly, was notorious as one of the worst-performing utilities in the country, unable to collect accounts, service debts or pay for fuel, which led to fuel shortages and frequent strikes by its workers. The territory is ideally placed, in terms of its proximity to the Pacific nations, for international trade, although the perception of widespread corruption restrained its development. A new railway crossing into China at Makhalino-Hunchun, which was expected to carry 3m. tons of cargo annually by 2002, opened in August 1998.

The economically active population in Maritime Krai was 922,600 in 1998, of whom 35,000 were unemployed. The average monthly wage at this time was 849.7 roubles. There was a budgetary deficit in 1998 of 41m. roubles. According to the European Bank for Reconstruction and Development, the Krai had huge investment potential: foreign investment in 1998 totalled US $46.1m. In August 1997 Hyundai (of South Korea), opened a $100m. hotel and business centre in Vladivostok. South Korea also planned to create an industrial park for high-technology industries over an 11-year period in the free economic zone of Nakhodka, although some analysts doubted the practicality of the project. At 1 January 1999 there were 10,100 small businesses registered in the territory.

Directory

Head of the Provincial Administration (Governor): SERGEI MIKHAILOVICH DARKIN; Primorskii krai, 690110 Vladivostok, ul. Svetlanskaya 22; tel. (4232) 22-38-00; fax (4232) 22-50-10; e-mail gubernator@primorsky.ru; internet www .primorsky.ru.

Chairman of the Provincial Duma: SERGEI VIKTOROVICH ZHEKOV; tel. (4232) 22-13-66; fax (4232) 22-52-77.

Head of the Provincial Representation in Moscow: MIKHAIL NIKOLAYEVICH MALGINOV; tel. (095) 254-81-27.

Head of the Vladivostok City Administration (Mayor): YURII MIKHAILOVICH KOPYLOV; Primorskii krai, Vladivostok, Okeanskii pr. 20; tel. (4232) 22-30-16; fax (4232) 22-68-40.

Stavropol Krai

Stavropol Krai is situated in the central Caucasus region and extends from the Caspian lowlands in the east to the foothills of the Greater Caucasus Mountains in the south-west. It is part of the North Caucasus Economic Area and the Southern Federal Okrug. Krasnodar Krai lies to the west, there is a short border with Rostov Oblast in the north-west of the Krai and it shares rather longer borders with Kalmykiya to the north-east and Dagestan to the east. Chechnya, North Osetiya (Ossetia)—Alaniya and Kabardino-Balkariya lie to the south. The autonomous republic of Karachayevo-Cherkessiya forms a south-western arm of the Krai, giving it an international border with Georgia further south still. The Krai's major rivers are the Kuban, the Kuma and the Yegorlyk. Much of its territory is steppe. Its total area, excluding that of Karachayevo-Cherkessiya, is 66,500 sq km (25,670 sq miles). It is divided into 26 administrative districts and 18 cities. The population of Stavropol Krai numbered 2,659,900 at 1 January 1999. The Krai's population density, therefore, was 40.0 per sq km. Its administrative centre is at Stavropol (known as Voroshilovsk 1935–43), which had an estimated population of 343,500. Other major cities are Nevinnomyssk (132,200), Pyatigorsk (128,600) and Kislovodsk (112,700).

History

Stavropol city was founded in 1777 as part of the consolidation of Russian rule in the Caucasus. The territory was created on 13 February 1924, although it was originally known as South-Eastern Oblast and, subsequently, the North Caucasus Krai. It was named Ordzhonikidze Krai in 1937–43, before adopting its current title.

On 27 March 1994 elections were held to a new representative body, the State Duma. In June 1995 the town of Budennovsk, situated about 150 km north of the Chechen border, was the scene of a massive hostage-taking operation by rebel Chechen forces; over 1,000 civilians were seized, but they were released after a few days. In the gubernatorial elections of November 1996 the Communist candidate, Aleksandr Chernogorov (a former State Duma deputy), defeated the government-backed incumbent, Petr Marchenko, winning 55% of the votes cast, compared with Marchenko's 40%. Marchenko was subsequently appointed the Permanent Representative of the federal President in many of the territories of the North Caucasus. In March 1998 Chernogorov came under attack by the Russian Prosecutor-General over the establishment of his own administration, which violated a number of local laws on the status of government and territorial government. This move also brought him into conflict with the provincial Duma, which wished to approve all the ministry heads, not just the premier. In late 1998, however, the courts supported the Governor. In September 1999 representatives of Cherkess and Abazin communities in the neighbouring Republic of Karachayevo-Cherkessiya campaigned for the restoration of the former Cherkess Autonomous Oblast within Stavropol Krai, following the defeat of the Cherkess candidate in a presidential election in the Republic. In August representatives of Chechnya and Stavropol Krai agreed to maintain order on their common border, following ongoing instances of theft and occupation of land by Chechen forces. In early October 2000 four people died, and more than 100 people were wounded, as a result of three simultaneous bomb explosions in Pyatigorsk and Nevinomyssk. There were a series of further attacks, including bombings and the hijacking of a bus, in the Krai during 2001, which official sources attributed to Chechen separatists, and in which more than 20 people died. In an attempt to calm the disorder in the region, Chernogorov demanded that the Krai to be granted special territorial status, and demanded the implementation of stricter immigration controls within the Krai, although these appeals were rejected by the State Duma. Chernogorov was re-elected for a further term as Governor in a second round of voting in December 2000. Elections to the State Duma took place in December 2001.

Economy

In 1997 Stavropol Krai's gross regional product was 25,6788,600m. old roubles, or 9,589,100 old roubles per head. Its main industrial centres are at Stavropol, Nevinnomyssk, Cherkessk (Kabardino-Cherkessiya), Georgiyevsk and Budennovsk. In September 1997 the federal Government announced that a new section of the petroleum pipeline from Baku, Azerbaijan, would cross Stavropol Krai, rather than run through Chechnya.

The Krai contains extremely fertile soil. Its agricultural production, which amounted to a value of 8,278m. roubles in 1998, consists mainly of grain, sunflower seeds, sugar beets and vegetables. Horticulture, viniculture and animal husbandry are also important. The sector employed 20.7% of the working population in 1998. The Krai's main industries are food processing, light manufacturing, mechanical engineering, chemicals and the production of natural gas, petroleum, non-ferrous metal ores and coal. Around 17.0% of the labour force worked in industry in 1998; total industrial output for that year was worth 11,633m. roubles.

The economically active population in Stavropol Krai in 1998 was 987,000, of whom 14,700 were registered unemployed, almost one-half of the 1996 figure. The average wage at that time was 632.3 roubles per month and there was a budgetary surplus of 147m. roubles. Foreign investment in the territory in 1998 amounted to US $67.3m. At 1 January 1999 there were 15,200 small businesses in operation.

Directory

Head of the Provincial Administration (Governor): ALEKSANDR LEONIDOVICH CHERNOGOROV; Stavropolskii krai, 355025 Stavropol, pl. Lenina 1; tel. (8652) 35-22-52; fax (8652) 35-06-60; e-mail stavadm@stavropol.net.

Chairman of the State Duma: ALEKSANDR AKIMOVICH SHIYANOV; tel. (8652) 34-82-55.

Krai Representation in Moscow: tel. (095) 203-55-36.

Head of Stavropol City Administration (Mayor): MIKHAIL VLADIMIROVICH KUZMIN; Stavropolskii krai, 355000 Stavropol, pr. Karla Marksa 95; tel. (8652) 26-03-10; fax (8652) 26-28-23; e-mail goradm@smtn.stavropol.ru; internet www.stavropol.net/stavropol.

OBLASTS (REGIONS)

Amur Oblast

Amur Oblast is situated in the south-east of the Russian Federation, to the west of Khabarovsk Krai. It forms part of the Far Eastern Economic Area and the Far Eastern Federal Okrug. The Jewish Autonomous Oblast lies to the south-east, Chita Oblast to the west and the Republic of Sakha (Yakutiya) to the north. Southwards it has an international border with the People's Republic of China. The Oblast's main river is the Amur, which is 2,900 km (1,800 miles) long. A large reservoir, the Zeya, is situated in the north of the region. A little under three-quarters of the Oblast's territory is forested. Its total area occupies 363,700 sq km (140,430 sq miles) and measures 750 km south to north and 1,150 km south-east to north-west. It is divided into 20 administrative districts and nine cities. The territory's inhabitants numbered some 1,007,700 at 1 January 1999 and the population density was, therefore, 2.8 per sq km. Most people (65.2%) lived in urban areas. Amur Oblast's administrative centre is at Blagoveshchensk, near the Chinese border, and it had an estimated population of 219,600 in 1999. Other major cities in the region are Belogorsk (74,500) and Svobodnyi (71,800).

History

The Amur region was first discovered by European Russians in 1639 and came under Russian control in the late 1850s. Part of the pro-Bolshevik Far Eastern Republic (based in Chita) until its reintegration into Russia in 1922, Amur Oblast was formed on 20 October 1932.

In the first year of post-Soviet Russian independence there was a struggle for power in the territory, which the federal President, Boris Yeltsin, decided should be resolved by a gubernatorial election in December 1992. However, his appointed head of the administration was defeated, leaving both executive and legislature in the region opposed to him. On 21 July 1993 Amur Oblast declared itself a republic, a move that was condemned by the federal authorities. During the constitutional crisis of September–October, President Yeltsin was denounced by all the regional authorities. The Governor was, therefore, later dismissed and the Regional Soviet dissolved. Contention between executive and legislative organs resumed following the election of a new Regional Assembly in 1994. In January 1996 the Regional Administration brought action against the Regional Assembly for adopting a Charter, a republican constitution, some of the clauses of which ran counter to federal laws and presidential decrees. In the same month, in accordance with the Charter, the Assembly changed its name to the Soviet of People's Deputies. In elections to the Soviet of People's Deputies, held in March, Communist Party candidates won between 35% and 40% of the votes cast. In response to these developments President Yeltsin again dismissed the Governor in June, and appointed Yurii Lyashko, formerly the chief executive of Blagoveshchensk city, in his place. A further gubernatorial election was held on 22 September. It was won by the Communist-backed candidate, Anatolii Belonogov, by a narrow margin, but the results were subsequently annulled because of alleged irregularities. Belonogov, hitherto speaker of the regional legislature and a Communist, succeeded in gaining a clear majority in the repeat election held in March 1997. In gubernatorial elections, held in two rounds in March–April 2001, Belonogov was defeated by Leonid Korotkov, hitherto a deputy in the State Duma, and a member of the Communist Party until 1999.

Economy

Amur Oblast's gross regional product was 15,664,700m. old roubles in 1997, equivalent to 15,248,400 old roubles per head. Its main industrial centres are at Blagoveshchensk, Belogorsk, Raichikhinsk, Zeya, Shimanovsk, Svobodnyi and Tynda. In 1998 there were 6,807 km of paved roads in the Oblast. Construction of a major highway, running from Chita to Khabarovsk, was under way on its territory. There were 2,982 km of railway track, including sections of two major railways, the Trans-Siberian and the Far Eastern (Baikal–Amur). There are five river-ports, at Blagoveshchensk, Svobodnensk, Poyarkovsk, Amursk (all of which transport cargo to and from the People's Republic of China) and Zeisk. There is an international airport at Blagoveshchensk which serves flights to Japan, the Democratic People's Republic of Korea (North Korea), the Republic of Korea (South Korea) and Turkey.

Agriculture in Amur Oblast, which employed 11.1% of its work-force in 1998, almost one-third less than in 1995, consists mainly of grain and vegetable production, animal husbandry and bee-keeping. The soil in the south of the region is particularly fertile—in 1998 Amur Oblast contained 57% of the arable land in the Russian Far East and produced 30% of its agricultural output. The value of output in this sector in 1998 was 3,196m. roubles. In 1998 timber reserves were estimated at 2,000m. cu m. The region is rich in mineral resources, but by the end of the 1990s it was estimated that only around 5% of these resources were exploited. None the less, the mining sector produced around 15% of gross regional product in the late 1990s. In the late 1990s around 10–12 metric tons of gold were extracted annually, making the Oblast the third-largest producer of gold in Russia. Other raw-material deposits in the Oblast include bituminous coal, lignite (brown coal) and kaolin. There are also substantial reserves of iron, titanium, silver and gold ores. Coal-mining is also important, as are mechanical engineering, electricity generation, electro-technical industry and the processing of agricultural and forestry products. Some 16.0% of the Oblast's work-force were employed in industry in 1998, when total output in the sector amounted to a value of 5,231m. roubles. The region contains the Amur Shipbuilding Plant. In 1997 the plant was contracted to build a 111-sq-km steel platform for a foreign consortium, intended to exploit the petroleum and natural-gas fields of Sakhalin Oblast. It has also proposed building nuclear-powered submarines for export to the People's Republic of China, in addition to those it continues producing for Russia, and a barge to contain nuclear waste. There is a hydroelectric power plant at Zeya, with a reservoir of 2,400 sq km. Another power-station under construction at Bureya, the first part of which was expected to commence operations in 2003. The Oblast's main trading partners were the People's Republic of China, Japan and North Korea.

Amur's economically active population numbered 428,700 in 1998, of whom 14,100 (3.3%) were officially registered as unemployed, less than one-half of the 1995 figure. Those in employment earned, on average, 712 roubles per month. There was a budgetary surplus of 203m. roubles in 1998, when foreign investment totalled US $414,000. At 1 January 1999 there was a total of 3,800 small businesses, with a combined work-force of 44,200 employees, registered in Amur.

Directory

Head of the Regional Administration: LEONID KOROTKOV; Amurskaya obl., 675023 Blagoveshchensk, ul. Lenina 135; tel. (4162) 44-03-22; fax (4162) 44-62-01.

Chairman of the Soviet of People's Deputies (Regional Assembly): VIKTOR VASILIYEVICH MARTSENKO; tel. (4162) 42-46-75; fax (4162) 44-38-58.

Regional Representation in Moscow: tel. (095) 299-38-63.

Head of Blagoveshchensk City Administration (Mayor): ALEKSANDR MIKHAI-LOVICH KOLYADIN; Amurskaya obl., 675000 Blagoveshchensk, ul. Lenina 133; tel. (4162) 42-49-85.

Archangel Oblast

Archangel Oblast is situated in the north of the Eastern European Plain. It lies on the White, Barents and Kara Seas (parts of the Arctic Ocean) and includes the archipelago of Zemlya Frantsa-Iosifa and the Novaya Zemlya islands. The Oblast forms part of the Northern Economic Area and the North-Western Federal Okrug. In the north-east the Nenets Autonomous Okrug, a constituent part of the Oblast, runs eastwards along the coast to end in a short border with the Yamal-Nenets AOk (part of Tyumen Oblast). The Republic of Komi lies to the south of the Nenets AOk and to the east of Archangel proper. Kirov and, mainly, Vologda Oblasts form the southern border and the Republic of Kareliya lies to the west. The Oblast contains several large rivers (the Severnaya Dvina, the Onega, the Mezen, the Pinega, the Vaga and the Pechora) and some 2,500 lakes. Some two-fifths of its entire area is forested—much of the north-west of the territory is taiga (forested marshland). The Oblast, including the autonomous okrug, occupies an area of 587,400 sq km (226,800 sq miles) and is divided into 20 administrative districts and 14 cities. It spans three climatic zones—arctic, sub-arctic and continental. The total population at 1 January 1999 was an estimated 1,478,000 and its population density, therefore, stood at 2.5 per sq km. Its administrative centre is at Archangel (Arkhangelsk), which had an estimated population of 367,200 at that time. Other major cities are Severodvinsk (237,000) and Kotlas (66,500).

History

The city of Archangel was founded in the 16th century, to further Muscovite trade. It was the first Russian seaport and the country's main one until the building of St Petersburg in 1703. The port played a major role in the attack by the Entente fleet (British and French navies) against the Red Army in 1918. It was an important route for supplies from the Allied Powers during the Second World War. Archangel Oblast was founded on 23 September 1937.

On 13 October 1993 the Archangel Regional Soviet transferred its responsibilities to the Regional Administration. Communist candidates initially formed the largest single group elected to the legislative chamber of the Regional Deputies' Assembly, which consisted of 39 members. However, supporters of the federal Government and the liberal reformists also enjoyed respectable levels of support in the cities. In March 1996 the unpopular head of the regional administration, Pavel Pozdeyev, a federal appointee nominated only one month previously, was forced to leave his position. His predecessor, Pavel Balakshin, who was being investigated on charges of misuse of federal funds, initially refused to step down from the Federation Council, as his demotion required, and was subsequently elected as Mayor of Archangel City; he was replaced by Oleg Nilov following an election held in December 2000. Anatolii Yefremov's position as Governor was confirmed by his popular election to the post in December 1997. He was re-elected to serve a further term of office in December 2000.

Economy

Including the Nenets district, Archangel Oblast's gross regional product totalled 19,245,200m. old roubles in 1997, equivalent to 12,831,800 old roubles per head. The Oblast's main industrial centres are at Archangel, Kotlas, Severodvinsk and Novodvinsk. Its main ports are Archangel, Onega, Mezen and Naryan Mar (sea- and river-ports).

The Oblast's agriculture, which employed just 5.6% of the labour force in 1998, consists mainly of grain and vegetable production, animal husbandry (livestock and reindeer) and hunting. Agricultural output in the Oblast, still including the autonomous okrug, amounted to a value of 2,449m. roubles in 1998. Its industry, which employed 27.4% of the working population in 1998, is based on the extraction of minerals (the Oblast's reserve of bauxite is the third-largest in the world), petroleum and natural gas, processing of agricultural and forestry products and mechanical engineering. Industrial output across the entire Oblast was worth 13,263m. roubles in 1998. In July it was announced that the federal finance ministry was to allocate credit worth US $30m. for development of a diamond field in the Oblast, one of Russia's largest, run by Severoalmaz as part of a multinational consortium. However, repeated licensing problems delayed progress.

In 1998 the Oblast's economically active population amounted to 567,100, with an unemployment rate of some 8.1% (45,800). The average monthly wage in 1998 was 710.6 roubles. There was a budgetary deficit in the Oblast in that year, amounting to 105m. roubles. At the end of 1998 Archangel was cited as the sixth-worst region in the Federation for wage-payment arrears (on average, almost six months behind). Total foreign investment in the Oblast in 1998 was US $22.78m., a 10fold increase compared with 1995. At 1 January 1999 there were 4,100 small businesses registered on its territory.

Directory

Head of the Regional Administration (Governor): ANATOLII ANTONOVICH YEFREMOV; Arkhangelskaya obl., 163004 Arkhangelsk, pr. Troitskii 49; tel. (8182) 65-30-41; fax (8182) 64-65-11; internet www.dvinaland.ru.

Chairman of the Regional Deputies' Assembly: (vacant); tel. (8182) 3-66-81; fax (8182) 3-73-03.

Principal Representative in Moscow: BORIS ALEKSANDROVICH GAGARIN; 103006 Moscow, ul. Malaya Dmitrovka 3/10; tel. (095) 209-45-94.

Head of Archangel City Administration: OLEG NILOV; Arkhangelskaya obl., 163061 Arkhangelsk, pl. Lenina 5; tel. (8182) 65-64-84; fax (8182) 65-20-71; e-mail webmaster@arhcity.ru; internet www.arhcity.ru.

Astrakhan Oblast

Astrakhan Oblast is situated in the Caspian lowlands and forms part of the Volga Economic Area and the Southern Federal Okrug. Lying between the Russian federal subject of Kalmykiya to the south and the former Soviet state of Kazakhstan to the east, Astrakhan is a long, relatively thin territory, which flanks the River Volga as it flows out of Volgograd Oblast in the north-west towards the Caspian Sea to the south-east via a large delta at Astrakhan. The delta is one of the largest in the world and occupies more than 24,000 sq km (9,260 sq miles) of the Caspian lowlands. It gives the Oblast some 200 km (over 120 miles) of coastline. It has one lake, the Baskunchak, measuring 115 sq km. Astrakhan occupies some 44,100 sq km (17,000 sq miles) and is divided into 11 administrative districts and six cities. At 1 January 1999 its total population was an estimated 1,019,500 and its population density, therefore, was 23.1 per sq km. The Oblast's administrative centre is at Astrakhan (formerly Khadzhi-Tarkhan), which had an estimated population of 483,700 at this time. The city lies at 22 m (72 feet) below sea level and is protected from the waters of the Volga delta by 75 km of dykes. Other major cities are Akhtubinsk (49,000) and Znamensk (36,100).

History

The Khanate of Astrakhan, which was formed in 1446 following the dissolution of the Golden Horde, was conquered by the Russians in 1556. The region subsequently became an important centre for trading in timber, grain, fish and petroleum. It was occupied by Bolshevik forces in 1917. Astrakhan Oblast was founded on 27 December 1943.

There was considerable hardship in the region with the dissolution of the USSR and the economic reforms of the early 1990s. Dissatisfaction was indicated by the relatively high level of support for the nationalist Liberal Democrats in the 1995 early federal parliamentary elections, although the Communists remained the leading party. The Governor, Anatolii Guzhvin, originally a federal appointment, retained his post in local elections in 1997, and was re-elected for a further term of office in December 2000, receiving 81% of the votes cast. In November 2001 an influx of Tajik refugees into the Oblast was reported, despite the temporary suspension of the railway link to the Tajik capital, Dushanbe, which prompted Guzhvin to request that the federal Government take measures to regulate illegal immigration.

Economy

Astrakhan Oblast's gross regional product was 11,223,100m. old roubles in 1997, equivalent to 10,900,400 old roubles per head. The Oblast's main industrial centres are at Astrakhan and Akhtubinsk. The rise in the level of the Caspian Sea (by some 2.6 m between the late 1970s and the late 1990s) and the resulting erosion of the Volga delta caused serious environmental problems in the region. These were exacerbated by the pollution of the water by petroleum products, copper, nitrates and other substances, which frequently contributed to the death of a significant proportion of fish reserves.

The Oblast remains a major producer of vegetables and cucurbits (gourds and melons). Grain production and animal husbandry are also important. Total agricultural production in 1998 amounted to a value of 1,300m. roubles. The sector employed 13.2% of the working population in that year. The Oblast is rich in natural resources, including gas and gas condensate, sulphur, petroleum and salt. Its main industries are light manufacturing, food processing, mechanical engineering, metal working, wood-working, pulp and paper manufacturing, chemicals and the production of petroleum and natural gas. It was hoped that this last activity would improve the economic fortunes of the region by the end of the 1990s, as the exploitation of Caspian hydrocarbons reserves increased. Industrial output in 1998 was worth 5,420m. roubles, and the sector employed 17.9% of the Oblast's labour force. Regional trade was also important to the economy of Astrakhan. The Lakor freight company established important shipping links with Iran, handling around 940,000 metric tons of cargo in 1996, and in early 2000 announced plans to develop a trade route with India. In September 1997 the company, with an Iranian group, Khazar Shipping, registered the Astrakhan–Nowshahr joint shipping line. Astrakhan's exports to Iran mainly comprised paper, metals, timber, mechanical equipment, fertilizers and chemical products.

Astrakhan Oblast's economically active population numbered 398,400 in 1998, of whom 18,900 were registered unemployed. The average monthly wage at that time was 636.3 roubles and there was a budgetary surplus of 118m. roubles. Foreign investment in the territory amounted to US $7.58m. At 1 January 1999 there were 3,600 small businesses in operation.

Directory

Head of the Regional Administration (Governor): ANATOLII PETROVICH GUZHVIN; Astrakhanskaya obl., 414008 Astrakhan, ul. Sovetskaya 15; tel. (8512)

22-85-19; fax (8512) 22-95-14; e-mail ves@astrakhan.ru; internet www.adm
.astranet.ru.

Chairman of the Representative Assembly: PAVEL PETROVICH ANISIMOV;
Astrakhanskaya obl., 414000 Astrakhan, ul. Volodarskogo 15; tel. (8512) 22-96-
44; fax (8512) 22-22-48; e-mail ootsops@astranet.ru.

Head of Astrakhan City Administration (Mayor): IGOR ALEKSANDROVICH
BEZRUKAVNIKOV; Astrakhanskaya obl., 414000 Astrakhan, ul. Chernyshevskogo
6; tel. (8512) 22-55-88; fax (8512) 24-71-76; e-mail munic@astranet.ru; internet
astrakhan.astranet.ru/munic.htm.

Belgorod Oblast

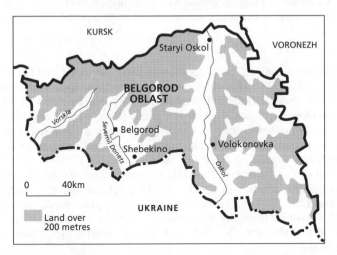

Belgorod Oblast is situated in the south-west of the Central Russian Highlands. It forms part of the Central Chernozem Economic Area and the Central Federal Okrug. The Oblast lies on the international border with Ukraine, with Kursk to the north and Voronezh to the east. Its main rivers are the Severnii Donets, the Vorskla and the Oskol. The territory occupies 27,100 sq km (10,460 sq miles) and measures around 260 km (160 miles) from west to east. It is divided into 21 administrative districts and nine cities. It had an estimated population of 1,489,500 at 1 January 1999, of whom some 65.7% inhabited urban areas, and a population density of 55.0 per sq km. According to the 1989 census, 92.9% of the Oblast's inhabitants were ethnic Russians. The Oblast's administrative centre is at Belgorod, which had an estimated 336,900 inhabitants in 1999. Other major cities include Staryi Oskol (211,200) and Gubkin (85,300).

History

Belgorod was established as a bishopric during the early days of Orthodox Christianity. The region was part of Lithuania until 1503, when it was annexed by the Muscovite state. The new city of Belgorod was founded in 1593. Belgorod Oblast was formally established on 6 January 1954. Briefly a 'White' stronghold in the civil wars following the 1917 Russian Revolution, in the 1990s the region remained a resolutely conservative part of the 'red belt' of loyal Communist support.

Following the 1993 confrontation of the federal presidency and parliament, Boris Yeltsin dismissed the region's governor and arranged for elections to a new Regional Duma in 1994. The Communists enjoyed a majority in this body too, and there was constant conflict with the administration, the head of which, however, also enjoyed popular support. For this reason, the Oblast was one of only 12 areas in the Federation to be permitted gubernatorial elections in December 1995. The incumbent, Yevgenii Savchenko, a supporter of the federal Government, was duly elected, despite the continued strength of the Communists. Savchenko was re-elected in May 1999, with the leader of the Liberal Democrat Party of Russia,

Vladimir Zhirinovskii, coming third in the poll, as part of his unsuccessful campaign to become a regional governor. In the elections to the Regional Duma of October 1997, the Communist Party increased its representation fivefold (securing 13 seats of the 35 in the Duma), becoming the only party to be represented in the parliament at that time.

Economy

In 1997 Belgorod Oblast's gross regional product amounted to 18,154,300m. old roubles, or 12,254,000 old roubles per head. The main industrial centres in the territory are situated at Belgorod, Shebekino, Alekseyevka and Valuiki.

Belgorod Oblast's principal crops are grain, sugar beets, sunflower seeds and essential-oil plants. Horticulture and animal husbandry are also important. In 1998 18.0% of the region's working population were engaged in the agricultural sector, which generated a total of 4,776m. roubles. There are substantial reserves of bauxite, iron ore and apatites. The Oblast's main industries are ore mining (iron ores), mechanical engineering, metal working, chemicals, the manufacture of building materials and food processing. There were plans to develop the mining and metal industries in the region between 1996 and 2000. Industry employed 22.4% of the work-force in 1998, and total industrial production was worth 17,943m. roubles.

The economically active population in Belgorod Oblast numbered 607,300 in that year, of whom 11,000 (1.8%) were registered unemployed. The average monthly salary was 718.7 roubles and there was a budgetary deficit of 149m. Foreign investment in the Oblast in 1998 totalled US $156.1m. In 1999 there were 6,800 small businesses, which employed 48,100 people.

Directory

Head of the Regional Administration (Governor): YEVGENII STEPANOVICH SAVCHENKO; Belgorodskaya obl., 308005 Belgorod, pl. Revolyutsii 4; tel. (0722) 22-42-47; fax (0722) 22-33-43; e-mail moscow@bel.ru; internet www.savchenko.ru.

Chairman of the Regional Duma: ANATOLII YAKOVLYEVICH ZELIKOV; tel. (0722) 22-42-60; fax (0722) 22-54-68.

Head of Belgorod City Administration: GEORGII GEORGIYEVICH GOLIKOV; Belgorodskaya obl., 308800 Belgorod, ul. Lenina 38; tel. (0722) 27-72-06.

Bryansk Oblast

Bryansk Oblast is situated in the central part of the Central Russian Highlands and is in the Central Economic Area and the Central Federal Okrug. It has international borders to its west (Belarus) and south (Ukraine), with Kursk and Orel Oblasts to the east, Kaluga to the north-east and Smolensk to the north-west. Bryansk's main river is the Desna, a tributary of the Dnepr (Dnieper), and just under one-third of its area is forested. The Oblast occupies 34,900 sq km (13,480 sq miles) of territory and measures 245 km (152 miles) from south to north and 270 km from west to east. It is divided into 27 administrative districts and 16 cities. At 1 January 1999 the region's estimated population was 1,451,000 (of whom some 68.7% inhabited urban areas) and the population density was, therefore, 41.6 per sq km. Bryansk, with an estimated population of 457,000 at 1 January 1999, is the Oblast's administrative centre. Other major cities are Klintsy (68,500) and Novozybkov (43,500).

History

The ancient Russian city of Bryansk was part of the independent principality of Novgorod-Serversk until 1356. It was an early Orthodox Christian bishopric. The Muscovite state acquired the city from Lithuania in the 16th century. After the German invasion during the Second World War had been repelled, Bryansk Oblast was founded on 5 July 1944.

In the 1990s the region was considered part of the Communist-dominated 'red belt'. Bryansk was one of the eight federal territories permitted gubernatorial elections in December 1992. The incumbent, a supporter of the federal President, Boris Yeltsin, was defeated by the Communist-backed candidate, Yurii Lodkin. During the constitutional crisis of 1993 the regional authorities were, thus, united in condemning President Yeltsin's Decree 1,400, which dissolved the all-Russian parliament. Lodkin was then dismissed and the Soviet disbanded, being replaced by a Regional Duma. The Communists secured about 35% of the votes cast in the region for the Federation Assembly in December 1995, with their preferred candidate, Gennadii Zyuganov, receiving almost one-half of the votes cast. After a series of scandals involving successive, short-lived (and non-Communist) governors, Lodkin returned to the post of governor, being elected to this position in December 1996. Relations with the federal centre improved after the signature of a power-sharing agreement in July 1997, although the Communists dominated the local elections held the previous month and maintained their influence in the federal presidential election of March 2000. Lodkin was re-elected as Governor in December 2000, although he gained only 29% of the votes cast.

Economy

Bryansk Oblast is one of the Russian Federation's major industrial regions. The territory's gross regional product was 12,336,600m. old roubles in 1997, equivalent to 8,395,100 old roubles per head. Its main industrial centres are at Bryansk and Klintsy. There are 1,037 km (644 miles) of railway track on its territory, and 5,939 km (3,690 miles) of paved roads.

The Oblast's agriculture, which employed 12.8% of its work-force in 1998, consists mainly of grain and vegetable production and animal husbandry. Around one-half of its area is used for agricultural purposes. Total production in the sector in 1998 was worth 4,533m. roubles. The Oblast's main industries are mechanical engineering, metal working, the manufacture of building materials, light manufacturing, food processing and timber working. Industry employed 22.3% of the work-force in 1998 and generated 5,896m. roubles.

At 1 January 1998 a total of 29,700, or 5.5% of the Oblast's work-force, were registered unemployed. In 1998 the average monthly wage was 554.1 roubles. There was a regional government budgetary surplus of 40m. roubles. In the late 1990s the economy of the Oblast was suffering severe difficulties, with a crisis in wage arrears and relatively little foreign investment (which in 1998 amounted to only US $596,000). International trade in 1998 was also relatively low, consisting of $64.4m. of exports and $141.5m. of imports. At 1 January 1999 there were 3,700 small businesses operating in the territory.

Directory

Head of the Regional Administration (Governor): YURII YEVGENIYEVICH LODKIN; Bryanskaya obl., 241002 Bryansk, pr. Lenina 33; tel. (095) 592-52-46; internet www.admin.debryansk.ru

Chairman of the Regional Duma: STEPAN NIKOLAYEVICH PONASOV; tel. (0832) 43-31-95.

Regional Representation in Moscow: tel. (095) 203-50-52.

Head of Bryansk City Administration: IVAN NIKOLAYEVICH TARUSOV; Bryanskaya obl., 241002 Bryansk, pr. Lenina 35; tel. (0832) 74-30-13; fax (0832) 74-47-30.

Chelyabinsk Oblast

Chelyabinsk Oblast is situated in the Southern Urals, in the Transural (Asian Russia). It forms part of the Urals Economic Area and the Urals Federal Okrug. Orenburg Oblast lies to the south, the Republic of Bashkortostan to the west, Sverdlovsk Oblast to the north and Kurgan Oblast to the east. There is an international border with Kazakhstan in the south-east. Much of the region lies on the eastern slopes of the southern Ural Mountains. The major rivers in the Oblast are the Ural and the Miass. It has over 1,000 lakes, the largest of which are the Uvildy and the Turgoyak. The Oblast covers an area of 87,900 sq km (34,940 sq miles) and is divided into 24 administrative districts and 30 cities. With an estimated population of 3,678,200 at 1 January 1999 (of whom 81.3% inhabited urban areas), the population density in the region was 41.8 per sq km. The Oblast's administrative centre is at Chelyabinsk, which had an estimated population of 1,085,800 at that time. Other major cities are Magnitogorsk (427,000), Zlatoust (198,700), Miass (166,200), Ozersk (88,900) and Troitsk (85,000).

History

Chelyabinsk city was established as a Russian frontier post in 1736, but was deep within Russian territory by the 19th century. The Oblast was created on 17 January 1934. The region was heavily industrialized during the Soviet period and was dominated by Communist cadres well into the 1990s. In December 1992, at elections for the head of the regional administration, the incumbent Governor, a supporter of Boris Yeltsin, the Russian President, was defeated. President Yeltsin re-established his authority in late 1993 and required the election of a Duma during

147

1994. Both in this body, and in the local results of the general election of 1995, pro-Yeltsin and reformist forces also gained significant levels of support. In the gubernatorial election of late 1996, however, Petr Sumin was returned to power. Sumin, a Communist, had been removed as head of the regional administration following the attempted Soviet coup of 1991. Sumin's pro-Communist movement 'For the Revival of the Urals' also won an absolute majority of seats in the legislature in the local elections held in December 1997. The administration was unable to prevent an accumulation in wage arrears, and there were strikes by coal-miners in mid-1998. Sumin was re-elected as Governor in December 2000.

Economy

Chelyabinsk Oblast became one of the most industrialized territories of the Russian Federation, following the reconstruction of plants moved there from further west during the Second World War. In 1998 31.2% of its economically active population worked in industry. The Oblast is, consequently, one of the most polluted in the Federation; in particular, high rates of disease and environmental despoliation resulted from the Kyshtym nuclear accident of 1957, in the north of the territory, when up to three times the levels of radiation emitted at the Chornobyl (Chernobyl) disaster in Ukraine in 1986 were released into the surrounding area. Approximately 180 sq km of agricultural land remained out of use because of radioactivity, while water supplies in many parts of the region were also unsafe. In 1997 the gross regional product of the Oblast amounted to 51,467,100m. old roubles, equivalent to 13,987,100 old roubles per head. The region's major industrial centres are at Chelyabinsk, Magnitogorsk, Miass, Zlatoust, Kopeisk, Korkino and Troitsk. Although output declined by one-half between 1989 and 1997, Magnitogorsk remains well-known as the city that produced the steel for over one-half of the tanks used by Soviet troops in the Second World War, and as the largest iron and steel production complex in the world. The Oblast is a major junction of the Trans-Siberian Railway. There are 1,793 km of railway track in the Oblast and 8,108 km of paved roads.

The Oblast's agriculture, which employed 7.9% of the working population in 1995, consists mainly of animal husbandry, horticulture and the production of grain and vegetables. Total agricultural output in 1998 was worth 5,790m. roubles. Its main industries are ferrous and non-ferrous metallurgy, ore mining, mechanical engineering, metal working, fuel and energy production and the manufacture of building materials. In the north-west, the closed city of Ozersk (formerly Chelya-binsk-40) is one of the Federation's major plutonium-processing and -storage sites, while in the west are centres for weapons manufacturing and space technology. The conversion of former military plants to civilian use in the 1990s meant that the former tank factory at Magnitogorsk began to produce tractors, and the Mayak nuclear armament plant (the location of the 1957 disaster) sought to become a recycling plant for foreign nuclear waste. In 1998 the industrial sector generated 50,956m. roubles.

The economically active population numbered 1,513,900 in 1998; some 33,300 of these were registered unemployed. Those in employment earned an average wage of 727.5 roubles per month. The 1998 budget showed a deficit of 171m. roubles. In order to create favourable conditions for economic growth in the region, the administration created two funds: one for the support of strategic sectors of the economy; the other concerned with development. Attempts to attract foreign investment in the Oblast in the mid-1990s were largely successful: foreign capital amounted to US $59.12m. in 1998. The Oblast contained the highest number of joint enterprises in the Urals Economic Area. At 1 January 1999 there were 17,700 small businesses registered on its territory.

Directory

Governor: PETR IVANOVICH SUMIN; Chelyabinskaya obl., 454089 Chelyabinsk, ul. Tsvillinga 28; tel. (3512) 33-92-41; fax (3512) 33-12-83; internet www .gubern.chel.su.

Chairman of the Regional Duma: VIKTOR FEDROVICH DAVIDOV.

Head of the Regional Representation in Moscow: OLEG NIKOLAYEVICH ANDREYEV; tel. (095) 977-08-35.

Head of Chelyabinsk City Administration (Mayor): VYACHESLAV MIKHAILOVICH TARASOV; Chelyabinskaya obl., 454113 Chelyabinsk, pl. Revolyutsii 2; tel. (3512) 33-38-05; fax (3512) 33-38-55; internet www.chelyabinsk.ru/adm.

Chita Oblast

Chita Oblast is situated in Transbaikal. It forms part of the Eastern Siberian Economic Area and the Siberian Federal Okrug. The Transbaikal region of Buryatiya lies to the west, Irkutsk Oblast in the north, Sakha and Amur to the east. To the south Chita has international borders with the People's Republic of China and Mongolia. The Aga-Buryat Autonomous Okrug lies within the Oblast, in the south. The western part of the region is situated in the Yablonovii Khrebet mountain range. Chita Oblast's major rivers are those in the Selenga, the Lena and the Amur basins. More than one-half of the Oblast's territory is forested. Excluding the Autonomous Okrug, the Oblast covers an area of 412,500 sq km (159,300 sq miles) and is divided into 28 districts and 10 cities. The population of the Oblast was estimated at 1,265,900 at 1 January 1999 and its population density was 2.9 per sq km (less than one-third of the national average). In the same year, some 62.7% of the region's inhabitants lived in urban areas. The Oblast's administrative centre is at Chita, which had an estimated population of 311,100 at that time. The region's other cities include Krasnokamensk (56,200) and Balei (renowned as the birthplace of Temujin—Chinghiz or Genghis Khan).

History

The city of Chita was established by the Cossacks in 1653, at the confluence of the Chita and Ingoda rivers. It was named Ingodinskoye Zirnove for a time. Chita was pronounced the capital of the independent, pro-Bolshevik Far Eastern Republic upon its establishment in April 1920. It united the regions of Irkutsk, Transbaikal, Amur and the Pacific coast (Maritime Krai, Khabarovsk Krai, Magadan and Kamchatka), but merged with Soviet Russia in November 1922. Chita Oblast was founded on 26 September 1937.

A new Regional Duma was elected in 1994. The Communists and the nationalist Liberal Democrats were the most popular parties in the mid- and late 1990s. In a gubernational election held on 29 October 2000 the incumbent Governor, Ravil Geniatulin, was re-elected with 57.4% of the votes cast.

Economy

Chita Oblast's gross regional product amounted to 12,737,800m. old roubles in 1997, equivalent to 9,938,200 old roubles per head. The region's main industrial centres are at Chita, Nerchinsk, Darasun, Olovyannaya and Tarbagatai. There are some 2,399 km (1,490 miles) of railway track in the territory, including sections of the Trans-Siberian and the Far Eastern (Baikal–Amur) Railways. There are also 9,626 km of paved roads, and 1,000 km of navigable waterways. The Chita–Khabarovsk highway (which would form part of a direct route between Moscow and Vladivostok) was under construction in the late 1990s.

Chita Oblast's agriculture, which employed some 12.6% of its working population in 1998, consists mainly of animal husbandry (livestock- and reindeer-breeding) and fur-animal hunting. In 1998 total agricultural output amounted to a value of 2,573m. roubles. The region's major industries are ferrous metallurgy, mechanical engineering, fuel extraction (including uranium), processing of forestry and agricultural products and ore mining. Industry employed some 15.8% of the work-force in 1998; total industrial production in that year was worth 4,494m. roubles. Coal mining in the Oblast was centred around the Vostochnaya mine; gold and tin mining were based at Sherlovaya Govra; and lead- and zinc-ore mines are situated at Hapcheranga, 200 km south-east of Yakutsk. In 1992 it was revealed that thorium and uranium had been mined until the mid-1970s at locations just outside Balei. The resulting high levels of radiation had serious consequences among the town's population, with abnormally high incidences of miscarriages and congenital defects in children. The regional Government lacked sufficient funds to relocate Balei's inhabitants and reduce radiation in the area. In 1997, however, the Australian mining company, Armada Gold, announced that it planned to seal the abandoned mines and exploit the nearby gold deposits. In 1998 the Oblast's exports, largely comprising timber, metals and radioactive chemicals, amounted to US $95.5m. The People's Republic of China was the Oblast's largest trading partner. A 'Chinese market' in Chita city reflects the importance of China as a source of imports.

The territory had an economically active population in 1998 of 427,900. Some 20,400 were registered unemployed at that time; the average monthly wage was 512.8 roubles (although, in the first quarter of 1997, it was reported that some 74% of the Oblast's economically active population earned less than the subsistence level, compared to 21% in Russia as a whole). In 1998 the budget showed a surplus of 87m. roubles. Foreign investment in the Oblast for much of the 1990s remained small, but increased over 40fold in 1998 compared with the previous year, to total $12.53m. At 1 January 1999 a total of 4,000 small businesses were in operation in Chita.

Directory

Head of the Regional Administration (Governor): RAVIL FARITOVICH GENIA-LUTIN; Chitinskaya obl., 672021 Chita, ul. Chaikovskogo 8; tel. (3022) 23-34-93; fax (3022) 23-02-22; internet www.adm.chita.ru.

Chairman of the Regional Duma: VITALII YEVGENIYEVICH VISHNYAKOV; tel. (3022) 26-58-59.

Representation in Moscow: tel. (095) 203-53-12.

Head of Chita City Administration (Mayor): ALEKSANDR FEDOROVICH SEDIN; Chitinskaya obl., 672000 Chita, ul. Butina 39; tel. (3022) 23-21-01.

Irkutsk Oblast

Irkutsk Oblast is situated in eastern Siberia in the south-east of the Central Siberian Plateau. Irkutsk Oblast forms part of the Eastern Siberian Economic Area and the Siberian Federal Okrug. The Republic of Sakha (Yakutiya) lies to the north-east, Krasnoyarsk Krai (including the Evenk AOk) to the north-west and Tyva to the south-west. Most of the long south-eastern borders are with the Transbaikal territories of Buryatiya and, in the east, Chita. Irkutsk Oblast includes the Autonomous Okrug of the Ust-Orda Buryats. Lake Baikal is the deepest in the world, possessing over 80% of Russia's, and 20% of the world's, freshwater resources. The Oblast's main rivers are the Angara (the only river to drain Lake Baikal), the Nizhnyaya Tunguska, the Lena, the Vitim and the Kirenga. More than four-fifths of the region's territory is covered with forest (mainly coniferous). The total area of the Oblast, including that of the autonomous okrug, is 767,900 sq km (296,490 sq miles) and stretches 1,400 km (850 miles) from south to north and 1,200 km west to east. It is divided into 33 administrative districts and 22 cities. The Oblast's estimated population was 2,758,200 in January 1999. The overall population density in the region was 3.6 per sq km. Its administrative centre is at Irkutsk, which had an estimated population of 592,400 in 1999. Other major cities in the region include Angarsk (266,400), Bratsk (254,400) and Ust-Ilimsk (106,600).

History

The city of Irkutsk was founded as an ostrog (military transit camp) in 1661, at the confluence of the Irkut and Angara rivers, 66 km to the west of Baikal. Irkutsk became one of the largest economic centres of eastern Siberia. After the collapse of the Russian Empire, the region was part of the independent, pro-Bolshevik Far Eastern Republic (based in Chita), which was established in April 1920 and merged with Soviet Russia in November 1922. On 26 September 1937 an Irkutsk Oblast was formed.

In late 1993, following the federal presidency's forcible dissolution of parliament, the executive branch of government secured the dissolution of the Regional Soviet, and in 1994 a Legislative Assembly was elected in its place. As a 'donor region' to the Russian Federation, central–regional relationships in Irkutsk Oblast were frequently strained. In May 1996 the regional and federal authorities signed a power-sharing agreement. The following year the Governor, Yurii Nozhikov, implemented a tax strike against Moscow in an attempt to compel the federal Government to pay greater attention to the Oblast's needs. Following Nozhikov's resignation in April 1997, the government-supported candidate, Boris Govorin (who also received Nozhikov's endorsement), was elected Governor, receiving 50.3% of the votes cast, in an election result that was interpreted as an endorsement of both the federal Government's reform programmes and Nozhikov's continuing popularity. At the gubernatorial election held in August 2001 Govorin was re-elected for a further term of office; however, the relatively high proportion of votes awarded to the Communist candidate, Sergei Levchenko, who received 45.3% (compared with the 47.6% received by Govorin), appeared to reflect increasing dissatisfaction with the economic situation in the region.

Economy

Irkutsk Oblast is, however, one of the most economically developed regions in Russia, largely owing to its significant fuel, energy and water resources, minerals and timber. In 1997 its gross regional product totalled 56,083,100m. old roubles, or 20,173,800 old roubles per head. The region's main industrial centres are at Irkutsk, Bratsk, Ust-Ilimsk, Angarsk and Usoliye Sibirskoye. The Oblast, which is traversed by the Trans-Siberian and the Far Eastern (Baikal–Amur) Railways, contains 2,481 km of railway track. There are almost 12,000 km of roads in the region, which carry some 40m. metric tons of freight annually. It has two international airports, at Irkutsk and Bratsk, from which there are direct and connecting flights to Japan, the People's Republic of China, the Republic of Korea (South Korea), Mongolia and the USA. In the late 1990s approximately one-10th of the region's freight was transported by river—there are two major river-ports on the Lena river at Kirensk and Osetrovo (Ust-Kut). These are used to transport freight to the Republic of Sakha (Yakutiya) and the northern seaport of Tiksi.

The Oblast's agriculture, which employed just 7.2% of its work-force in 1995, consists mainly of grain production, animal husbandry (fur-animal- reindeer- and livestock-breeding), hunting and fishing. Total agricultural production in the territory generated 6,635m. roubles in 1998. The region contains the huge Kovyikinskoye oilfield, which was awaiting an international consortium with the resources to construct an export pipeline across the People's Republic of China. The Oblast's development as a centre for heavy industry originated in the city of Irkutsk's position as a major junction on the Trans-Siberian Railway. In the late 1990s more than 45% of its fixed assets were concentrated in its industrial sector and more than 20% of its working population were engaged in industrial production. Its main industries were mining (coal, iron ore, gold, muscovite or mica, gypsum, talc and salt), mechanical engineering, metal working, chemicals and petrochemicals, petroleum refining, non-ferrous metallurgy, fuel extraction, electricity generation, the manufacture of building materials and the processing of forestry products. The total value of manufactured goods in the Oblast in 1998 was 31,393m. roubles, of which processing by the fuel industry contributed 31%, electricity generation 20%, the non-ferrous metallurgy industry 25%, and the timber and timber-processing industries 17%.

The economically active population in Irkutsk Oblast totalled 1,099,900 in 1998. Some 34,200 (3.1%) in the entire territory were unemployed at this time. For those in employment, the average wage amounted to some 1,064.8 roubles per month. In 1998 there was a budgetary deficit of 314m. roubles. Foreign investment in the territory was worth some US $135.24m. The value of exports from the territory in 1998 amounted to some $2,147.1m. At 1 January 1999 there was a total of 12,000 small businesses in operation.

Directory

Governor: BORIS ALEKSANDROVICH GOVORIN; Irkutskaya obl., 664027 Irkutsk, ul. Lenina 1a; tel. (3952) 27-67-60; fax (3952) 24-33-40; internet www.admirk.ru.

Chairman of the Legislative Assembly: VIKTOR MITROFANOVICH BOROVSKII; tel. (3952) 24-17-60; fax (3952) 27-35-09; internet irk.gov.ru.

Head of the Regional Representation in Moscow: NIKOLAI VLADIMIROVICH YEROSHCHENKO; tel. (095) 915-70-58.

Head of Irkutsk City Administration (Mayor): VLADIMIR VIKTOROVICH YAKU-BOVSKII; tel. (3952) 27-56-90.

Ivanovo Oblast

Ivanovo Oblast is situated in the central part of the Eastern European Plain. It forms part of the Central Economic Area and the Central Federal Okrug. It is surrounded by the Oblasts of Kostroma (to the north), Nizhnii Novgorod (east), Vladimir (south) and Yaroslavl (north-west). Its main river is the Volga and one-half of its territory is forested. The Oblast covers a total area of 21,800 sq km (9,230 sq miles), which includes 21 administrative districts and 17 cities. Its estimated population at 1 January 1999 was 1,232,300, of whom as many as 82.4% inhabited urban areas; its population density was 56.5 per sq km. Its administrative centre, Ivanovo, had an estimated population of 460,700 in 1996.

History

The city of Ivanovo was founded in 1871 and was known as Ivanovo-Voznesensk until 1932. It was an important centre of anti-government activity during the strikes of 1883 and 1885 and in the 1905 Revolution. Ivanovo Oblast was founded on 20 July 1918.

In the post-Soviet era the region displayed support for political diversity and increasingly became associated with moderation. Whereas, in the 1994 regional Legislative Assembly election and the 1995 general election a similar level of support was displayed for both the Communist Party and Vladimir Zhirinovskii's Liberal Democrats, moderates subsequently triumphed. This was the case in the gubernatorial and legislative elections of 1996, and the elections to the Federal Duma in December 1999. In the gubernatorial elections held in two rounds in December 2000, the Communist candidate, Vladimir Tikhonov, defeated the Oblast's Prime Minister, Vladimir Golovkov. Legislative elections took place in the same month.

Economy

In 1997 Ivanovo Oblast's gross regional product totalled 8,847,000m. old roubles, equivalent to 7,071,900 old roubles per head. The region's main industrial centres are at Ivanovo (a major producer of textiles), Kineshma, Shuya, Vichuga, Furmanov,

Teikovo and Rodniki. There are well-developed rail, road and river transport networks in the region and the largest international airport in central Russia.

Ivanovo Oblast was the historic centre of Russia's cotton-milling industry and was known as the 'Russian Manchester' at the beginning of the 20th century. Flax production was still an important agricultural activity in the region in the 1990s, as were grain and vegetable production and animal husbandry. Owing to the Oblast's high degree of urbanization, agriculture employed just 8.5% of its work-force in 1998, and total agricultural production in that year amounted to a value of 1,988m. roubles. The region's main industries were light manufacturing (especially textiles), mechanical engineering, chemicals, food processing, wood-working and handicrafts (especially lacquerware). Some 34.1% of its working population were engaged in the sector, which generated 6,886m. roubles in 1998.

The economically active population in that year amounted to 479,000, of whom 29,400 (6.1%) were registered as unemployed, although in the mid-1990s the unemployment rate was around twice this amount. The average wage was 529.8 roubles per month. The 1998 budget showed a deficit of 77m. roubles. Although foreign investment totalled only US $120,000 in 1998, the previous year Alfabank and the federal Chamber of Commerce and Industry had initiated a campaign to attract foreign capital to the Oblast, in conjunction with the adoption of federal and regional laws to protect the interests of overseas investors. In December 1999 the Regional Administration signed an agreement on trade, economic, scientific, technical and cultural co-operation with the Government of neighbouring Belarus, in an attempt to increase trade in the region. At 1 January 1999 there was a total of 5,200 small businesses registered in the region.

Directory

Head of the Regional Administration (Governor): VLADIMIR ILYICH TIKHONOV; Ivanovskaya obl., 153000 Ivanovo, ul. Baturina 5; tel. (0932) 41-77-05; fax (0932) 41-92-31; e-mail adminet@ivanovo.ru; internet ivadm.ivanovo.ru:8001.

Chairman of the Legislative Assembly: VALERII GRIGORIYEVICH NIKOLOGOR-SKII; Ivanovskaya obl., Ivanovo, ul. Pushkina 9; tel. (0932) 41-60-68.

Representation in Moscow: tel. (095) 292-19-73.

Head of Ivanovo City Administration: ALEKSANDR VASILIYEVICH GROSHEV; Ivanovskaya obl., 153001 Ivanovo, pl. Revolyutsii 6; tel. (0932) 32-70-20; fax (0932) 41-25-12; e-mail office@ivgoradm.ivanovo.ru; internet ivgoradm .ivanovo.ru.

Kaliningrad Oblast

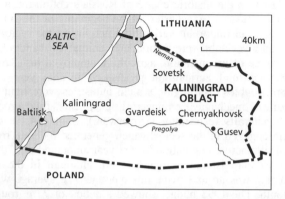

Kaliningrad Oblast forms the westernmost part of the Russian Federation, being an enclave separated from the rest of the country by Lithuania (which borders it to the north and east) and Belarus. Poland lies to the south. It falls within the North-Western Federal Okrug and is sometimes included in the North-Western Economic Area. The city of Kaliningrad (formerly Königsberg) is sited at the mouth of the River Pregolya (Pregel), where it flows into the Vistula Lagoon, an inlet of the Baltic Sea. The other main river is the Neman (Memel). The Oblast occupies 15,100 sq km (5,830 sq miles), of which only 13,300 sq km are dry land, the rest of its territory comprising the freshwater Kurshskaya Lagoon, in the north-west, and the Vistula Lagoon. The coastline is 140 km (87 miles) long. The Oblast is divided into 13 administrative districts and 22 cities. It had an estimated population of 951,300 at 1 January 1999 (of whom some 77.3% inhabited urban areas) and its population density was, therefore, 63.0 per sq km. Its administrative centre is at Kaliningrad, which had an estimated population of 426,500 at 1 January 1999. Other major cities in the Oblast are Sovetsk (formerly Tilsit—44,200), and Chernyakhovsk (formerly Insterburg—43,300).

History

The city of Kaliningrad was founded in 1255, as Königsberg, during German expansion eastwards. The chief city of East Prussia, it was the original royal capital of the Hohenzollerns (from 1871 the German Emperors). After the Second World War it was annexed by the USSR and received its current name (1945). Most of the German population was deported and the city almost completely rebuilt. On 7 April 1946 the region became an administrative-political entity within the Russian Federation.

In mid-1993 Kaliningrad Oblast requested the status of a republic, a petition refused by the federal authorities. On 15 October the Regional Soviet was disbanded by the head of the regional administration for failing to support the state presidency's struggle against the federal parliament. A new regional legislature, the Duma, was later formed. On 12 January 1996 Yurii Matochkin was one of the very first oblast governors to sign a power-sharing agreement with the federal Government. Elections to the governorship were held in October, and were won by Leonid Gorbenko, an independent candidate.

Despite ambitions to transform the enclave into a free-trade zone, Kaliningrad was bedevilled by corruption and excessive and arbitrary taxation. Power struggles in local and regional government bodies further affected the stability of the region during the late 1990s. On several occasions the Russian Government threatened to curtail the Oblast's special economic regulations, because of the competitive advantage given to Kaliningrad-based companies in the Russian market. Relations with the enclave's neighbours were also troubled at times. German groups in Russia (primarily those resident along the River Volga) and ultra-nationalists supported by the leader of the Liberal Democratic Party of Russia, Vladimir Zhirinovskii, made demands for increased German influence in the management of the Oblast, but little seemed likely to come of them. In July 1998 a proposal that the region be awarded the status of an autonomous Russian Baltic republic within Russia was submitted to the Federation Council. However, Governor Gorbenko opposed plans for greater autonomy, instead supporting the growth of closer ties with Belarus. In July 1999 Gorbenko visited the Belarusian capital, Minsk, and appeared to support the wish of that country's President Alyaksandr Lukashenka that Kaliningrad become the port of Belarus. The previous winter the regional authorities had declared a state of emergency as the population became dependent on food aid from Lithuania and Poland. In late 1999 it was suggested that Russia might conclude a special treaty with the European Union (EU) to protect the interests of the region as the EU expanded eastwards. The EU's policy towards the Kaliningrad region was widely expected to influence the future of EU–Russia relations. In gubernatorial elections held in two rounds in November 2000, Gorbenko was defeated by Adm. Vladimir Yegorov, the former Commander of the Baltic Fleet. Yegorov was regarded as a pro-Kremlin candidate, and was elected largely on the basis of his anti-corruption campaign.

Economy

Kaliningrad Oblast is noted for containing more than 90% of the world's reserves of amber. Within Russia it is also noted for its reputedly flourishing parallel ('black') market, with federal officials suggesting in January 1999 that the region had become a major transhipment point for illegal drugs. In 1997 its gross regional product totalled 8,466,100m. old roubles, or 9,011,300 old roubles per head. Its main industrial centres are at Kaliningrad, Gusev, Sovetsk and Chernyakhovsk. There are rail services to Lithuania and Poland and the Oblast's road network consisted of 4,567 km (2,837.9 miles) of paved roads in 1998. Its main ports are at Kaliningrad and Baltiisk.

Kaliningrad Oblast's agricultural sector, which employed some 10.1% of its work-force in 1998, consists mainly of animal husbandry, vegetable growing and fishing. Total agricultural output in 1998 was worth 1,697m. roubles. The Oblast has substantial reserves of petroleum (around 275m. metric tons), more than 2,500m. cu m in peat deposits and 50m. tons of coal. The industrial sector employed 18.3% of its working population and generated 4,678m. roubles in 1998. The region's main industries are mechanical engineering, electro-technical industry, the processing of agricultural and forestry products, natural-gas production, light manufacturing and the production and processing of amber. In 1996 some 757,000 tons of petroleum were extracted, but were refined outside the Oblast. The continuing strategic geopolitical situation of Kaliningrad Oblast meant that demilitarization proceeded at a much slower pace than it did elsewhere in the former USSR; in 1998 there were around 200,000 members of military units in the Oblast.

The economically active population, of whom 13,400 (3.4%) were registered unemployed, numbered 399,600 in 1998. The average monthly wage at that time was 629.6 roubles. The 1998 regional budget, as in several previous years, showed a deficit, in that year amounting to 84m. roubles, and the region is largely dependent on federal subsidies. In the late 1990s there was some foreign investment (US $39.37m. in 1998) and hopes continued that the region would be favoured as an entry point to the Russian market. In 1998 the value of imported goods outnumbered that of exports by a ratio of more than three to one, and over one-half of the exports came from the fishing industry. Much of the foreign investment was from Germany, which alarmed nationalist Russians, anxious that the ethnic Germans expelled 50 years previously might wish to return. At 1 January 1999 there was a total of 9,200 small businesses registered in the region.

Directory

Head of the Regional Administration (Governor): VLADIMIR GRIGORYEVICH YEGOROV; Kaliningradskaya obl., 236007 Kaliningrad, ul. Dmitriya Donskogo 1; tel. (0112) 46-46-49; fax (0112) 46-38-62; e-mail egorov@kaliningrad.ru; internet www.gov.kaliningrad.ru.

Chairman of the Regional Duma: VALERII NIKOLAYEVICH USTYUGOV; tel. (0112) 46-46-32; fax (0112) 46-35-54.

Regional Representation in Moscow: tel. (095) 959-41-40.

Head of Kaliningrad City Administration (Mayor): YURII ALEKSEYEVICH SAVENKO; Kaliningradskaya obl., 236040 Kaliningrad, ul. Pobedy 1; tel. (0112) 21-48-98; fax (0112) 21-16-77; e-mail mayor@klgd.ru; internet www.klgd.ru.

Kaluga Oblast

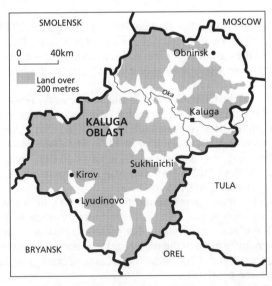

Kaluga Oblast is situated in the central part of the Eastern European Plain, its administrative centre, Kaluga, being 188 km (177 miles) south-west of Moscow. It forms part of the Central Economic Area and the Central Federal Okrug. Tula and Orel Oblasts lie to the south-east, Bryansk Oblast to the south-west, Moscow Oblast to the north-east and Smolensk Oblast to the north-west. Kaluga's main river is the Oka and some two-fifths of its territory is forested. It occupies 29,900 sq km (11,540 sq miles) and is divided into 23 administrative districts and 17 cities. The Oblast had a population of 1,087,500 in 1999 (74.4% of whom inhabited urban areas) and a population density, therefore, of 36.4 per sq km. Its administrative centre is at Kaluga, a river-port on the Oka river, which had an estimated population of 341,300 in 1999. Other major cities in the Oblast include Obninsk (108,100), the site of the world's first nuclear power-station and Lyudinovo (44,000).

History

The city of Kaluga, first mentioned in the letters of a Lithuanian prince, Olgerd, in 1371, was founded as a Muscovite outpost. The region was the scene of an army mutiny in 1905 and was seized by Bolshevik troops at the end of 1917. Kaluga Oblast was founded on 5 July 1944.

In the early 1990s Communist-affiliated managers of industrial and agricultural bodies dominated the new representative body, the Legislative Assembly, elected in March 1994. The Communist Party won over one-quarter of the region's votes in the 1995 elections to the State Duma of the Federation. Further elections to the Legislative Assembly took place in 1996, being marked by low participation rates and the failure of either the Communist Party or the Liberal Democrats to win any seats. Valerii Sudarenkov, the Governor from 1996, had previously been the Deputy Prime Minister of the Uzbek Soviet Socialist Republic (SSR). Sudarenkov did not stand for re-election in November 2000; his former deputy, Anatolii Artamonov, was elected with 57% of the votes cast.

Economy

In 1997 gross regional product in Kaluga Oblast totalled 10,919,000m. old roubles, equivalent to 9,972,600 old roubles per head. Apart from Kaluga, the region's main industrial centres are at Lyudinovo, Kirov, Maloyaroslavets, Sukhinichi and Borovsk. In 1998 there were 855 km of railway track in the Oblast and 4,737 km of paved roads.

Only some areas of the Oblast contain fertile black earth (*chernozem*). Agriculture employed just 9.0% of the work-force in 1998 and consists mainly of animal husbandry and production of vegetables, grain and flax. Agricultural output amounted to a value of 3,100m. roubles in 1998. The Oblast's main industries are mechanical engineering, wood-working, chemicals and light manufacturing. Industry as a whole employed 25.7% of the working population in 1998, when the industrial sector generated 6,653m. roubles.

The economically active population totalled 473,000, of whom 11,000 (2.3%) were registered as unemployed. The average monthly wage in Kaluga Oblast in 1998 was 639.5 roubles. There was a budgetary surplus of 40m. roubles in that year. Total foreign investment in the region in 1998 amounted to some US $65.45m. In 1999 there were around 4,700 small businesses operating in the region, with a combined work-force of 70,000.

Directory

Head of the Regional Administration (Governor): ANATOLII DMITRIYEVICH ARTAMONOV; Kaluzhskaya obl., 248661 Kaluga, pl. Staryi torg 2; tel. (0842) 56-23-57; fax (0842) 53-13-09.

Chairman of the Legislative Assembly: VIKTOR MIKHAILOVICH KOSLESNIKOV; tel. (0842) 57-52-31.

Regional Representation in Moscow: tel. (095) 229-98-25; e-mail kaluga@orc.ru.

Head of Kaluga City Administration: VALERII GRIGORIYEVICH BELOBROVSKII; Kaluzhskaya obl., 248600 Kaluga, ul. Lenina 93; tel. (0842) 56-26-46; fax (0842) 24-41-78; e-mail uprava@kaluga.ru; internet users.kaluga.ru/uprava.

Kamchatka Oblast

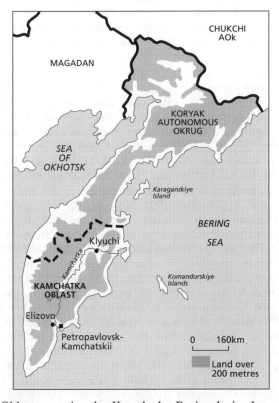

Kamchatka Oblast occupies the Kamchatka Peninsula in the easternmost part of Russia and is, therefore, part of the Far Eastern Economic Area and the Far Eastern Federal Okrug. The Peninsula, some 1,600 km (1,000 miles) in length and 130 km (80 miles) in width, separates the Sea of Okhotsk, in the west, from the Bering Sea, in the east. The Oblast also includes the Karaginskiye and Komandorskiye Islands and the southernmost part of the Chukhotka Peninsula. In the latter area there are land borders with other Russian federal territories, the Chukchi AOk to the north and Magadan Oblast to the west. This part of the Oblast, together with the northern section of the Kamchatka Peninsula, comprises the Koryak Autonomous Okrug. The region is dominated by the Sredinnii Khrebet mountain range, which is bounded to the west by a broad, poorly drained coastal plain, and to the east by the Kamchatka river valley. The territory's other main river is the Avacha. Two-thirds of its area is mountainous (including the highest point in the Russian Far East, Mt Klyuchevskaya, at 4,685 m—15,961 feet) and it contains many hot springs. Kamchatka Oblast covers an area of 472,300 sq km (182,350 sq miles), including the autonomous okrug, and is divided into 11 administrative districts and four cities. There is a high annual rate of precipitation in the region, sometimes as much as 2,000 mm, and temperatures vary considerably according to region. January temperatures are between –9°C and –22°C, while those for July are between 11°C and 34°C. At 1 January 1999 the estimated total population in the region was 396,100 and the population density, therefore, was just 0.8 per sq km. An estimated 80.7% of the region's population inhabited urban areas. The Oblast's administrative centre is at Petropavlovsk-Kamchatskii, in the south-east, which was inhabited by around 199,700 people. The Oblast's other cities are Elizovo (38,700), Vilyuchinsk (34,700) and Klyuchi (9,700).

History

The Kamchatka Peninsula was first sighted in 1697 and was annexed by Russia during the 18th century. Petropavlovsk came under Russian control in 1743. After the Russian Revolution Kamchatka was part of the short-lived Far Eastern Republic (which had its capital at Chita). A distinct Kamchatka Oblast was formed on 20 October 1923, but as part of Khabarovsk Krai until 23 January 1956.

Following the dissolution of the USSR in 1991, Kamchatka tended to be supportive of the federal Government (both the regional administration and the Soviet supported President Boris Yeltsin during the 1993 constitutional crisis). In the general election of December 1995, however, the most successful party was the liberal, and usually anti-government, Yabloko bloc, which gained 20% of the votes cast in the Oblast (a higher proportion than the reformists gained even in the great cities). This success was because the local candidate, Mikhail Zadornov, was a popular figure, who was subsequently appointed as the country's finance minister in 1997. Yabloko repeated this success in the highly competitive regional legislative elections of December 1997, in which it gained nine seats, coming second only to the Communists, with 10. Although a relatively wealthy region, by the late 1990s public patience was tried by the continued lack of economic and social stability in the Federation—one of the main issues for Kamchatka was the shortage of fuel during the winter months. Continued difficulties with fuel supplies led the federal Prime Minister, Sergei Stepashin, to threaten to implement federal rule over the region in July 1999. At the gubernatorial election held in December 2000, the Communist candidate, Mikhail Mashkovtsev, was elected Governor; the incumbent, Vladimir Biryukov, had declined to stand.

Economy

The waters around Kamchatka Oblast (the Sea of Okhotsk, the Bering Sea and the Pacific Ocean) being extremely rich in marine life, make fishing, especially of crabs, the dominant sector of Kamchatka Oblast's economy, accounting for over 90% of its trade in the mid-1990s. The region's fish stocks comprise around one-half of Russia's total. In 1997 the Oblast's gross regional product (GRP) amounted to 8,146,400m. old roubles, or 20,360,800 old roubles per head (one of the highest per-head GRPs in the Russian Federation). These figures all include the Koryak AOk. Petropavlovsk is one of two main industrial centres and ports in the territory, the other being Ust-Kamchatka. There is an international airport, Yelizovo, situated 30 km from Petropavlovsk-Kamchatskii.

Apart from fishing, agriculture in Kamchatka Oblast consists of animal husbandry (livestock, reindeer, mostly in the Koryak AOk, and fur animals), poultry farming and hunting. Just 4.7% of the working population were employed in agriculture in 1998. Agricultural output for the entire territory amounted to a value of 1,277m. roubles in that year. There are deposits of gold, silver, natural gas, sulphur and other minerals in Kamchatka Oblast, which by the late 1990s had been explored and were in the process of development. Industry had been developed in the Soviet period, but only to a limited extent. The sector, which employed 23.1% of the work-force in 1998, is based on the processing of agricultural and forestry products and coal production. Total industrial output was worth 6,878m. roubles in 1998. With trade dominated by the fishing industry, one of the Oblast's main foreign markets was Japan.

In 1998 the economically active population of Kamchatka region numbered 183,700; some 10,300 inhabitants of the entire territory were registered unemployed. Those in employment in Kamchatka Oblast earned an average of 1,560.9 roubles per month, a relatively high wage compared to the rest of the Russian Federation, but one balanced by the high cost of living in the Oblast. In November 1999 groceries that cost 549.59 roubles as an average across the Federation cost some 891.21 roubles in Petropavlovsk-Kamchatskii. There was a budgetary deficit of 282m. roubles in 1998. In May 1998 10-hour reductions in power and heating supplies to homes were introduced, owing to debts owed by the region's energy supplier, Kamchatenergo. Shortages of fuel remained a problem in 2001. Foreign investment in the Oblast amounted to US $42.91m. in 1998, although international trade was limited, amounting to just $121.6m. during that year. The European Bank for Reconstruction and Development provided a loan of $100m. for the development of a geothermal energy plant in the region by the end of 2001. At 1 January 1999 there were some 2,100 small businesses registered in the region.

Directory

Governor: MIKHAIL BORISOVICH MASHKOVTSEV; Kamchatskaya obl., 683040 Petropavlovsk-Kamchatskii, pl. Lenina 1; tel. (4152) 11-20-96; fax (41522) 7-38-43.

Chairman of the Legislative Assembly: LEV NIKOLAYEVICH BOITSOV; Kamchatskaya obl., 683040 Petropavlovsk-Kamchatskii, pl. Lenina 1; tel. (4152) 11-28-95.

Head of the Regional Representation in Moscow: MIKHAIL MIKHAILOVICH SITNIKOV; tel. (095) 241-39-29; fax (095) 244-54-04.

Head of Petropavlovsk-Kamchatskii City Administration: YURII IVANOVICH GOLENICHTCHEV; Kamchatskaya obl., 683040 Petropavlovsk-Kamchatskii, ul. Leninskaya 14; tel. (41522) 2-49-13; e-mail citiadm@svyaz.kamchatka.su.

Kemerovo Oblast

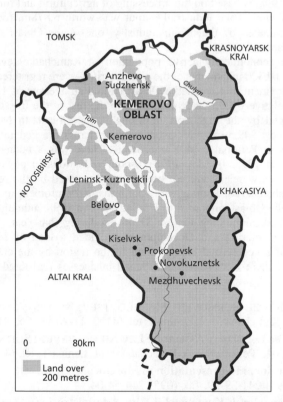

Kemerovo Oblast, also known as the Kuzbass (a Russian acronym for the Kuznetsk coalfields) region, is situated in southern central Russia and forms part of the Western Siberian Economic Area and the Siberian Federal Okrug. It lies to the west of Krasnoyarsk Krai and Khakasiya (an autonomous republic, nominally part of that province). Tomsk lies to the north, Novosibirsk to the west and Altai (including the Republic of Altai) to the south-west. The region lies in the Kuznetsk basin, the area surrounding its main river, the Tom. The territory of the Oblast occupies 95,500 sq km (36,870 sq miles) and is divided into 19 administrative districts and 20 cities. At 1 January 1999 the total population was 3,002,100 and the population density in the region was 31.4 per sq km. Some 86.8% of the population inhabited urban areas. The region's administrative centre is at Kemerovo, which had an estimated population of 494,000 at this time. Other major cities are Novokuznetsk (565,000), Prokopevsk (237,800), Leninsk-Kuznetskii (115,000), Kiselevsk (110,600) and Mezhdurechensk (104,600).

History

Kemerovo (formerly Shcheglovsk) was founded in 1918 and became the administrative centre of the Oblast at its formation on 26 January 1943. The city was at the centre of Russia's principal coal-mining area, the Kuzbass. Although disaffection in the region was instrumental in the disintegration of the USSR, it maintained its strong Communist tradition throughout the 1990s. In the first part of the decade a former head of the Kuzbass workers, Mikhail Kislyuk, was Governor of the region. In July 1997 he was dismissed by President Boris Yeltsin, whom he had previously supported, as the result of a dispute over unpaid pensions arrears. He had earned criticism, as had the federal authorities, for refusing to schedule elections to a new duma (to replace the bicameral Regional Assembly—elected in March 1994, its activities suspended in 1995).

In the December 1995 federal general election, the Communists won 48% of the regional vote, their highest proportion (and the highest of any party) in the Federation, outside the ethnic republic of North Osetiya—Alaniya. Much of this support was secured because of the leadership of Amangeldy Tuleyev, speaker of the suspended local assembly (and a candidate in the federal presidential election of mid-1996). Tuleyev, who stood for the position of federal President in all three of the elections that followed the collapse of the USSR (in 1991, 1996 and 2000), and who spent 11 months in 1996–97 as the Minister for Co-operation with Members of the CIS, amassed a considerable support in Kemerovo Oblast. Having been appointed Governor by Yeltsin, following the removal of Kislyuk, Tuleyev's position was confirmed by an overwhelming victory in popular elections to the post in October 1997. (He received 94.6% of the votes cast.) In April 1999 his electoral bloc went on to win 34 of the 35 seats available in elections to the regional council, and all 11 seats in the local legislative elections. These results were considered by many to reflect a desire for more paternalistic, economically interventionalist policies, as social conditions in the region worsened. In May 1998 widespread industrial action by coal-miners in Anzhero-Sudzhensk and Prokopevsk over wage arrears threatened to bring the regional administration into direct confrontation with the federal Government. The workers blockaded a section of the Trans-Siberian Railway, which seriously affected rail transportation throughout the country. Failure by the federal Ministry of Fuel and Energy to comply with a schedule of payment resulted in Tuleyev threatening legal action and the continuation of the strike until the end of July. At this time Tuleyev's administration signed a framework agreement (negotiated by a commission headed by the energy ministry) with the federal Government on the delimitation of powers, and accompanied by 10 accords aimed at strengthening the economy of the region. None the less, during 1998 Kemerovo was regarded as the federal unit with the fourth-worst record on wage arrears, and its economy remained troubled. However, despite this, Tuleyev was widely considered to be the country's most popular regional leader. When Tuleyev stood for the presidency of the Russian Federation in March 2000, he received 51.6% of the votes cast in Kemerovo Oblast, more than twice the number of votes cast there for Vladimir Putin (in the presidential election of 1991 Tuleyev had also taken first place in the Oblast's poll, with 44.7%, while in 1996 he had stood down in support of Gennadii Zhuganov, the leader of the Communist Party). Before the 2000 election Tuleyev spoke in favour of reducing the number of federal subjects from 89 to between 30 and 35. In January 2001 Tuleyev announced his resignation, in order to bring forward the gubernatorial election to April of that year, several months earlier than had been previously scheduled. His opponents criticized this decision as a tactic to ensure his re-election, as the Governor had widespread popular support at that time. In the election, held on 22 April, Tuleyev received 93.5% of the votes cast.

Economy

The economy of Kemerovo Oblast is based on industry. It is rich in mineral resources, particularly coal, containing the Kuzbass basin, one of the major coal reserves of the world. The region produced 38% of Russia's coal in 1997, but intensive mining in the Soviet period had resulted in severe environmental degradation. In 1997 Kemerovo's gross regional product amounted to 48,778,600m. old roubles, equivalent to 16,083,100 old roubles per head. The Oblast's main industrial centres are at Kemerovo, Novokuznetsk, Prokopevsk, Kiselevsk, Leninsk-Kuznetskii, Anzhero-Sudzhensk and Belovo. The region has 1,755 km (1,091 miles) of railway track and 5,485 km (3,408 miles) of paved roads on its territory in 1998.

Kemerovo Oblast's agriculture, which employed just 4.9% of the work-force in 1998, consists mainly of vegetable production, animal husbandry, bee-keeping and fur-animal hunting. The value of agricultural output for 1998 stood at 4,946m. roubles. In the mid-1990s reserves of coal to a depth of 1,800 m (5,900 feet) were estimated at 733,400m. metric tons. In the same period deposits of iron ore were considered to amount to some 5,250m. tons. Production of complex ores, ferrous and non-ferrous metallurgy, chemicals, mechanical engineering, metal working, food processing, light manufacturing and wood-working are also important industries in the region. The industrial sector as a whole employed 32.4% of the working population in 1998 and generated 40,313m. roubles.

The economically active population in 1998 numbered 1,249,200, of whom 35,700 were registered unemployed. The average monthly wage was 988.8 roubles. The 1998 annual regional budget, like several preceding it, showed a relatively large deficit, on this occasion amounting to 604m. roubles. From the mid-1990s foreign investors showed some interest in exploiting the region's coal reserves. Total foreign investment in the Oblast in 1998 amounted to US $8.07m. Economic reforms introduced after 1992 were fairly effective; by 1995 some 61% of employees were working in the private sector. In the late 1990s the regional Government aimed to promote small businesses, of which there were 10,300 in operation at 1 January 1999.

Directory

Head of the Regional Administration (Governor): AMANGELDY MOLDAGAZYE-VICH TULEYEV; Kemerovskaya obl., 650099 Kemerovo, pr. Sovetskii 62; tel. (3842) 36-34-09; fax (3842) 36-48-33; internet www.kemerovo.su.

Chairman of the Legislative Assembly: GENNADII TIMOFEYEVICH DYUDYAYEV; tel. (3842) 23-41-42; fax (3842) 23-57-32.

Head of the Regional Representation in Moscow: SERGEI VLADIMIROVICH SHATIROV; tel. (095) 953-54-89.

Head of Kemerovo City Administration (Mayor): VLADIMIR VASILIYEVICH MIKHAILOV; Kemerovskaya obl., 650099 Kemerovo, pr. Sovetskii 54; tel. (3842) 36-46-10; fax (3842) 23-18-91; e-mail sityadm@kuzbass.net.

Kirov (Vyatka) Oblast

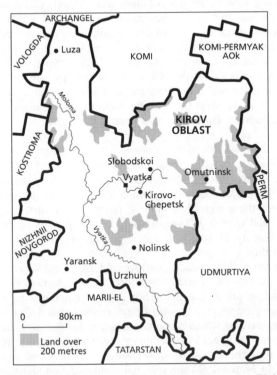

Kirov Oblast is situated in the east of the Eastern European Plain. It forms part of the Volga-Vyatka Economic Area and the Volga Federal Okrug. It is bordered by Archangel and Komi to the north, the Komi-Permyak AOk (part of Perm Oblast) and Udmurtiya to the east, Tatarstan and Marii-El to the south, and Nizhnii Novgorod, Kostroma and Vologda to the west. Its main rivers are the Kama and the Vyatka; in addition there are almost 20,000 rivers and more than 1,000 lakes on its territory. Kirov occupies a total area of 120,800 sq km (46,640 sq miles) and measures 570 km (354 miles) from south to north and 440 km from west to east. It is divided into 39 administrative districts and 18 cities. The total population at 1 January 1999 was 1,603,200 and the population density was 13.3 per sq km. Around 71.0% of the population inhabited urban areas at this time. At the census of 1989 ethnic Russians comprised 90.4% of the population. The Oblast's administrative centre is at Vyatka (formerly Kirov), a river-port, which had an estimated 465,600 inhabitants in 1999. Other major cities are Kirovo-Chepetsk (92,700) and Vyatskiye Polyany (42,500).

History

The city and its region were known as Kirov from the formation of the latter on 7 December 1934, but the city was renamed Vyatka in 1992. In September 1993 a draft constitution for Kirov Oblast was prepared; this referred to the Oblast as Vyatka Krai and provided for a universally elected governor and a new legislature,

169

a provincial duma. On 18 October the Kirov Regional Soviet voted to disband itself. The federal authorities refused to acknowledge the area's redesignation as a krai and, during 1994, a Regional Duma was elected. The most popular party in the mid-1990s was that of the nationalist supporters of Vladimir Zhirinovskii, although members of the old Communist establishment were well represented in its ranks. Election to the governorship of the Oblast was held in October 1996 and was won by the Communist candidate, Vladimir Sergeyenkov, by a narrow margin; he was re-elected, with 58% of the votes cast, on 26 March 2000. In October 1997 the Governor of the Oblast signed a power-sharing treaty with federal President Boris Yeltsin, with the specific hope that investment in the extraction of raw materials and health care would benefit the region.

Economy

In 1997 the Oblast's gross regional product (GRP) stood at 17,369,000m. old roubles, equivalent to 10,733,500 old roubles per head. Its main industrial centres are at Vyatka, Slobodskoi, Kotelnich, Omutninsk, Kirovo-Chepetsk and Vyatskiye Polyany. In 1998 there were 1,093 km of railway track in the region, 8,784 km of paved roads and over 2,000 km of navigable waterways on the Vyatka river. Owing to the density of rivers in the region its soil is high in mineral salts, reducing its fertility.

The Oblast's agriculture, which employed 13.3% of the working population in 1998, consists mainly of animal husbandry and production of grain, flax and vegetables. Total output within the sector in 1998 amounted to 5,253m. roubles. Kirov Oblast has significant deposits of peat, estimated at 435m. metric tons, and phosphorites, reserves of which amounted to some 2,000m. tons in the mid-1990s. Its main industries are mechanical engineering, metal working, ferrous and non-ferrous metallurgy, chemicals, the processing of agricultural products and light manufacturing. In March 1998 the regional administration signed a protocol with the federal ministries of defence and economy on the restructuring of the Oblast's military-industrial complex, which was significantly underachieving (in 1997 the sector accounted for just one-10th of the Oblast's GRP, despite owning 58% of its main assets). The region was also renowned for the manufacturing of toys and wood products (especially skis). Industry employed 27.8% of the work-force in 1998 and generated 12,012m. roubles. In 1997 exports largely comprised chemical and petrochemical goods, while imports were dominated by automobiles and equipment and food products.

In 1998 the economically active population numbered 682,400, with 41,200 registered as unemployed, almost one-third less than in 1995. Average earnings and government finances remained weak into the late 1990s. In 1998 the average monthly wage was just 598.4 roubles, while the budget surplus was 152m. roubles. Economic reform in the region was, nevertheless, well advanced by the mid-1990s: in 1996 the private sector accounted for some 90% of total industrial output, while in 1999 there were some 4,100 small businesses operating in Kirov Oblast, employing around 35,000 people.

Directory

Head of the Regional Administration (Governor): VLADIMIR NILOVICH SERGE-YENKOV; Kirovskaya obl., 610019 Vyatka, ul. Karla Libknekhta 69; tel. (8332) 62-95-64; fax (8332) 62-89-58; e-mail region@gov-vyatka.ru; internet gov-vyatka.ru.

Chairman of the Regional Duma: MIKHAIL ALEKSANDROVICH MIKHEYEV; tel. (8332) 62-48-00.

Head of Vyatka (Kirov) City Administration: VASILII ALEKSEYEVICH KISELEV; Kirovskaya obl., 610000 Vyatka, ul. Vorovskogo 39; tel. (8332) 62-89-40; fax (8332) 67-69-91.

Kostroma Oblast

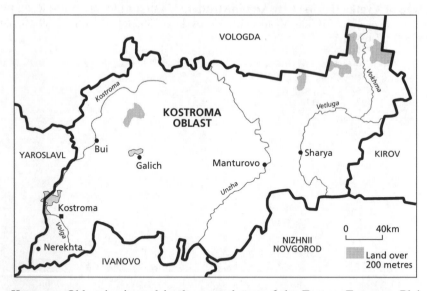

Kostroma Oblast is situated in the central part of the Eastern European Plain. It forms part of the Central Economic Area and the Central Federal Okrug. It is bordered by Vologda Oblast to the north, Kirov Oblast to the east, Nizhnii Novgorod and Ivanovo Oblasts to the south and Yaroslavl Oblast to the west. Its main rivers are the Volga, the Kostroma, the Unzha, the Vokhma and the Vetluga. It has two major lakes—the Galichskoye and the Chukhlomskoye. The total area of Kostroma Oblast is 60,100 sq km (23,200 sq miles), almost three-quarters of which is forested. It is divided into 24 administrative districts and 12 cities. The region had an estimated population of 786,900 at 1 January 1999, some 65.7% of whom inhabited urban areas. Its population density at this time was 13.1 per sq km. The Oblast's administrative centre is at Kostroma, a river-port situated on both banks of the Volga, and a popular tourist resort as part of the 'Golden Ring', which had an estimated 288,400 inhabitants in 1999.

History

The city of Kostroma was founded in the 12th century. In the Russian heartland, Kostroma Oblast was formed on 13 August 1944. The region remained loyal to the Communist nomenklatura in the 1990s—its local council supported the federal parliament in its 1993 defiance of the Russian President, Boris Yeltsin, and was replaced by a new representative body in 1994. The main party was the Communists; its domination of the region was confirmed in the gubernatorial election of December 1996, although Yeltsin was the preferred candidate in the presidential election of June of that year. The incumbent Governor, Viktor Shershunov, was re-elected in December 2000, defeating the mayor of Kostroma City, Boris Korobov.

Economy

In 1997 gross regional product in Kostroma Oblast amounted to 8,835,400m. old roubles, or 11,056,700 old roubles per head. The Oblast's main industrial centres are at Kostroma, Sharya, Nerekhta, Galich, Bui, Manturovo and Krasnoye-on-Volga (Krasnoye-na-Volge). The region has major road and rail networks—there are 646 km (401 miles) of railways in use on its territory and 5,366 km of paved roads. There are also 985 km of navigable waterways.

Agriculture in Kostroma Oblast, which employed 10.2% of the work-force in 1998, consists mainly of production of grain, flax (the region is one of Russia's major producers of linen) and vegetables and animal husbandry. Total agricultural output in 1998 was worth 2,870m. roubles, while industrial production amounted to a value of 6,198m. roubles. The region has an energy surplus, exporting some four-fifths of electrical energy produced. Electricity generation comprised 42.3% of total industrial production in Kostroma Oblast in 1998. The other main industries in the region are light manufacturing, wood-working, mechanical engineering, food and timber processing and handicrafts (especially jewellery). The territory is also an important military centre, with numerous rocket silos, of which 23 had already been converted to agricultural use by early 1996, with plans to recultivate a further 20. Some 23.1% of the Oblast's working population was engaged in industry in 1998.

The economically active population numbered 325,100 in 1998, of whom 11,700 (3.6%) were registered unemployed, a percentage that had decreased considerably since the mid-1990s. The average wage in the Oblast was 586.1 roubles per month in 1998. There was a budgetary deficit of some 134m. roubles in that year. Although foreign trade amounted to some US $100m., foreign investment was equivalent to only $1.88m. in 1998. At 1 January 1999 there were 3,100 small businesses in operation.

Directory

Head of the Regional Administration (Governor): VIKTOR ANDREYEVICH SHERSHUNOV; Kostromskaya obl., 156006 Kostroma, ul. Dzerzhinskogo 15; tel. (0942) 31-34-72; fax (0942) 31-33-95; e-mail shershunov@kos-obl.kmtn.ru; internet www.region.kostroma.net.

Chairman of the Regional Duma: ANDREI IVANOVICH BYCHKOV; Kostromskaya obl., 156000 Kostroma, Sovetskaya pl. 2; tel. (0942) 57-62-52.

Head of the Regional Representation in Moscow: GALINA MIKHAILOVNA PSHENITSYNA; tel. (095) 203-42-44.

Head of Kostroma City Administration: BORIS KONSTANTINOVICH KOROBOV; Kostromskaya obl., 156000 Kostroma, pl. Sovetskaya 1; tel. (0942) 31-44-40; fax (0942) 31-39-32; internet www.boriskorobov.ru.

Kurgan Oblast

Kurgan Oblast is situated in the south of the Western Siberian Plain. It forms part of the Urals Economic Area and the Urals Federal Okrug. Chelyabinsk Oblast lies to the west, Sverdlovsk Oblast to the north and Tyumen Oblast to the north-east. There is an international border with Kazakhstan to the south. The main rivers flowing through Kurgan Oblast are the Tobol and the Iset and there are numerous lakes (more than 2,500) in the south-east of the region. The Oblast occupies 71,000 sq km (27,400 sq miles) and measures 290 km (180 miles) from south to north and 430 km from east to west. It is divided into 24 administrative districts and nine cities. It had an estimated population of 1,102,100 at 1 January 1999 (of whom some 55.6% inhabited urban areas, the lowest urban population of any region in the Urals Economic Area) and a population density of 15.5 per sq km. Its administrative centre is at Kurgan, which had an estimated population of 365,400. The second-largest city in the Oblast is Shadrinsk (88,000).

History

The city of Kurgan was founded as a tax-exempt settlement in 1553, on the edge of Russian territory. By the Soviet period, when there was some industrialization, it was a firmly ethnically Russian area. Kurgan Oblast was formed on 6 February 1943. In the 1990s it was still dominated by the Communists, who led the Regional Duma elected on 12 December 1993. Two years later, as indicated by the regional results of the all-Russian parliamentary election, the Communists remained the most popular party, but were closely followed by the Liberal Democrats, an immoderate nationalist grouping. In the gubernatorial election of late 1996 the Communist candidate, Oleg Bogomolov, hitherto speaker of the Regional Duma, was voted into office, running unopposed in the second round of the election after his opponent stood down. Bogomolov was re-elected in December 2000.

Economy

Kurgan Oblast, with its fertile soil and warm, moist climate, is the agricultural base of the Urals area, producing around one-10th of the region's grain, meat and milk. In 1997 its gross regional product amounted to 9,088,300m. old roubles, equivalent to 8,215,800 old roubles per head. Its main industrial centres are at Kurgan, a river-port in the south-east of the region, and Shadrinsk. The Trans-

Siberian Railway passes through the Oblast's territory, as do several major petroleum and natural-gas pipelines.

The Oblast's important agricultural sector employed 19.2% of the work-force in 1998 and consists mainly of grain production and animal husbandry. Total agricultural production in the region was worth 3,076m. roubles in 1998. Its main industries are mechanical engineering, metal working, manufacturing of building materials, light manufacturing and food and timber processing. The industrial sector employed 21.1% of the working population and generated 6,941m. roubles in 1998.

The economically active population in 1998 numbered 420,800; around 15,200 of these were registered unemployed. Those in employment earned, on average, 534.9 roubles per month. There was a budgetary surplus of 58m. roubles in 1998, and foreign investment totalled US $910,000. Government deficit problems had been problematic during the second half of the 1990s and, in January 1999, with wage arrears having provoked teachers' strikes, the central Government announced that federal transfers to the region would be increased in that year. In 1999 there were around 3,700 small businesses operating in the Oblast, employing some 32,000 people.

Directory

Head of the Regional Administration (Governor): OLEG ALEKSEYEVICH BOGO-MOLOV; Kurganskaya obl., 640000 Kurgan, ul. Gogolya 56; tel. (3522) 41-70-30; fax (3522) 41-71-32.

Chairman of the Regional Duma: LEV GRIGORIYEVICH YEFREMOV; tel. (3522) 41-72-17.

Head of the Regional Representation in Moscow: OLEG YEVGENIYEVICH PANTELEYEV; tel. (095) 200-39-78.

Head of Kurgan City Administration (Mayor): ANATOLII FEDOROVICH YELCH-ANINOV; Kurganskaya obl., 640000 Kurgan, pl. Lenina; tel. (35222) 2-24-52; fax (35222) 2-42-88; internet www.munic.kurgan.ru.

Kursk Oblast

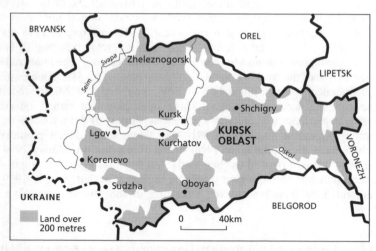

Kursk Oblast is situated within the Central Russian Highlands. It forms part of the Central Chernozem Economic Area and the Central Federal Okrug. An international boundary with Ukraine lies to the south-west, with neighbouring Russian federal territories consisting of Bryansk in the north-west, Orel and Lipetsk in the north, Voronezh in the east and Belgorod in the south. Its main river is the Seim. The Oblast measures 171 km (106 miles) from south to north and 305 km from west to east. It occupies 29,800 sq km (11,500 sq miles) and is divided into 28 administrative districts and 10 cities. It had a population of 1,323,500 in 1999, of whom some 61.2% inhabited urban areas. Its population density was, therefore, 44.4 per sq km. The Oblast's administrative centre is at Kursk, which had an estimated 441,200 inhabitants at 1 January 1999. Other major cities in the region are Zheleznogorsk (97,000) and Kurchatov (48,300).

History

The city of Kursk, one of the most ancient in Russia, was founded in 1032 and became famous for its nightingales and Antonovka apples. The region was the scene of an army mutiny in 1905 and, in 1943, of a decisive battle against German forces during the Second World War. Kursk Oblast was formed on 13 July 1934. The Communists dominated the regional assembly, a Duma, elected in 1994. In December 1995 the party's candidates to the federal State Duma secured 28% of the regional votes. The former Russian Vice-President, Aleksandr Rutskoi, was elected regional Governor on 20 October 1996. However, he was prevented from standing as a candidate in the election of 22 October 2000, one day before the election, owing to a legal technicality. In a second round of voting on 5 November, the Communist candidate, Aleksandr Mikhailov, defeated the pro-Government, former Federal Security Service (FSB) General, Viktor Surzhikov. Immediately after being elected, Mikhailov provoked controversy by making a number of anti-Semitic remarks, prompting Rutskoi (who had a Jewish mother) to threaten to take legal action.

Economy

Kursk Oblast's gross regional product in 1995 stood at 15,404,400m. old roubles, equivalent to 11,499,300 old roubles per head. Its main industrial centres are at Kursk and Zheleznogorsk.

The region's agriculture, which employed 17.8% of the working population in 1998, consists mainly of sugar beets and grain production, horticulture and animal husbandry. Total agricultural production in 1998 amounted to a value of 5,063m. roubles. The territory contains a major iron-ore basin, with significant deposits of Kursk magnetic anomaly. Kursk Oblast's main industries were production and enrichment of iron ores, mechanical engineering, electro-technical products and chemicals, food processing, light manufacturing and production of building materials. Some 22.3% of the work-force was engaged in industry, while output within the sector was worth 12,755m. roubles in 1998. From the mid-1990s the Oblast's main foreign trading partners were Poland and the Czech Republic, although it also had economic links with other European countries, North America, India and Turkey. It exports largely comprised iron ore and concentrate, automobiles and machinery.

The economically active population in Kursk Oblast was 564,900 strong in 1998, of whom 11,300 (1.9%) were registered unemployed at that time. The average monthly wage in the region was 633.7 roubles and there was a budgetary deficit of 216m. roubles. Foreign investment in that year amounted to US $13.85m. At 1 January 1999 around 2,900 small businesses were operating in the Oblast.

Directory

Head of the Regional Administration (Governor): ALEKSANDR NIKOLAYEVICH MIKHAILOV; Kurskaya obl., 305002 Kursk, Krasnaya pl., Dom Sovetov; tel. (0712) 2-62-62; fax (0712) 56-58-89; e-mail intercom@region.kursk.ru.

Chairman of the Regional Duma: VIKTOR DMITRIYEVICH CHERNYKH; tel. (0712) 56-09-91; fax (0712) 56-20-06; internet www.oblduma.kursknet.ru.

Representation in Moscow: tel. (095) 917-08-69.

Head of Kursk City Administration: SERGEI IVANOVICH MALTSEV; Kurskaya obl., 305000 Kursk, ul. Lenina 1; tel. (07122) 2-63-63; fax (07122) 2-43-16; e-mail kursk@pub.sovest.ru; internet www.sovtest.ru/kursk.

Leningrad Oblast

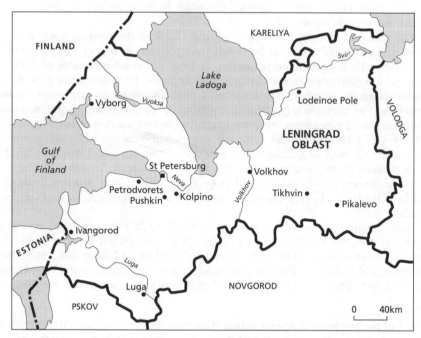

Leningrad Oblast is situated in the north-west of the Eastern European Plain. It lies on the Gulf of Finland, an inlet of the Baltic Sea, and forms part of the North-Western Economic Area and the North-Western Federal Okrug. The Republic of Kareliya (Karelia) lies to the north and the oblasts of Volodga to the east and Novgorod and Pskov to the south. There is an international border with Estonia to the west and with Finland to the north-west. Two-thirds of the Oblast is forested and over one-10th is swampland. Its main rivers are the Neva, the Sayas, the Luga and the Vuoksa. Lake Ladoga (Ladozhskoye), the largest lake in Europe, with a surface area of 17,800 sq km, forms a partial border with Kareliya, and the southern tip of Lake Onega (Onezhskoye—9,700 sq km) also lies within Leningrad. The Oblast occupies 84,500 sq km (32,620 sq miles) and is divided into 17 administrative districts and 29 cities. Its total population at 1 January 1999, excluding the St Petersburg city region, was 1,673,700, of whom 66.0% inhabited urban areas. Its administrative centre is at St Petersburg, now a federal city in its own right. The largest cities within the Oblast proper are Gatchina (population 82,300) and Vyborg (80,500).

History

The city of St Petersburg (known as Petrograd 1914–24 and Leningrad until 1991) was built in 1703. Leningrad Oblast, which was formed on 1 August 1927 out of the territories of five regions (Cherepovetskoi, Leningrad, Murmansk, Novgorod and Pskov), was heavily industrialized during the Soviet period, particularly during 1926–40. The region did not change its name when the city reverted to the name of St Petersburg in October 1991.

Although the city was a strong base for reformists and supporters of the federal Government in the early and mid-1990s, and the Oblast evinced a greater degree of approval for the Communists, the region generally produced a significant number of votes for Our Home is Russia and Yabloko. The former, led by the federal premier, won 11% of the poll in December 1995, while the reformists gained 8%. In mid-1996 an agreement delimiting the division of powers between the federal and regional governments was signed. Later that year gubernatorial elections were held, which were won by an independent candidate, Vladimir Gustov. On 24 September 1998 the federal President, Boris Yeltsin, approved a proposal to merge the Oblast with the federal city of St Petersburg, although any immediate implementation seemed unlikely. Gustov resigned to take up the position of Deputy Prime Minister in September 1998, and his replacement, Valerii Serdyukov, confirmed his position on 5 September 1999 by securing 30% of the votes cast in an election contested by 16 candidates.

Economy

Leningrad Oblast's gross regional product amounted to 19,456,200m. old roubles in 1997, equivalent to 11,580,400 old roubles per head. Its main industrial centres are at St Petersburg, Vyborg (both major seaports), Sestroretsk and Kingisepp. At the beginning of 1999 the region contained 2,810 km (1,746 miles) of railway track, of which 1,352 km (840 miles) were electrified, and 10,375 km (6,447 miles) of paved roads.

The Oblast's agriculture, which employed 9.5% of the working population in 1998, consists mainly of animal husbandry and vegetable production. Total agricultural output was worth 5,582m. roubles in 1998. The region's timber reserves are estimated to cover 6.1m. ha (15m. acres). Its major industries are mechanical engineering, ferrous and non-ferrous metallurgy, chemicals and petrochemicals, petroleum refining, the processing of forestry and agricultural products, production of electrical energy, light manufacturing and the production of building materials, bauxites, slate and peat. Some 24.3% of the Oblast's work-force was engaged in industry in 1998. Industrial output in that year amounted to a value of 17,265m. roubles.

The economically active population numbered 671,100, of whom 35,700 were registered unemployed. The average monthly wage in 1998 was 648.6 roubles. The budget for 1998 showed a deficit of 406m. roubles. At the beginning of 1997 there were over 200 joint enterprises, which were mainly in the Vyborg raion, bordering Finland, and established with over US $150m. of foreign investment. In 1998 there was $190.7m.-worth of foreign investment in the region, primarily in the timber, chemical and petrochemicals industries. In that year exports from the region amounted to $1,447.8m.

Directory

Head of the Regional Administration (Governor): VALERII PAVLOVICH SERD-YUKOV; Leningradskaya obl., 193311 St Petersburg, Suvorovskii pr. 67; tel. (812) 274-35-63; fax (812) 271-56-27; internet www.lenobl.ru.

Chairman of the Regional Legislative Assembly: VITALII NIKOLAYEVICH KLIMOV; tel. (812) 274-65-31.

Regional Representation in Moscow: tel. (095) 951-82-39.

Lipetsk Oblast

Lipetsk Oblast is situated within the Central Russian Highlands, some 508 km (315 m) south-east of Moscow. It forms part of the Central Chernozem Economic Area and the Central federal district. It is bordered by Voronezh and Kursk Oblasts to the south, Orel Oblast to the west, Tula Oblast to the north-west, Ryazan Oblast to the north and Tambov Oblast to the east. Its main rivers are the Don and the Voronezh. The Oblast occupies 24,100 sq km (9,300 sq miles) and is divided into 18 administrative districts and eight cities. It had an estimated population of 1,244,900 at 1 January 1999, of whom some 64.6% inhabited urban areas. Its population density at this time was 51.7 per sq km. Its administrative centre is at Lipetsk, which had an estimated population of 519,200 in 1999. Other cities include Yelets (119,300) and Gryazi (48,300).

History

Lipetsk was founded in the 13th century and was later famed for containing one of Russia's oldest mud-bath resorts and spas. In the late tsarist and Soviet period the region became increasingly industrialized. Lipetsk Oblast was formed on 6 January 1954. By the 1990s it was considered part of the 'red belt' of Communist support across central Russia. Thus, in December 1992, when Lipetsk was one of eight territorial units permitted to hold gubernatorial elections (in an attempt to resolve the dispute between the head of the administration and the regional assembly), the incumbent, a supporter of the federal Government, was defeated by the Communist candidate. In September 1993 both the Regional Soviet and the Governor, therefore, denounced the Russian President's dissolution of the federal parliament. Subsequently, the territory was obliged to comply with the directives of the federal Government. Legislative elections were held in the region on 6 March 1994, but were invalidated, owing to a low level of attendance. Further elections were held later that year. Political apathy also contributed to a low level of support, compared to other regions on the red belt, for the Communists in the federal general election of December 1995—a still high 29%. In the Russian presidential election of March 2000, Lipetsk Oblast gave the Communist candidate, Gennadii Zyuganov, a higher proportion of the votes cast (47.4%) than did any other federal subject. On 12 April 1998 the Chairman of the Regional Assembly, Oleg Korolev, won an overwhelming victory (some 79% of the votes cast) in the gubernatorial election. He was supported primarily by the Communist Party, but also by the local branch of Yabloko and other political movements.

Economy

In 1997 Lipetsk Oblast's gross regional product totalled 15,736,900m. old roubles, or 12,604,700 old roubles per head. Its main industrial centres are at Lipetsk, Yelets, Dankov and Gryazi. Yelets and Gryazi contain the region's major railway junctions.

The region's agriculture consists mainly of animal husbandry, horticulture and the production of grain, sugar beets, makhorka tobacco and vegetables. Some 14.4% of the work-force was engaged in agriculture in 1998. Agricultural output in that year amounted to a value of 4,231m. roubles. The Oblast's main industries are ferrous metallurgy (ferrous metallurgy comprised over one-half of the region's total industrial output in 1998), mechanical engineering, metal working, electro-technical industry, food processing and the production of building materials. Novolipetsk Metallurgical Group, based in the region, is one of the country's major industrial companies. The industrial sector employed 25.6% of the region's working population and generated 20,139m. roubles.

The economically active population in 1998 totalled 514,600; 6,300 of these were registered unemployed. Those in employment earned, on average, 749.6 roubles per month. The regional budget recorded a deficit of 80m. roubles in 1998. Foreign investment in Lipetsk Oblast in 1998 amounted to US $14.76m. The value of exported goods from the Oblast in 1998 totalled some $1,018.4m. At 1 January 1999 there were around 4,100 small businesses registered in the territory.

Directory

Head of the Regional Administration (Governor): OLEG PETROVICH KOROLEV; Lipetskaya obl., 398014 Lipetsk, Sobornaya pl. 1; tel. (0742) 24-15-71; fax (0742) 72-24-26; e-mail 4800024@lipadm.lipetsk.ru; internet www.admlr.lipetsk.ru.

Chairman of the Regional Assembly: ANATOLII IVANOVICH SAVENKOV.

Head of Lipetsk City Administration (Mayor): ALEKSANDR SERGEYEVICH KOROBEINIKOV; Lipetskaya obl., 398600 Lipetsk, ul. Sovetskaya 22; tel. (0742) 77-66-17; fax (0742) 77-44-30.

Magadan Oblast

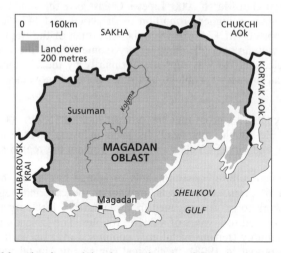

Magadan Oblast is situated in the north-east of Russia and forms part of the Far Eastern Economic Area and the Far Eastern Federal Okrug. To the north-east, on the Chukotka Peninsula, lies the Chukchi AOk, which, until 1992, formed part of Magadan Oblast. The rest of its border with territory on Chukotka is with the Koryak AOk (Kamchatka Oblast), which lies to the east. Magadan has a coastline on the Sea of Okhotsk in the south-east. Khabarovsk Krai lies to the south-west of the region and the Republic of Sakha (Yakutiya) to the north-west. Its main river is the Kolyma, which flows northwards and drains into the Arctic Ocean by way of Yakutiya. A considerable proportion of the territory of the region is mountainous, while the area around the Anadyr estuary is low marshland. Much of the Oblast is tundra or forest-tundra. The Oblast occupies a total area of 461,400 sq km (178,150 sq miles—much reduced from when it included the Chukchi, or Chukot, AOk). It is divided into eight administrative districts and two cities. The climate in the region is severe, with winters lasting from six to over seven months. The average annual temperature in all areas of the region is below nought (Celsius). The Oblast had an estimated population of 246,100 at 1 January 1999. It is one of the most sparsely populated regions, with a population density of just 0.5 per sq km. The majority of the population (91.3%) inhabited urban areas. Its administrative centre is at the only large city in the Oblast, Magadan, which had an estimated population of 121,700 in 1999.

History

Russians first reached the Magadan region in the mid-17th century. At the start of the Soviet period it was in the Far Eastern Republic, which in 1922 was reintegrated into Russia. A distinct Magadan Oblast was formed on 3 December 1953, although it then included the Chukot (now Chukchi) AOk. The successful rejection of Magadan's jurisdiction on the Chukotka Peninsula (acknowledged by the federal authorities in 1992) massively reduced Magadan's territory and contributed to local feeling of remoteness and of neglect by the centre. Thus, in the elections to the State Duma of the Federation Assembly of December 1995, candidates of the nationalist Liberal Democrats secured 22% of the votes cast in the region and remained relatively popular there during the late 1990s. Both the Communists and the existing federal authorities were also identified with the political establishments. However, the Regional Duma (elected in 1994) was still dominated by the old nomenklatura class. The gubernatorial election of 3 November 1996 was won by Valentin Tsvetkov, a candidate backed by the Communist-dominated Popular-Patriotic Union. In June 1999 a special economic zone was created in the Oblast, in the hope that investors would facilitate the exploitation of the region's rich natural resources. Tsvetkov was re-elected as Governor in November 2000.

Economy

Magadan Oblast is Russia's principal gold-producing region. Its gross regional product in 1997 amounted to 6,402,400m. old roubles, equivalent to 25,774,500 old roubles per head. The Oblast's main industrial centres are at Magadan and Susuman. Magadan and Nagayevo are its most important ports. There are no railways in the territory, but there are 2,653 km (1,648 miles) of paved roads. There is an international airport at Magadan.

The region's primary economic activities are fishing, animal husbandry and hunting. These and other agricultural activities, which employed just 3.8% of the region's work-force, generated 222m. roubles in 1998. Ore mining is also important: apart from gold, the region contains considerable reserves of silver, tin and wolfram (tungsten). It is also rich in peat and timber. In early 1998 the regional Government hired a prospecting company to explore offshore petroleum deposits in the Sea of Okhotsk, in a zone thought to hold around 5,000m. metric tons of petroleum and natural gas. The Kolyma river is an important source of hydroelectric energy. In 1997 the Pan American Silver Corporation of Canada purchased a 70% stake in local company ZAO Dukat, to reopen a defunct silver mine in the Oblast, which contained an estimated 477m. troy ounces of silver and 1m. troy ounces of gold. However, licensing and other bureaucratic obstacles delayed operations. Other industry includes food processing, mechanical engineering and metal working. Some 18.6% of the working population was engaged in industry in 1998. Total industrial output in that year was worth 4,022m. roubles.

In 1998 a total of 118,200 of the Oblast's inhabitants were economically active, of whom 6,400 (5.4%) were registered unemployed. The average monthly wage in 1998 was some 1,621.9 roubles, one of the highest figures in the Federation, while the budget showed a surplus of 67m. roubles. Earlier in the 1990s persistent deficit problems, not helped by high wages, meant continuing problems with payment arrears and in December 1998 Magadan was cited as the fifth-worst territory in the Federation for wage arrears. In late 1998 the Russian branch of the International Committee of the Red Cross (ICRC) requested food and medical aid to help alleviate the deteriorating conditions in the region, as elsewhere in the Russian Far East. The cost of living in the region is among the highest in the Russian Federation. Foreign investment in the Oblast amounted to US $53.72m. in 1998. At 1 January 1999 there were an estimated 2,200 small businesses in operation.

Directory

Governor: VALENTIN IVANOVICH TSVETKOV; Magadanskaya obl., 685000 Magadan, ul. Gorkogo 6; tel. (41300) 2-31-34; fax (41300) 2-04-25.

Chairman of the Regional Council of Deputies: ILYA SEMENOVICH ROZEN-BLYUM.

Regional Representation in Moscow: tel. (095) 203-92-82.

Head of Magadan City Administration (Mayor): NIKOLAI BORISOVICH KARPENKO; Magadanskaya obl., 685000 Magadan, pl. Gorkogo 1; tel. (41300) 2-50-47; fax (41322) 2-49-40; e-mail admin@cityadm.magadan.ru.

Moscow Oblast

Moscow Oblast is situated in the central part of the Eastern European Plain, at the Volga-Oka confluence. It forms part of the Central Economic Area and the Central Federal Okrug. Moscow is surrounded by seven other oblasts: Tver and Yaroslavl to the north, Vladimir and Ryazan to the east, Tula and Kaluga to the south-west and Smolensk to the west. Most of the region is forested and its main rivers are the Moskva and the Oka. The territory of the Oblast (excluding Moscow City) covers an area of 46,000 sq km (17,760 sq miles) and has 39 administrative districts and 74 cities. Its total population at 1 January 1999 was estimated at 6,500,500. The population density was 138.4 inhabitants per sq km. Inhabitants of urban areas comprise around 79.8% of the region's total population. The Oblast's administrative centre is in Moscow City. Within the Oblast proper, there are several cities with a population of over 100,000 including (in order of size) Podolsk, Lyubertsy, Mytishchi, Kolomna, Elektrostal and Orekhovo-Zuyevo.

History

The city of Moscow was established in the mid-12th century and became the centre of a burgeoning Muscovite state. The region soon became an important trade route between the Baltic Sea in the north and the Black and Caspian Seas in the south. It first became industrialized in the early 18th century, with the development of the textile industry, in particular the production of wool and cotton. The region and the city of Moscow were captured by the troops of Emperor Napoleon I of France in 1812, but the invaders were forced to retreat later that year. German invaders reached the Moscow region (which had been formed as Moscow Oblast on 14 January 1929) in 1941, and the Soviet Government removed from the city until 1943. In the winter of 1941/42 the German forces were driven from the Oblast's territory. Otherwise, the region and the city have benefited from Moscow being the Soviet, and the Russian, capital.

185

As the seat of government, in the 1990s the federal executive could rely on a reasonable level of support in the Moscow region. Our Home is Russia, the party of Viktor Chernomyrdin, the federal Prime Minister, achieved 14% of the votes cast in the general election (not as high as in the city itself, and not as high as the Communists, with 22%) in 1995. In simultaneous local elections for a governor, the pro-Government incumbent won, but only after a second round of voting. The gubernatorial elections of December 1999–January 2000 were similarly closely fought, with Col-Gen. Boris Gromov, an ally of Moscow City Mayor Yurii Luzhkov, and a former State Duma deputy and Deputy Minister of Defence, emerging the victor. Relative prosperity kept discontent to a minimum and the region did not experience the problems of wage arrears to the same extent as elsewhere in the Federation—it was among the three regions with the best record for timely payment during 1998.

Economy

Moscow Oblast's gross regional product (GRP) amounted to 97,419,500m. old roubles, or 14,824,100 old roubles per head in 1998. The main industrial centres are at Podolsk, Lyubertsy, Kolomna, Mytishchi, Odintsovo, Noginsk, Serpukhov, Orekhovo-Zuyevo, Shchelkovo and Sergiyev-Posad (formerly Zagorsk). The latter city is an important centre of Russian Orthodoxy, containing Russia's foremost monastery and two medieval cathedrals.

The Oblast's agriculture, which employed just 5.9% of the region's work-force in 1998, consists mainly of animal husbandry and the production of vegetables and grain. Total agricultural production generated 9,618m. roubles in 1998. Moscow Oblast's industry, in which some 24.1% of the working population were engaged in 1998, mainly comprised heavy industry (which accounted for approximately one-third of GRP during the mid-1990s). The region's major industries are mechanical engineering, radio electronics, chemicals, light manufacturing, textiles, ferrous metallurgy, metal working, the manufacture of building materials, wood-working and handicrafts (ceramics, painted and lacquered wooden ornaments). The region's military-industrial complex is also important. Industrial output in 1998 was worth 42,812m. roubles.

The economically active population in the Oblast in 1998 was 2,331,500, of whom 73,900 were registered unemployed. The average monthly wage at that time was 703.3 roubles. There was a regional budgetary deficit of 766m. roubles. Total foreign investment in Moscow Oblast amounted to US $708.70m. in 1998. External trade with the region increased significantly during the late 1990s, amounting to $3,159.3m. in 1998, of which just under 60% represented imports. In 1997 there was a total of 110 joint enterprises operating in the Oblast, of which 78 had foreign partners, particularly from Germany, Italy and the USA.

Directory

Governor: BORIS VSEVOLODOVICH GROMOV; Moskovskaya obl., 103070 Moscow, Staraya pl. 6; tel. (095) 206-60-93, 206-62-78; fax (095) 975-26-42; e-mail amo@obladm.msk.su; internet www.mosreg.ru.

Deputy Governor: MIKHAIL ALEXANDROVICH MEN; tel. (095) 206-65-49; internet www.menn.ru.

First Deputy Governors: VASILII YURIEYEVICH GOLUBEV; tel. (095) 206-02-06; MIKHAIL VIKTOROVICH BABICH; tel. (095) 206-60-95; VALENTINA MATVEY-EVNA DANILINA; tel. (095) 206-66-13.

Chairman of the Regional Duma: ALEKSANDR YEVGENIYEVICH ZHAROV.

Murmansk Oblast

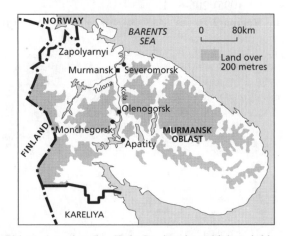

Murmansk Oblast occupies the Kola Peninsula, which neighbours the Barents Sea to the north and the White Sea to the east. It forms part of the Northern Economic Area and the North-Western Federal Okrug. It has international borders with Norway and Finland to the west and the Russian federal subject of Kareliya (Karelia) lies to the south. Much of its territory lies within the Arctic Circle. The major rivers in the Oblast are the Ponoi, the Varguza, the Umba, the Kola, the Niva and the Tulona. It has several major lakes, including the Imandra, Umbozero and Lovozero. The territory of the Oblast covers an area of 144,900 sq km (55,930 sq miles), extending some 400 km (250 miles) from south to north and 500 km from west to east. The climate in the Oblast is severe and changeable, influenced by cold fronts from the Arctic and warm, moist weather from the Atlantic. Its total population was estimated at 1,018,100 at 1 January 1999 (of whom 91.9% inhabited urban areas) and it had a population density, therefore, of 7.0 per sq km. It is divided into five districts and 16 cities. Its administrative centre is at Murmansk, a major seaport and tourist centre, with an estimated population of 381,800 in 1999. Other major cities in the region are Apatity (70,100), Monchegorsk (59,100) and Severomorsk (56,100).

History

Murmansk city was founded in 1916, as a fishing port on the Barents Sea and was known as Romanov-on-Murman (Romanov-na-Murmane) until the following year. After the Bolshevik Revolution of 1917 Murmansk region was a centre of anti-Communist resistance until a peace treaty was signed with the Soviet Government on 13 March 1920. Murmansk Oblast was formed on 28 May 1938.

The development of industry in the region, particularly after the Second World War, resulted in a steady increase in population until the late 1950s. However, heavy industry, particularly the sulphurous emissions from the vast nickel-smelting works on the Kola Peninsula, were accused of causing major environmental damage by the neighbouring Nordic nations (agreement on the monitoring and limiting of this was achieved, to an extent, in mid-1996). The concentration of nuclear reactors on the Kola Peninsula, considered to be the world's most hazardous, is also a major source of concern—in 1993–97 Norway, Finland and the European Bank for Reconstruction and Development committed considerable funds to improving atomic safety in the region.

In the 1990s political allegiances in the Oblast as a whole were fairly evenly balanced, with both the reformist Yabloko movement and the nationalist Liberal Democrats receiving over 10% of the votes cast overall in both the 1995 and, more unusually, the 1999 general elections, although disparity by area was immense. A candidate favoured by Aleksandr Lebed, Yurii Yevdokimov, was elected in the Oblast's first ever direct poll to the governorship, held in November 1996, after a second round; he was re-elected, with 86% of the votes cast, on 26 March 2000. A power-sharing agreement was signed between the federal and regional authorities in November 1997.

Economy

Murmansk Oblast's gross regional product in 1997 stood at 19,017,900m. old roubles, or 18,561,300 old roubles per head. The Oblast's principal industrial centres are at Murmansk, Monchegorsk, Kirovsk, Zapolyarnyi, Apatity and Kandalaksha. There are 891 km of railway track in the region, with Murmansk, Apatity, Olenegorsk and Kandalaksha the main railway junctions, and 2,500 km of paved roads. The port at Murmansk is Russia's sole all-weather Northern port, through which some 12m. metric tons of cargo pass every year. This is also the base for the world's only nuclear ice-breaker fleet, the Northern Fleet, and the scene of the 'Kursk' submarine disaster in August 2000. There is an international airport at Murmansk, which operates flights to destinations in Finland, Norway and Sweden.

The Oblast's agricultural sector, which, owing to its extreme climate, employed just 1.7% of the work-force in 1998, consists mainly of fishing (the region produces 45% of the country's fish supplies) and animal husbandry. The territory is rich in natural resources, including phosphates, iron ore and rare and non-ferrous metals. In 1985 the Shtokmanovsk gas-condensate deposit, the world's largest, was opened on the continental shelf of the Barents Sea. It was hoped that by 2005 the deposit would supply most of the north and north-west of the country. The region produces almost all of Russia's apatites, 43.4% of its nickel, 14.4% of its refined copper and 11.7% of its concentrates of iron. Some 27.2% of the Oblast's working population was engaged in industry in 1998, when the industrial sector generated 17,587m. roubles. Its major industries are the production and enrichment of ores and ferrous metals, ore mining, ferrous metallurgy, the manufacture of building materials and food processing. In 1995 the United Nations Development Programme approved a project to strengthen the economy of the area and encourage sustainable development. In 1999 LUKoil, the domestic petroleum producer, signed an agreement with Governor Yevdokimov, which made Murmansk a base for exploration of the Barents Sea, in association with the natural-gas producer, Gazprom. LUKoil also agreed to accept payment in barter, in addition to money, for supplies of petroleum to the region. The Oblast's major exports, worth US \$770m. in 1998, are non-ferrous metals, fish products and apatite concentrate.

In 1998 the region's economically active population numbered 423,200, of whom some 34,200 (8.1%) were registered unemployed. The average monthly wage in the Oblast was some 1,532.9 roubles. The 1995 budget showed a deficit of 23m. roubles. Foreign investment in 1998 amounted to \$9.58m. The Kola Centre for Business Development, employing Russian and US specialists, opened in Murmansk in 1997. It holds annual conventions bringing together companies from across and outside the Barents Region. At 1 January 1999 there were some 3,900 small businesses operating in the Oblast.

Directory

Head of the Regional Administration (Governor): YURII ALEKSEYEVICH YEVDOKIMOV; Murmanskaya obl., 183006 Murmansk, pr. Lenina 75; tel. (8152) 47-65-40; fax (8152) 47-65-03; e-mail evdokimov@murman.ru; internet gov .murman.ru.

Chairman of the Regional Duma: PAVEL ALEKSANDROVICH SAZHINOV.

Head of the Regional Representation in Moscow: PETR IVANOVICH ZELENOV; tel. (095) 299-46-17.

Head of Murmansk City Administration: OLEG PETROVICH NAIDENOV; Murmanskaya obl., 183006 Murmansk, pr. Lenina 75; tel. (8152) 45-81-60.

Nizhnii Novgorod Oblast

Nizhnii Novgorod (Nizhegorod) Oblast is situated on the middle reaches of the Volga river. It forms part of the Volga-Vyatka Economic Area and the Volga Federal Okrug. Mordoviya and Ryazan lie to the south, Vladimir and Ivanovo to the west, Kostroma to the north-west, Kirov to the north-east and Marii-El and Chuvashiya to the east. Its major rivers are the Volga, the Oka, the Sura and the Vetluga. The terrain in the north of the Oblast is mainly low lying, with numerous forests and extensive swampland. The southern part is characterized by fertile black soil (*chernozem*). The Oblast occupies a total area of 76,900 sq km (29,690 sq miles) and measures some 400 km (250 miles) from south to north and 300 km from east to west. It is divided into 48 administrative districts and 26 cities. At 1 January 1999 it had an estimated total population of 3,687,700 and a population density, therefore, of 48.0 per sq km, making it one of Russia's most densely populated regions. Some 78.3% of the Oblast's inhabitants resided in urban areas. Its administrative centre is at Nizhnii Novgorod (formerly Gorkii), which lies at the confluence of the Volga and Oka rivers. The city is Russia's fourth-largest, with an estimated population of 1,361,500 in 1999. Other major cities include Dzerzhinsk (formerly Chernorech—279,200), Arzamas (110,800), Sarov (formerly Arzamas-16—83,800) and Pavlovo (70,700).

History

Nizhnii Novgorod city was founded in 1221 on the borders of the Russian principalities. With the decline of Tatar power the city was absorbed by the Muscovite state. The Sarov Monastery, one of Russian Orthodoxy's most sacred sites, was founded in the region. Industrialization took place in the late tsarist period. In 1905 mass unrest occurred among peasants and workers in the region, which was one of the first areas of Russia to be seized by the Bolsheviks in late 1917. Nizhnii Novgorod Oblast was formed on 14 January 1929. From 1932 until 1990 the city and region were named Gorkii, and for much of the time the city was 'closed', owing to the importance of the defence industry.

In 1991 the Russian President, Boris Yeltsin, appointed a leading local reformer, Boris Nemtsov, Head of the Regional Administration (Governor). Nemtsov instituted a wide-ranging programme of economic reform, which was widely praised by liberals and by the federal Government. Nemtsov, however, was careful not to be identified with any one party, but secured popular election in December 1995 with 60% of the votes cast. Although occasionally accused of authoritarian tendencies, he was a prominent advocate of democratization and decentralization in the Federation. On 8 June 1996 Nemtsov signed a treaty on the delimitation of powers with the federal Government, giving the Oblast greater budgetary independence and more control over its public property. In April 1997 Nemtsov was appointed to the federal Government; gubernatorial elections were subsequently held, in which the pro-Government candidate, Ivan Sklyarov (former Mayor of Nizhnii Novgorod), defeated Gennadii Khodyrev (who was supported both by the Communists and the Liberal Democrats) after a 'run-off' vote in mid-July. His victory was claimed by the federal Government as an endorsement of President Yeltsin's reform programme and a rejection of political extremism. The Oblast's economic situation subsequently deteriorated somewhat; in late 1998 defence-sector workers took industrial action over wage arrears, and the withholding of funds by the federal Government for the continuing conversion of the Oblast's defence industry. Continued dissatisfaction with economic progress was reported as a major concern prior to the gubernatorial elections held in July 2001. In the second round of voting, held on 30 July, Khodyrev, by this time a Communist member of the State Duma, was elected Governor, gaining almost 60% of the votes cast; Sklyarov gained only 19% of the votes. The rate of participation in the elections was notably low, at around 38%. Following his election, Khodyrev suspended his membership of the Communist Party, apparently in response to allegations that the federal Government was to transfer the administrative centre of the Volga Federal Okrug to another city in the event of the election of a Communist governor. In mid-September the regional Legislative Assembly voted in favour of a proposal made by Khodyrev that he act both as Governor and as Prime Minister of the Oblast.

Economy

The Oblast's gross regional product in 1997 amounted to 52,943,700m. old roubles, or 14,293,700 old roubles per head. Its principal industrial centres are at Nizhnii Novgorod, Dzerzhinsk and Arzamas. Nizhnii Novgorod contains a major river-port, from which it is possible to reach the Baltic, Black, White and Caspian Seas and the Sea of Azov. There are over 12,000 km of paved roads and 1,215 km of railway track in the region. In 1985 an underground railway system opened in Nizhnii Novgorod and in 1994 an international airport was opened, from which Lufthansa (of Germany) operates flights to the German city of Frankfurt. In late 1996 plans to extend the Second Trans-European Corridor to Nizhnii Novgorod were initiated by the Russian Government and the European Union.

Reform of the farming sector in the 1990s involved extensive privatization and investment in rural infrastructure. Agriculture in the region, which employed 8.5%

of the working population in 1998, consists mainly of the production of grain, sugar beets, flax and onions and other vegetables, although the Oblast lacks many areas with the fertile black topsoil typical of the European Plain. Animal husbandry and poultry farming are also important. Total agricultural output in 1998 was worth 5,660m. roubles. As one of the three most industrially developed regions in Russia, however, it was the Oblast's industry that provided some 80% of total production (industrial output generated as much as 43,437m. roubles in 1998). The principal industries of the Oblast include the manufacture of automobiles, mechanical engineering, metal working, ferrous metallurgy, chemicals, petrochemicals, the processing of agricultural and forestry products, the production of building materials and light manufacturing. The Italian automobile company, Fiat, announced a joint venture with the Gorkii automobile plant (GAZ) for the production, sale and servicing of three models of car in Nizhnii Novgorod by 2002. In 1998 some 30.0% of the working population was engaged in industry. During the Soviet period the region was developed as a major military-industrial centre, with the defence sector accounting for around three-quarters of the regional economy, and Gorkii became a 'closed' city. The Oblast also contains the secret city of Arzamas-16 (now Sarov), a centre of nuclear research. In the early 1990s much of Governor Nemtsov's reform programme was aimed at the conversion of as much of the industrial base to civilian use as possible, but this process was made increasingly difficult as federal funds became less readily available. Indeed, defence-industry production in the region increased by 130% in 1999 compared with the previous year, although, overall, the Oblast was among those that dealt most successfully with the transition from military to civilian industry. The Oblast exports principally to Belarus, Belgium, France, Kazakhstan, Switzerland and the United Kingdom and imports goods from Austria, Belarus, the People's Republic of China, Germany, Kazakhstan, the Netherlands, Ukraine and the USA. In 1997 there were 1,153 joint-stock companies in the region, as well as 34 commercial banks and 35 insurance companies. Nizhnii Novgorod Oblast is the only Russian federal subject, other than the two federal cities to have issued Eurobonds.

In 1998 the economically active population numbered 1,643,200, of whom 41,400 (2.5%) were registered unemployed. The average monthly wage in the Oblast was 655.3 roubles. The 1998 budget showed a deficit of 474m. roubles. Foreign investment in the region in that year totalled US $149.70m. Infrastructure for small-business development had resulted in the emergence of 13,900 small businesses, employing 191,500 people, at the end of 1998.

Directory

Head of the Regional Administration (Governor and Prime Minister): GENNADII MAKSIMOVICH KHODYREV; Nizhegorodskaya obl., 603082 Nizhnii Novgorod, Kreml, korp. 1; tel. (8312) 39-13-30; fax (8312) 39-06-29; e-mail official@kreml.nnov.ru; internet www.gubernia.nnov.ru.

Chairman of the Legislative Assembly: ANATOLII ALEKSANDROVICH KOZERADSKII.

Regional Representation in Moscow: tel. (095) 203-77-41.

Head of Nizhnii Novgorod City Administration (Mayor): YURII ISAAKOVICH LEBEDEV; Nizhegorodskaya obl., 603082 Nizhnii Novgorod, Kreml, korp. 5; tel. (8312) 39-15-06; fax (8312) 39-13-02; e-mail lebedev@admgor.nnov.ru; internet www.admcity.nnov.ru.

Novgorod Oblast

Novgorod Oblast is situated in the north-west of the Eastern European Plain, some 500 km (just over 300 miles) north-west of Moscow and 180 km south of St Petersburg. It forms part of the North-Western Economic Area and the North-Western Federal Okrug. Tver Oblast lies to the south-east, Pskov Oblast to the south-west and Leningrad and Vologda Oblasts to the north. The territory's major rivers are the Msta, the Lovat and the outlet of Lake Ilmen, the Volkhov. Just over two-fifths of its territory is forested (either taiga—forested marshland—or mixed forest). The region contains the Valdai state national park. Its territory covers an area of 55,300 sq km (21,350 sq miles) and extends 250 km from south to north and 385 km from west to east. It is divided into 21 administrative districts and 10 cities. At 1 January 1999 the population of the Oblast was estimated at 733,900 and its population density, therefore, was 13.3 per sq km. The urban population was reckoned at 71.1% of the total. The region's administrative centre is at Great (Velikii) Novgorod, which lies on the River Volkhov, some 6 km from Lake Ilmen (it had an estimated population of some 230,600 in 1999).

History

One of the oldest Russian cities, Great Novgorod remained a powerful principality after the dissolution of Kievan Rus and even after the Mongol incursions further to the south-west. In 1478 Ivan III ('the Great'), prince of Muscovy and the first Tsar of All Russia, destroyed the Republic of Novgorod, a polity sometimes used as evidence for the rather spurious claim of a democratic tradition in Russia. Its wealth and importance, based on trade, declined after the foundation of St Petersburg. Novgorod Oblast was formed on 5 July 1944.

In the mid-1990s the region displayed a relatively high level of support for reformists and the centrist supporters of the federal Government of President Boris Yeltsin. The Oblast was permitted gubernatorial elections in December 1995, which were won by the pro-Yeltsin incumbent, Mikhail Prusak. Prusak's regime was characterized by his policy of pragmatic compromise with regard to the economy, spreading the region's economic benefits as widely as possible. Similar policies prevailed in the Duma, the members of which did not bear allegiance to any national political party. Prusak, whose policies were widely admired by national political leaders, including the federal President elected in 2000, Vladimir Putin, was re-elected for a further term of office on 5 September 1999, with approximately 90% of the votes cast. Prusak combined demands for regional governors to be appointed rather than elected with support for the (historical) 'Novgorod model' of federalism, property rights and subsidiarity.

Economy

In 1997 Novgorod Oblast's gross regional product amounted to 7,728,500m. old roubles, equivalent to 10,460,800 old roubles per head. The Oblast's major industrial centres are at Great Novgorod and Staraya Russa (a 19th century resort town famous for its mineral and radon springs and therapeutic mud). The major Moscow–St Petersburg road and rail routes pass through the region. The road system, comprising 8,513 km of paved roads, is the Oblast's major transport network.

The region's agriculture, which employed 12.1% of the work-force in 1998, consists mainly of flax production and animal husbandry. Its major natural resource is timber: in the late 1990s some 2.5m. cu m were produced annually, but it was thought that there was potential for this amount to be expanded by four or five times. In 1998 total agricultural production amounted to a value of 1,638m. roubles. The region's major industries include mechanical engineering, chemicals, wood-working, light manufacturing and the processing of forestry and agricultural products. The industrial sector employed 24.1% of the working population in 1998 and generated 7,678m. roubles. Great Novgorod city is an important tourist destination, attracting around 1m. visitors annually.

The economically active population in 1998 totalled 302,700. Some 12,000 (4.0%) of these were registered unemployed. Those in employment earned an average wage of 895.6 roubles per month. The 1998 regional budget showed a surplus of 56m. roubles. Legislative conditions for foreign investors in Novgorod Oblast were considered to be favourable in the 1990s, owing to a foreign company's exemption from all local taxes until its project returned a profit. In 1998 total foreign investment in the region amounted to US $44.46m., approximately five times as much per head as the average for the Federation. It was reported that, while Russia's GDP per head declined by 2.7% overall between 1995 and 1998, that of Novgorod Oblast increased by 3.8% annually. By the end of 1997 a total of 197 foreign companies were established in the region, accounting for around 40% of Novgorod Oblast's output and more than 83% of exports (compared to figures of 3% and 9%, respectively, for Russia as a whole). The multinational company Cadbury's Schweppes invested $150m. in a chocolate factory in the region, which opened in 1996 and was the largest project the company had been involved in, outside the United Kingdom. At 1 January 1999 there were an estimated 2,700 small businesses registered in the region.

Directory

Head of the Regional Administration (Governor): MIKHAIL MIKHAILOVICH PRUSAK; Novgorodskaya obl., 173005 Novgorod, Sofiiskaya pl. 1; tel. (8162) 13-12-02; internet region.adm.nov.ru.

Chairman of the Regional Duma: ANATOLII ALEKSANDROVICH BOITSEV.

Head of the Regional Representation in Moscow: VLADIMIR NIKOLAYEVICH PODOPRIGORA; fax (095) 200-45-38.

Head of Great (Velikii) Novgorod City Administration (Mayor): ALEKSANDR VLADIMIROVICH KORSUNOV; Novgorodskaya obl., 173007 Novgorod, ul. Bolshaya Vlasevskaya 4; tel. (81622) 7-30-58; fax (8162) 13-25-99; e-mail mayor@ adm.nov.ru; internet www.adm.nov.ru/web.nsf/pages/framesmain.

Novosibirsk Oblast

Novosibirsk Oblast is situated in the south-east of the Western Siberian Plain, at the Ob-Irtysh confluence. The Oblast forms part of the Western Siberian Economic Area and the Siberian Federal Okrug. Its south-western districts lie on the international border with Kazakhstan. The neighbouring federal territories are Omsk Oblast to the west, Tomsk Oblast to the north, Kemerovo Oblast to the east and Altai Krai to the south. The region's major rivers are the Ob and the Om. The Oblast has around 3,000 lakes, the four largest being Chany, Sartlan, Ubinskoye and Uryum. About one-third of its territory is swampland. It occupies a total area of 178,200 sq km (68,800 sq miles) and measures over 400 km (250 miles) from south to north and over 600 km from west to east. It is divided into 30 administrative districts and 14 cities. At 1 January 1999 the Oblast had an estimated population of 2,748,200 (of whom some 74.0% inhabited urban areas) and a population density of 15.4 per sq km. There is a small German community in the Oblast, constituting 2.2% of its population. Just over one-half of the region's inhabitants live in its administrative centre, Novosibirsk, which had an estimated population of 1,402,100 in 1999. Other major cities are Berdsk (86,300), Iskitim (68,300) and Kuibyshev (52,400).

History

The city of Novosibirsk (known as Novonikolayevsk until 1925) was founded in 1893, during the construction of the Trans-Siberian Railway. It became prosperous through its proximity to the Kuznetsk coal basin (Kuzbass). The Oblast, which was officially formed on 28 September 1937, increased in population throughout the Soviet period as it became heavily industrialized, and was a major centre of industrial production during the Second World War.

In October 1993 the Russian President, Boris Yeltsin, dismissed the head of the regional administration, Vitalii Mukha, because of the latter's outspoken criticism of the President. In the same month the Regional Soviet refused to disband itself until new elections were held. In 1994 elections were held to a new representative body. The region was considered part of the 'red belt' of Communist support, and that party dominated the new Regional Soviet after elections in 1994 and 1998. It was constantly in dispute with the regional administration, the head of which was a presidential appointment. In an effort to resolve this power struggle, and in the hope that the incumbent would win, the President permitted the Oblast a gubernatorial election in December 1995. It was the Communist candidate, Mukha, who was returned to his former post by the electorate. Despite his support for the Communists, Mukha failed publicly to endorse any federal presidential candidates prior to the June 1996 elections. He was involved in further disagreements, primarily over unpaid debts, with the federal authorities during the late 1990s. In January 2000 another politician regarded as a left-wing statist, despite his reported closeness to business magnate Boris Berezovskii, was elected as the new regional Governor. Viktor Tolokonskii, who had previously served as Mayor of Novosibirsk City, defeated Ivan Starikov, the federal deputy economy minister, by a margin of just 2% in the second round of voting. Communist support declined somewhat in the regional legislative elections of December 2001, in which the Party secured 12 of the 49 seats available, compared with the 16 seats they had previously held. The Agrarian Party of Russia, an ally of the Communist Party, secured six seats, and the remainder were filled by independent candidates.

Economy

In 1997 Novosibirsk Oblast's gross regional product stood at 39,072,600m. old roubles, or 14,220,100 old roubles per head. Novosibirsk city is a port on the Ob river, and is also the region's principal industrial centre. There are four airports in the region, including Tolmachevo, an international airport.

The Oblast's agriculture employed 12.1% of its working population in 1998 and consists mainly of animal husbandry, fur-animal breeding and the production of grain, vegetables, potatoes and flax. Agriculture generated 6,397m. roubles in 1998, compared to a total of 15,730m. roubles contributed by the industrial sector. Extraction industries involved the production of coal, petroleum, natural gas, peat, marble, limestone and clay. Manufacturing industry includes ferrous and non-ferrous metallurgy, mechanical engineering, metal working, chemicals, electricity generation, food processing, light manufacturing, timber production and the manufacture of building materials. Industry employed some 21.4% of the region's workforce in 1998. In the mid-1990s the region's defence industry was largely converted to civilian use—by 1999 only 15% of the output from the former military-industrial complex was for military purposes.

The Oblast's economically active population totalled 1,060,500 in 1998, of whom 19,400 were registered unemployed. The average monthly wage in the region was 777.7 roubles. The 1998 budget showed a surplus of 61m. roubles. In February 1996 a 'social contract' was agreed between the region's trade unions, administration and employers' union, according to which average civil-service pay was to be maintained at no less than 85% of the average wage in industry and unemployment was to be kept below 6% of the able-bodied population. Some commentators claimed that this arrangement contributed to the problem of the late payment of wages, with arrears provoking teachers into withdrawing their labour in January 1999, for instance. The regional and federal governments each blamed the other, but one pertinent statistic was that 56% of the regional budget was expended on servicing the state debt and only 23% on wages. Foreign investment in Novosibirsk Oblast totalled some US $186.18m. roubles in 1998. At 1 January 1999 there were some 20,400 small businesses registered in the region.

Directory

Head of the Regional Administration (Governor): VIKTOR ALEKSANDROVICH TOLOKONSKII; Novosibirskaya obl., 630011 Novosibirsk 11, Krasnyi pr. 18; tel. (3832) 23-08-62; fax (3832) 23-57-00; internet www.adm.nso.ru

Chairman of the Regional Soviet: VIKTOR VASILIYEVICH LEONOV.

Head of the Regional Representation in Moscow: NINA MIKHAILOVNA PIRYA-ZEVA; tel. (095) 203-27-20.

Head of Novosibirsk City Administration (Mayor): VLADIMIR FILIPPOVICH GORODETSKII; Novosibirskaya obl., 630099 Novosibirsk, Krasnyi pr. 34; tel. (3832) 22-49-32; fax (3832) 22-08-58; e-mail cic@municipal.gcom.ru; internet novosibirsk.sol.ru.

Omsk Oblast

Omsk Oblast is situated in the south of the Western Siberian Plain on the middle reaches of the Irtysh river. Kazakhstan lies to the south. Other federal subjects that neighbour the Oblast are Tyumen to the north-west and Tomsk and Novosibirsk to the east. Omsk forms part of the Western Siberian Economic Area and the Siberian Federal Okrug. Its major rivers are the Irtysh, the Ishim, the Om and the Tara. Much of its territory is marshland and about one-quarter is forested. The total area of Omsk Oblast covers some 139,700 sq km (53,920 sq miles). It measures some 600 km (370 miles) from south to north and 500 km from west to east and is divided into 30 administrative districts and 14 cities. At 1 January 1999 the region had a total population of 2,179,700 and a population density, therefore, of 15.6 per sq km. Of the Oblast's inhabitants, some 67.3% lived in urban areas. Its administrative centre is at Omsk, which lies at the confluence of the Ob and Irtysh rivers and had an estimated population of 1,157,600 in 1999.

History

The city of Omsk was founded as a fortress in 1716. In 1918 it became the seat of Admiral Aleksandr Kolchak's 'all-Russian Government' (in which he was 'Supreme Ruler'). However, Omsk fell to the Bolsheviks in 1919 and Kolchak 'abdicated' in January 1920. Omsk Oblast was formed on 7 December 1934.

In the 1990s the region was generally supportive of the Communists, although the nationalist, anti-government Liberal Democrats also enjoyed a significant level of popularity. The regional Governor, Leonid Polezhayev, although a supporter of the federal state President, Boris Yeltsin, was well respected locally and, in December 1995, was re-elected to his post, one year in advance of the gubernatorial elections scheduled for most territories. In May 1996 the regional and federal administrations signed a treaty on the delimitation of powers. Legislative elections were held in the Oblast on 22 March 1998, in which the Communists and other leftist candidates won 30 assembly seats and a majority of seats on Omsk city council. Polezhayev was re-elected on 5 September 1999, defeating the regional leader and chief ideologist of the Communist Party, Aleksandr Kravets. Nevertheless, Omsk was one of four regions in which the Communist candidate, Gennadii Zyuganov, received a larger proportion of the votes cast than Vladimir Putin in the federal presidential election of March 2000. The Oblast abolished its power-sharing treaty with the Federal Government in mid-2001.

Economy

Omsk Oblast's gross regional product in 1997 amounted to 33,787,100m. old roubles, equivalent to 15,526,500 old roubles per head. Omsk is one of the highest-ranking cities in Russia in terms of industrial output. The region lies on the Trans-Siberian Railway and is a major transport junction, containing 775 km of railway track, 7,511 km of paved roads and 1,252 km of navigable waterways. There are also 580 km of pipeline on its territory, carrying petroleum and petroleum products. There are two airports—a third, international one was under construction in the late 1990s.

The Oblast's soil is the fertile black earth (*chernozem*) characteristic of the region. Its agriculture, which generated a total of 5,999m. roubles in 1998 and employed some 15.3% of the work-force, consists mainly of the production of grain, flax, sunflower seeds and vegetables, and animal husbandry and hunting. The region's mineral reserves include clay, peat and lime. There are also deposits of petroleum and natural gas. Industry employed 19.7% of the work-force in 1998. The Oblast's main industries are electricity generation, fuel, chemical and petrochemical production, processing of forestry products, mechanical engineering, petroleum refining, light manufacturing, the manufacture of building materials and food processing. Total industrial production amounted to a value of 13,366m. roubles in 1998. The Omsk petroleum refinery is one of Russia's largest and most modern and is part of Sibneft, one of the country's newer, vertically integrated petroleum companies. The region's exports primarily comprise chemical, petro-chemical and petroleum products. External trade in 1998 amounted to US $731.3m. The Oblast's main trading partners include the People's Republic of China, Cyprus, Germany, Kazakhstan, Spain, Switzerland and the United Kingdom.

The economically active population in 1998 numbered 937,400, of whom 20,000 were registered unemployed. In 1998 the average wage in the Oblast was 784.6 roubles per month, although in late 1999 the Oblast was named as one of the worst regions in Russia for wages arrears. The 1998 budget showed a deficit of 241m. roubles. Foreign investment in the region in 1998 totalled some $452.21m. and was growing; by 1997 some 500 companies had been established with foreign participation. At 1 January 1999 there was a total of 12,000 small businesses registered in the region.

Directory

Head of the Regional Administration (Governor): LEONID KONSTANTINOVICH POLEZHAYEV; Omskaya obl., 644002 Omsk, ul. Krasnyi Put 1; tel. (3812) 24-14-15; fax (3812) 24-23-72; internet region.omskelecom.ru.

Chairman of the Legislative Assembly: VLADIMIR ALEKSEYEVICH VARNAVSKII.

Regional Representation in Moscow: tel. (095) 921-65-54.

Head of Omsk City Administration (Mayor): YEVGENII IVANOVICH BELOV; Omskaya obl., 644099 Omsk, ul. Gagarina 34; tel. (3812) 24-30-33; fax (3812) 24-49-34.

Orel Oblast

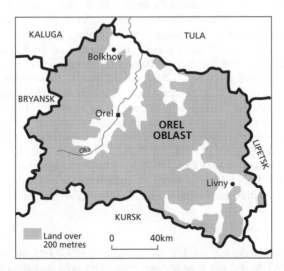

Orel Oblast is situated in the central part of the Eastern European Plain within the Central Russian Highlands. The Oblast forms part of the Central Economic Area and the Central Federal Okrug. It is surrounded by five other oblasts: Kursk (to the south), Bryansk (west), Kaluga (north-west), Tula (north-east) and Lipetsk (east). The Ukrainian border lies some 180 km (just over 100 miles) to the south-west. The Oblast's major river is the Oka, the source of which is found in the south-west. There are a total of around 2,000 rivers, with a combined length of 9,100 km, although none are navigable. Just over 7% of the Oblast's area is forested. The territory of Orel Oblast covers an area of 24,700 sq km (9,530 sq miles) and is divided, for administrative purposes, into 24 districts and seven cities. At 1 January 1999 the estimated population of the Oblast was 902,600 (the smallest of any oblast in Russia) and the population density was 36.5 per sq km. Some 63.0% of the inhabitants of the region lived in urban areas at this time. The Oblast's administrative centre is at Orel, which had an estimated 342,800 inhabitants in 1999. Other major cities are Livny (53,700) and Mtsensk (51,000).

History

Orel was founded as a fortress in 1566. In the 1860s it served as a place of exile for Polish insurgents and was later a detention centre for prisoners on their way to exile in Siberia. Orel Oblast was formed on 27 September 1937. In the newly independent, post-Soviet Russia it formed part of the political 'red belt'. The Communist candidate defeated the pro-Government incumbent in elections for a head of the regional administration in December 1992. The victor was eventually dismissed and the regional legislature dissolved by presidential decree, following their criticism of the federal Government during the constitutional crisis of 1993. A 50-seat Regional Duma was elected in March 1994, but remained dominated by the Communists. That party received 45% of the votes cast in the Oblast during the 1995 elections to the State Duma of the Federal Assembly. Despite the loyalty to President Yeltsin shown by the head of the regional administration, Yegor Stroyev (a former cabinet member and the speaker of the upper house of the Russian parliament, the Federation Council), the greatest show of support in the presidential election of 1996 was for Gennadii Zyuganov, the Communist candidate. Although Orel Oblast was Zyuganov's home region, he received 44.6% of the regional votes cast in the federal presidential election of 26 March 2000, which was 1.2% fewer than the number of votes cast in support of Vladimir Putin. In the regional legislative elections of March 1998 just 11 Communist deputies were elected, compared to the 37 seats won by candidates nominated by initiative groups. Stroyev was re-elected Governor by a convincing majority in October 1997. He was one of the most consistent opponents of power-sharing agreements between regional and federal government, and in September 2000 he advocated closer co-operation with the People's Republic of China and other Asian countries. Following his re-election as Governor in October 2001, Stroyev resigned from the federation Council in early December, in order to comply with legislation introduced by President Putin, which prevented regional governors from holding seats in the Council.

Economy

Orel Oblast's gross regional product amounted to 8,889,700m. old roubles in 1997, equivalent to 9,779,700 old roubles per head. The principal industrial centres in the region are at Orel, Livny and Mtsensk. Orel city lies on the Moscow–Simferopol (Crimea, Ukraine) highway and is an important railway junction. There are 585 km of railway track in the Oblast and 3,869 km of paved roads.

Orel Oblast is an important agricultural trade centre. At 1 January 1999 around 16.7% of the economically active population were engaged in agriculture. Agricultural production consists mainly of grain, sugar beets, sunflower seeds, potatoes, vegetables, hemp and animal husbandry and amounted to a value of 3,049m. roubles in 1998. There are some 17.5m. cu m of timber reserves in the Oblast and a major source of iron ore, at Novoyaltinskoye. However, this and reserves of other minerals in the region have generally not been exploited to their full potential. The industrial sector employed around 22.2% of the economically active population in 1998 and generated some 5,258m. roubles in that year. The Oblast's main industries are mechanical engineering, metallurgy, chemicals, light manufacturing and food processing. It produces around one-third of its electrical-energy requirements, the remainder being supplied by neighbouring Oblasts (Tula, Kursk and Lipetsk).

The region's economically active population numbered 374,000 in 1998, of whom 6,500 (1.7%) were registered unemployed, while those in employment earned an average of 692.8 roubles per month. There was a budgetary deficit of 89m. roubles in that year, while total foreign investment in Orel Oblast amounted to US $33.04m. At 1 January 1999 there were some 2,700 small businesses in operation.

Directory

Head of the Regional Administration (Governor): YEGOR SEMENOVICH STROYEV; Orlovskaya obl., 302021 Orel, pl. Lenina 1; tel. (0862) 41-63-13; fax: (0862) 41-25-30; e-mail post@adm.oryol.ru; internet www.adm.orel.ru.

Chairman of the Regional Duma: NIKOLAI ANDREYEVICH VOLODIN.

Regional Representative in Moscow: MARINA GEORGIYEVNA ROGACHEVA; tel. (095) 915-86-14.

Head of Orel City Administration (Mayor): YEFIM NIKOLAYEVICH VILKOVSKII; Orlovskaya obl., 302000 Orel, Proletarskaya gora 1; tel. (08622) 6-33-12.

Orenburg Oblast

Orenburg Oblast is situated in the foothills of the Southern Urals. It forms part of the Urals Economic Area and the Volga Federal Okrug. Orenburg sprawls along the international border with Kazakhstan, which lies to the south and east. Samara Oblast lies to the west, and in the north-west of the territory there is a short border with the Republic of Tatarstan. The Republic of Bashkortostan and Chelyabinsk Oblast neighbour the north of the Oblast. Orenburg's major river is the Ural. The region occupies a total area of 124,000 sq km (47,860 sq miles) and is divided into 35 districts and 12 cities. At 1 January 1999 the total population of the Oblast was 2,225,500 and the population density was, therefore, 17.9 per sq km. Its administrative centre is at Orenburg, which had an estimated population of 524,200 in 1999. Other major cities are Orsk (275,100), Novotroitsk (109,700) and Buzuluk (87,000).

History

The city of Orenburg originated, as a fortress, in 1743. During the revolutionary period Orenburg was a headquarters of 'White' forces and possession of it was fiercely contested with the Bolsheviks. The city was also a centre of Kazakh (then erroneously known as Kyrgyz) nationalists and was the capital of the Kyrgyz ASSR in 1920–25. The region was then separated from the renamed Kazakh ASSR. Orenburg Oblast was formed on 7 December 1934.

The Communists remained the most popular party into the 1990s, winning 24% of the votes cast in the region at the general election of December 1995. Simultaneous elections to the post of governor, however, were won by the incumbent, Vladimir Yelagin, who was popular, despite expressing support for the Russian President, Boris Yeltsin. He was, however, defeated in the gubernatorial elections of December 1999 by the former chair of the State Duma Committee on Agrarian Issues, Aleksei Chernyshev. The region was considered strategically important, owing to its proximity to Kazakhstan, a fact that led to the signature, on 30 January 1996, of an agreement between the regional administration and President Yeltsin. The accord defined the powers and areas of remit of the federal and local authorities. In regional legislative elections held at the end of March 1998 the Communists maintained their relatively high level of support, winning 16 out of 47 seats.

Economy

The Oblast's gross regional product was 30,594,000m. old roubles in 1997, or 13,729,800 old roubles per head. Its principal industrial centres are at Orenburg, Orsk, Novotroisk, Mednogorsk, Buzuluk, Buguruslan and Gai. Owing to the region's high degree of industrialization, and that of its neighbours, Chelyabinsk and Bashkortostan, there is a high level of pollution in the atmosphere. Around 1m. metric tons of harmful substances are emitted annually, including almost 700 tons of nickel and one ton of lead. In addition, the intensive exploitation of petroleum and gas deposits have caused serious damage to the land—around 60% of arable land is eroded or in danger of suffering erosion.

Agriculture in Orenburg Oblast, which employed some 16.7% of the work-force in 1998, consisted mainly of grain, vegetable and sunflower production and animal husbandry. Agricultural output in the region in 1998 amounted to a value of 4,001m. roubles. The Oblast's major industries are ferrous and non-ferrous metallurgy, mechanical engineering, metal working, natural-gas production, chemicals, light manufacturing, food processing and the production of petroleum, ores, asbestos (the region produces around two-fifths of asbestos produced in Russia) and salt. In 1998 some 22.5% of the working population was engaged in industry, which generated a total of 22,381m. roubles.

The economically active population at this time stood at 929,600, some 9,600 (1.0%) of whom were registered unemployed. The regional average monthly wage was 642.5 roubles. The Oblast's budget for 1998 showed a deficit of 665m. roubles. Total foreign investment in the region in 1998 amounted to some US $130.04m. At 1 January 1999 there were some 7,300 small businesses in operation.

Directory

Head of the Regional Administration (Governor): ANDREI ANDREYEVICH CHERNYSHEV; Orenburgskaya obl., 460015 Orenburg, Dom Sovetov; tel. (3532) 77-69-31; fax (3532) 77-38-02; e-mail office@gov.orb.ru; internet www.orb.ru.

Chairman of the Legislative Assembly: VALERII NIKOLAYEVICH GRIGOREV.

Head of the Regional Representation in Moscow: VYACHESLAV SEMENOVICH RYABOV; tel. (095) 203-59-76.

Head of Orenburg City Administration (Mayor): YURII MISCHERYAKOV; Orenburgskaya obl., 461300 Orenburg, ul. Sovetskaya 60; tel. (3532) 77-50-55; fax (3532) 77-60-58; e-mail glava@admin.orenburg.ru.

Penza Oblast

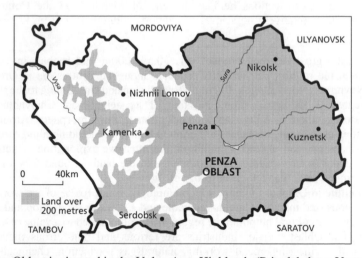

Penza Oblast is situated in the Volga Area Highlands (Privolzhskaya Vozvyshennost), to the south of the Republic of Mordoviya. It forms part of the Volga Economic Area and the Volga Federal Okrug and shares borders with Ulyanovsk Oblast to the east, Saratov Oblast to the south, Tambov Oblast to the south-west and touches Ryazan Oblast to the north-west. Penza's major river is the Sura, a tributary of the River Volga. Its territory covers an area of 43,200 sq km (16,750 sq miles) and is divided into 28 districts and 11 cities. At 1 January 1999 the population of the Oblast was estimated to be 1,541,800 (of whom some 64.5% inhabited urban areas) and its population density, therefore, stood at 35.7 per sq km. Its administrative centre, Penza, had an estimated population of 528,700 in 1999. The region's other major cities are Kuznetsk (99,100) and Zarechnyi (63,900).

History

The city of Penza was founded in 1663 as an outpost on the south-eastern border of the Russian Empire. The region was annexed by Bolshevik forces in late 1917 and remained under the control of the Red Army throughout the period of civil war. Penza Oblast was formed on 4 February 1939. Described as part of the 'red belt' of Communist support in the 1990s, in 1992 the Communist candidate defeated the pro-Yeltsin Governor in elections to head the regional administration. The Communists controlled the Legislative Assembly, elected in 1994 (although the federal presidency replaced the governor), and, almost exactly three years after the gubernatorial elections, gained some 37% of the local vote in the federal general elections of December 1995. Although the presidentially appointed Governor, Anatolii Kovlyagin, was a member of the pro-Government movement, Our Home is Russia, he failed to give public support to the federal Government's reforms during the mid-1990s. On 12 April 1998 a new Governor, Vasilii Bochkarev, was elected. His campaign promoted effective management and pragmatism, and he contested the election as an independent.

Economy

In 1997 Penza's gross regional product was 12,951,200m. old roubles or 8,345,400 per head. The Oblast's principal industrial centres are at Penza and Kuznetsk. There are 829 km (448 miles) of railway track in the region, which include lines linking the territory to central and southern Russia as well as the Far East and Ukraine and Central Asia. Some 5,804 km of paved roads include several major highways.

Around three-quarters of the agricultural land in the Oblast consists of fertile black earth (*chernozem*). Agricultural activity, which employed 16.8% of the workforce in 1998, consists mainly of the production of grain, sugar beets, potatoes, sunflower seeds and hemp. Animal husbandry is also important. Total agricultural production amounted to a value of 3,364m. roubles in 1998. The main industries are mechanical engineering, light manufacturing, the processing of timber and agricultural products and the production of building materials. Industry employed some 25.5% of the working population in 1998 and generated 7,596m. roubles.

In 1998 the economically active population in Penza Oblast numbered 633,700, of whom around 26,500 were registered unemployed. Those in employment earned an average of just 452.5 roubles per month. International trade figures were, similarly, below the average for the Russian Federation, amounting to just US $93.4m. in 1998. The 1998 local budget showed a surplus of 42m. roubles. Foreign investment in the Oblast in 1998 amounted to $5.21m. In 1999 there was a total of 4,600 small businesses registered.

Directory

Head of the Regional Administration (Governor): VASILII KUZMICH BOCH-KAREV; Penzenskaya obl., 440025 Penza, ul. Moskovskaya 75; tel. (8412) 55-04-11; fax (8412) 63-35-75; e-mail pravobl@sura.com.ru; internet www.penza.ru.

Deputy Governor and Chairman of the Government: NIKOLAI SERGEYEVICH OVCHINNIKOV; tel. (8412) 55-11-41.

Chairman of the Legislative Assembly: YURII IVANOVICH VECHKASOV; Penzenskaya obl., 440025 Penza, ul. Moskovskaya 75; tel. (8412) 66-22-66; fax (8412) 55-25-95; e-mail zsobl@sura.com.ru.

Head of the Regional Representation in Moscow: MELS UMRALYEVICH NOS-INOV; 103025 Moscow, ul. Novii Arbat 19; tel. (095) 203-62-45; fax (095) 203-48-93.

Head of Penza City Administration: ALEKSANDR SERAFIMOVICH KALASH-NIKOV; Penzenskaya obl., 440064 Penza, Gorodskaya Duma, pl. Marshala Zhukova 4; tel. (8412) 66-29-85; fax (8412) 6-65-88.

Perm Oblast

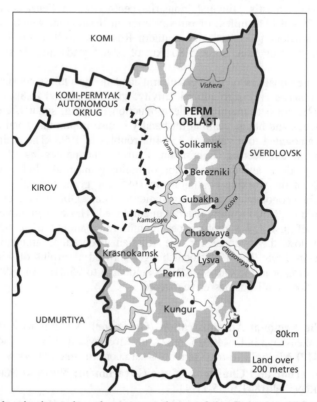

Perm Oblast is situated on the western slopes of the Central and Northern Urals and the eastern edge of the Eastern European Plain. It forms part of the Urals Economic Area and the Volga Federal Okrug. The Komi-Permyak Autonomous Okrug (AOk) forms the north-western part of the Oblast, providing part of the northern border with the Republic of Komi and most of the western border with Kirov Oblast. The Republic of Udmurtiya also lies to the west, the Republic of Bashkortostan to the south and Sverdlovsk Oblast to the east. Apart from the Kama, its major rivers are the Chusovaya, the Kosva and the Vishera. The Kamsk reservoir lies in the centre of the region. Its territory, including that of the autonomous okrug, occupies an area of 160,600 sq km (61,990 sq miles) and extends some 600 km (370 miles) from south to north and 400 km from west to east. It is divided into 36 districts and 25 cities. Its total population at 1 January 1999 was estimated at 2,969,700, some 75.7% of whom inhabited urban areas, and its population density at that time was 18.5 per sq km. The Oblast's administrative centre is at Perm, which had an estimated population of 1,018,100. Other major cities include Berezniki (183,100), Solikamsk (106,400) and Chaikovskii (89,900).

History

Perm city was founded in 1723, with the construction of a copper foundry. Industrial development was such that by the latter part of the 20th century the city extended for some 80 km along the banks of the Kama. Perm Oblast was formed on 3 October 1938. The city was called Molotov in 1940–57 and entry was forbidden to foreigners until 1989. Until 1991 it was the site of the last Soviet camp for political prisoners (Perm-35). In December 1993 there were regional elections for a new parliament, the Legislative Assembly. On 31 May 1996 the regional administration signed a power-sharing treaty with the Russian President, Boris Yeltsin. In December the Governor, Genadii Igumnov, retained his post in direct elections, and pro-reform candidates loyal to Igumnov were successful in gaining an absolute majority of seats in elections to the regional legislature in December 1997. Following the gubernatorial election held in December 2000, Igumnov was replaced as Governor by Yurii Trutnev, hitherto the mayor of Perm City. Elections to a new Legislative Assembly were held in December 2001.

Economy

In 1997 Perm Oblast's gross regional product, including that of the Komi-Permyak Aok, amounted to 51,331,400m. old roubles, or 17,223,100 old roubles per head. Its major industrial centres are at Perm, Berezniki, Solikamsk, Chusovoi, Krasnokamsk and Chaikovskii.

Agriculture in the Oblast, which in 1998 employed just 8.4% of the working population, consists mainly of grain and vegetable production and animal husbandry. In 1998 agricultural production in the entire Oblast was worth 5,909m. roubles, compared to a total in the industrial sector of 41,582m. roubles. The main industries are coal, petroleum, natural-gas, potash and salt production, mechanical engineering, electro-technical industries, chemicals and petrochemicals, petroleum refining, the processing of forestry products, ferrous and non-ferrous metallurgy and printing. Some 26.1% of the working population were engaged in industry in 1998.

The economically active population in 1998 numbered 1,275,300. There were 19,400 registered unemployed at this time. The average wage was above the national average, amounting to 1,000.9 roubles per month. In 1998 there was a budgetary surplus of 156m. roubles for the entire Oblast. Foreign investment in 1998 amounted to US $42.74m., and the region was named as the eighth-highest in Russia, in terms of investment potential late the following year. Perm is also one of 13 'donor regions' in the Federation. In 1998 exports were valued at some $1,525.4m. At 1 January 1999 there were some 9,600 small businesses registered in the region.

Directory

Governor: YURII PETROVICH TRUTNEV; Permskaya obl., 614006 Perm, ul. Kuibysheva 14; tel. (3422) 34-07-90; fax (3422) 34-89-52; internet www.trutnev.ru.

Chairman of the Legislative Assembly: NIKOLAI ANDREYEVICH DEVYATKIN; Permskaya obl., 614006 Perm, ul. Lenina 51; tel. (3422) 12-60-81; fax (3422) 34-27-47; e-mail parliament@perm.ru; internet www.parliament.perm.ru.

Principal Regional Representative in Moscow: NIKOLAI PETROVICH ARTAMONOV; Moscow, ul. Malaya Dmitrovka 3; tel. (095) 299-48-36; fax (095) 209-08-97.

Head of Perm City Administration: ARKADII KAMENEV; Permskaya obl., 614000 Perm, ul. Lenina 15; tel. (3422) 12-44-01; fax (3422) 34-94-11; e-mail permduma @nevod.ru; internet www.gorodperm.ru.

Pskov Oblast

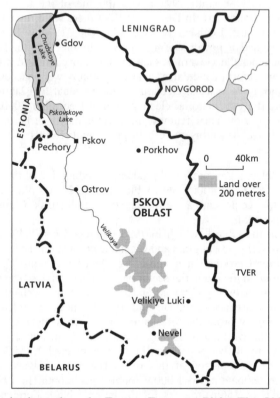

Pskov Oblast is situated on the Eastern European Plain. The Oblast forms part of the North-Western Economic Area and the North-Western Federal Okrug. It has international borders with Belarus to the south and Latvia and Estonia to the west. During the first half of the 1990s Estonia and Latvia questioned Russia's sovereignty of parts of Pskov Oblast and by late 2000 there had still been no formal ratification of the now accepted border delimitations. Smolensk Oblast lies to the south-east, Tver and Novgorod Oblasts to the east and Leningrad Oblast to the north-east. Pskov's major river is the Velikaya and around two-fifths of its territory is forested. On its border with Estonia lie the Pskovskoye (Pihkva) and Chudskoye (Peipsi) lakes. Pskov Oblast covers an area of 55,300 sq km (21,350 sq miles) and measures 380 km (236 miles) from south to north and 260 km from west to east. It is divided into 24 districts and 14 cities. The population at 1 January 1999 was estimated at 811,100 and the population density was, therefore, 14.7 per sq km. Around 94.3% of the territory's inhabitants were ethnic Russian and 66.1% inhabited urban areas in 1999. The Oblast's administrative centre is at Pskov, which had an estimated population of 202,600 in 1999. The second-largest city is Velikiye Luki (116,700).

History

Pskov region was acquired by the Muscovite state in 1510. Previously, in 1242, it was the area in which Russian Prince Aleksandr Nevskii defeated an army of

Teutonic knights, who sought to expand eastwards. The Oblast was formally created on 23 August 1944. Some territory to the south of Lake Pskov was transferred from Estonia to Pskov Oblast in 1945, remaining a cause for dispute between the newly independent Estonia and the Russian Federation in the 1990s. In 1995 Estonia formally renounced any territorial claim, but it remained eager to secure Russian acknowledgement of the 1920 Treaty of Tartu (by which Estonia had been awarded the disputed territory), which would render the Soviet occupation illegal. The Oblast was a traditional bastion of support for the extreme nationalist policies of Vladimir Zhirinovskii; a gubernatorial election was held on 21 October 1996, which was won by Yevgenii Mikhailov, a former Liberal Democrat deputy. The eastward expansion of the North Atlantic Treaty Organization (NATO) was a major issue in the election campaign, as were proposals that the regional Government receive a share of the customs revenue generated by trade with the Baltic States. As Governor, Mikhailov visited both the Chechen Republic of Ichkeriya (Chechnya) and the Serbian province of Kosovo and Metohija in the Federal Republic of Yugoslavia, reflecting the high levels of support for him among the military (accounting for approximately one-10th of the population of Pskov Oblast). Mikhailov was re-elected as Governor in November 2000.

Economy

In 1997 Pskov Oblast's gross regional product amounted to 6,956,400m. old roubles, equivalent to 8,445,300 old roubles per head. The Oblast's principal industrial centres are at Pskov and Velikiye Luki. There are 1,092 km of railway track in the region and 9,925 km of paved roads. There is an airport at Pskov, which was to be upgraded to international status in the late 1990s.

Agricultural activity, which employed 13.2% of the work-force in 1998, consists mainly of animal husbandry and the production of grain, potatoes, vegetables and flax. Total output in the sector amounted to a value of 2,045m. roubles in 1998. The region's major industries are the manufacture of building materials, mechanical engineering, light manufacturing, food processing and wood-working. Industry employed some 22.2% of the working population in 1998 and generated 3,556m. roubles. According to local official sources, industry in the Oblast was completely privatized by 1995, although it was severely affected by the 1998 financial crisis. Owing to its three international borders, there are two representatives of foreign consulates, Latvian and Estonian, operating in the region. Customs duties from the city of Pskov alone amounted to some US $5m. in 1997. None the less, foreign trade in 1998 amounted to just $142.4m. Pskov's main trading partners are Estonia, Finland and Germany.

At 1 January 1999 there were 17,200 registered unemployed in the Oblast, representing some 5.7% of an economically active population of 301,800. In 1995 those in employment earned, on average, 543.7 roubles per month, reflecting Pskov's status as one of the poorer areas of the Russian Federation. There was a budgetary deficit of 28m. roubles. In 1996–98 a federal programme for the socio-economic development of Pskov Oblast invested some 1,500,000m. old roubles in the improvement of agriculture in the region. In 1998 foreign investment in the region totalled $3.67m. At 1 January 1999 there were some 2,700 small businesses in operation.

Directory

Head of the Regional Administration (Governor): YEVGENII EDUARDOVICH MIKHAILOV; 180001 Pskovskaya obl., Pskov, ul. Nekrasova 23; tel. (8122) 16-22-03; fax (8122) 16-03-90; e-mail glava@obladmin.pskov.ru; internet www.pskov.ru.

Chairman of the Regional Assembly: YURII ANISIMOVICH SHCHMATOV; tel. (8122) 16-24-44.

Regional Representation in Moscow: tel. (095) 234-96-31.

Head of Pskov City Administration (Mayor): MIKHAIL YAKOVLEVICH KHO-RONEN; Pskovskaya obl., 180000 Pskov, ul. Nekrasova 22; tel. (8122) 16-26-67.

Rostov Oblast

Rostov Oblast is situated in the south of the Eastern European Plain, in the North Caucasus Economic Area and the Southern Federal Okrug. It lies on the Taganrog Gulf of the Sea of Azov. Krasnodar and Stavropol Krais lie to the south and the Republic of Kalmykiya to the east. Volgograd Oblast lies to the north-east and Voronezh Oblast to the north-west. The region has an international border with Ukraine to the west. Its major rivers are the Don and the Severnii Donets. The Volga–Don Canal runs through its territory. Rostov Oblast covers an area of 100,800 sq km (38,910 sq miles) and consists of 43 districts and 23 cities. The region is densely populated, having an estimated 4,367,900 inhabitants at 1 January 1999, giving it a population density of 43.3 per sq km. Some 66.1% of the region's inhabitants resided in urban areas. Its administrative centre is at Rostov-on-Don (Rostov-na-Donu), which had an estimated population of 1,005,800. Other major cities are Taganrog (286,400), Shakhty (222,800), Novocherkassk (185,400), Volgo-donsk (180,200) and Novoshakhtinsk (102,200).

History

Rostov-on-Don was established as a city in 1796. It became an important grain-exporting centre in the 19th century, and increased in economic importance after the completion of the Volga–Don Canal. Rostov Oblast was formed on 13 September 1937. The region became heavily industrialized after 1946 and, therefore, considerably increased in population.

In the mid-1990s the liberal Yabloko bloc enjoyed its highest level of support outside the two federal cities and Kamchatka, and it managed to gain over 15% of the votes cast in some parts of the Oblast in the federal parliamentary elections of December 1999. The regional Government signed a power-sharing treaty with the federal authorities in June 1996. The Oblast directly elected the incumbent,

Vladimir Chub, as Governor on 29 September. In regional legislative elections held on 29 March 1998 the Communists gained just nine out of 45 seats to the Legislative Assembly, the majority being won by local business leaders. The incumbent Governor was re-elected for a further term of office on 23 September 2001, as the candidate of the Yedinstvo (Unity) party, receiving 78% of the votes cast.

Economy

In 1997 Rostov Oblast's gross regional product stood at 35,062,000m. old roubles, or 7,947,100 old roubles per head. The Oblast's main industrial centres are at Rostov-on-Don, Taganrog, Novocherkassk, Shakhty, Kamensk-Shakhtinskii, Novo-shakhtinsk and Volgodonsk. Its ports are Rostov-on-Don (connected by shipping routes to 16 countries) and Ust-Donetskii, both of which are river-ports.

The Oblast is one of the major grain-producing regions in Russia, with agricultural land comprising some 85% of its territory. The production of sunflower seeds, coriander, mustard, vegetables and cucurbits (gourds and melons) is also important, as are viniculture and horticulture. The sector employed some 14.1% of the working population in 1998. Total agricultural output amounted to a value of 10,600m. roubles in that year. The Oblast is situated in the eastern Donbass coal-mining region and contains some 6,500m. metric tons of coal, as well as significant deposits of anthracite. It is also rich in natural gas, reserves of which are estimated at 54,000m. cu m. Its other principal industry is mechanical engineering: Rostov-on-Don contained some 50 machine-building plants. In the early 1990s the industrial association, Rostselmash, produced 70% of all grain combines in Russia (although the quantity produced in 1999 was less than one-50th of that achieved 15 years earlier) and Krasnyi Aksai manufactured 50% of all tractor-mounted cultivators (although from 1997 it specialized in the assembly of automobiles for Daewoo of the Republic of Korea); in Novocherkassk, Krasnyi Kotelshchik produced 70% of Russia's electric locomotives, and is now a joint-stock company; and 60% of the country's steam boilers were made in Taganrog. Food processing, light manufacturing, chemicals and ferrous and non-ferrous metallurgy are also major economic activities.

In 1998 some 21.6% of the Oblast's working population were employed in industry, and industrial production was worth 21,762m. roubles. In 1998 the economically active population numbered 1,752,200, of whom some 26,000 were unemployed. Those in employment earned an average monthly wage of 718.3 roubles. The 1998 budget showed a surplus of 72m. roubles. Total foreign investment in the region amounted to US $16.79m. in 1998. At 1 January 1999 there were some 27,300 small businesses operating in the Oblast.

Directory

Head of the Regional Administration (Governor): VLADIMIR FEDOROVICH CHUB; Rostovskaya obl., 344050 Rostov-on-Don, ul. Sotsialisticheskaya 112; tel. (8632) 44-18-10; fax (8632) 44-12-24.

Chairman of the Regional Government: VIKTOR NIKOLAYEVICH ANPILOGOV; tel. (8632) 66-61-44; fax (8632) 65-36-26.

Chairman of the Legislative Assembly: ALEKSANDR VASILIYEVICH POPOV; tel. (8632) 65-04-26.

Regional Representation in Moscow: tel. (095) 203-94-71; fax (095) 203-89-58.

Head of Rostov-on-Don City Administration (Mayor): MIKHAIL ANATOLIYE-

VICH CHERNYSHEV; Rostovskaya obl., 344007 Rostov-on-Don, ul. Bolshaya Sado-
vaya 47; tel. (8632) 44-13-23; fax (8632) 66-62-62; internet www.rostov-gorod.ru.

Ryazan Oblast

Ryazan Oblast is situated in the central part of the Eastern European Plain and forms part of the Central Economic Area and the Central Federal Okrug. It lies some 192 km (just under 120 miles) south-east of Moscow. The other neighbouring regions are Vladimir (to the north), Nizhnii Novgorod (north-east), the Republic of Mordoviya (east), Penza (south-east), Tambov and Lipetsk (south), and Tula (west). There are some 2,800 lakes in the region (the largest being the Velikoye and the Dubovoye) and its major rivers are the Oka and the Don and their tributaries. The Oka extends 489 km (304 miles) along the borders with Moscow and Vladimir Oblasts. Its catchment area amounts to over 95% of the region's territory, which occupies an area of 39,600 sq km (15,290 sq miles) and is divided into 25 administrative districts and 12 cities. At 1 January 1999 its population was estimated at 1,298,300 (of whom some 68.7% inhabited urban areas) and its population density was 32.8 per sq km.

History

Ryazan city was an early Orthodox Christian bishopric. The Oblast was formed on 26 September 1937. In the 1990s it was described as part of the 'red belt' of Communist support across the Russian heartland. With 31% of the Oblast's participating electorate voting for the Communists in the general election of December 1995, this party was also able to dominate the Regional Duma. In October 1998 the incumbent Governor was removed by the federal Government; the acting Governor, Igor Ivlev, lost the subsequent election (held in December) to the Communist candidate, Vyacheslav Lyubimov. The region co-operated in a federal experiment with jury trials from 1993, but they were abolished, apparently for financial reasons, in December 1998. In April 1999, at the time of the aerial bombardment of Serbia, the Federal Republic of Yugoslavia, by NATO forces, Lyubimov was one of the leading supporters in the Federation Council of the expansion of the Russia–Belarus Union to include Yugoslavia. Lyubimov was re-elected as Governor in December 2000.

Economy

In 1997 Ryazan Oblast's gross regional product amounted to 14,404,600m. old roubles, or 10,981,600 per head. The Oblast's industrial centres are at Ryazan, Skopin, Kasimov and Sasovo.

Its warm, moist climate is conducive to agriculture, which consists mainly of grain and vegetable production, horticulture and animal husbandry, and employed 12.6% of the work-force in 1998. Total agricultural production amounted to a value of 5,426m. roubles in that year. There are 162.8m. cu m of timber reserves in the region and substantial reserves of brown coal and peat, estimated at around 302m. metric tons and 222m. tons, respectively. Deposits of peat are concentrated in the north, the east and the south-west of the region. The Oblast's main industries are mechanical engineering, petroleum processing, chemicals, the production of building materials, light manufacturing and food processing. In 1998 some 27.5% of the working population was engaged in industry, which generated a total of 10,844m. roubles.

The economically active population numbered 520,200 at this time. Some 12,600 of these were registered unemployed, while those in employment earned, on average, 568.4 roubles per month. The 1998 budget showed a surplus of 51m. roubles. Foreign investment in the region totalled US $4.87m. in 1998, while at 1 January 1999 there were some 6,400 small businesses registered on its territory.

Directory

Head of the Regional Administration (Governor): VYACHESLAV NIKOLAYE-VICH LYUBIMOV; Ryazanskaya obl., 390000 Ryazan, ul. Lenina 30; tel. (0912) 27-45-07; fax (0912) 44-25-68; e-mail postmaster@adm1.ryazan.su; internet www.gov.ryazan.ru.

Chairman of the Regional Duma: VLADIMIR NIKOLAYEVICH FEDOTKIN.

Regional Representation in Moscow: tel. (095) 203-61-78.

Head of Ryazan City Administration (Mayor): PAVEL DMITRIYEVICH MAM-ATOV; Ryazanskaya obl., 390000 Ryazan, ul. Radishcheva 28; tel. (0912) 77-34-02; fax (0912) 24-05-70; e-mail glava@cityadmin.ryazan.ru.

Sakhalin Oblast

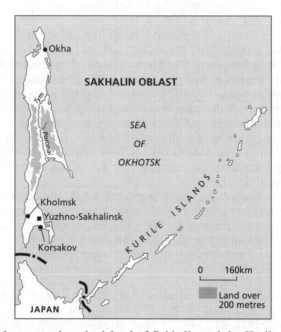

Sakhalin Oblast comprises the island of Sakhalin and the Kurile (Kuril) Islands in the Pacific Ocean. It forms part of the Far Eastern Economic Area and the Far Eastern Federal Okrug. The island of Sakhalin lies off the coast of Khabarovsk Krai, separated from the mainland by the Tatar Strait. Eastward lie the Kurile Islands (annexed by the USSR in 1945, but claimed by Japan), which are an archipelago of some 56 islands extending from the Kamchatka Peninsula in the north-east, to Hokkaido Island (Japan) in the south-west. Sakhalin Island is 942 km (just over 580 miles) in length and contains two parallel mountain ranges running north to south and separated by a central valley. The highest peaks on the island, both belonging to the eastern range of mountains, are Lopatin (1,609 m or 5,281 feet) and Nevelskogo (1,397 m). The north-west coast of the island is marshland, and much of its area is forested. The Kurile Islands are actively volcanic and contain many hot springs. There are some 60,000 rivers on Sakhalin Island, the major ones being the Poronai (350 km in length), the Tym (330 km), the Viakhtu (131 km) and the Lyutoga (130 km), all of which are frozen during the winter months, December–April/May. The Kurile Islands contain around 4,000 rivers and streams and the largest waterfall in the Russian Federation, Ilya Muromets. Sakhalin Oblast covers a total area of 87,100 sq km (33,620 sq miles) and is divided into 17 districts and 18 cities. The estimated total population at 1 January 1999 was 608,500, the region's population density being 7.0 per sq km. Some 86.5% of the region's total population at that time was found to reside in urban areas. The population of the Oblast was reported to have declined by some 110,000, or 15%, between 1991 and 1998, largely reflecting migration from the region as a result of the decline of its industrial base. The Oblast's administrative centre is at Yuzhno-

Sakhalinsk, which had an estimated population of 176,900. Other cities include Kholmsk (40,900) and Korsakov (39,100). All these settlements are on Sakhalin Island.

History

Sakhalin was traditionally known as a place of exile for political opponents to the tsars. It was originally inhabited by the indigenous Gilyak people; Russians first reached the island in 1644, although the region was assumed to be a peninsula until the early 19th century. The island was conquered by the Japanese at the end of the 18th century, but Russia established a military base at Korsakov in 1853. Joint control of the island followed until 1875, when it was granted to Russia in exchange for the Kurile Islands. Karafuto, the southern part of the island, was won by Japan during the Russo-Japanese War (1904–05), but the entire island was ceded to the USSR in 1945. The Kurile Islands, which were discovered for Europeans by the Dutch navigator, Martin de Vries, in 1634, were divided between Japan and Russia in the 18th century and ruled jointly until 1875. Russia occupied the islands in 1945 and assumed full control in 1947. The southern Kuriles remained disputed between Japan and the newly independent Russia. Sakhalin Oblast had been formed on 20 October 1932 as part of Khabarovsk Krai. It became a separate administrative unit in 1947, when the island was united with the Kuriles.

On 16 October 1993 the head of the regional administration disbanded the Regional Soviet; a Regional Duma was elected in its place. In May 1995 a major earthquake, one of the largest ever to occur in Russia, destroyed the town of Neftegorsk in the north of the region, and claimed an estimated 2,000 lives. In May 1996 the then Russian President, Boris Yeltsin, signed a power-sharing treaty with the regional Government. The gubernatorial elections of 21 October 1996 and 22 October 2000 were won by the incumbent, Igor Farkhutdinov. In 1998 Russia and Japan agreed to attempt to settle their territorial dispute by 2000. However, in September 2000 President Vladimir Putin rejected continuing Japanese demands for the sovereignty of four of the Southern Kuriles (known as the 'Northern Territory' to Japan), and the continuing dispute meant that the two countries had still to sign a peace treaty officially to mark the end of the Second World War. In December 1998 the Oblast authorities signed a friendship and economic co-operation accord with the Japanese province of Hokkaido, and a further agreement was signed in January 2000. A special economic zone in the Southern Kuriles was established in the late 1990s, in order to encourage foreign investment.

Economy

In 1997 Sakhalin Oblast's gross regional product amounted to 13,368,800m. old roubles, or 21,335,500 old roubles per head. The Oblast's principal industrial centres are at Yuzhno-Sakhalinsk, Kholmsk, Okha (the administrative centre of the petroleum-producing region), Nevelsk, Dolinsk and Poronaisk. Its ports are Kholmsk (from where the Kholmsk-Vanino ferry connects Sakhalin Island with the mainland) and Korsakov. There are flights to Moscow, Khabarovsk, Vladivostok, Petropavlovsk-Kamchatskii and Novosibirsk and international services to Alaska, the USA, the Republic of Korea (South Korea) and Japan.

Agriculture in the region is minimal, owing to its unfavourable climatic conditions—agricultural land occupies only 1% of its territory. It employed just 4.6% of its working population and consists mainly of potato and vegetable production, animal husbandry and fur farming. Total agricultural production amounted to a value of 1,298m. roubles in 1998. Annual catches of fish and other marine life amount to around 400,000 metric tons. Fishing and fish processing is the major traditional industry, accounting for two-fifths of industrial production. The entire industrial sector employed some 25.3% of the region's work-force and generated 6,236m. roubles in 1998. There is some extraction of coal and, increasingly, petroleum and natural gas in and to the north of Sakhalin Island. Some petroleum is piped for refining to a plant in Komsomolsk-na-Amure (Khabarovsk Krai), although from 1994 the territory had its own refinery, with a capacity of some 200,000 tons per year. Coal was the territory's primary source of energy, but in the late 1990s a gradual conversion to gas was initiated. The further development of Sakhalin's rich hydrocarbons reserves was the subject of negotiations between a number of Russian and foreign companies in the mid-1990s. By 1999 four major consortia had been formed. Sakhalin-1, a project to produce petroleum on the continental shelf of Sakhalin Island, comprised Rosneft (of which Sakhalinmorneftegas is a local subsidiary and which had a 40% stake), Exxon (of the USA) and Sodeco (of Japan), both of which had a 30% stake. Sakhalin-2, two fields containing an estimated 1,000m. barrels of petroleum and 408,000m. cu m of natural gas, was run by Sakhalin Energy Investment, comprising Mitsui and Mitsubishi (of Japan), Marathon (of the USA) and the Anglo-Dutch company, Shell. Sakhalin-3, backed by Mobil and Texaco (of the USA), was seeking to develop what was potentially the largest field on the Sakhalin shelf, containing an estimated 320m. tons of recoverable reserves. It was hoped that the proceeds from the ongoing projects would help to alleviate the high level of poverty in the region. In July 1998 the federal premier, Sergei Kiriyenko, signed a resolution extending a federal programme on social and economic development of the Oblast, to be financed by proceeds from Sakhalin-1 and Sakhalin-2, until 2005. In 2001 Exxon Mobil was undertaking a project to examine the feasibility of constructing a pipeline to export petroleum and gas from Sakhalin to Japan.

In 1998 the Oblast's economically active population totalled 265,300, of whom 18,600 were unemployed. The average monthly wage in the region amounted to some 1,112.5 roubles. The 1998 budget showed a surplus of 92m. roubles. In 1998 exports from the Oblast were valued at US $211m. and imports to the Oblast were worth $474m. Total foreign investment in the region was equivalent to some $136.10m. in 1998. At 1 January 1999 there was a total of 4,100 small businesses.

Directory

Governor: IGOR PAVLOVICH FARKHUTDINOV; Sakhalinskaya obl., 693011 Yuzhno-Sakhalinsk, Kommunisticheskii pr. 39; tel. (4242) 43-14-02; fax (4242) 23-60-81; internet www.adm.sakhalin.ru.

Chairman of the Regional Duma: BORIS NIKITOVICH TRETYAK; tel. (4242) 42-15-75.

Regional Representation in Moscow: tel. (095) 973-19-95.

Head of Yuzhno-Sakhalinsk City Administration (Mayor): FEDOR ILYCH SIDORENKO; Sakhalinskaya obl., Yuzhno-Sakhalinsk, ul. Lenina 173; tel. (4242) 72-25-11; fax (4242) 23-00-06.

Samara Oblast

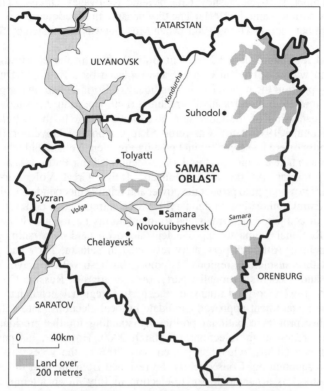

Samara Oblast (known as Kuibyshev between 1935 and 1991) is situated in the south-east of the Eastern European Plain on the middle reaches of the Volga river. It forms part of the Volga Economic Area and the Volga Federal Okrug. Its southernmost tip lies on the border with Kazakhstan. Saratov lies to the south-west, Ulyanovsk to the west, Tatarstan to the north and Orenburg to the east. The Volga snakes through the west of the territory. The Oblast's other major rivers are the Samara, the Sok, the Kunel, the Bolshoi Igruz and the Kondurcha. The region occupies an area of 53,600 sq km (20,690 sq miles). It is divided into 27 districts and 10 cities. Owing to its proximity to the Kazakh desert, the southernmost part of the Oblast is prone to drought. The region is densely populated, with an estimated population of 3,305,300 at 1 January 1999 (of whom 80.5% inhabited urban areas) and a population density, therefore, of 61.7 per sq km. The majority of the population, 83.4%, was ethnic Russian. Mordovians and Chuvash comprised 3.6% apiece, 3.5% were Tatars and 2.5% were Ukrainians. The administrative centre is at Samara (formerly Kuibyshev), which had an estimated 1,170,800 inhabitants in 1999. The region's other major towns are Tolyatti (719,100), Syzran (187,000) and Novokuibyshevsk (115,900).

History

Samara city was founded in 1586 as a fortress. It increased in prosperity after the construction of the railways in the late 19th century. Samara Oblast was founded on 14 May 1928, as the Middle Volga (Sredne-Volzhskaya) Oblast. In 1929 it was upgraded to the status of a krai, which was renamed Kuibyshev Krai in 1935. On 5 December 1936 Kuibyshev Krai became Kuibyshev Oblast. (The territory assumed its current name in 1991.) The city became the headquarters of the Soviet Government between 1941 and 1943, when Moscow was threatened by the German invasion.

The local legislature defied President Boris Yeltsin in the constitutional crisis of 1993 and was dissolved in October and replaced by a Regional Duma. There was more support in the region for the candidacy of Boris Yeltsin in the presidential election of mid-1996 than for his Communist rival, Gennadii Zyuganov, owing to the strong leadership of the Governor, Konstantin Titov. In the popular election held in December 1996 Titov was returned to the post of Governor. Titov, who was reportedly offered a senior cabinet post by President Yeltsin and who expressed a willingness to take a senior post under President Vladimir Putin, was an ambitious economic reformer. As the informal head of the 'Great Volga' interregional association, Titov sought to protect the power and relative independence of governors from the central authorities. In January 1998 he introduced a policy to defer the tax arrears of companies that managed to maintain tax payments. He also strongly urged the Regional Duma to approve legislation on land ownership, which was achieved in June. Although personally respected in Samara, Titov had to contend not only with a suspicious regional assembly, but also with a mayor of Samara from Aleksandr Lebed's nationalist party, the Congress of Russian Communities. On 13 July 1997 Georgii Limanskii, the party's regional head, had decisively defeated the government-approved candidate in local elections. Titov attempted to gain a higher profile in national politics by standing for the presidency of the Russian Federation at the elections of March 2000. However, his performance, even in Samara Oblast, where he gained only 20% of the votes cast and came third, was disappointing. Consequently, he resigned from the post of Governor in April, but stood as a candidate for re-election in July, in an attempt to confirm his legitimacy; he was re-elected with 53% of the votes cast. In local legislative elections, held in December 2001, supporters of Limanskii increased their representation threefold, to hold about one-third of the seats in the Regional Duma.

Economy

Economic growth in Samara Oblast during 1997 was 6%, in real terms, compared to around 1% in Russia as a whole. In 1997 its gross regional product amounted to 72,603,400m. old roubles, or 21,935,200 old roubles per head. The Oblast's major industrial centres are at Samara, Tolyatti, Syzran and Novokuibyshevsk.

Agriculture in the Oblast, which employed just 7.4% of the working population in 1998, consists mainly of animal husbandry and the production of grain, sugar beets and sunflower seeds. Total agricultural production in 1998 was worth 6,530m. roubles. There are some reserves of petroleum and natural gas in the region. Its main industries are petroleum production and refining, food processing, mechanical engineering, metal working, petrochemicals and the manufacture of building materials. The Oblast's principal company is Avtovaz, manufacturer of the Lada automobile, which accounts for around 43% of industrial output in the region and is the largest automobile manufacturer in Russia. In that year some 29.8% of the region's work-force was engaged in industry, which generated 57,317m. roubles.

In 1998 the economically active population numbered 1,443,500, of whom

65,700 were unemployed. Those in employment earned an average wage of 1,163.7 roubles per month, well above the national average. In 1998 the rate of spending per head in the Oblast was one of the highest in the Federation, and the 1998 budget showed a surplus of 79m. roubles. Moreover, in December 1998 Samara was one of the three regions with the best record on the timely payment of wages (most Russian regions owed significant arrears). In December 2001, however, the Governor, Konstantin Titov, issued a decree introducing state control over the finances of Samara city and two rural districts of the Oblast, the debts of which exceeded 10% of their total consolidated budgets. In 1998 total foreign investment in the region amounted to US $192.86m. By August 1998 some 300 foreign companies, including some of the world's largest, such as Coca-Cola and General Motors of the USA and Nestle of Switzerland, had invested in the region, attracted by its technologically advanced industrial base, reputation for creditworthiness and well-educated, urbanized labour force. Foreign trade in the region amounted to some $2,209.4m. in 1998. At 1 January 1999 there were some 21,700 small businesses in operation.

Directory

Governor: KONSTANTIN ALEKSEYEVICH TITOV; Samarskaya obl., 443006 Samara, ul. Molodogvardeiskaya 210; tel. (8462) 32-22-68; fax (8462) 32-13-40; e-mail governor@samara.ru; internet www.adm.samara.ru.

Chairman of the Regional Duma: (vacant); Samarskaya obl., 443110 Samara, ul. Molodogvardeiskaya 187; tel. (8462) 32-75-06; fax (8462) 42-38-08; e-mail samgd@duma.sam-reg.ru; internet www.duma.sam-reg.ru.

Regional Representation in Moscow: tel. (095) 973-19-95.

Head of Samara City Administration (Mayor): GEORGII SERGEYEVICH LIMAN-SKII; Samarskaya obl., 443010 Samara, ul. Kuibysheva 135/137; tel. (8462) 32-20-68; fax (8462) 33-67-41; e-mail city@vis.infotel.ru.

Saratov Oblast

Saratov Oblast is situated in the south-east of the Eastern European Plain. It forms part of the Volga Economic Area and the Volga Federal Okrug. On the border with Kazakhstan (to the south-east), the federal territories adjacent to Saratov are Volgograd (south), Voronezh and Tambov (west), and Penza, Ulyanovsk and Samara (north). Its main river is the Volga. The west of the Oblast (beyond the left bank of the Volga) is mountainous, the east low-lying. The region's territory occupies an area of 100,200 sq km (38,680 sq miles). It comprises 38 districts and 17 cities. At 1 January 1999 it had a total of 2,719,000 inhabitants (of whom some 73.2% inhabited urban areas) and a population density of 27.1 per sq km. Its administrative centre is at Saratov, a major river-port on the Volga, with an estimated population of 878,800 in 1999. Other major cities were Balakovo (208,200), Engels (189,900) and Balashov (95,300).

History

Saratov city was founded in 1590 as a fortress city, to protect against nomad raids on the Volga trade route. Strategically placed on the Trans-Siberian Railway, it was seized by Bolshevik forces in late 1917 and remained under Communist control, despite attacks by the 'White' forces under Adm. Aleksandr Kolchak during 1918 and 1919. The Oblast was formed in 1936, having formed part of a Saratov Krai from 1934. The region became heavily industrialized in the Soviet period, before the Second World War.

Saratov remained an important centre for the military and for Communist support into the 1990s. However, in September 1996 Dmitrii Ayatskov, a presidential appointment, retained his post heading the regional administration, having secured 81.35% of the popular vote to become the first popularly elected regional leader in Russia. He was re-elected for a further term in April 2000, amid accusations of electoral manipulation, which removed all other serious candidates from the contest, and press censorship. As Governor, Ayatskov carried out extensive reform to the region's agro-industrial sector, which culminated, in November 1997, in the

226

passing in the Oblast of the first law in Russia to provide for the purchase and sale of agricultural land. The law greatly diminished the power base of Communists and nationalists in the region and by April 1998 land sales had already generated 3m. roubles for the regional economy. A series of bilateral trade agreements signed with the Mayor of Moscow, Yurii Luzhkov, in August 1996, also benefited the economy of Saratov Oblast.

Economy

Saratov Oblast's gross regional product in 1997 totalled 31,767,600m. old roubles, equivalent to 11,654,800 old roubles per head. The region's major industrial centres are at Saratov, Engels and Balakovo. The Oblast was the major Soviet/Russian arsenal for chemical weapons, provoking some local concern. In January 1996 it was announced that chemical weapons stored near the village of Gornyi would be destroyed, in accordance with international agreements. In November 2001 it was reported that some 2,000m. roubles was to be allocated for the construction of a chemical weapons-processing plant in 2002.

Its agriculture, which employed some 18.2% of the working population in 1998, consists primarily of animal husbandry and the production of grain (the Oblast is one of Russia's major producers of wheat), sunflower seeds and sugar beets. Total agricultural production in 1998 amounted to a value of 5,471m. roubles. Its main industries are mechanical engineering, petroleum refining, chemicals, the manufacture of building materials, wood-working, light manufacturing, food processing and the production of petroleum and natural gas. In the late 1990s the region produced over 30% of the cement and 20% of the mineral fertilizer produced in the Volga Economic Area. Total industrial production was worth 17,562m. roubles in 1998, and some 20.7% of the work-force was engaged in industry at that time. Foreign-trade turnover in 1998 amounted to US $448m.

In 1998 the region's economically active population numbered 1,163,700; some 20,300 (1.7%) of these were registered unemployed, while those in employment earned an average wage of 645.7 roubles per month. The regional budget for 1998 showed a surplus of 29m. roubles. Foreign investment in the Oblast amounted to $37.31m. In 1997 there were around 100 joint enterprises registered in the region, involving eight different countries. At 1 January 1999 there were some 13,100 small businesses in operation in the region.

Directory

Head of the Regional Administration (Governor): DMITRII FEDOROVICH AYAT-SKOV; Saratovskaya obl., 410042 Saratov, ul. Moskovskaya 72; tel. (8452) 72-20-86; fax (8452) 72-52-54; internet www.gov.saratov.ru.

Chairman of the Regional Duma: ALEKSANDR PETROVICH KHARITONOV; internet www.srd.ru.

Regional Representation in Moscow: tel. (095) 917-05-42.

Head of Saratov City Administration (Mayor): YURII NIKOLAYEVICH AKSENENKO; Saratovskaya obl., 410600 Saratov, ul. Pervomaiskaya 78; tel. (8452) 24-02-49; fax (8452) 24-84-44; e-mail mayor@admsaratov.ru; internet www .admsaratov.ru.

Smolensk Oblast

Smolensk Oblast is situated in the central part of the Eastern European Plain on the upper reaches of the Dnepr (Dnieper). It forms part of the Central Economic Area and the Central Federal Okrug. The former Soviet state of Belarus lies to the south-west, while neighbouring Russian territories are Pskov and Tver Oblasts to the north, Moscow in the north-east and Kaluga and Bryansk to the south-east. The Oblast covers an area of 49,800 sq km (19,220 sq miles) and extends for some 280 km (175 miles) from south to north and 250 km from west to east. It is divided into 25 districts and 15 cities. The estimated population was 1,142,700 at 1 January 1999 and the population density 22.9 per sq km. Some 70.4% of the region's inhabitants lived in urban areas at this time. Its administrative centre is at Smolensk, a river-port on the Dnepr with an estimated 352,900 inhabitants in 1999. The Oblast's other major cities are Vyazma (60,200), Roslavl (59,300), Yartsevo (57,400) and Safonovo (53,600).

History

Smolensk city was first documented in 863, as the chief settlement of the Krivichi, a Slavic tribe. It became an Orthodox Christian bishopric in 1128. It achieved prosperity during the 14th and 15th centuries as it was situated on one of the Hanseatic trade routes. Smolensk was the site of a major battle in 1812, between the Russian imperial army and the forces of Emperor Napoleon I of France, who subsequently went on to occupy the city of Moscow for a time. It was seized by the Bolsheviks in late 1917 and remained under their control for the duration of the civil war. Smolensk Oblast was formed on 27 September 1937.

The Communist establishment remained in control of the region in the early years of Russia's restored independence. The Party won the most seats in the Regional Duma elected in 1994 and secured the highest proportion of the votes of any party in elections to the State Duma in both 1995 and 1999. In the gubernatorial election of April–May 1998, after a second round of voting, the Communist candidate and mayor of Smolensk, Aleksandr Prokhorov, defeated the incumbent.

Economy

Smolensk Oblast's gross regional product amounted to 12,029,800m. old roubles in 1997, or 10,352,700 old roubles per head. Its major industrial centres are at Smolensk, Roslavl, Safonovo, Vyazma, Yartsevo, Gagarin and Verkhnedneprovskii. At 1 January 1999 there were 8,819 km of paved roads in the Oblast.

Agriculture in Smolensk Oblast, which employed 13.2% of the work-force in 1998, mainly consists of animal husbandry and the production of grain, sugar beets and sunflower seeds. Total agricultural output in 1998 was worth 2,680m. roubles. Its main industries are textiles, mechanical engineering, chemicals, light manufacturing, food processing, electrical-energy production and the production of coal and peat. In 1998 24.2% of the work-force was engaged in industry. Total industrial production in that year amounted to a value of 9,962m. roubles.

The region's economically active population numbered 446,800 in 1998, of whom some 4,700 were registered unemployed. The average wage in the Oblast at that time stood at 712.1 roubles per month. The 1998 budget showed a deficit of 32m. roubles. Total foreign investment in the region in 1998 amounted to US $26.63m. At 1 January 1999 there were 3,000 small businesses in operation.

Directory

Head of the Regional Administration (Governor): ALEKSANDR DMITRIYEVICH PROKHOROV; Smolenskaya obl., 214008 Smolensk, pl. Lenina 1; tel. (08100) 3-66-11; fax (08100) 3-68-51; internet admin.smolensk.ru.

Chairman of the Regional Duma: VLADIMIR IVANOVICH ANISIMOV; Smolenskaya obl., 214008 Smolensk, pl. Lenina 1; tel. (08122) 3-67-00; fax (08122) 3-71-85; e-mail duma@admin.smolensk.ru; internet admin.smolensk.ru/duma/index.html.

Head of Smolensk City Administration: IVAN ALEKSANDROVICH AVERCHENKOV; Smolenskaya obl., 214000 Smolensk, ul. Oktyabrskaya revolyutsii 1–2; tel. and fax (08100) 3-11-81; internet admin.smolensk.ru/~smol/.

Sverdlovsk Oblast

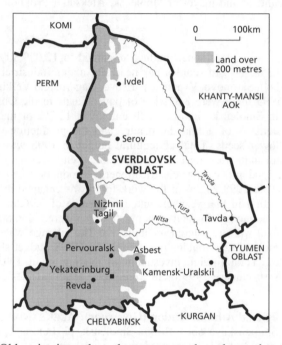

Sverdlovsk Oblast is situated on the eastern, and partly on the western, slopes of the Central and Northern Urals and in the Western Siberian Plain. It forms part of the Urals Economic Area and the Urals Federal Okrug. Tyumen Oblast lies to the east (with its constituent district of the Khanty-Mansii AOk to the north-west), there is a short border with the Republic of Komi in the north-west and Perm Oblast lies to the west. To the south are Bashkortostan, Chelyabinsk and Kurgan. The region's major rivers are those of the Ob and Kama basins. The west of the region is mountainous, while much of the eastern part is taiga (forested marshland). The territory of the Oblast covers an area of 194,800 sq km (75,190 sq miles) and is divided into 30 districts and 47 cities. At 1 January 1999 the estimated population totalled 4,631,000 and the population density was 23.8 per sq km. As many as 87.5% of the region's inhabitants lived in urban areas. The Oblast's administrative centre is at Yekaterinburg (formerly Sverdlovsk), which had an estimated population of 1,270,700 in 1996. Other major cities are Nizhnii Tagil (407,300), Kamensk-Uralskii (195,000), Pervouralsk (137,100) and Serov (100,400).

History

Yekaterinburg city was founded in 1821 as a military stronghold and trading centre. Like the Oblast (formed on 17 January 1934) it was named Sverdlovsk in 1924 but, unlike the Oblast, reverted to the name of Yekaterinburg in 1991. The city was infamous as the location where the last Tsar, Nicholas II, and his family were assassinated in 1918. The region became a major industrial centre after the Second World War.

Following the disintegration of the USSR, Sverdlovsk Oblast was among the most forthright in demanding regional rights from the centre. On 29 September 1993 the Sverdlovsk Regional Soviet adopted a draft constitution for a 'Ural Republic'. The 'Republic' was officially proclaimed on 27 October by the Regional Soviet and the head of the regional administration. The Ural Republic was dissolved by presidential decree, however, and Eduard Rossel, the head of the regional administration, was dismissed on 9 November. In 1994 elections were held to a Regional Duma. In August 1995 Rossel was reinstated as Governor, having won the direct election to head the regional administration. His popularity enabled him to establish an independent 'Transformation of the Urals Movement' that eclipsed support for the national parties in the region in the federal elections of December 1995.

As Governor, Rossel continued to strive for more autonomy for the Oblast, one of the most powerful and potentially most prosperous regions in the Federation. On 12 January 1996 Rossel signed an agreement on the division of powers and spheres of competence between federal and regional institutions. This accord was the first of its kind to be signed with a federal territory that did not have republican status. On 7 April elections were held to the Regional Duma. Less than one-third of the electorate participated, but some 35% voted for Rossel's Transformation bloc. Subsequently, however, the Governor's popularity began to decline: in April 1998, following student protests in Yekaterinburg against delayed payment of grants and government plans to introduce tuition fees for higher education in the region, the Transformation bloc won just 9.3% of the votes to the regional legislature and claimed just two seats in the lower house; it had previously held the majority there. Rossel subsequently established a new party, May, or the Movement of Labourers for Social Guarantees, in April 1999, headed by the unexpected runner-up in the gubernatorial election of that year, the factory director, Anton Burkov. Although attempts by Rossel to establish a Ural Republic alongside neighbouring regions came to naught, he was re-elected as Governor of Sverdlovsk Oblast on 12 September 1999.

Economy

Sverdlovsk Oblast is a leading territory of the Russian Federation in terms of industry, producing around 5% of the country's total industrial output during the mid-1990s. The concentration of industry in the Oblast is around four times the average for a federal unit. In 1997 the territory's gross regional product amounted to 73,923,200m. roubles, equivalent to 15,853,500 roubles per head. Its most important industrial centres are at Yekaterinburg, Nizhnii Tagil, Pervouralsk, Krasnouralsk, Serov, Alapayevsk and Kamensk-Uralskii. There is an international airport, Koltsovo.

The Oblast's agriculture, which employed just 4.8% of its work-force in 1998, consists of grain production and animal husbandry. Total agricultural output in 1998 was worth 7,831m. roubles. There is some extraction of gold and platinum in the Oblast. Its main industries are ferrous and non-ferrous metallurgy, mechanical engineering (the most important plant being the Yekaterinburg-based Uralmash), chemicals, the processing of forestry and agricultural products, light manufacturing and the production of copper and other ores, bauxite, asbestos, petroleum, peat and coal. Industry employed some 32.0% of the working population in 1998 and generated as much as 66,697m. roubles. The services sector was also of increasing significance in the regional economy; the Oblast was given approval to issue US \$500m.-worth of Eurobonds.

Sverdlovsk's economically active population numbered 1,953,300 in 1998, of whom some 59,500 were registered unemployed. The average monthly wage in the region at that time was 793.7 roubles. The 1998 budget showed a deficit of 133m. roubles. Total foreign investment in that year was US \$120.65m., and international trade amounted to some \$3,346.2m., of which over two-thirds was generated by exports. At 1 January 1999 there were 25,900 small businesses registered in the region.

Directory

Governor: EDUARD ERGARTOVICH ROSSEL; Sverdlovskaya obl., 620031 Yekaterinburg, pl. Oktyabrskaya 1; tel. (3432) 51-13-65; fax (3432) 70-54-72; e-mail press-center@midural.ru; internet www.rossel.ru.

Chairman of the Government: ALEKSEI PETROVICH VOROBEV; Sverdlovskaya obl., 620031 Yekaterinburg, pl. Oktyabrskaya 1; tel. (3432) 51-29-20.

Legislative Assembly: Sverdlovskaya obl., Yekaterinburg; e-mail duma@midural.ru; internet wwwduma.midural.ru.

   Chairman of the House of Representatives: ALEKSANDR YURIYEVICH SHASPOSHNIKOV; tel. (3432) 51-56-60.

   Chairman of the Regional Duma: VYACHESLAV SERGEYEVICH SURGANOV; tel. (3432) 58-91-63; fax (3432) 58-92-79.

Head of the Regional Representation in Moscow: VLADIMIR SERAFIMOVICH MELENTIYEV; Moscow, ul. Novyi Arbat 21; tel. and fax (095) 291-90-72.

Head of Yekaterinburg City Administration (Mayor): ARKADII MIKHAILOVICH CHERNETSKII; Sverdlovskaya obl., 620014 Yekaterinburg, pr. Lenina 24; tel. (3432) 56-29-90; fax (3432) 71-79-26; e-mail glava@sov.mplik.ru; internet www.sov .mplik.ru.

Tambov Oblast

Tambov Oblast is situated in the central part of the Oka-Don plain. It forms part of the Central Chernozem Economic Area and the Central Federal Okrug. Penza and Saratov Oblasts lie to the east, Voronezh Oblast to the south, Lipetsk Oblast to the west and Ryazan Oblast to the north. Tambov city lies 480 km south-east of Moscow. Its major rivers are the Tsna and the Vorona. Its territory occupies 34,300 sq km (13,240 sq miles) and measures around 250 km from south to north and 200 km from west to east. The Oblast is divided into 23 districts and eight cities. At 1 January 1999 its population was estimated at 1,283,700, of whom some 58.3% inhabited urban areas, and it had a population density of 37.4 per sq km. The administrative centre is at Tambov, which had an estimated population of 314,100 in 1999. Other major cities are Michurinsk (119,200), Morshansk (49,200) and Rasskazovo (48,600).

History

Tambov city was founded in 1636 as a fort to defend Moscow. The region was the scene of an army mutiny during the anti-tsarist uprising of 1905, and came under Bolshevik control immediately following the October Revolution in 1917. The Oblast was formed on 27 September 1937. It was still considered part of the 'red belt' of committed Communist adherence in the 1990s. The dissolution of the local council in October 1993, and its replacement by a Regional Duma, did not ease the tension between the Communist-led assembly with the regional administration. Having appointed Oleg Betin, a locally respected Governor, President Boris Yeltsin permitted a gubernatorial election in Tambov in December 1995. However Betin lost to the Communist candidate, Aleksandr Ryabov, and

233

was, instead, appointed as presidential representative to the region. Betin, thus, remained visible in the political life of the Oblast prior to his election as governor in December 1999, with the support of both Yurii Luzhkov's Fatherland (Otechestvo) movement, and Unity (Yedinstvo) leader Sergei Shoigu, in December 1999. In elections held to the Regional Duma in March 1998 (at which the rate of participation was just over 25%), the greatest number of seats was won by the Common Sense Party, comprised largely of young directors of firms and enterprises. New elections to the Regional Duma were held in December 2001; the rate of voter participation was unexpectedly high, at some 40%.

Economy

In 1997 Tambov Oblast's gross regional product amounted to 9,434,400m. old roubles, equivalent to 7,272,300 old roubles per head. The region's industrial centres are at Tambov, Michurinsk, Morshansk, Kotovsk and Rasskazovo. It is situated on the ancient trading routes from the centre of Russia to the lower Volga and Central Asia and contains several major road and rail routes.

The Oblast's agriculture, which employed a relatively high proportion of the work-force (some 20.8% in 1998) consists mainly of the production of grain, sugar beets, sunflower seeds and vegetables. Animal husbandry and horticulture are also important. Total agricultural output in 1998 was worth 3,254m. roubles. The principal industries in the Oblast are mechanical engineering, metal working, chemicals and petrochemicals, the production of electrical energy, light manufacturing and food processing. In 1998 19.8% of the working population was engaged in industry. Total industrial production in that year amounted to a value of 5,605m. roubles.

In 1998 around 23,400 of the economically active population of 476,000 was unemployed. In that year the average monthly wage in the Oblast was 596.2 roubles and there was a budgetary surplus of 116m. roubles. At 1 January 1999 there were some 3,000 small businesses operating in the region, while foreign investment in the Oblast during 1998 stood at a mere US $67,000.

Directory

Head of the Regional Administration (Governor): OLEG IVANOVICH BETIN; Tambovskaya obl., 392017 Tambov, ul. Internatsionalnaya 14; tel. (0752) 72-25-18; e-mail post@regadm.tambov.ru; internet www.regadm.tambov.ru.

Chairman of the Regional Duma: VLADIMIR NIKOLAYEVICH KAREV; tel. (0752) 71-23-70; fax (0752) 71-07-72.

Head of Tambov City Administration (Mayor): ALEKSEI YURIYEVICH ILYIN; tel. (0752) 72-20-30; internet www.cityadm.tambov.ru.

Tomsk Oblast

Tomsk Oblast is situated in the south-east of the Western Siberian Plain. It forms part of the Western Siberian Economic Area and the Siberian Federal Okrug. The regions of Kemerovo and Novosibirsk lie to the south, Omsk Oblast to the south-west, the Khanty-Mansii AOk (part of Tyumen Oblast) to the north-west and Krasnoyarsk Krai to the east. Its major rivers are the Ob, the Tom, the Chulym, the Ket, the Tym and the Vasyugan. The Ob flows for about 1,000 km (almost 400 miles) from the south-east to the north-west of the territory. Its largest lake is the Mirnoye. Almost all the Oblast's territory taiga (forested marshland), and over one-half of its total area is forested. It occupies 316,900 sq km (122,320 sq miles) and is divided into 16 districts and six cities. At 1 January 1999 its total population was 1,072,200, of whom 66.8% inhabited urban areas. The region's population density was 3.4 per sq km. Around 88.2% of the population were ethnic Russian at this time, 2.6% were Ukrainian and 2.1% Tatar. The administrative centre of the Oblast is at Tomsk, which had an estimated population of 481,100 in 1999. Other major cities are Seversk (119,000) and Strezhevoi (44,000).

History

Tomsk city was founded as a fortress in 1604. It was a major trading centre until the 1890s, when the construction of the Trans-Siberian Railway promoted other centres. Tomsk Oblast was formed on 13 August 1944. In 1993 the Regional Soviet was initially critical of President Boris Yeltsin's forcible dissolution of the federal parliament. It too, therefore, was disbanded and replaced (in elections on 12 December) by a Regional Duma. The Communists remained the most popular party in the region, securing 19% of the votes cast in federal elections two years later. However, in a simultaneous gubernatorial election for the Oblast, the pro-Yeltsin incumbent, Viktor Kress, won the popular mandate to head the regional administration. Kress, the Chairman of the inter-regional association 'Siberian Accord', and a member of Our Home is Russia, was re-elected with a clear majority at the gubernatorial election of 5 September 1999. In elections to the regional legislature in January 1998, independent candidates fared well, with the business lobby winning 30 of the 42 seats.

Economy

In 1997 the gross regional product of Tomsk Oblast amounted to 21,299,900m. old roubles, equivalent to 19,836,000 old roubles per head. The industrial sector plays a dominant role in the economy of Tomsk Oblast. Its major industrial centres are at Tomsk, Kopashevo, Asino and Strezhevoi.

The Oblast's agricultural sector, which generated 2,501m. roubles in 1998, consists mainly of animal husbandry, the production of grain, vegetables and flax, fishing, hunting and fur farming. Some 7.2% of the Oblast's working population was engaged in agriculture in 1998. Around 1.4m. ha (3.4m. acres) of the Oblast's territory was used for agricultural purposes, of which one-half was arable land. The Oblast has substantial reserves of coal as well as of petroleum and natural gas (estimated at 333.7m. metric tons and 300,000m. cu m, respectively). Its other main industries are mechanical engineering, metal working, the electro-technical industry, the processing of forestry and agricultural products and chemicals. Industry employed 23.4% of the working population in 1998, and industrial output amounted to a value of 12,331m. roubles in that year.

In 1998 around 20,300 (4.6%) of the economically active population of 445,600 were registered unemployed. The average monthly wage was 804.5 roubles, and there was a budgetary deficit of 140m. roubles. Total foreign investment in 1998 amounted to US $96.95m. The Oblast's most significant partners in international trade are the USA and the Republic of Korea, with the chemical industry accounting for the majority of this activity. At 1 January 1999 there were some 4,700 small businesses in operation in the region.

Directory

Head of the Regional Administration (Governor): VIKTOR MELKHIOROVICH KRESS; Tomskaya obl., 634050 Tomsk, pl. Lenina 6; tel. (3822) 51-05-05; fax (3822) 51-03-23; e-mail ato@tomsk.gov.ru; internet www.tomsk.gov.ru.

Chairman of the Legislative Assembly (Regional Duma): BORIS ALEKSEYEVICH MALTSEV; tel. (3822) 51-01-47; fax (3822) 51-06-02; e-mail duma@tomsk.gov.ru; internet duma.tomsk.gov.ru.

Representation in Moscow: tel. (095) 200-39-80.

Head of Tomsk City Administration (Mayor): ALEKSANDR SERGEYEVICH MAKAROV; Tomskaya obl., 634050 Tomsk, pr. Lenina 73; tel. (3822) 52-68-99; fax (3822) 52-68-60; e-mail pmayor@admin.tomsk.ru; internet admin.tomsk.ru.

Tula Oblast

Tula Oblast is situated in the central part of the Eastern European Plain in the northern section of the Central Russian Highlands. It forms part of the Central Economic Area and the Central Federal Okrug. Ryazan Oblast is bordered by Tula to the east, Lipetsk Oblast to the south-east, Orel Oblast to the south-west, Kaluga Oblast to the north-west and Moscow Oblast to the north. Tula city is 193 km (about 120 miles) south of Moscow. The region's major rivers are the Oka, the Upa, the Don and the Osetr. The territory of the Oblast covers an area of 25,700 sq km (9,920 sq miles) and extends for 230 km from south to north and 200 km from west to east. It is divided into 23 administrative districts and 21 cities. It is a highly populated area, with a total population of 1,763,400 at the beginning of 1999 and a population density of 68.6 per sq km. At 1 January 1999 some 81.5% of the Oblast's population inhabited urban areas. The Oblast's administrative centre is at Tula, a military town, which had an estimated population of 509,600 in 1999. Other major cities are Novomoskovsk (with an estimated 139,000 inhabitants), Aleksin (70,300), Shchekino (65,100), Uzlovaya (60,300) and Yefremov (54,100).

History

The city of Tula was founded in the 12th century. It became an important economic centre in 1712, with the construction of the Imperial Small Arms Factory. Tula Oblast was founded on 26 September 1937. Tula's armaments industry meant that it was closed to foreigners for most of the Soviet period.

On 7 October 1993 the Tula Regional Soviet refused to disband itself, but was subsequently dissolved and its functions transferred to the Regional Administration. A new representative body, the 48-seat Regional Duma, was later elected and remained dominated by members of the former Communist nomenklatura. That

237

party remained the most widely supported in the Oblast throughout the 1990s, receiving the largest proportion of the votes cast for any party in the State Duma elections of both 1995 and 1999. The Oblast also had a high-profile Communist Governor, following the election of Vasilii Starodubtsev in March 1997. He had previously been known nationally as a participant in the coup organized against the Soviet leader, Mikhail Gorbachev, in August 1991, in an attempt to prevent the fragmentation of the USSR. Starodubtsev's continuing reputation as a radical Communist was reflected in his standing as the sole 'red belt' governor to support the candidacy of Gennadii Zyuganov in the presidential election of 26 March 2000. Starodubtsev was also elected as a Communist member of the State Duma in the legislative election of December 1999, but he refused to take his seat as, to do so, he would have been required to relinquish his position as Governor of Tula. Like his predecessor, Nikolai Sevryugin (who was subsequently detained on charges of bribe-taking and theft), Starodubtsev was accused of corruption, in regard to alleged tax evasion worth US $5m. during his tenure at the Lenin Collective Farm, prior to his election as Governor. Starodubtsev also implemented controversial policies as Governor; within seven months of taking office his generous support for the agrarian sector, in particular, had added $68m. to the Oblast's existing debts of $10m. In July 1999 representatives of various political and social organizations in the Oblast wrote to President Yeltsin to request, unsuccessfully, that Starodubtsev be removed from office. Gubernatorial elections, held in two rounds in April 2001, aroused widespread controversy. One day before the first round of the elections a meeting of the electoral commission, which reportedly had been convened to consider withdrawing the right of one candidate, Andrei Samoshin, to participate in the election, was attacked by a group of men, and fighting ensued; the commission had previously accused Samoshin of misusing electoral funds and violating campaign procedures. In the event, Samoshin was permitted to participate, coming in second place, with 21.0% of the votes cast, behind Starodubtsev, with 49.4%, less than the 50% of the votes required for an outright victory. However, Samoshin withdrew his candidacy on 19 April, three days before the 'run-off' election was due to take place, citing his dissatisfaction with the conduct of the electoral commission. Despite his reluctance to participate, the commission ruled that the third-placed candidate, Viktor Sokolovskii, who had received 18.6% of the votes cast in the first round of voting, was to stand against Starodubtsev in the 'run-off' election. On 22 April Starodubtsev received over 71% of the votes cast in the second round of voting, for which his opponent had refused to campaign.

Economy

Tula Oblast's gross regional product amounted to 16,577,100m. old roubles, or 9,244,400 old roubles per head in 1997. Its important industrial centres are at Tula, Novomoskovsk, Shchekino, Aleksin, Uzlovaya and Yefremov.

Around 73.7% of the Oblast's territory is used for agricultural purposes. Agricultural activity, in which some 9.4% of the working population were engaged in 1998, consists primarily of animal husbandry and production of grain, potatoes and sugar beets. Agricultural production was worth 5,714m. roubles in 1998. The Oblast's main industries are mechanical engineering, metal working, chemicals, ferrous metallurgy, manufacture of building materials, light manufacturing, food processing and the production of brown coal (lignite). Industry employed approximately 28.5% of the working population in 1998, and total industrial production amounted to a value of 16,118m. roubles. Ferrous metallurgy, mechanical engineering and metal working dominated exports in the region. A tourism sector is encouraged by the city's history and the Yasnaya Polyana country estate of Count Leo Tolstoy (1828–1910), the writer. The main foreign trading partners of the Oblast are Germany, Italy, the Republic of Korea (South Korea), Switzerland and the USA.

In 1998 the economically active population in the Oblast numbered 765,000, of whom around 14,800 (1.9%) were registered unemployed. Those in employment at that time earned an average monthly wage of 720.9 roubles. The 1998 budget showed a surplus of 13m. roubles. Total foreign investment in Tula Oblast in 1998 amounted to US $31.45m. By 1997 around 350 companies in the Oblast had economic links with 75 foreign countries. At 1 January 1999 there were some 7,400 small businesses in operation on its territory.

Directory

Head of the Regional Administration (Governor): VASILII ALEKSANDROVICH STARODUBTSEV; Tulskaya obl., 300000 Tula, pl. Lenina 2; tel. (0872) 27-84-36; internet www.starodubtsev.tula.ru.

Chairman of the Regional Duma: IGOR VIKTOROVICH IVANOV; tel. (0872) 20-52-24.

Representation in Moscow: tel. (095) 978-14-56.

Head of Tula City Administration (Mayor): SERGEI IVANOVICH KAZAKOV; tel. (0872) 27-80-85.

Tver Oblast

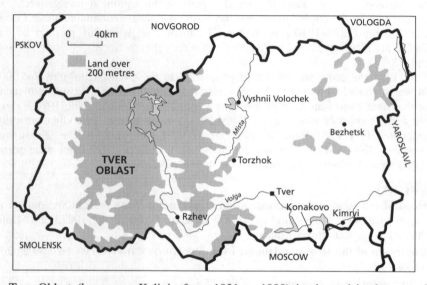

Tver Oblast (known as Kalinin from 1931 to 1990) is situated in the central part of the Eastern European Plain. It forms part of the Central Economic Area and the Central Federal Okrug. Moscow and Smolensk Oblasts lie to the south, Pskov Oblast to the west, Novgorod and Vologda Oblasts to the north and Yaroslavl Oblast to the east. Its westernmost point lies some 50 km (just over 30 miles) from the border with Belarus. The major rivers in the region are the Volga, which rises within its territory, the Mologa and the Tvertsa. The Zapadnaya Dvina and the Msta rivers also have their sources in the Oblast. It has more than 500 lakes, the largest of which is the Seliger, and contains nine reservoirs. The western part of the territory is mountainous, containing the Valdai Highlands (Valdaiskaya Vozvyshennost). About one-third of the territory of the Oblast is forested. It occupies 84,100 sq km (32,460 sq miles) and is divided into 36 districts and 23 cities. The region had an estimated 1,613,500 inhabitants in 1999, of whom 73.5% inhabited urban areas, and its population density was 19.2 per sq km. The administrative centre is at Tver (formerly Kalinin), a river-port, which at the beginning of January 1999 had an estimated population of 451,900. Other major cities are Rzhev (68,800) and Vyshnii Volochek (60,600).

History

The city of Tver was founded as a fort in the 12th century. The Oblast was officially formed on 29 January 1935. In the 1990s the region's relations with the federal Government, led by President Boris Yeltsin, were not always cordial. Having criticized Yeltsin for his policy towards the federal parliament, in October 1993 the Tver Regional Soviet refused to disband itself. It was subsequently obliged to comply with the directives of the federal authorities and a new body, the Legislative Assembly, was elected the following year. This, too, was dominated by the Communists and was obstructive of executive action. President Yeltsin appointed a respected local figure to head the regional administration and decided to permit a gubernatorial election in December 1995. The incumbent was defeated by Vladimir Platov, then a member of the Communist Party; in the simultaneous election to the Russian State Duma, the Communists secured 27% of the regional vote, compared to only 8% for the pro-Yeltsin bloc. The federal Government attempted to placate local opinion, therefore, and in June 1996 the regional authorities were granted greater autonomy with the signing of a power-sharing treaty. Platov, by then one of the founders of the pro-Vladimir Putin Unity electoral bloc, won a second term in office in the second round of voting at the gubernatorial election held on 9 January 2000, narrowly defeating the Communist candidate and promising reform and improved living standards. Unity also gained the largest number of votes cast for any party in elections to the State Duma the previous month.

Economy

In 1997 Tver Oblast's gross regional product amounted to 16,213,100m. old roubles, equivalent to 9,896,900 old roubles per head. Industry is the dominant branch of the Oblast's economy. The principal industrial centres are Tver, Vyshnii Volochek, Rzhev, Torzhok and Kimryi. The region is crossed by road and rail routes between Moscow and Rīga, Latvia, and a highway between Moscow and St Petersburg. The total length of railway track in the Oblast is 1,789 km, while the network of paved roads is 14,830 km long. There are 924 km of navigable waterways in the region, mainly on the Volga. There is an international airport at Tver.

Around 2.4m. ha (5.9m. acres) of the Oblast's territory is used for agricultural purposes, of which two-thirds is arable land. Agriculture in Tver Oblast, which employed around 12.4% of the work-force in 1998, consists mainly of animal husbandry and the production of vegetables, potatoes and flax (the region grows around one-quarter of flax produced in Russia). Total agricultural output in 1998 amounted to a value of 4,229m. roubles. The region contains deposits of peat, lime and coal and is famous for its mineral-water reserves. Its major industries are mechanical engineering, metal working, light manufacturing, chemicals, wood-working, the processing of forestry and agricultural products, printing and glass-, china- and faience-making. In 1998 some 25.4% of the Oblast's working population was engaged in industry, while total industrial production was worth 11,659m. roubles. Its main trading partners in the late 1990s were the People's Republic of China, Germany, Switzerland, Turkey and the USA. In 1998 there were 20 commercial banks and 100 insurance companies and branches in operation on its territory.

In 1998 the region's economically active population numbered 631,400, of whom 11,000 (1.7%) were registered unemployed. The average wage at this time amounted to 537.3 roubles per month. The 1998 regional budget showed a surplus of 47m. roubles. In 1998 a social and cultural development programme for Tver Oblast (for 1998–2005) was adopted by the federal Government, which gave tax incentives to foreign investors. Total foreign investment in the Oblast in 1998 amounted to US $4.92m. In 1999 3,600 small businesses were operating in the region, employing 38,000 people.

Directory

Head of the Regional Administration (Governor): VLADIMIR IGNATEVICH PLATOV; Tverskaya obl., 170000 Tver, ul. Sovetskaya 44; tel. (0822) 33-10-51; fax (0822) 42-55-08; e-mailtradm@tversa.ru; internet www.region.tver.ru.

Chairman of the Legislative Assembly: VYACHESLAV ALEKSANDROVICH MIRONOV; tel. (0822) 33-10-11.

Regional Representation in Moscow: tel. (095) 926-65-19.

Head of Tver City Administration (Mayor): ALEKSANDR PETROVICH BELOUSOV; Tverskaya obl., 170640 Tver, ul. Sovetskaya 11; tel. (0822) 33-01-31; fax (0822) 42-59-39; e-mail info@www.tver.ru; internet www.tver.ru.

Tyumen Oblast

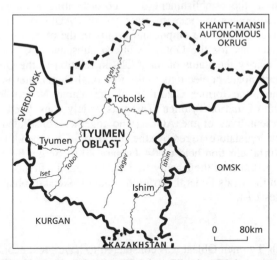

Tyumen Oblast is situated in the Western Siberian Plain, extending from the Kara Sea in the north to the border with Kazakhstan in the south. It forms part of the Western Siberian Economic Area and the Urals Federal Okrug. Much of its territory comprises the Khanty-Mansii and Yamal-Nenets Autonomous Okrugs (AOks). To the west (going south to north) lie Kurgan, Sverdlovsk, Komi and the Nenets AOk (part of Archangel Oblast); to the east lie Omsk, Tomsk and Krasnoyarsk (in the far north the border is with Krasnoyarsk's Taimyr AOk). The region has numerous rivers, its major ones being the Ob, the Taz, the Pur and the Nadym. Much of its territory is taiga (forested marshland). The territory of the Oblast, including that of the AOks , occupies an area of 1,435,200 sq km (554,130 sq miles) and is divided into 38 districts and 26 cities. It is a sparsely populated region: the estimated total population at 1 January 1999 was 3,243,500 and the population density was 2.3 per sq km. Some 76.2% of the Oblast's inhabitants lived in urban areas. The Oblast's administrative centre is at Tyumen, which then had an estimated population of 502,500. Other major cities outside the AOks are Tobolsk (98,000) and Ishim (61,100).

History

Tyumen city was founded in 1585 on the site of a Tatar settlement. It subsequently became an important centre for trade with the Chinese Empire. Tyumen Oblast was formed on 14 August 1944. The region became industrialized after the Second World War. On 21 October 1993 the Regional Soviet in Tyumen Oblast repealed its earlier condemnation of government action against the federal parliament but refused to disband itself. Legislative elections were held in the Oblast on 6 March 1994, but the results in several constituencies were declared invalid, owing to a low level of participation. Eventually a new assembly, the Regional Duma, was elected. It remained Communist-led, but the pro-Government faction was well represented. This position was confirmed by regional results in the general election of 1995. During the mid-1990s the exact nature of the relationship between Tyumen

Oblast proper and the two AOks, which wished to retain a greater share of the income from their wealth of natural resources, became a source of intra-élite contention, despite the establishment of a co-ordinating administrative council between the three bodies in 1995. In 1997 the two AOks (which between them accounted for over 90% of the output and profits in the oblast) had boycotted the gubernatorial elections for the Oblast, while a subsequent Constitutional Court ruling failed to clarify the status of the AOks in relation to the Oblast. However, the AOks did participate in elections to the Regional Duma later in 1997. In 1998 Sergei Korepanov, the former Chairman of the Yamal-Nenets legislature, was elected Chairman of that of Tyumen. This was widely considered to form part of a plan by representatives of the AOks (who together constituted a majority of seats in the oblast legislature) to remove the Governor of Tyumen, Leonid Roketskii. At the gubernatorial election held on 14 January 2001, Sergei Sobyanin, a former speaker in the legislature of the Khanty-Mansi AOk and the first deputy presidential representative in the Urals Federal Okrug, defeated Roketskii, obtaining more than 51% of the votes cast.

Economy

In the mid-1990s Tyumen Oblast was considered to have great economic potential, owing to its vast hydrocarbons and timber reserves (mainly located in the Khanty-Mansii and Taimyr AOks). In 1997 its gross regional product amounted to 209,198,000m. old roubles, equivalent to 65,460,300 old roubles per head (by far the highest figure in the Russian Federation). Its main industrial centres are at Tyumen, Tobolsk, Surgut, Nizhnevartovsk and Nadym.

The Oblast's agriculture, which employed just 4.5% of its work-force in 1998, consists mainly of animal husbandry (livestock- and reindeer-breeding), fishing, the production of grain, flax and vegetables, fur farming and hunting. In 1998 agricultural production throughout the entire territory was worth 4,764m. roubles. In the late 1990s the Oblast's reserves of petroleum, natural gas and peat were estimated at 60%, 90% and 36%, respectively, of Russia's total supply. The Tyumen Oil Company (TNK), formed in 1995 from nine other companies, is among the largest petroleum companies in Russia and produced 156m. barrels of crude petroleum in 1996. From 1997, when the state's share in the company was reduced to less than one-half, TNK became increasingly market-driven and dismissed around a quarter of its work-force by 1999, as one of its largest subsidiaries, Nizhnevartovskneftegaz (NNG) became subject to bankruptcy procedures. Overall petroleum output in the region for 1997 was forecast at 191.6m. metric tons. The Oblast's other major industries are mechanical engineering, metal-working, chemicals and the processing of agricultural and forestry products. Industry employed some 17.8% of the Oblast's working population in 1998 and generated a total of 126,924m. roubles, by far the highest level of any federal subject.

The economically active population in 1998 totalled 1,676,000. There was a total of 63,700 (3.8%) registered unemployed in the region at the time, a figure that grew steadily during the 1990s. The average monthly wage in 1998 was 2,793 roubles, the highest in the Federation. The budget for that year showed a deficit of 327m. roubles. Total foreign investment in the Oblast amounted to US $182.29m. in 1998, while by the beginning of the next year there were some 16,800 small businesses in operation on its territory. Trade figures for 1998 showed the Oblast to have generated some \$8,220.7m. in exports (of which approximately two-thirds were destined for non-CIS countries) and to have purchased \$1,077.5m. of imports.

Directory

Governor: SERGEI SEMENOVICH SOBYANIN; Tyumenskaya obl., 625004 Tyumen, ul. Volodarskogo 45; tel. (3452) 46-77-20; fax (3452) 29-32-05; internet www .adm.tyumen.ru.

Chairman of the Regional Duma: SERGEI YEVGENIYEVICH KOREPANOV; Tyumenskaya obl., 625018 Tyumen, ul. Respubliki 52, Dom Sovetov; tel. (3452) 46-51-31; internet www.tmn.ru/~tyumduma.

Head of the Regional Representation in Moscow: GEORGII VASILIYEVICH GLYBIN; tel. (095) 291-71-94.

Head of Tyumen City Administration: STEPAN MIKHAILOVICH KIRICHUK; Tyumenskaya obl., 625036 Tyumen, ul. Pervomaiskaya 20; tel. (3452) 24-67-42; fax 46-42-72; e-mail ves@tyumen-city.ru; internet www.tyumen-city.ru.

Ulyanovsk Oblast

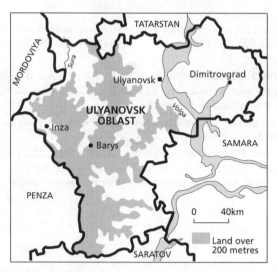

Ulyanovsk Oblast is situated in the Volga Highlands. It forms part of the Volga Economic Area and the Volga Federal Okrug. The Republics of Mordoviya and of Chuvashiya and Tatarstan lie to the north-west and to the north, respectively. There are also borders with Samara Oblast in the south-east, Saratov Oblast in the south and Penza Oblast in the south-west. The region's major river is the Volga. The region occupies an area of 37,300 sq km (14,400 sq miles) and is divided into 21 districts and six cities. The estimated total population of the Oblast was 1,472,100 in January 1999, of whom some 73.1% inhabited urban areas. It had a population density of 39.5 per sq km. The administrative centre at Ulyanovsk (formerly Simbirsk) had an estimated population of 620,200 at this time.

History

Simbirsk city was founded in 1648. Lenin (Vladimir Ulyanov) was born there in 1870, and it was his home until 1887. The city assumed his family name following his death in 1924. Ulyanovsk Oblast, which was formed on 19 January 1943, formed part of the 'red belt' of Communist support in post-Soviet Russia. Thus, it refused to revert to its old name and also gave the party 37% of the regional vote in the 1995 elections to the federal State Duma. In December 1996 the Communist-backed candidate, Yurii Goryachev, won the election to the governorship of the Oblast. Goryachev, whose support came largely from the Oblast's rural community, banned local privatization and collective-farm reforms, imposed restrictions on imports and exports, and subsidized bread prices until early 1997. Goryachev was defeated in the gubernatorial elections held in December 2000, and replaced by Gen. Vladimir Shamanov.

Economy

In 1997 Ulyanovsk Oblast's gross regional product amounted to 16,564,600m. old roubles, or 11,141,100 old roubles per head. The Oblast's major industrial centres are at Ulyanovsk and Melekess.

Around 1.5m. ha of its territory is used for agricultural purposes, of which over four-fifths is arable land. Agriculture in the region, which employed some 13.2% of the working population in 1998, consists primarily of animal husbandry and the production of grain, sunflower seeds and sugar beets. Total agricultural production amounted to a value of 2,445m. roubles in 1998. The Oblast's main industries are mechanical engineering and metal working, food processing, light manufacturing, the manufacture of building materials and wood-working. The region's major companies included the UAZ automobile plant and the Aviastar aeroplane manufacturer (both of which were working at 50% capacity in the late 1990s). Industry employed 29.0% of the working population in 1998 and generated some 13,647m. roubles.

The economically active population in Ulyanovsk Oblast in that year numbered 594,100, of whom 15,700 were registered unemployed. Those in employment at this time earned an average of 616.8 roubles per month. There was a budgetary surplus in 1998 of 220m. roubles. Total foreign investment in the Oblast in 1998 amounted to only US $153,000. At 1 January 1999 there were some 4,600 small businesses in operation.

Directory

Head of the Regional Administration (Governor): VLADIMIR ANATOLYEVICH SHAMANOV; Ulyanovskaya obl., 423700 Ulyanovsk, pl. Lenina 1; tel. (8422) 41-20-78; fax (8422) 31-27-65; internet www.admobl.mv.ru.

Chairman of the Legislative Assembly: SERGEI NIKOLAYEVICH RYABUKHIN.

Head of the Regional Representation in Moscow: GENNADII VASILIYEVICH SAVINOV; tel. (095) 241-312-42.

Head of Ulyanovsk City Administration (Mayor): PAVEL ROMANENKO; Ulyanovskaya obl., 432700 Ulyanovsk, ul. Kuznetsova 7; tel. (8422) 41-20-78; fax (8422) 31-90-64.

Vladimir Oblast

Vladimir Oblast is situated in the central part of the Eastern European Plain. It forms part of the Central Economic Area and the Central Federal Okrug. It shares borders with Ryazan and Moscow to the south-west, Yaroslavl and Ivanovo to the north and Nizhnii Novgorod to the east. The Oblast's main rivers are the Oka and its tributary, the Klyazma. Over one-half of its territory is forested. It occupies a total of 29,000 sq km (11,200 sq miles) and measures around 170 km (over 100 miles) from south to north and 280 km from west to east. The Oblast is divided into 19 administrative districts and 22 cities. It had an estimated population of 1,617,700 at 1 January 1999, of whom 80.5% inhabited urban areas. Its population density in 1999 was 55.8 per sq km. Its administrative centre is at Vladimir, which had an estimated population of 336,100. Other major cities are Kovrov (161,900), Murom (141,400), Gus-Khrustalnyi (73,500) and Aleksandrov (65,900).

History

Founded in 1108 as a frontier fortress by Prince Vladimir Monomakh, after the disintegration of Kievan Rus, Vladimir city was the seat of the principality of Vladimir-Suzdal and an early Orthodox Christian bishopric. Vladimir fell under the rule of Moscow in 1364 and was supplanted by that city as the seat of the Russian Orthodox patriarch, although Vladimir was chosen for the coronations of several Muscovite princes. It declined in importance from the 15th century. Vladimir Oblast was formed on 14 August 1944.

In the 1990s it awarded a respectable level of support to all the main national parties. In the December 1995 parliamentary election, the Communists, the nationalist Liberal Democrats, and the pro-Kremlin Our Home is Russia, all gained more than 10% of the votes cast, while in the December 1999 election the Communists obtained only a slightly higher share of the votes cast than the pro-Kremlin party, Unity. The Communists, however, secured the election of Nikolai Vinogradov, former Chairman of the Legislative Assembly, to the post of Governor in late 1996. Vinogradov was re-elected as Governor in December 2000, with some 66% of the votes cast, defeating Yurii Glasov, who had held the post in 1991–96.

Economy

Vladimir Oblast's gross regional product in 1997 totalled 15,265,000m. old roubles, or 9,342,700 old roubles per head. The Oblast's main industrial centres are at Vladimir, Kovrov, Murom, Aleksandrov, Kolchugino, Vyazniki and Gus-Khrustalnyi. There are 928 km of railway track and 5,509 km of paved roads on its territory.

Agriculture in the region, which employed just 7.6% of its work-force in 1998, consists mainly of animal husbandry, vegetable production and horticulture. Total agricultural output in 1998 stood at 3,249m. roubles. Vladimir is rich in peat deposits and timber reserves, but relies on imports for around 70% of its energy supplies. The Oblast's main industries are mechanical engineering, manufacture of building materials, metal working, light manufacturing, chemicals, glass-making and handicrafts. Industrial output in 1998 was worth 13,660m. roubles. In that year a total of 34.3% of the working population was engaged in industry. Vladimir city's largest employer is the Vladimir Tractor Factory, which struggled to adapt to the new economic conditions from the 1990s.

In 1998 41,300 (5.9%) of the economically active population of 699,000 were registered as unemployed. The average monthly wage in the Oblast in 1998 was 589.0 roubles. In 1998 there was a regional deficit of 83m. roubles. Total foreign investment in Vladimir Oblast in that year amounted to some US $198.86m. In 1997 organizations with private or mixed forms of ownership, which employed 400,000 people, contributed around 90% of the Oblast's economic output. At 1 January 1999 there was a total of 6,600 small businesses registered on its territory.

Directory

Head of the Regional Administration (Governor): NIKOLAI VLADIMIROVICH VINOGRADOV; Vladimirskaya obl., 600000 Vladimir, Oktyabrskaya pr. 21; tel. (0922) 33-15-52; fax (0922) 23-34-45; e-mail post@obladm.vladimir.ru; internet avo.ru.

Chairman of the Legislative Assembly: VITALII YAKOVLEVICH KOTOV; Vladimirskaya obl., 600000 Vladimir, Oktyabrskaya pr. 21; tel. (0922) 22-64-42; fax (0922) 22-60-13.

Regional Representation in Moscow: tel. (095) 926-64-57.

Head of Vladimir City Administration: IGOR VASILIYEVICH SHAMOV; Vladimirskaya obl., 600000 Vladimir, ul. Gorkogo 36; tel. (0922) 23-28-17; fax (0922) 23-85-54; e-mail mayor@cityadmin.vladimir.su; internet www.cityadm.vladimir.su.

Volgograd Oblast

Volgograd Oblast is situated in the south-east of the Eastern European Plain. It forms part of the Volga Economic Area and the Southern Federal Okrug. The Oblast has an international border with Kazakhstan to its east. The federal subjects of Astrakhan and Kalmykiya lie to the south-east, Rostov to the south-west, Voronezh to the north-west and Saratov to the north. The Oblast's main rivers are the Volga and the Don. Its terrain varies from fertile black earth (*chernozem*) to semi-desert. Volgograd city is the eastern terminus of the Volga–Don Canal. The region occupies an area of 113,900 sq km (43,980 sq miles) and is divided into 33 administrative districts and 19 cities. At 1 January 1999 it had an estimated total of 2,693,000 inhabitants, of whom some 74.1% lived in urban areas, and a population density of 23.6 per sq km. In 1989 around 89% of the population were ethnic Russians, while 3% were Ukrainians, 2% were Kazakhs and 1% were Tatars. Subsequently, there was an influx of immigrants to the Oblast from more unstable areas of the Caucasus. The Oblast's administrative centre is at Volgograd, which had an estimated population of 995,800 in 1999. Other major cities are Volzhskii (287,200) and Kamyshin (126,700).

History

The city of Volgograd (known as Tsaritsyn until 1925 and Stalingrad from 1925 until 1961) was founded in the 16th century, to protect the Volga trade route. It was built on the River Volga, at the point where it flows nearest to the Don (the two river systems were later connected by a canal). The Oblast was formed on 10 January 1934. In 1942–43 the city was the scene of a decisive battle between the forces of the USSR and Nazi Germany.

In October 1993 the Regional Soviet in Volgograd Oblast eventually agreed to a reform of the system of government in the Oblast. It decided to hold elections to a new 30-seat Regional Duma, which took place the following year. The Communist Party was the largest single party. The continued pre-eminence of the old ruling élite was confirmed by the 27% share of the regional poll secured by the Communist list in the 1995 federal parliamentary election. Furthermore, the December 1996 gubernatorial election was won by Nikolai Maksyuta, a Communist and former speaker of the regional assembly. In December 1998 Communist candidates won a convincing 23 of the 32 seats in the regional legislative elections. On 24 September the Duma had voted for the principle of restoring the Oblast's previous name of Stalingrad, and this notion remained popular in 2001. Maksyuta was re-elected for a second term as Governor on 19 December 1999.

Economy

In 1997 Volgograd Oblast's gross regional product amounted to 32,496,300m. old roubles, or 12,026,300 old roubles per head. Its main industrial centres are at Volgograd, Bolzhskii and Kamyshyn. In 1999 there were 8,467 km of paved roads and 1,619 km of railways. In 1996 construction began of a road bridge across the Volga river into Volgograd.

The region's principal agricultural products are grain, sunflower seeds, fruit, vegetables, mustard and cucurbits (gourds and melons). Horticulture and animal husbandry are also important. In 1998 some 14.2% of the Oblast's work-force were engaged in agriculture. Total agricultural production amounted to a value of 6,568m. roubles in that year. The agricultural sector suffered a major reverse in mid-1998, however, when drought destroyed more than 1m. ha of grain, 200,000 ha of fodder crops and 80,000 ha of mustard. The Oblast's mineral reserves include petroleum, natural gas and phosphorites. The main industries in the Oblast are petroleum refining, chemicals and petrochemicals, mechanical engineering, metal working, ferrous and non-ferrous metallurgy, the manufacture of building materials, wood-working, light manufacturing, food processing and the production of petroleum and natural gas. Industry employed approximately 24.0% of the working population in 1998, while total industrial production was worth 22,630m. roubles.

In 1998 the economically active population in the Oblast numbered 1,081,800, of whom 15,500 (1.4%) were unemployed. The local average monthly wage was 639.4 roubles. There was a budgetary deficit of 147m. roubles in that year. Total foreign investment in 1998 amounted to US $82.56m. In 1997 there were more than 250 joint and foreign enterprises in the region. The joint enterprises had largely been established with investment from Bulgaria, Germany, Greece, Italy and the USA. At the beginning of the 1999 there were some 13,500 small businesses in the region.

Directory

Head of the Regional Administration (Governor): NIKOLAI KIRILLOVICH MAKSYUTA; Volgogradskaya obl., 400098 Volgograd, pr. Lenina 9; tel. (8442) 33-66-88; fax (8442) 93-62-12; e-mail glava@volganet.ru; internet www.volganet.ru.

Chairman of the Regional Duma: VIKTOR IVANOVICH PRIPISNOV; tel. and fax (8442) 36-52-79.

Regional Representation in Moscow: tel. (095) 229-96-73.

Head of Volgograd City Administration (Mayor): YURII VIKTOROVICH CHEKHOV; Volgogradskaya obl., 400066 Volgograd, ul. Sovetskaya 11; tel. (8442) 33-50-10; internet www.volgadmin.ru.

Vologda Oblast

Vologda Oblast is situated in the north-west of the Eastern European Plain. It forms part of the Northern Economic Area and the North-Western Federal Okrug. It has a short border, in the north-west, with the Republic of Kareliya, which includes the southern tip of Lake Onega (Onezhskoye). Onega also forms the northern end of a border with Leningrad Oblast, which lies to the west of the Vologda region. Novgorod Oblast lies to the south-west and Tver, Yaroslavl and Kostroma Oblasts to the south. Kirov Oblast forms an eastern border and Archangel Oblast lies to the north. The region's main rivers are the Sukhona, the Yug, the Sheksna and the Mologa. There are three major lakes, in addition to Lake Onega— Beloye, Bozhe and Kubenskoye. Vologda Oblast occupies 145,700 sq km (56,250 sq miles) and extends for 385 km (240 miles) from south to north and 650 km from west to east. It is divided into 26 administrative districts and 15 cities. The Oblast's population at the beginning of 1999 was estimated at 1,328,100 and the population density was, therefore, 9.1 per sq km. Some 68.7% of the total population inhabited urban areas. The Oblast's administrative centre is at Vologda, which had an estimated population of 301,300 in 1999. Its other major city is Cherepovets (323,600).

History

Vologda province was annexed by the state of Muscovy in the 14th century. The city was, for a time, the intended capital of Tsar Ivan IV ('the Terrible', 1533–84). Until the Bolshevik Revolution of 1917 the province was administered by governors appointed by the Tsar. Vologda Oblast was formed on 23 September 1937.

In 1991 the newly elected Russian President, Boris Yeltsin, appointed a new head of administration of Vologda Oblast. In mid-1993 the Vologda Oblast declared itself a republic but failed to be acknowledged as such by the federal authorities. On 13 October the Regional Soviet transferred its responsibilities to the Regional Administration and elections were later held to a Legislative Assembly. In 1995 ballots implemented the Statutes of Vologda Oblast, according to which the region's

Governor would lead the executive. In the Russia of the 1990s many in the region considered Vologda neglected by the federal centre. There was, therefore, a high level of support for the nationalist Liberal Democrats, particularly in the countryside. In June 1996 Boris Yeltsin dismissed the local Governor, who was subsequently arrested and imprisoned on charges of corruption. His successor, Vyacheslav Pozgalev, won 80% of votes cast in a direct election in late 1996, and was re-elected for a further term of office on 19 December 1999, with 83% of the votes cast.

Economy

In 1997 Vologda Oblast's gross regional product amounted to 20,802,900m. old roubles, equivalent to 15,508,300 old roubles per head. Its main industrial centres are at Vologda, Cherepovets, Velikii Ustyug and Sokol. There are 768 km of railway track in general use on its territory, as well as 11,472 km of paved roads and 1,800 km of navigable waterways, including part of the Volga–Baltic route network.

Agriculture in Vologda Oblast, which employed 9.6% of the work-force in 1998, consists mainly of animal husbandry and production of flax and vegetables. The region is famous for its butter. In 1998 total agricultural output was worth 3,899m. roubles. The territory imports around one-half of its electrical energy from other Oblasts (Kostroma, Kirov, Leningrad, Tver and Yaroslavl). Its main industries are ferrous metallurgy (the region produces 20% of Russia's iron, 19% of its rolled stock and 18% of its steel), chemicals (11% of the country's mineral fertilizers are manufactured in Vologda Oblast), the processing of forestry products, mechanical engineering, pharmaceuticals, glass-making, light manufacturing, food processing and handicrafts, such as lace-making. In 1998 28.8% of the region's working population were engaged in industry. The industrial sector generated a total of 29,382m. roubles.

The Oblast's economically active population numbered 571,900 in 1998, of whom 21,600 were registered unemployed. Those in employment earned, on average, 799.9 roubles per month. The 1998 budget showed a deficit of 160m. roubles. Total foreign investment in the Oblast in 1998 amounted to US $7.93m. Export trade amounted to some $1,501.7m. In January 1999 there were some 4,100 small businesses in operation.

Directory

Governor: VYACHESLAV YEVGENIYEVICH POZGALEV; Vologodskaya obl., 160035 Vologda, ul. Gertsena 2; tel. (8172) 72-07-64; fax (8172) 25-15-54; e-mail governor@vologda-oblast.ru; internet www.vologda-oblast.ru.

Chairman of the Legislative Assembly: GENNADII TIMOFEYEVICH KHRIPEL; tel. (8172) 25-11-33.

Head of the Regional Representation in Moscow: VLADIMIR SERGEYEVICH SMIRNOV; tel. (095) 201-73-03; fax (095) 201-55-24.

Head of Vologda City Administration: ALEKSEI SERGEYEVICH YAKUNICHEV; Vologodskaya obl., 160035 Vologda, ul. Kamennyi most 4; tel. (8172) 72-00-42; fax (8172) 72-25-59.

Voronezh Oblast

Voronezh Oblast is situated in the centre of the Eastern European Plain on the middle reaches of the Volga. It forms part of the Central Chernozem Economic Area and the Central Federal Okrug. There is a short border with Ukraine in the south. Of the neighbouring Russian federal territories, Belgorod and Kursk lie to the west, Lipetsk and Tambov to the north, a short border with Saratov in the north-east, Volgograd to the east and Rostov to the south-east. The west of the territory is situated within the Central Russian Highlands and the east in the Oka-Don Lowlands. Its main rivers are the Don, the Khoper and the Bityug. The Voronezh region occupies an area of 52,400 sq km (20,230 sq miles) and is divided into 32 administrative districts and 15 cities. The Oblast's estimated population at 1 January 1999 was 2,471,700, of whom 62.0% lived in urban areas; its population density was 47.2 per sq km. The region's administrative centre is at Voronezh, which had an estimated population of 903,800 at that time. Other major cities are Borisoglebsk (65,100) and Rossosh (63,500).

History
Voronezh city was founded in 1586 as a fortress. The centre of a fertile region, the city began to industrialize in the tsarist period. Voronezh Oblast was formed on 13 June 1934. In the immediate post-Soviet years the region remained committed to the Communist Party, which controlled the Regional Duma. The region also largely supported the Communist leader, Gennadii Zyuganov, in the presidential election of June 1996, although this level of support was not repeated in the election of March 2000. A Communist and former speaker of the Oblast assembly, Ivan Shabonov, was elected Governor in December 1996. At the gubernatorial election held in December 2000 Shabonov received only 15% of the votes cast, and was defeated by Federal Security Service (FSB) General Vladimir Kulakov, who obtained some 60% of the votes.

Economy
In 1997 Voronezh Oblast's gross regional product amounted to 25,737,400m. old roubles, equivalent to 10,326,800 old roubles per head. The important industrial

centres in the Oblast are at Voronezh, Borisoglebsk, Georgii u-Dezh, Rossosh and Kalach. The territory contains some 1,189 km of railway track (of which 60.2% are electrified) and 9,012 km of paved roads. The road network includes sections of major routes, such as the Moscow–Rostov, Moscow–Astrakhan and Kursk–Saratov highways. There are 640 km of navigable waterways.

Around 4.7m. ha (11.6m. acres—90% of the total) of Voronezh's territory is used for agricultural purposes, of which 3.1m. ha is arable land. In 1998 around 20.6% of the Oblast's working population were employed in the agricultural sector. The Oblast's agriculture consists mainly of the production of grain, sugar beets, sunflower seeds, fruit and vegetables. Animal husbandry was also important. Total agricultural production in 1998 amounted to a value of 6,805m. roubles. Its main industries are mechanical engineering, metal working, chemicals and petro-chemicals, the manufacture of building materials and food processing. In 1998 some 21.3% of the work-force were engaged in industry, the output of which was valued at a total of 15,072m. roubles. In 1997 there were five commercial banks, 18 insurance companies and six investment funds in operation on the Oblast's territory. Turnover from foreign trade in 1998 amounted to US $314m.

The Oblast's economically active population numbered 988,600 in 1998, of whom around 19,600 were registered unemployed. The Oblast's average wage in that year was 632.2 roubles per month. There was a budgetary deficit of 118m. roubles in 1998. By 1997 some sectors of the economy, such as light industry, food processing and construction materials, had been almost entirely privatized. Foreign investment in the region increased dramatically during the mid-1990s: while total foreign capital in 1995 amounted to just $23,000, by 1997 there were 200 joint or foreign enterprises, established primarily with funds from Belarus, Bulgaria, the Czech Republic, Germany, Liechtenstein, Ukraine, the USA and Uzbekistan. In 1998 foreign investment in the region amounted to $3.95m. At 1 January 1999 there were around 9,400 small businesses operating in the region.

Directory

Head of the Regional Administration: VLADIMIR GRIGORYEVICH KULAKOV; Voronezhskaya obl., 394018 Voronezh, pl. Lenina 1; tel. (0732) 55-27-37; fax (0732) 55-38-78; internet admin.vrn.ru.

Chairman of the Regional Duma: ANATOLII SEMENOVICH GOLIUSOV; Voronezh-skaya obl., 394018 Voronezh, ul. Kirova 2; tel. (0732) 55-06-88; fax (0732) 55-38-78.

Head of the Regional Representation in Moscow: VLADISLAV IVANOVICH LEONOV; tel. (095) 299-67-35.

Head of Voronezh City Administration (Mayor): ALEKSANDR KOVALEV; Voronezhskaya obl., 394067 Voronezh, ul. Plekhanovskaya 10; tel. (0732) 55-34-20; fax (0732) 55-47-16; e-mail admin@city.vrn.ru; internet www.city.vrn.ru.

Yaroslavl Oblast

Yaroslavl Oblast is situated in the central part of the Eastern European Plain. It forms part of the Central Economic Area and the Central Federal Okrug. Ivanovo Oblast lies to the south-east, Vladimir and Moscow Oblasts to the south, Tver Oblast to the west, Vologda Oblast to the north and Kostroma Oblast to the east. Yaroslavl city, which lies on the Volga, is 282 km (175 miles) north-east of Moscow. The region has 2,500 rivers and lakes, its major two lakes being Nero and Pleshcheyevo, and there is a large reservoir at Rybinsk. The Volga river flows for 340 km through the region. Its territory, just over two-fifths of which is forested, covers a total area of 36,400 sq km (14,050 sq miles) and is divided into 17 administrative districts and 11 cities. The estimated total population in the Oblast at the beginning of 1999 was 1,425,100, of whom 80.6% inhabited urban areas. The population density in the region was 39.2 per sq km. The Oblast's administrative centre is at Yaroslavl, which had an estimated population of 616,100 in 1999. Other major cities are Rybinsk (242,600), Tutayev (45,700) and Pereslavl-Zalesskii (44,900).

History

Yaroslavl city is reputed to be the oldest town on the River Volga, having been founded *circa* 1024. The region was acquired by the Muscovite state during the reign of Ivan III (1462–1505). Yaroslavl Oblast was formed on 11 March 1936. In the 1990s the region developed a liberal and diverse political climate. A range of interests was represented in the new, 23-seat Regional Duma elected on 27 February 1994. Thus, in December 1995 the federal President, Boris Yeltsin, permitted his appointed Governor, Anatolii Listisyn, to contest a direct election for the post, which he won. He was re-elected for a further term on 19 December 1999, gaining around 65% of the votes cast.

Economy

In 1997 Yaroslavl Oblast's gross regional product amounted to 21,093,400m. old roubles, equivalent to 14,659,400 old roubles per head. The major industrial centres in the region are at Yaroslavl itself, Rybinsk, Tutayev, Uglich, Pereslavl-Zalesskii, Rostov and Gavrilov-Yam. There are river-ports at Yaroslavl, Rybinsk and Uglich. Its total length of railway track amounts to 650 km. The Oblast lies on the main Moscow–Yaroslavl–Archangel and Yaroslavl–Kostroma highways. The total length of paved roads in the territory is 6,221 km. There are also 789 km of navigable waterways.

The climate and soil quality in the region is not favourable to agriculture. Agricultural activity, which employed just 7.3% of the working population in 1998, consists primarily of animal husbandry and the production of vegetables, flax and grain. Total agricultural output in 1998 was worth 2,922m. roubles. The main industries are mechanical engineering (Rybinsk Motors is Russia's largest manufacturer of aircraft engines), chemicals and petrochemicals, petroleum refining, light manufacturing, peat production and the processing of agricultural and forestry products. In 1998 industrial output in the region amounted to a value of 16,768m. roubles and industry employed some 30.7% of the work-force.

The economically active population, of whom around 18,900 (3.0%) were registered unemployed, numbered 634,600 in 1998. The average wage was 741.2 roubles per month. There was a regional budgetary deficit in 1998 of 86m. roubles. However, Yaroslavl was considered sufficiently viable to have its federal transfers reduced in amount for 1999. Total foreign investment in the region in 1998 amounted to US $22.97m., while at 1 January 1999 there were some 8,900 small businesses in operation.

Directory

Governor: ANATOLII IVANOVICH LISITSYN; Yaroslavskaya obl., 150000 Yarovslavl, Sovetskaya pl. 3; tel. (0852) 72-81-28; fax (0852) 32-84-14; internet www.adm.yar.ru.

Deputy Governor: VLADIMIR ALEKSANDROVICH KOVALYEV; tel. (0852) 72-84-55.

Chairman of the Regional Duma: (vacant); tel. (0852) 30-39-36; fax (0852) 72-72-04.

Regional Representation in Moscow: tel. (095) 253-45-18.

Head of Yaroslavl City Administration (Mayor): VIKTOR VLADIMIROVICH VOLONCHUNAS; Yaroslavskaya obl., 150000 Yaroslavl, ul. Andropova 6; tel. (0852) 30-46-41; fax (0852) 30-52-79; e-mail ird@gw.city.yar.ru; internet www.city.yar.ru.

FEDERAL CITIES

Moscow

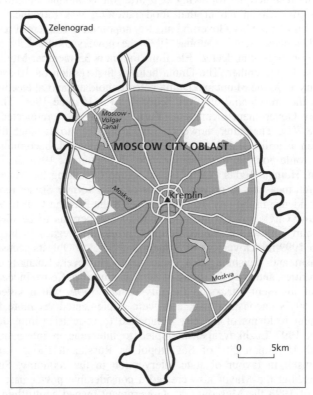

Moscow (Moskva) is located in the west of European Russia, on the River Moskva, which crosses the city from the north-west to the south-east. It is connected to the Volga river system by the Moscow–Volga Canal. Moscow is included in the Central Economic Area and the Central Federal Okrug. The city's total area is 994 sq km (384 sq miles), and it consists of nine administrative districts and the town of Zelenograd (which alone had a population of 207,300 in 1999). Moscow is the largest city in the Russian Federation and had an estimated total population of 8.3m. at 1 January 1999; from 1996 its population had contracted by over 360,000, marking a continuing trend. In 1999 around 89.7% of the city's population were ethnic Russians, 2.9% were Ukrainians and 2.0% were Jews.

History

Moscow city was founded in about 1147. In 1325 it became the seat of the Eastern Orthodox Metropolitan of Russia (from 1589–1721 and after 1917 the Patriarch of the Russian Orthodox Church) and the steadily expanding Muscovite state became the foundation for the Russian Empire. The centre of tsarist government was moved to St Petersburg in 1712, but Moscow was restored as the Russian and Soviet capital in March 1918.

In the 1980s and 1990s, while reformists enjoyed considerable support in the city, there were also powerful forces of conservatism. On 12 June 1991 the first mayoral elections were held in the city. They were won by the democrat Gavriril Popov, but he resigned the following year after the economic situation of the city deteriorated to such an extent that food rationing was introduced, and Yurii Luzhkov, head of the City Government, was appointed by federal President Boris Yeltsin in his place. On 7 October 1993 the powers of the City Soviet were suspended by presidential decree. Elections to a new 35-member Municipal Duma were held on 12 December. The Duma held its first session on 10 January 1994.

In February 1996 the Municipal Duma voted to hold a mayoral election simultaneously with the presidential election, scheduled for 16 June 1996. The reformist, generally pro-Government incumbent, Yurii Luzhkov, was re-elected by a large majority (88.7%). Thereafter, however, Luzhkov began to distance himself from his reputation as a liberal and criticized central government, becoming an increasingly high-profile political figure nationwide. In September 1997 the international organization, Human Rights Watch, issued a report accusing the Mayor of implementing tough measures to prevent citizens of other former Soviet republics from taking up residence in the city. In February 1998 the Russian Constitutional Court ruled Moscow City's strict controls over residence permits to be illegal and the Supreme Court outlawed residence permits (*propiski*, a legacy of the Soviet era) that July. In 1999 the Governors of Samara and Saratov Oblasts accused Luzhkov of chauvinism and racism against Caucasians. However, Luzhkov opposed or ignored his critics, and even the ruling of the Constitutional Court. Indeed, following a number of dissident attacks in the city in late 1999, which killed over 200 people, the city's unconstitutional laws were implemented yet more firmly, with non-permanent residents of the city compelled to re-register immediately or be deported. In 1997 Luzhkov also attempted to intervene in international affairs, claiming the Ukrainian city of Sevastopol as Russian territory. Luzhkov also declared himself in favour of state intervention in the economy. Such policies were popular, but the Mayor also created a considerable power base in the city: by the end of 1998 the Moscow City Government owned controlling stakes in a television station, a bank, a car factory, a chain of convenience food stores and a network of petrol stations. In June 1998 Luzhkov signed a power-sharing treaty with the federal authorities, following a protracted period of negotiation that resulted in the city receiving taxation and budget privileges. None the less, in municipal elections held in December 1997 the majority of seats were won by the Democratic Choice bloc. Luzhkov became increasingly involved in national politics, and concluded a number of trade agreements with other regions. In late 1998 he founded a nationwide political movement, Fatherland, which subsequently joined with St Petersburg Mayor Vladimir Yakovlev's All Russia, to contest the December 1999 State Duma elections as a centrist, anti-Kremlin electoral bloc. Luzhkov had also been expected to stand as a candidate in the 2000 elections for the federal presidency. Although Luzhkov was re-elected as Mayor by a clear majority on 19 December 1999, in the simultaneous nationwide elections to the State Duma Fatherland—All Russia came third, behind the Communists and the newly formed pro-Kremlin bloc, Unity. Many of Luzhkov's supporters in the regions backed the candidacy of Vladimir Putin in the presidential campaign, and, after a period of neutrality, Luzhkov and the Fatherland movement also gave their backing to Putin. Preliminary results of the elections to the Municipal Duma held in December 2001 indicated that the Fatherland and Unity parties had each secured seven seats, followed by the Union of Rightist Forces with six seats, and the liberal Yabloko with four seats.

Economy

In 1997 the city of Moscow's gross regional product amounted to 320,084,800m. old roubles, equivalent to 37,073,000 old roubles per head (the second-highest rate in the Russian Federation after the petroleum-producing Tyumen oblast). There are nine railway termini in the city and 11 electrified radial lines. The metro system includes 11 lines and over 150 stations and extends for 244 km (152 miles). Its trolleybus and tram routes are 1,700 km long, its bus routes 5,700 km. The public-transport system carries around 6.5m. passengers per day. Moscow's waterways connect with the Baltic, White, Caspian and Black Seas and the Sea of Azov. There are also four airports on the city's territory.

Moscow's industry consists primarily of mechanical engineering, electro-technical metallurgy, production of chemicals, petroleum refining, the manufacture of building materials, light industry and food processing. Industry employed around 14.7% of the city's working population in 1998 (in contrast to the 0.1% engaged in agriculture) and generated 81,435m. roubles, a figure surpassed in the Russian Federation only by Tyumen Oblast, which has the majority of gas and petroleum deposits in the Federation. The Moskvich Automobile Plant, in which the City Government held a controlling stake from 1998, is one of Moscow's principal companies, although at the end of 1997 it was producing just 3,000 cars per month, compared with its maximum capacity of 160,000, a situation that necessitated the restructuring of the plant's production. The services sector was also significant in the city economy, with the city authorities having successfully consolidated its leading position within Russia during the reform period of the 1990s: in 1992–95 significant changes occurred in the structure of Moscow's economy—industrial production declined by 52%, while financial institutions, such as commercial banks, joint-stock companies and commodities and stock exchanges increased. By 1997 there were around 1,000 commercial banks in the city. Although the financial crisis of August 1998 led to a restructuring of the sector, the city was sufficiently resourced to recover. As the Russian capital, the city was the site of a large number of government offices, as well as the centre for major business and financial companies. Tourism was another important service industry.

The economic problems of the 1990s were less accentuated in Moscow than in the rest of Russia. In 1998, of an economically active population of 5.51m., the registered unemployed accounted for 52,500. Those in employment earned, on average, 4,017.1 roubles per month, one of the highest rates in the Federation. The 1998 budget, like its immediate predecessors, was relatively well-balanced, showing a surplus of 110m. roubles, but the city finances, while undoubtedly healthy, are notoriously lacking in transparency. Capital investment in the city represents around one-10th of that in Russia as a whole. More than one-half of Russian enterprises and organizations involving foreign capital were situated in Moscow. Total foreign investment in the city amounted to US $5,860m. in 1998. In that year international trade amounted to a value of some $34,717.3m., by far the highest level of any federal subject, of which 56% was accounted for by exports. In September 1997 Moscow became the first city in Russia to enter the international capital market and place a Eurobonds issue. Local companies also flourished, in one of the few regions of Russia that could claim significant economic growth during the 1990s. At the beginning of 1999 there were 175,200 small companies registered in the city.

Directory

Mayor and Prime Minister of the Government of Moscow: YURII MIKHAILO-VICH LUZHKOV; 103032 Moscow, ul. Tverskaya 13; tel. (095) 229-48-87; internet www.mos.ru.

Deputy Mayor: VALERII PAVLINOVICH SHANTSEV; tel. (095) 290-77-35.

Speaker of the Municipal Duma: VLADIMIR MIKHAILOVICH PLATONOV; 101498 Moscow, ul. Petrovka 22; tel. (095) 292-15-16; fax (095) 921-92-02; e-mail speaker@mcd.mos.ru; internet duma.mos.ru.

St Petersburg

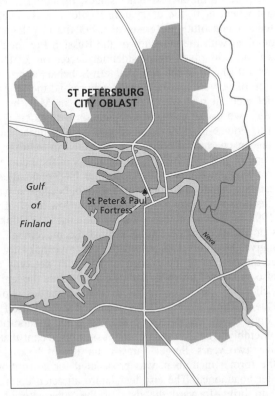

St Petersburg (Sankt Peterburg) is a seaport at the mouth of the River Neva, which drains into the easternmost part of the Gulf of Finland (part of the Baltic Sea). St Petersburg is included in the North-Western Economic Area and the North-Western Federal Okrug. The city's territory, including a total of 42 islands in the Neva delta, occupies an area of 570 sq km (220 sq miles—making it the smallest of the Russia's federal subjects), of which its waterways comprise around 10%. There are more than 580 bridges in the city and surrounding area, including 20 drawbridges. The population of the city was an estimated 4.70m. at 1 January 1999, making it Russia's second-largest city.

History

St Petersburg was founded by the Tsar, Peter (Petr) I ('the Great') in 1703, as a 'window on the West', and was the Russian capital from 1712 to 1918. At the beginning of the First World War, in 1914, the city was renamed Petrograd. Following the fall of the Tsar and the Bolshevik Revolution in 1917, the Russian capital was moved back to Moscow. In 1924 the city was renamed Leningrad. During the Second World War it was besieged by German troops for 870 days, between November 1941 and January 1944. In June 1991 the citizens of Leningrad voted to restore the old name of St Petersburg and their decision was effected in

October. On 24 September 1998 the federal President, Boris Yeltsin, approved the administrative merger of the city with Leningrad Oblast, although actual implementation required a number of other stages, including a referendum; there was no indication when, or if, the unification would actually occur.

During the federal constitutional crisis of 1993 the city legislature variously opposed and complied with the demands of the Russian President, Boris Yeltsin. The Soviet was finally dissolved by presidential decree on 22 December. On 24 April 1996 the liberal Mayor of the city, Anatolii Sobchak, approved a draft treaty on the delimitation of powers between St Petersburg and the federal Government. Sobchak was defeated in a mayoral election held in May by another liberal, Vladimir Yakovlev, who soon acquired a reputation for autocracy in government. Sobchak moved to France in 1997, after allegedly suffering a heart attack during police questioning on charges of corruption, and died in February 2000.

The city was one of just two constituent members of the Federation to give the reformist Yabloko bloc a majority in the December 1995 general election. A series of corruption scandals damaged support for Yabloko, because it was the dominant party, but also disillusioned potential voters (thus, a low level of participation in the December 1998 legislative election was to the cost of Yabloko). In addition, the Mayor was powerful in campaigning against the movement. On 14 January 1998 the Legislative Assembly had passed the controversial City Charter, which greatly restricted the powers of the executive. Yakovlev not only challenged it in the courts, but also sponsored his own 'list' of candidates in the legislative election, distancing himself from the Moscow-based political parties. Following a poor performance at the election, Yabloko subsequently distanced itself from Yakovlev and went into opposition; supporters of the Governor in non-party blocs now dominated the assembly. The divisions in the Assembly meant that it was without a speaker for over two years. Sergei Tarasov, an ally of Yakovlev, was elected in June 2000; the former incumbent was prosecuted for corruption, although the charges were later abandoned. The city legislature attracted controversy in 1999, as it attempted to bring forward the date of the gubernatorial election, amid allegations of irregularities in the vote that confirmed this decision. However, the Supreme Court ruled that attempts to hold the election earlier than originally scheduled, believed to be of benefit to the incumbent Governor, Yakovlev, were invalid. None the less, Yakovlev won the election, which was finally held in May 2000, obtaining around 73% of the votes cast and gaining the support of the Communist Party and nationalist elements.

Economy

In 1997 St Petersburg's gross regional product amounted to 75,783,500m. old roubles, or 15,908,500 old roubles per head, less than one-half of the figure recorded in Moscow. All transport systems in the city have been privatized.

Industry in St Petersburg, which employed around 20.4% of its work-force in 1998 (compared to the 0.5% engaged in agriculture), consists mainly of mechanical engineering, ferrous and non-ferrous metallurgy, electricity generation, manufacture of chemicals and petrochemicals, rubber production, light manufacturing, the manufacture of building materials, food and timber processing, and printing. Total industrial production in the city amounted to a value of 46,038m. roubles in 1998. The city is also an important centre for service industries, such as tourism, financial services and leisure activities. At the beginning of 1996 there were 117 commercial banks registered in the city, including 54 local banks. The city is an important centre of trade: turnover from foreign trade in 1998 amounted to US $5,220.6m.; however, this figure represented less than one-sixth of the value of Moscovite trade in that year. In the late 1990s around 30% of Russia's imports and 20% of its exports passed through the city.

At the end of 1998 the economically active population in St Petersburg amounted to 2.3m., of whom around 40,600 (1.7%) were officially registered as unemployed. The average wage in St Petersburg in 1998 was 1,060.1 roubles, considerably higher than the national average. The 1998 city budget showed a surplus of 376m. roubles. However, the city had a US $300m. Eurobond debt, which was due to be repaid by June 2002; in 1999 some 9% of the city's budget was devoted to repaying and servicing its debts. In 1998 foreign investment in St Petersburg amounted to $413.28m. Despite its significance as a trading centre, by the beginning of 2000 St Petersburg was not a strong commercial capital—the number of Western companies it had attracted and the extent of its property development failed to rival those of Moscow. The renationalization of the famous Lomonosov Porcelain Factory, which took place following a court ruling in St Petersburg in October 1999, annulled its privatization six years earlier, and caused concern to foreign investors that a new precedent was being set.

Directory

Mayor (Governor and Premier of the City Government): VLADIMIR ANATOLI-YEVICH YAKOVLEV; 193060 Saint Petersburg, Smolnyi; tel. (812) 278-59-24, fax (812) 278-18-27; e-mail gov@gov.spb.ru; internet www.government.spb.ru.

Senior Vice-Governor: YURII VASILIYEVICH ANTONOV; tel. (812) 273-4893; e-mail vg_office@gov.spb.ru.

Speaker of the Legislative Assembly: SERGEI TARASOV; tel. (812) 319-8455; e-mail starasov@assembly.spb.ru; internet www.assembly.spb.ru.

City Representation in Moscow: tel. (095) 290-17-94.

AUTONOMOUS OBLAST

Jewish Autonomous Oblast

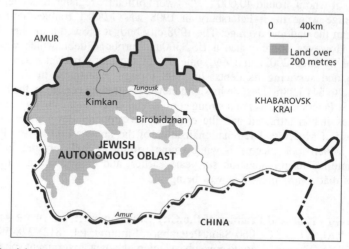

The Jewish Autonomous Oblast (AO—Birobidzhan) is part of the Amur river basin, and is included in Russia's Far Eastern Economic Area and Far Eastern Federal Okrug. It is situated to the south-west of Khabarovsk Krai (of which it formed a part until 1991), on the international border with the People's Republic of China. There is a border with Amur Oblast in the north-west. Apart from the River Amur, which is frozen for around five months of the year, the region's major river is the Tungusk. Forest, which is particularly concentrated in the north-west, covers more than one-third of its territory. Around one-half is mountainous, with the south and east occupying the western edge of the Central Amur Lowlands. It occupies 36,000 sq km (13,900 sq miles) and has five administrative districts and two cities. The Jewish AO had an estimated population of 200,900 in January 1999 and a population density, therefore, of 5.2 per sq km. Around 67.6% of its population inhabited urban areas at this time. The census of 1989 found that ethnic Russians accounted for some 83.2% of the AO's population and ethnic Jews for 4.2% (although this figure can be expected to have decreased subsequently; in the early 1950s the Jews had constituted around one-quarter of the population of the Oblast). Indeed, in 1990 alone, around 1,000 of the 9,000 Jews resident in the Oblast the previous year emigrated to Israel. The regional capital is at Birobidzhan, which had an estimated population of 80,800 in January 1999.

History

The majority of Russian Jews came under Russian control following the Partitions of Poland in 1772–95. The Soviet regime established an autonomous Jewish province at Birobidzhan in 1928, but it never became the centre of Soviet (or Russian) Jewry, largely because of its remote location and the absence of any prior Jewish settlement there. (In Imperial Russia between 1835 and 1917, Jews

266

were required to receive special permission to live outside the 'Pale of Settlement' to the south-west of the Empire, which constituted territories largely in present-day Belarus, Lithuania, Poland and Ukraine.) This province was renamed the Jewish AO on 7 May 1934 and formed part of Khabarovsk Krai until 25 March 1991. In the early post-Soviet period the region remained a redoubt of Communist support. Despite the advice of the Russian President, Boris Yeltsin, at a session on 14 October 1993 the Regional Soviet announced that it would not disband itself. Subsequently, however, the council was replaced by a new body, the Legislative Assembly, elections to which confirmed Communist domination. A gubernatorial election held on 20 October 1996 was won by the incumbent, Nikolai Volkov; he was re-elected with 57% of the votes cast on 26 March 2000. A wage crisis in the region in May 1998 resulted in a decree by the Governor that the salaries of local-government officials be put towards repayment of wage arrears.

Economy

In 1997 the Jewish AO's gross regional product stood at 1,300,100m. old roubles, equivalent to 6,302,200 old roubles per head. Birobidzhan is the region's main industrial centre. There are 312 km (194 miles) of railway track, including a section of the Trans-Siberian Railway, and 1,593 km (990 miles) of paved roads on the Autonomous Oblast's territory. In February 2000 the opening of a bridge across the Amur river provided improved road and rail links with the city of Khabarovsk and the People's Republic of China. There are around 600 km of navigable waterways in the south of the Jewish AO.

Agriculture, which employed 11.5% of the region's work-force in 1998, and generated a total of 390m. roubles in that year, consists mainly of grain, soybean, vegetable and potato production, animal husbandry, bee-keeping, hunting and fishing. Total agricultural production in 1998 amounted to 389.7m. roubles. There are major deposits of coal, peat, iron ore, manganese, tin, gold, graphite, magnesite and zeolite, although they are largely unexploited. The main industries are mechanical engineering, the manufacture of building materials, wood-working, light manufacturing and food processing. Industry employed around 15.2% of the Autonomous Oblast's working population and generated a total of 565m. roubles in 1998. In the mid-1990s the region's foreign economic activity was largely concentrated in the Far East, including the People's Republic of China and Japan.

Its economically active population numbered 69,400 in 1998, of whom 1,300 were registered unemployed. The average monthly wage in the Autonomous Oblast was 630.2 roubles at this time. The 1998 budget showed a surplus of 56m. roubles. On 1 January 1999 around 400 small businesses were registered in the region.

Directory

Head of the Regional Administration: NIKOLAI MIKHAILOVICH VOLKOV; Yevreiskaya avtonomnaya obl., 682200 Birobidzhan, pr. 60-letiya SSSR 18; tel. (42622) 6-02-42; fax (42622) 4-04-93; e-mail gov@eao.ru; internet www.eao.ru.

Chairman of the Legislative Assembly: STANISLAV VLADIMIROVICH VAVILOV; Yevreiskaya avtonomnaya obl., 682200 Birobidzhan, pr. 60-letiya SSSR 18; tel. (42622) 6-44-27.

Head of Birobidzhan City Administration: (vacant); Yevreiskaya avtonomnaya obl., 682200 Birobidzhan, ul. Lenina 29; tel. (42622) 6-22-02; fax (42622) 4-04-93.

AUTONOMOUS OKRUGS (DISTRICTS)

Aga-Buryat Autonomous Okrug

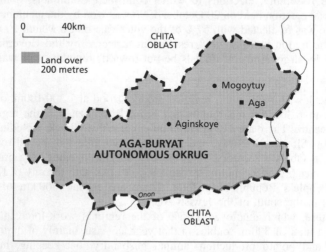

The Aga-Buryat AOk is situated in the south-east of Transbaikal, in the southern part of Chita Oblast. It forms part of the Eastern Siberian Economic Area and the Siberian Federal Okrug. Its major rivers are the Onon and the Ingoda, and about one-third of its territory is forested. Aga settlement is about 550 km (just under 350 miles) to the east of Ulan-Ude, the capital of Buryatiya (which lies to the west of Chita Oblast). The Autonomous Okrug contains varied terrain, ranging from desert to forest-steppe. The Aga-Buryat AOk occupies a total of 19,000 sq km (7,340 sq miles) and extends for about 250 km from south to north and 150 km from west to east. It has three administrative districts and four 'urban-type settlements' (towns). Its climate is severe and annual precipitation is as little as 250–380 mm (about 100–150 inches) per year. Its population at 1 January 1999 was estimated at 79,100, of whom just 32.3% inhabited urban areas; the population density was, therefore, 4.3 per sq km. In 1989 ethnic Buryats were found to make up some 54.9% of the population, and ethnic Russians 40.8%. The Buryats inhabiting the district are Transbaikal Buryats, who are more closely related to their Mongol ancestors than their western counterparts, the Irkutsk Buryats. The Autonomous Okrug's administrative centre is at Aga settlement, which had an estimated population of just 9,400 in January 1999.

History

The Aga-Buryat-Mongol AOk was created on 26 September 1937, as part of Stalin—Iosif Dzhugashvili's policy of dispersing the Buryat population, whom he perceived as a threat because of their ethnic and cultural links with the Mongolian

People's Republic (Mongolia). Its formation occurred as part of the division of the Eastern Siberian Oblast into Chita and Irkutsk Oblasts (the former of which it became a part). It assumed its current name on 16 September 1958.

Under the Federation Treaty of March 1992, the Autonomous Okrug was recognized as one of the constituent units of the Russian Federation. The old Communist élite remained pre-eminent in the district, mainly represented by the Communist Party of the Russian Federation. The area attracted some notoriety in late 1997, when Iosif Kobzon, a popular singer frequently referred to as the 'Russian Frank Sinatra', beat four rival candidates in a by-election for an okrug seat in the federal State Duma; he won 84% of the votes cast. Kobzon attracted controversy, owing to his reputedly close connections with organized crime both within Russia and in the USA. The incumbent Head of the District Administration, Bair Zhamsuyev, was re-elected in October 2000, obtaining more than 89% of the votes cast.

Economy

The Autonomous Okrug's transport infrastructure is relatively unsophisticated—there are only 71 km of railway track and 903 km of paved roads. The economy of the Aga-Buryat AOk is based on agriculture, which consists mainly of animal husbandry (particularly sheep-rearing), fur-animal farming and grain production. Agricultural production amounted to a value of 350m. roubles in 1998 and employed some 35.6% of the Okrug's work-force. The territory is rich in reserves of wolfram (tungsten) and tantalum. Its main industries are non-ferrous metallurgy, ore mining, the manufacture of building materials and the processing of forestry and agricultural products. Industry employed just 8.9% of the Okrug's work-force in 1998, and produced output worth 45m. roubles. The district's main foreign trading partners are the People's Republic of China and Mongolia. The transport, trade and services sectors were fully privatized by 1995. The Aga-Buryat AOk is one of the most under-developed federal territories in terms of its health and social-security provision and educational establishments.

There were some 2,100 registered unemployed in the territory (of an economically active population of 22,500) in 1998. The average monthly wage in that year was 269.9 roubles. The 1998 district budget showed a surplus of 23m. roubles. Approximately 600 small businesses were registered in the territory by 1999.

Directory

Head of the District Administration: BAIR BAYASKHALANOVICH ZHAMSUYEV; Chitinskaya obl., Aginskii Buryatskii a/o, 674460 pos. Aginskoye, ul. Bazara Rinchino 92; tel. (30239) 3-41-52; fax (30239) 3-49-59.

Chairman of the Duma: DASHI TSYDENOVICH DUGAROV.

Head of the District Representation in Moscow: VLADIMIR DYMBRYLOVICH SHOIZHILZHAPOV; tel. (095) 203-95-09.

Chukchi Autonomous Okrug

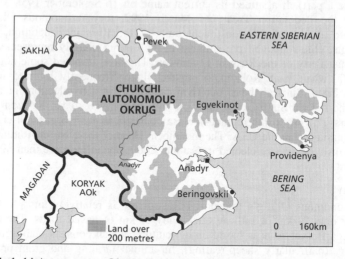

The Chukchi Autonomous Okrug (AOk—formerly known as the Chukot Autonomous Okrug) is situated on the Chukotka Peninsula and an adjacent section of the mainland. The Okrug forms part of the Far Eastern Economic Area and the Far Eastern Federal Okrug. It is the easternmost part of Russia and faces the Eastern Siberian Sea (Arctic Ocean) to the north and the Bering Sea to the south; the Anadyr Gulf, part of the Bering Sea, cuts into the territory from the south-east. The USA (Alaska) lies eastwards across the Bering Straits. The western end of the district borders the Republic of Sakha (Yakutiya), to the west, and Magadan Oblast (of which Chukotka formed a part until 1992), to the south. Also to the south lies the Koryak AOk (part of Kamchatka Oblast). The district's major river is the Anadyr. The Chukchi AOk occupies an area of 737,700 sq km (284,830 sq miles), of which approximately one-half lies within the Arctic Circle, and is divided into eight administrative districts and three cities. Its climate is severe, with the average annual temperature ranging from −4.1°C to −14.0°C. The Autonomous Okrug is a sparsely populated area, with an estimated total of 83,000 inhabitants at 1 January 1999, and a population density of 0.1 per sq km. Approximately 69.2% of the territory's population inhabited urban areas at this time. Around 80,000 people left the Autonomous Okrug between 1985 and 1999, reducing the population by about one-half. According to the census of 1989, ethnic Russians represented 66.1% of the region's total population, while only 7.3% were Chukchi. The Chukchi speak the Chukotic language as their native tongue, which belongs to the Paleo-Asiatic linguistic family. Until the 20th century the Chukchi (who call themselves the Lyg Oravetlyan, and are also known as the Luoravetlan, Chukcha and Chukot) could be subdivided into several distinct tribal groups. Traditionally they were also divided into two economic groups, the nomadic and semi-nomadic reindeer herders (the Chavchu or Chavchuven), and the coastal dwellers (known as the An Kalyn). The district's administrative centre is at Anadyr, which had an estimated population of 13,000 in 1999.

History

Russian settlers first arrived in the territories inhabited by Chukchi tribes in the mid-17th century. Commercial traders, fur trappers and hunters subsequently established contact with the Chukchi and many were forcibly converted to Orthodox Christianity and enserfed. Economic co-operation continued to expand and reached its height in 1905, with the construction of the Trans-Siberian Railway. A Chukchi Okrug was created as part of Magadan Oblast by the Soviet Government on 10 December 1930, as part of its policy to incorporate the peoples of the north of Russia into the social, political and economic body of the USSR. It later acquired autonomous status. Simultaneously, collectivization was introduced into the district, which encouraged the assimilation of the Chukchi into Russian life. Throughout the 1950s and 1960s eastern Siberia was rapidly industrialized, resulting in extensive migration of ethnic Russians to the area and a drastic reduction of the territory available to the Chukchi for herding reindeer. Many abandoned their traditional way of life to work in industry.

After 1985 the Chukchi, in common with the rest of the Soviet population, experienced more political freedom. On 31 March 1990 the Chukchi participated in the creation of the Association of the Peoples of the North. They also campaigned for the ratification of two international conventions, which would affirm their right to the ownership and possession of the lands they traditionally inhabited. In the early 1990s the Chukchis began to demand real political autonomy: in February 1991 the legislature of the Chukchi AOk seceded from Magadan Oblast and declared the territory the Chukchi Soviet Autonomous Republic (the word 'Soviet' was dropped from the district's title following the disintegration of the USSR in December). This measure failed to be recognized by the federal Government, although the district was acknowledged as a constituent member of the Federation by the Treaty of March 1992 and, subsequently, as free from the jurisdiction of Magadan Oblast. At the gubernatorial election held in December 2000, The incumbent Governor, Aleksandr Nazarov, withdrew his candidacy. Roman Abramovich, an 'oligarch' associated with the petroleum company Sibneft, was elected in his place, receiving 91% of the votes cast.

Economy

Alone among the autonomous okrugs, Chukotka is no longer included in a larger territory and there has been, therefore, fuller coverage of it in official statistics. In 1997 the Chukchi AOk's gross regional product amounted to 2,388,800m. roubles, equivalent to 28,745,400 roubles per head. Although relatively high, this level of regional wealth was highly dependent on federal transfers. The territory has 652 km of paved roads and a relatively undeveloped infrastructure. Anadyr is one of the district's major ports, the others being Pevek, Providenya, Egvekinot and Beringovskii.

The Autonomous Okrug's agricultural sector, which employed 6.0% of its workforce in 1998, consists mainly of fishing, animal husbandry (especially reindeer-breeding) and hunting. Total agricultural production in 1998 was worth 44,200m. roubles. In 1992 it was estimated that some 500,000 reindeers were raised in state-controlled breeding areas. In the early 1990s increasing demands were made by Chukchi activists for the privatization of reindeer herds, but the usefulness of state support was apparent in the winter of 1996/97, when the lives of some 30,000 reindeer were threatened after heavy rains were followed by freezing temperatures and blizzards, covering the grazing areas in a thick sheet of ice. The region contains reserves of coal and brown coal (lignite), petroleum and natural gas, as well as gold, tin, wolfram (tungsten), copper and other minerals. It is self-sufficient in energy, containing two coal-mines, six producers of electricity and one nuclear power-station. Its main industries are ore mining and food processing. Industry employed some 14.4% of the Autonomous Okrug's working population in 1998 and generated 108,000m. old roubles during the previous year.

Its economically active population numbered 35,200 in 1998, of whom 2,000 (5.7%) were officially registered as unemployed. Those in employment earned an average of 1,685.7 roubles per month, well above the national average, although this was counterbalanced by some of the highest living costs in the Federation; in November 1999 a typical 'consumer basket' cost about three times as much in Anadyr as the national average and, indeed, considerably more than elsewhere in the Russian Far East. The 1998 district government budget showed a deficit of 27m. roubles, representing a considerable improvement on earlier records; in 1994 and 1995 the deficit had exceeded the entire gross output of the district. In December 1998 the federal authorities claimed that the payment of wages in the district was, on average, just over seven months late—the worst record on payment arrears of any region of the Federation. At 1 January 1999 there were about 100 small businesses registered in the Autonomous Okrug; an extra-budgetary fund was created for the support and development of small business during 1996 and 1997, although little success was evident.

Directory

Head of the Region Administr ition (Governor): ROMAN ARKADYEVICH ABRA-MOVICH; 689000 Chukotskii a/o, Anadyr, ul. Beringa 20; tel. (42722) 2-42-62; fax (42722) 2-24-66.

Chairman of the District Du ʏ a: VASILII NIKOLAYEVICH NAZARENKO; tel. and fax (42722) 2-44-70.

Head of the District Representation in Moscow: VLADIMIR SERGEYEVICH VILDIAAIKIN; 101000 Moscow, ul. Miasnitskaia 26/2; tel. and fax (095) 925-95-13.

Head of Anadyr City Administration: VIKTOR ALEKSEYEVICH KHVAN; Chukotskii a/o, 689000 Anadyr, ul. Beringa 45; tel. (41361) 4-45-33; fax (41361) 4-22-16.

Evenk Autonomous Okrug

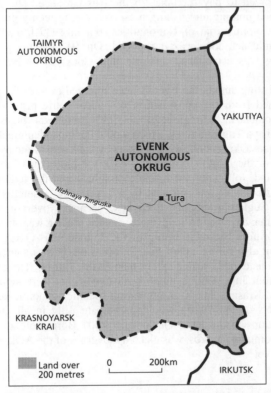

The Evenk Autonomous Okrug is a land-locked territory situated on the Central Siberian Plateau. It is part of the Eastern Siberian Economic Area and the Siberian Federal Okrug. The district forms the central-eastern part of Krasnoyarsk Krai, with the core territories of the province lying to the west and south and the other autonomous okrug, the Taimyr (Dolgan-Nenets) AOk, to the north. Sakha (Yakutiya) adjoins to the east. It has numerous rivers, the largest being the Nizhnaya Tunguska and the Podkammenaya Tunguska, both tributaries of the Yenisei river. The Evenk district occupies a total area of 767,600 sq km (296,370 sq miles), of which almost three-quarters is forested, and comprises three administrative districts and one 'urban-type settlement' (town). At 1 January 1999 the Autonomous Okrug's population was estimated at 19,400, of whom just 28.9% inhabited urban areas. Its population density, of 0.03 per sq km, was the lowest in the Federation. According to the 1989 census, ethnic Russians comprised some 67.5% of the district's population and ethnic Evenks 14.0%. The Evenks' native tongue is part of the Tungusic group of the Tungusic-Manuchu division of the Uralo-Altaic language family. The region's administrative centre is at Tura settlement, which had an estimated population of just 5,700 on 1 January 1999.

History

The Evenks, who are thought to be descended from a mixture of Tungus and Yukagir culture, were first identified as a distinct group in the 14th century. Their first contact with Russians occurred in the early 17th century, as Russian Cossacks and fur trappers advanced eastwards through Siberia. By the mid-1620s many Evenks were forced to pay fur taxes to the Russian state. The Evenks' right to land, pasture, and hunting and fishing preserves was officially guaranteed in 1919 by the Soviet Commissariat of Nationalities, but in 1929 forced collectivization of their economic activities was introduced. On 10 December 1930 the Evenk National Okrug was established and the first Congress of Evenk Soviets was convened.

Nationalist feeling among the Evenks later emerged as a result of environmental damage sustained from the construction of hydroelectric projects and extensive mineral development in the region. In the 1980s there were plans to build a dam across the Nizhnaya Tuguska river, which would have flooded much of the territory of the Autonomous Okrug. Following protests by the Evenks, and by the Association of the Peoples of the North (formed in 1990), the project was abandoned. In the post-Soviet period, following the forcible dissolution of the federal parliament in 1993, the District Soviet was replaced by a Legislative Assembly or Suglan. The speaker of the Suglan, Aleksandr Bokivkov, became Governor of the Okrug in March 1997, after an election held three months earlier was annulled, owing to various irregularities. The relationship of the Autonomous Okrug to Krasnoyarsk Krai, of which it also forms a part, has, on occasion, been a source of difficulties, although to a considerably lesser extent than in the Taimyr (Dolgan-Nenets) AOk (see below). From June 1997 a number of agreements were signed between the Evenk AOk and Krasnoyarsk Krai, regulating specific economic issues and stating that the residents of the Okrug would participate fully in all gubernatorial and legislative elections in the Krai. On 8 April 2001 Boris Zolotarev, a director of the petroleum company, Yukos, was elected Governor of the AOk, receiving 51.8% of the popular vote.

Economy

Despite its size and, indeed, its potential wealth, the Evenk AOk remains an undeveloped and economically insignificant producer. In 1998 7.1% of its working population were occupied in agriculture, producing total output worth 25m. roubles. The Autonomous Okrug's agriculture consists mainly of fishing, hunting, reindeer-breeding and fur farming. The estimated combined hydroelectric potential of the district's two major rivers is 81,300m. kWh. Its main industries otherwise are the production of petroleum, natural gas, graphite and Iceland spar, and food processing. In 1998, however, industry employed just 4.1% of the Okrug's work-force, and generated only 30m. roubles.

Of the economically active population of 9,800, there were 600 registered unemployed in 1998. The average monthly wage in that year was some 1,008.0 roubles. The 1998 budget showed a deficit of 7m. roubles. At 1 January 1999 there were no small businesses registered in the Autonomous Okrug.

Directory

Head of the District Administration: BORIS ZOLOTAREV; Krasnoyarksii krai, Evenkiiskii a/o, 663370 pos. Tura, ul. Sovetskaya 2; tel. (39113) 2-21-35; fax (39113) 2-26-55.

Chairman of the Legislative Assembly (Suglan): ANATOLII YEGOROVICH AMOSOV.

Head of the District Representation in Moscow: GALINA FEDOROVNYA
SEMENOVA; tel. (095) 203-50-41.

Khanty-Mansii Autonomous Okrug

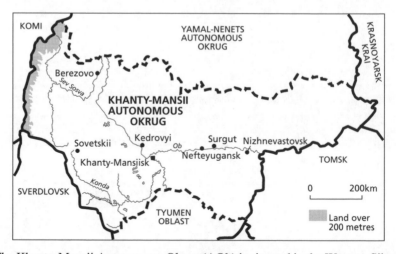

The Khanty-Mansii Autonomous Okrug (AOk) is situated in the Western Siberian Plain and the Ob-Irtysh river basin. The district forms part of the Western Siberian Economic Area and the Siberian Federal Okrug, and lies within the territory of Tyumen Oblast. The other autonomous okrug within Tyumen Oblast, the Yamal-Nenets AOk, lies to the north, while to the south of the district's centre lies the region of Tyumen proper. Komi is to the west and Sverdlovsk to the south-west; to the south-east lies Tomsk and east Krasnoyarsk. Apart from the Ob and the Irtysh, the district's other major rivers are the Konda, the Sosva, the Vakh, the Agan and the Bolshoi Yugan. It has numerous lakes, and much of its territory is Arctic tundra (frozen steppe) and taiga (forested marshland). More than one-third of the territory of the Khanty-Mansii district is forested. It occupies a total of 523,100 sq km (201,970 sq miles) and measures about 900 km (560 miles) from south to north and 1,400 km from east to west. There are nine administrative districts in the Autonomous Okrug and 15 towns. Its estimated total number of inhabitants was 1,383,500 at 1 January 1999, of whom as many as 91.1% lived in urban areas. The population density was 2.6 per sq km. Ethnic Khants and Mansis, collectively known as Ob-Ugrian peoples, are greatly outnumbered by ethnic Russians in the district: the census of 1989 found that some 66.3% of total inhabitants were Russians, 11.6% Ukrainians, 7.6% Tatars, 2.4% Bashirs, 2.2% Belarusians, compared with just 0.9% Khants and 0.5% Mansi. The Khanty and the Mansii languages are grouped together as an Ob-Ugrian sub-division of the Ugrian division of the Finno-Ugrian group. The Autonomous Okrug's administrative centre is at the town of Khanty-Mansiisk, which had an estimated 38,200 inhabitants at 1 January 1999. Other major, and larger, cities in the Okrug are Surgut (278,400), Nizhnevartovsk (238,900) and Nefteyugansk (96,100).

History

The Khanty-Mansii region, known as the Yugra region in the 11th to 15th centuries, came under Russian control in the late 16th and early 17th centuries as Russian

276

fur traders established themselves in western Siberia. Attempts were made to assimilate the Khants and Mansi into Russian culture, and many were forcibly converted to Orthodox Christianity. The territory was created on 10 December 1930, as the East Vogul (Ostyako-Vogulskii) National Autonomous Okrug (adopting its current name in 1940).

From about the time of the Second World War the district became heavily industrialized, causing widespread damage to fish catches and reindeer pastures. Consequently, during the period of *glasnost* (openness) in the late 1980s, many of the indigenous inhabitants of the area began to demand more cautious development policies that would guarantee the survival of their livelihood and cultures. In the mid-1990s the okrug authorities sought to establish local control over natural resources. In 1996 they appealed to the Constitutional Court against Tyumen Oblast's attempt to legislate for district petroleum and natural-gas reserves, and a protracted dispute ensued. As in the neighbouring Yamal-Nenets AOk, the exact nature of the constitutional relationship between Khanty-Mansii and Tyumen Oblast remained obscure. Even the exact geographical delineation of the Okrug remained uncertain in the late 1990s, with disputes over which jurisdiction had the authority to develop oilfields in the regions. This dispute partly reflected the domination of different interest groups in the two administrations—the district authorities favoured the federal Government and the energy industry, while the Communists still had strong support in Tyumen Oblast generally. Aleksandr Filipenko, the moderate head of the district administration, was returned to power in the gubernatorial election held in late 1996. He was re-elected, with 91% of the votes cast, in an election held simultaneously with the federal presidential election of 26 March 2000, in which he was a vocal supporter of Vladimir Putin's candidacy.

Economy

The Autonomous Okrug's economy is based on industry, particularly on petroleum extraction and refining. In the late 1990s it produced around 5% of Russia's entire industrial output and over 50% of its petroleum. Its main industrial centre is at the petroleum-producing town of Surgut. Its major river-port is at Nizhnevartovsk. There are 1,073 km of railway track in the district and 1,458 km of paved roads, many of which were constructed during the 1990s. In September 2000 a long-awaited road bridge across the River Ob was opened.

Agriculture in the Khanty-Mansii AOk, which employed just 1.1% of the work-force in 1998, consists mainly of fishing, reindeer-breeding, fur farming, hunting and vegetable production. Total agricultural output in that year was worth 601m. roubles, while industrial production amounted to a value of some 84,093m. roubles, a larger amount than that generated individually by five of the 11 economic regions in the Russian Federation. Industry, which employed some 20.4% of the work-force in 1998, is based on the processing of agricultural and forestry products, and the extraction of petroleum and natural gas. Khanty-Mansiisk Oil Company (KMOC) was formed in 1997 by the merger of Khanty-Mansiiskneftegazgeologiya (KMNNG)—a petroleum exploration company in possession of oilfields containing up to 3,000m. barrels of petroleum—and UPC (of Delaware, USA). KMOC is one of Russia's largest independent exploration companies. Despite this industrial wealth, unemployment increased rapidly during the second half of the 1990s, reaching a figure of 35,700 in 1998, representing 4.4% of the economically active population of 802,500. It was thought that the high price of petroleum in the late

1990s might help reverse this trend. The average monthly wage in 1998 was some 2,697.7 roubles. The local budget in that year showed a surplus of 209m. roubles. There was considerable foreign investment in the Okrug during the late 1990s, totalling some US $106.61m. in 1998. On 1 January 1999 there were some 7,800 small businesses registered on the territory.

Directory

Governor: ALEKSANDR VASILIYEVICH FILIPENKO; Tyumenskaya obl., Khanty-Mansiiskii a/o, 628001 Khanty-Mansiisk, ul. Mira 5; tel. (34671) 3-31-47; fax (34671) 3-34-60; e-mail kominf@hmansy.wsnet.ru; internet www.hmao.wsnet.ru/index.htm.

Chairman of the District Duma: SERGEI SEMENOVICH SEBYANIN; tel. (34671) 3-06-00; fax (34671) 3-16-84.

Head of the District Representation in Tyumen Oblast: NIKOLAI MIKHAILOVICH DOBRYNIN; 626002 Tyumen, ul. Komsomolskaya 37; tel. (3452) 46-67-79; fax (3452) 46-00-91.

Head of the District Representation in Moscow: VLADIMIR ALEKSEYEVICH KHARITON; 109004 Moscow, ul. Bolshaya Kommunisticheskaya 33/1; tel. (095) 911-04-13; fax (095) 232-34-77.

Head of Khanty-Mansiisk City Administration: VLADIMIR GRIGORIYEVICH YAKOVLEV; Tyumenskaya obl., Khanty-Mansiisk a/o, 626200 Khanty-Mansiisk, ul. Dzerzhinskogo 6; tel. (34671) 3-23-80; fax (34671) 3-21-74.

Komi-Permyak Autonomous Okrug

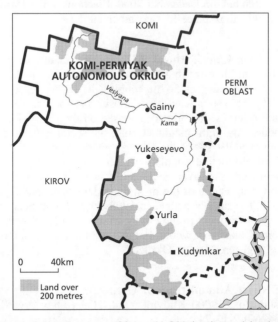

The Komi-Permyak Autonomous Okrug (AOk) is situated in the Urals area on the upper reaches of the Kama river and forms the north-western part of Perm Oblast. The region is part of the Urals Economic Area and the Volga Federal Okrug. The other neighbouring federal territories are Komi to the north and north-west and Kirov to the west. A largely forested territory, it occupies an area of 32,900 sq km (12,700 sq miles) and comprises six administrative districts and one city. The region's population was estimated at 151,400 at 1 January 1999, of whom 28.3% inhabited urban areas, and the population density was 4.6 per sq km. According to the 1989 census, of the district's total population, some 60.2% were Komi Permyak and 36.1% ethnic Russian. The Komi Permyaks speak two dialects of the Finnic division of the Uralo-Altaic linguistic family. The district's administrative centre is at Kudymkar, which had an estimated population of 34,400 at 1 January 1999.

History

The Komi Permyaks became a group distinct from the Komis in around 500, when some Komi (Zyryans) migrated from the upper Kama river region to the Vychegda basin, while the Komi Permyaks remained. The Komi-Permyak AOk was established on 26 February 1925. The area frequently perceived the central authorities to be neglectful of their interests, and the harsh economic conditions of the late 1990s doubtless contributed to the dissatisfaction that had earlier produced a significant level of support for the nationalist Liberal Democratic Party. In May 1996 the Autonomous Okrug's administration signed a treaty with the federal Government on the delimitation of powers between the two bodies. An August presidential decree permitted a gubernatorial election to be held in November; the post was

279

retained by the incumbent, Nikolai Poluyanov. Poluyanov was defeated by the deputy president of the audit chamber of Perm Oblast, Gennadii Savelyev, in the gubernatorial election held in December 2000. Elections to the 15-member regional Legislative Assembly took place in December 2001.

Economy

The agriculture of the Komi Permyak AOk consists mainly of grain production, animal husbandry and hunting. In 1998 it occupied 17.0% of the work-force and produced output to the value of 567m. roubles. Its timber reserves are estimated at 322m. cu m. There are significant peat deposits and approximately 12.1m. metric tons of petroleum reserves. Its industry is based on the processing of forestry and agricultural products and light manufacturing; the sector generated 267m. roubles in 1998 and employed 19.4% of the Okrug's work-force.

Of the economically active population of 50,100 in 1998, 1,900 (3.8%) were registered unemployed. The average monthly wage in that year was just 327.4 roubles, and the Okrug is one of the most underdeveloped and deprived European regions of Russia. The district budget in 1998 showed a surplus of 22m. roubles. Figures on foreign investment in the Okrug were unavailable, being included with those for the Perm Oblast as a whole, but in 1998 there were approximately 2,000 small businesses registered in the Okrug.

Directory

Head of the District Administration: GENNADII SAVELYEV; Permskaya obl., Komi-Permyatskii a/o, 619000 Kudymkar, ul. 50 let Oktyabrya 33; tel. (34260) 2-09-03; fax (34260) 2-12-74.

Chairman of the Legislative Assembly: IVAN VASILIYEVICH CHETIN; tel. (32460) 2-24-70.

Head of the District Representation in Moscow: TAMARA ALEKSANDROVNA SYSTEROVA; tel. (095) 203-94-08.

Head of Kudymkar City Administration: ALEKSANDR ALEKSEYEVICH KLIMO-VICH; Permskaya obl., Komi-Permyatskii a/o, 617240 Kudymkar, ul. M. Gorkogo 3; tel. (34260) 2-00-47.

Koryak Autonomous Okrug

The Koryak Autonomous Okrug (AOk) comprises the northern part of the Kamchatka Peninsula and the adjacent area of mainland. It forms part of the Far Eastern Economic Area, the Far Eastern Federal Okrug, and Kamchatka Oblast. Its eastern coastline lies on the Bering Sea, and its western shores face the Shelekhov Gulf (Sea of Okhotsk). South of the district lies the rest of Kamchatka Oblast. In the north it is bordered by the Chukchi AOk and Magadan Oblast, to the north and to the west, respectively. The Koryak AOk occupies 301,500 sq km (116,410 sq miles) and is divided, for administrative purposes, into four districts and two 'urban-type settlements' (towns). At 1 January 1996 its estimated total population was 30,800 (of whom just 24.7% inhabited urban areas) and its population density, therefore, stood at just 0.1 per sq km. The 1989 census showed that 62.0% of its population were ethnically Russian, 7.2% Ukrainian, 16.4% Koryak, 3.6% Chukchi, 3.0% Itelmeni and 1.8% Eveni. The administrative centre of the district is at Palana settlement, which had an estimated population of just 4,100 on 1 January 1999.

History

The area was established as a territorial unit on 10 December 1930. Like the Chukchis, the Koryaks have always been divided into nomadic and semi-nomadic hunters and more sedentary coastal dwellers. They first encountered ethnic Russians in the 1640s, when Cossacks, commercial traders and fur trappers arrived in the district. The Soviet Government attempted to collectivize the Koryaks' economic activity, beginning with the fishing industry in 1929, and continuing with reindeer hunting in 1932, a measure that was violently opposed by the Koryak community. After the Second World War large numbers of ethnic Russians moved to the area, which was becoming increasingly industrialized. The resultant threat to the Koryaks' traditional way of life, and environmental deterioration, became a source of contention between the local community and the federal Government during the period of *glasnost* (openness) in the late 1980s. In the first years of independence, however, the local élite were sufficiently placated to be generally supportive of both the federal Government and, indeed, of the reformists. An independent candidate, Valentina Bronevich, was elected Governor in late 1996, the first woman to head the administration of a territorial unit in the Russian Federation. On 5 May 1999 Bronevich signed a co-operation agreement with the Governor of Kamchatka Oblast, Vladimir Biryukov. On 3 December 2000 a local businessman, Vladimir Loginov, defeated Bronevich in a single round of voting in the gubernatorial election, receiving 51% of the votes cast.

Economy

Much economic data on the Koryak Autonomous Okrug is incorporated into the figures for Kamchatka Oblast, although certain indicators are available. Fishing is the most important economic activity in the district, contributing 60% of total industrial output.

The Autonomous Okrug's agriculture, which employed 6.8% of the work-force in 1998, consists mainly of reindeer-breeding, fur farming and hunting. Total agricultural output was worth 53m. roubles in that year. The main industries are the production of non-ferrous metals (primarily palladium and platinum), food processing, the production of electrical energy and the extraction of brown coal (lignite). Industry employed 22.3% of the work-force and generated a total of 1,559m. roubles in 1998.

In 1998, of an economically active population of 17,600, around 1,700 (9.7%) were registered unemployed. The average monthly wage in that year was some 1,319.7 roubles. The 1998 budget showed a deficit of 41m. roubles. By 1997 just under two-thirds of enterprises in the Koryak district had been privatized. However, it remained impoverished and dependent on federal subsidies; in December 1998 the Koryak AOk was reckoned to be the second-worst region in the Federation for the late payment of wages (on average, 6.6 months behind). In 1999 it was also named as being among the federal subjects with the highest rate of inflation and the least promising opportunities for investment. None the less, in 1998 the region attracted foreign investment worth US $7.146m., with about 100 small businesses registered on the territory at the start of the following year.

Directory

Governor: VLADIMIR LOGINOV; Kamchatskaya obl., Koryakskii a/o, 688000 pos. Palana, ul. Porotova 22; tel. (41543) 3-13-80; fax (41543) 3-13-70.

Chairman of the District Duma: VLADIMIR NIKOLAYEVICH MIZININ; tel. (41543) 3-10-30.

Head of the District Representation in Moscow: IRINA VLADIMIROVNA YEVDO-KIMOVA (acting); tel. (095) 921-90-96.

Head of Palana Settlement Administration: YURII ALEKSEYEVICH KHNAYEV; tel. (41543) 3-10-22.

Nenets Autonomous Okrug

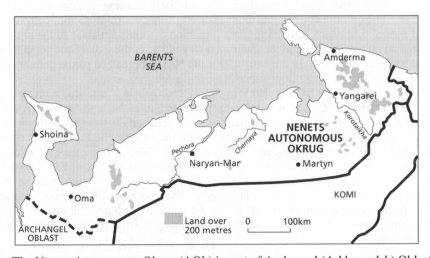

The Nenets Autonomous Okrug (AOk) is part of Archangel (Arkhangelsk) Oblast and, hence, the Northern Economic Area and the North-Western Federal Okrug. It is situated in the north-east of European Russia, its coastline lying, from west to east, on the White, Barents and Kara Seas, parts of the Arctic Ocean. Most of the territory lies within the Arctic Circle. Archangel proper lies to the south-west, but most of the Nenets southern border is with the Republic of Komi. At its eastern extremity the district touches the Yamal-Nenets AOk (part of Tyumen Oblast). The major river is the Pechora, which drains into the Pechora Gulf of the Barents Sea just north of Naryan-Mar. The territory occupies an area of 176,700 sq km (68,200 sq miles) and extends some 300 km (190 miles) from south to north and 1,000 km from west to east. For administrative purposes it is divided into one city and two 'urban-type settlements' (towns). At 1 January 1999 the estimated total population of the Nenets AOk was 45,500 and its population density was 0.3 per sq km. Around 59.5% of the population inhabited urban areas at this time. At 1 January 1997 estimated figures showed some 70.0% of the region's population were ethnic Russian, while 15.6% were Nenets and 9.5% Komi. The language spoken by the Nenets belongs to the Samoyedic group of Uralian languages, which is part of the Uralo-Altaic linguistic group. In 1997 a Norwegian anthropologist claimed to have discovered a forgotten tribe of nomads in the Autonomous Okrug, the Nentser, hitherto unrecognized by the Russian authorities. The Nentser inhabit a vast area south of the Novaya Zemlya islands and comprise around 200 reindeer herders. The district capital is at Naryan-Mar, the only city, which had an estimated population of 18,500 at 1 January 1999.

History

The Nenets were traditionally concerned with herding and breeding reindeer. A Samoyedic people, they are believed to have broken away from other Finno-Ugrian groups in around 3000 BC and migrated east where, in around 200 BC, they began to mix with Turkish-Altaic people. By the early 17th century their territory had

283

come entirely under the control of the Muscovite state. The Russians established forts in the region, from which they collected fur tax.

The Nenets AOk was formed on 15 July 1929. During the Soviet period, collectivization of the Nenets' economic activity, and the exploitation of petroleum and natural gas, which resulted in mass migration of ethnic Russians to the region, posed an increasing threat to the traditional way of life of the indigenous population and to the environment. In the early 1990s the Nenets organized public demonstrations against the federal Government's development projects.

On 11 March 1994 the Russian President, Boris Yeltsin, suspended a resolution by the District Administration ordering a referendum to be held on the territory of the Autonomous Okrug. Participants in the referendum were to vote on the status of the district within the Russian Federation. Despite the President's move, however, the district maintained its style of the 'Nenets Republic'. A district Deputies' Assembly replaced the old legislature and election results in the mid-1990s indicated continued disaffection with federal policies—there was strong support for the party of Vladimir Zhirinovskii. The December 1996 election to head the district administration was won by an independent candidate and businessman, Vladimir Butov, who was re-elected on 14 January 2001, with some 68% of the votes cast.

Economy

As part of Archangel Oblast, the Nenets Okrug is usually subsumed into the region's overall statistics, so few separate details are available. The Autonomous Okrug's major ports are Naryan-Mar and Amderma.

Its agriculture, which employed 12.1% of the work-force in 1998 and produced goods to a value of 71m. roubles in 1998, consists mainly of reindeer-breeding (around two-thirds of its territory is reindeer pasture), fishing, hunting and fur farming. There are substantial reserves of petroleum, natural gas and gas condensate. These have yet to be fully exploited. Exxon Arkhangelsk Ltd, an affiliate of Exxon (of the USA), in 1997 purchased a 50% stake in the development of oilfields in Timan-Pechora, although they were forced to withdraw after problems with tender arrangements. In 1998 Bukov gave support to plans for the construction of a petroleum transportation terminal on the Barents Sea coast, allowing the Okrug to benefit from the potential wealth to be generated by the exploitation of the Timan-Pechora oilfields. These plans met with hostility from various sources, including the former federal Prime Minister, Viktor Chernomyrdin, but more particularly from the administration of the neighbouring Komi Republic, which lies on the route of the existing Kharyaga-Usinsk pipeline. Although Bukov's relations with the major fuel companies Gazprom and LUKoil were reported to be strained during the late 1990s, and petroleum deposits in the region were developed only slowly, a new sea terminal for petroleum transportation was opened at Varandey in August 2000. The annual capacity of this terminal, which was constructed by LUKoil and which was to be served by its fleet of ice-breaking tankers, was over 1m. metric tons, although this was expected to expand. Other sectors of the district's industry included the processing of agricultural products and the generation of electricity. Industry employed 12.5% of the Okrug's work-force in 1998, and produced output worth 1,136m. roubles in that year.

Of an economically active population of 19,800 in 1998, there were some 1,900 registered unemployed, while those in work earned an average monthly wage of

1,184.9 roubles. The Nenets government budget managed to record a small surplus of 17m. roubles. In the late 1990s the Okrug was successful in attracting foreign investment, which totalled US $2.6m. in 1998. In January 1999 there were approximately 100 small businesses registered in the territory.

Directory

Head of the District Administration: VLADIMIR YAKOVLEVICH BUTOV; Arkhangelskaya obl., Nenetskii a/o, 166000 Naryan-Mar, ul. Smidovicha 20; tel. (81853) 4-21-13; fax (81853) 4-22-69.

Chairman of the Deputies' Assembly: VYACHESLAV ALEKSEYEVICH VYUCHEISKII; Arkhangelskaya obl., Nenetskii a/o, 164700 Naryan-Mar, ul. Smidovicha 20; tel. (81853) 2-21-59; fax (095) 253-51-00.

Head of the District Representation in Moscow: TATYANA ALEKSEYEVNA MALYSHEVA; 103025 Moscow, ul. Novii Arbat 19; tel. (095) 203-90-39; fax (095) 203-91-74; e-mail neninter@atnet.ru.

Head of Naryan-Mar City Administration: GRIGORII BORISOVICH KOVALENKO; Arkhangelskaya obl., Nenetskii a/o, 164700 Naryan-Mar, ul. Lenina 12; tel. (81853) 2-21-53; fax (095) 253-51-00.

Taimyr (Dolgan-Nenets) Autonomous Okrug

Taimyr (Dolgan-Nenets) Autonomous Okrug (AOk) is situated on the Taimyr Peninsula, which abuts into the Arctic Ocean, separating the Kara and Laptev Seas. The district comprises the northern end of Krasnoyarsk Krai and, in common with its south-eastern neighbour, the Evenk AOk, forms part of the Eastern Siberian Economic Area and the Siberian Federal Okrug. The Yamal-Nenets AOk, in Tyumen Oblast, lies to the west and the Republic of Sakha (Yakutiya) is located to the south-east. The Taimyr district's major rivers are the Yenisei (which drains into the Kara Sea in the west of the region), the Pyasina and the Khatanga. The district is mountainous in the south and in the extreme north and just under one-half of it is forested. It has numerous lakes, the largest being Lake Taimyr. The territory occupies a total area of 862,100 sq km (332,860 sq miles), which is divided into three administrative districts and one city. There are 262 km (163 miles) of paved roads. The climate in the Autonomous Okrug is severe, with snow for an average of 280 days per year. The Taimyr AOk had an estimated population of 44,300 at 1 January 1999. Its population density, therefore, was 0.05 per sq km, one of the lowest of any federal unit. Some 65.1% of the total population inhabited urban areas at that time. In 1989 some 67.1% of the district's inhabitants had been ethnic Russians, 8.8% Dolgans, 8.6% Ukrainians and 4.4% Nenets. The Autonomous Okrug's administrative centre is at Dudinka, its only city, which had an estimated population of 27,200 in 1999.

History

The territory of the Taimyr district was first exploited by Russian settlers in the 17th century. An autonomous okrug was founded on 10 December 1930, as part of Krasnoyarsk Krai. In 1993, following Russian President Boris Yeltsin's forcible dissolution of the Russian parliament and his advice to the federal units, on 18 October the Taimyr District Soviet voted to disband itself and a District Duma was subsequently elected as the legislature. The administration was generally supportive of the federal regime of Boris Yeltsin, but there was also significant popular support for the nationalist Liberal Democratic Party. Tensions arose between Taimyr and Krasnoyarsk Krai, within which it is contained, in addition to being a federal subject in its own right. In October 1997 then federal President Boris Yeltsin and first deputy premier Boris Nemtsov signed a power-sharing treaty with the leaders of the Taimyr AOk, Krasnoyarsk Krai and the other autonomous okrug within the Krai, the Evenk AOk. The first of its kind, this treaty clearly delineated authority between the national, krai and okrug authorities, and ensured that some of the wealth generated by the local company Norilsk Nickel, the world's largest producer of nickel, went to pay salaries and other benefits within the Okrug. None the less, the attitudes of Taimyr leaders towards the Krai were variable; the Okrug did not participate in elections to the Krai legislature in 1997 or 2000, although it did participate in the gubernatorial election of the Krai in April 1998. The victor in that election, Aleksandr Lebed, unilaterally cancelled the previous power-sharing agreement in October 1999, fuelling suspicions that he wished the Krai to reimpose greater control over the Okrug. At the gubernatorial election held in the AOk on 28 January 2001, Aleskandr Khloponin, hitherto the General Director of Norilsk Nickel, was elected as Governor, with some 63% of the votes cast, defeating the incumbent Governor, Gennadii Nedelin.

Economy

As with most of the national territorial formations (excluding the republics), separate economic data are scarce, the district being part of Krasnoyarsk Krai. The major ports in the Taimyr (Dolgan-Nenets) Autonomous Okrug are Dudinka, Dikson and Khatanga. There is limited transport—only the Dudinka–Norilsk railway line (89 km, or 55 miles, long) operates throughout the year. The district's roads, which total 262 km in length, are concentrated in its more populous areas.

Agricultural production was valued at just 11m. roubles in 1998, mainly provided by fishing, animal husbandry (livestock- and reindeer-breeding) and fur-animal hunting. Agriculture employed just 3.9% of the Okrug's work-force in 1998. There are extensive mineral reserves, however, including those of petroleum and natural gas. The main industries are ore mining (coal, copper and nickel) and food processing. In 1998 industry provided employment to some 23.7% of the work-force and produced an output equivalent to 60m. roubles. Norilsk Nikel accounted for some 20% of the world's, and 80% of Russia's, nickel output in the mid-1990s. The plant also produced 19% of the world's cobalt (70% of Russia's), 42% of the world's platinum (100% of Russia's) and 5% of the world's copper (40%

of Russia's). Its activity, however, caused vast environmental damage to its surroundings, in the form of sulphur pollution.

In 1998, of an economically active population of 20,700 in the region, there were 1,400 registered unemployed. The average monthly wage in the region during that year was some 1,007.5 roubles. The district administrative budget for that year showed a surplus of 10m. roubles.

Directory

Head of the District Administration (Governor): ALEKSANDR GENNADYEVICH KHLOPONIN; Krasnoyarskii krai, Taimyrskii (Dolgano-Nenetskii) a/o, 663210 Dudinka, ul. Sovetskaya 35; tel. (39111) 2-53-74; fax (39111) 2-52-74.

Chairman of the District Duma: VIKTOR VLADIMIROVICH SITNOV; Krasnoyarskii krai, Taimyrskii (Dolgano-Nenetskii) a/o, 663210 Dudinka, ul. Sovetskaya 35; tel. (39111) 2-37-37; fax (39111) 2-12-30.

Head of the District Representation in Moscow: OLEG YEVGENIYEVICH MORGUNOV; tel. (095) 120-45-36.

Head of Dudinka City Administration: SERGEI MATVEYEVICH MOSHKIN; Krasnoyarskii krai, Taimyrskii (Dolgano-Nenetskii) a/o, 663210 Dudinka, ul. Sovetskaya 35; tel. (39111) 2-13-30; fax (39111) 2-55-52.

Ust-Orda Buryat Autonomous Okrug

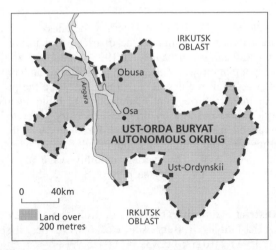

The Ust-Orda Buryat Autonomous Okrug (AOk) is situated in the southern part of the Lena-Angara plateau. The district forms part of Irkutsk Oblast and, hence, the Eastern Siberian Economic Area and the Siberian Federal Okrug. It lies to the north of Irkutsk city, west of Lake Baikal. Its major rivers are the Angara and its tributaries, the Osa, the Ida and the Kuda. Most of its terrain is forest-steppe. It occupies an area of 22,400 sq km (8,650 sq miles) and comprises six administrative districts. At 1 January 1999 the estimated population was 143,200 and the population density stood at 6.4 per sq km. In 1992, the last year for which comprehensive demographic statistics were available, just 18.4% of the population of the Okrug lived in urban areas. According to the 1989 census, some 56.5% of the Okrug's population were ethnic Russians and 36.3% were western or Irkutsk Buryats. The capital is at Ust-Ordynskii settlement, which had a population of under 20,000.

History

The Buryat-Mongol Autonomous Soviet Socialist Republic (BMASSR), created in 1923, was restructured by Stalin (Iosif Dzhugashvili) on 26 September 1937. Anxious to discourage nationalism and links with Mongolia, Stalin had resolved to divide the Buryat peoples administratively. The Ust-Orda Buryat AOk, which represented the four western counties of the BMASSR, was established on the territory of Irkutsk Oblast. The Communists remained the most popular party in the Legislative Assembly (which replaced the District Soviet in 1994), although the federal Government also had important local supporters. In 1996 the federal President, Boris Yeltsin, had signed an agreement with the Okrug's administration on the delimitation of powers between the federal and district authorities. Later that year an independent candidate, Valerii Maleyev, was elected Governor. In October 1999 the Governor of Irkutsk Oblast, Boris Govorin, stated that the Autonomous Okrug (70% of the budget of which consisted of federal transfers) should be re-incorporated into the Oblast proper, as the Oblast provided fuel and other resources to the Okrug and there were concerns that Buryat nationalists might seek to unite the three different nominally Buryat federal subjects. Maleyev was re-elected Governor in November 2000.

Economy

Statistical information for Irkutsk Oblast generally includes data on the autonomous district, so separate figures are limited. The district's agriculture consists mainly of grain production and animal husbandry. In 1998 some 42.2% of the Autonomous Okrug's working population was engaged in agriculture, and production in that year was valued at 1,475m. roubles. Its main industries are the production of coal and gypsum, light manufacturing, the manufacture of building materials and the processing of agricultural and forestry products. Industry generated 170m. roubles in 1998 and employed just 6.6% of the work-force. In 1998 there were around 1,600 registered unemployed among an economically active population of 45,000 in the Ust-Orda Buryat AOk. The average monthly wage in that year was just 284.0 roubles. There was a budgetary surplus of 34m. roubles.

Directory

Head of the District Administration: VALERII GENNADIYEVICH MALEYEV; Irkutskaya obl., Ust-Ordynskii Buryatskii a/o, 666110 pos. Ust-Ordynskii, ul. Lenina 18; tel. (39541) 2-10-62; fax (39541) 2-25-93.

Chairman of the District Duma: LEONID ALEKSANDROVICH KHUTANOV; tel. (39541) 2-20-18.

Head of the District Representation in Moscow: OLEG BORISOVICH BATOROV; tel. (095) 203-64-04.

Head of Ust-Ordynsk City Administration: KARL PROKOPIYEVICH BORISOV; Irkutskaya obl., Ust-Ordynskii Buryatskii a/o, 666110 pos. Ust-Ordynskii, ul. Baltakhinova 19; tel. (39541) 2-10-42.

Yamal-Nenets Autonomous Okrug

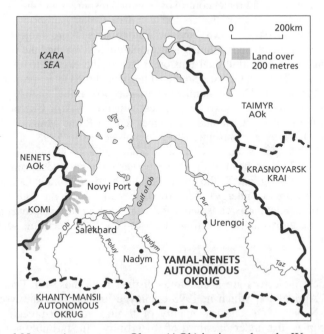

The Yamal-Nenets Autonomous Okrug (AOk) is situated on the Western Siberian Plain on the lower reaches of the Ob river. It forms part of Tyumen Oblast and, therefore, the Western Siberian Economic Area and the Siberian Federal Okrug. The territory lies on the Asian side of the Ural Mountains and has a deeply indented northern coastline, the western section, the Yamal Peninsula, being separated from the eastern section by the Ob bay. The rest of Tyumen Oblast, immediately the Khanty-Mansii Autonomous Okrug, lies to the south. To the west lie the Nenets AOk (part of Archangel Oblast) and the Republic of Komi, to the east Krasnoyarsk Krai (including the Taimyr AOk in the north-west). Apart from the Ob, the Yamal-Nenets district's major rivers are the Nadym, the Taz and the Pur. Around one-10th of its area is forested. The territory of the Yamal-Nenets AOk occupies 750,300 sq km (289,690 sq miles). It comprises seven administrative districts and seven cities. It had an estimated total population (at 1 January 1999) of 506,800 inhabitants, of whom 82.8% inhabited urban areas. The population density of the region was 0.7 per sq km. In the 1989 census, ethnic Russians represented some 59.3% of the population, Ukrainians 17.2% and Tatars 5.3%, while Nenets represented just 4.2%, although the proportion of Nenets was thought to have increased subsequently. The district administrative centre is at Salekhard, which had an estimated population of 32,900 in January 1999. Its other major cities are Noyabrsk (98,500) and Novyi Urengoi (91,800).

History

The Nenets were traditionally a nomadic people, who were totally dominated by Russia from the early 17th century. The Yamal-Nenets AOk was formed on 10

December 1930. Environmental concerns provoked protests in the 1980s and 1990s, and prompted the local authorities (consisting of an administration and, from 1994, an elected Duma) to seek greater control over natural resources and their exploitation. The main dispute was with the central Tyumen Oblast authorities (more pro-Communist than the okrug's own), and the Autonomous Okrug's rejection of oblast legislation on petroleum and natural-gas exploitation first reached the Constitutional Court during 1996. Constitutional tensions between the two Autonomous Okrugs contained within Tyumen Oblast, and the authorities of the Oblast proper, continued throughout the 1990s. The economic importance of the fuel industry in Yamal-Nenets was reflected in the Okrug's political situation. Viktor Chernomyrdin, the leader of Our Home Is Russia and the former federal Prime Minister, was elected to the State Duma as a representative of Yamal-Nenets in 1998, and he retained his seat until his appointment as Russia's ambassador to Ukraine in May 2001. He had previously been head of the domestic gas monopoly, Gazprom, the largest employer in the Okrug, and in the Duma became head of an inter-factionary group of deputies, Energiya (Energy). Moreover, in early 2000 the Governor of the Okrug, Yurii Neyelov, was considered for a directorship at Gazprom; he retained his post in the gubernatorial election of 26 March 2000, securing some 90% of the votes cast.

Economy

Few statistical indicators are available as distinct from those for Tyumen Oblast in general. Agriculture, which in 1998 employed just 1.4% of the work-force in the Yamal-Nenets AOk consists mainly of fishing, reindeer-breeding (reindeer pasture occupies just under one-third of its territory), fur farming and fur-animal hunting. Total agricultural production amounted to a value of just 135m. roubles in 1998. Its main industries are the production of natural gas and petroleum, and the processing of agricultural and forestry products. In 1998 the industrial sector employed 19.2% of the work-force and generated a total of some 35,254m. roubles, a considerably larger amount than that generated by many oblasts or republics in the Russian Federation. The potential wealth of the district generated foreign interest. In January 1997 a loan of US $2,500m. to Gazprom was agreed by the Dresdner Bank group (of Germany), to support construction of the 4,200-km (2,610-mile) Jagal pipeline from the Autonomous Okrug to Frankfurt-an-der-Oder on the German border with Poland. This was to be the world's largest gas-transport project and was expected to be fully operational by 2005.

In 1998, of a 314,400-strong economically active population, there were some 14,200 registered unemployed in the Autonomous Okrug, while the district government budget showed a deficit of 558m. roubles. These statistics, like the high average monthly wage of 3,398.2 roubles in 1998, have far more in common with those of the Khanty-Mansii AOk than those of the Tyumen Oblast as a whole. The Okrug has also been successful in attracting foreign investment, receiving US $28.18m. in 1998. At 1 January 1999 there were 3,000 small businesses registered in the Yamal-Nenets Autonomous Okrug.

Directory

Governor: YURII VASILIYEVICH NEYELOV; Tyumenskaya obl., Yamalo-Nenetskii a/o, 626608 Salekhard, ul. Respubliki 72; tel. (34591) 4-46-02; fax (34591) 4-52-89; internet www.yamal.ru.

Chairman of the Yamal-Nenets Autonomous District Duma: ALEKSEI VLAD-IMIROVICH ARTEEV; tel. and fax (34591) 4-51-51.

Permanent Representative of the President of the Russian Federation: SERGEI IVANOVICH LOMAKHIN; tel. (34591) 4-55-63; fax (34591) 4-55-20.

Head of the District Representation in Moscow: NIKOLAI ARKADIYEVICH BORODULIN; tel. (095) 924-67-89; fax (095) 925-83-38

Head of Salekhard City Administration: ALEKSANDR MIKHAILOVICH SPIRIN; Tyumenskaya obl., Yamalo-Nenetskii a/o, 629000 Salekhard, ul. Respubliki 72; tel. (34591) 4-50-67; fax (34591) 4-01-82; e-mail salekhard@ytc.ru.

KRASNOYARSK KRAI

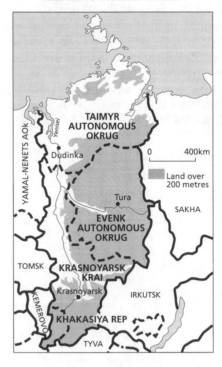

ARCHANGEL OBLAST

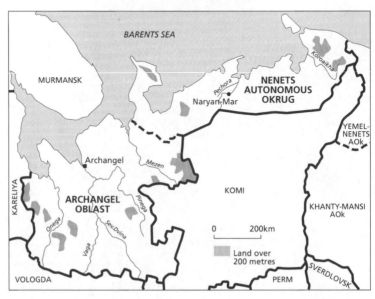

TYUMEN OBLAST

PART THREE
Select Bibliography

Select Bibliography

Alekseev, M. A., (Ed.). *Centre–Periphery Conflict in Post-Soviet Russia: A Federation Imperilled*. Basingstoke, Macmillan, 1999.

Bahry, D. *Outside Moscow: Power, Politics and Budgetary Policy in the Soviet Republics*. New York, NY, Columbia University Press, 1987.

Bassin, M. *Imperial Visions: Nationalist Imagination and Geographical Expansion in the Russian Far East*. Cambridge, Cambridge University Press, 1999.

Baxendale, J., Dewar, S., and Gowan, D. *The EU and Kaliningrad: Kaliningrad and the Impact of EU Enlargement*. London, Kogan Page, 2000.

Blum, D., (Ed.). *Russia's Future: Consolidation of Disintegration*. Oxford, Westview, 1994.

Bradshaw, M. J. *Regional Patterns of Foreign Investment in Russia*. London, Royal Institute of International Affairs, 1995.

The Russian Far East. London, Royal Institute of International Affairs, 1999.

Bradshaw, M. J., (Ed.). *The Soviet Union: A New Regional Geography?* London, Belhaven Press, 1991.

The Russian Far East and Pacific Asia. Richmond, Curzon Press, 2001.

Bukharayev, Ravil. *The Model of Tatarstan: Under Mintimer Shaimiyev*. Richmond, Curzon Press, 2001.

Centre for Co-operation with Non-members. *A Regional Approach to Industrial Restructuring in the Tomsk Region*. Paris, Organisation for Economic Co-operation and Development, 1998.

Chenciner, R., (Ed.). *Daghestan: Tradition and Survival*. London, Caucasus World, 1997.

Colton, T. *Moscow: Governing the Socialist Metropolis*. Cambridge, MA, Harvard University Press, 1995.

Dellenbrant, J. A. *The Soviet Regional Dilemma: Planning, People and Natural Resources*. London, M. E. Sharpe, 1986.

Easter, G. M. *Reconstructing the State: Personal Networks and Elite Identity in Soviet Russia*. Cambridge, Cambridge University Press, 2000.

Forsyth, J. *A History of the Peoples of Siberia*. Cambridge, Cambridge University Press, 1994.

Fowkes, B. *Russia and Chechnia: The Permanent Crisis*. Basingstoke, Macmillan, 1998.

Freinkman, L. *Subnational Budgeting in Russia*. Washington, DC, World Bank, 2000.

Friedgut, T. H., and Hahn, J. W., (Eds). *Local Power and Post-Soviet Politics*. Armonk, NY, M. E. Sharpe, 1995.

Gall, C., and de Waal, T. *Chechnya: Calamity in the Caucasus*. New York, NY, New York University Press, 1998.

Gibson, J., and Hanson, P., (Eds). *Transformation from Below: Local Power and the Political Economy of Post-Communist Transitions*. Cheltenham, Edward Elgar, 1996.

Glatter, P. *Tyumen: The West Siberian Oil and Gas Province*. London, Royal Institute of International Affairs, 1997.

Grant, B., and Pika, A., (Ed.). *Neotraditionalism in the Russian North*. Washington, DC, University of Washington Press, 1999.

Hahn, J., (Ed.). *Democratization in Russia: The Development of Legislative Institutions*. Armonk, NY, M. E. Sharpe, 1996.

    Regional Russia in Transformation. Washington, DC, Woodrow Wilson Center Press, 2001.

Hanson, P. *Regions, Local Power and Economic Change in Russia*. London, Royal Institute of International Affairs, 1994.

Hanson, P., and Bradshaw, M. J., (Eds). *Regional Economic Change in Russia*. Cheltenham, Edward Elgar, 2000.

Hill, F. *Russia's Tinderbox: Conflict in the North Caucasus and its Implications for the Future of the Russian Federation*. Cambridge, MA, Harvard University Press, 1995.

Human Rights Watch. *Russia, the Ingush–Ossetian Conflict in the Prigordnyi Region*. New York, NY, Human Rights Watch, 1996.

Huskey, E. *Presidential Power in Russia*. Armonk, NY, M. E. Sharpe, 1999.

Jacobs, E. M., (Ed.). *Soviet Local Politics and Government*. London, HarperCollins, 1983.

Jaimoukha, A. *The Circassians*. London, Caucasus World, 2001.

Joenniemi, P., and Prawitz, J. *Kaliningrad: The European Amber Region*. Aldershot, Ashgate, 1998.

Kirkow, P. *Russia's Provinces: Authoritarian Transformation versus Local Autonomy*. London, Macmillan, and New York, NY, St Martin's Press, 1998.

Kondrashev, S. *Nationalism and the Drive for Sovereignty in Tatarstan, 1988–92: Origins and Development (Studies in Diplomacy)*. New York, NY, St Martin's Press, 1999.

Koropeckyi, I. S., and Schroeder, G. E., (Eds). *Economics of Soviet Regions*. New York, NY, Praeger, 1981.

Kotkin, S., and Wolff, D., (Eds). *Rediscovering Russia in Asia: Siberia and the Russian Far East*. New York, NY, M. E. Sharpe, 1995.

Lapidus, G. W., (Ed.). *The New Russia: Troubled Transformation*. Boulder, CO, Westview, 1995.

Lavrov, A. M., Makushkin, A. G., *et al. The Fiscal Structure of the Russian Federation: Financial Flows between the Centre and the Regions*. Armonk, NY, M. E. Sharpe, 2001.

Lieven, A. *Chechnya: Tombstone of Russian Power*. New Haven, CT, Yale University Press, 1998.

Lincoln, W. B. *The Conquest of a Continent: Siberia and the Russians*. New York, NY, Random House, 1994.

McAuley, M. *Russia's Politics of Uncertainty*. Cambridge, Cambridge University Press, 1997.

Mandelstam Balzer, M. *The Tenacity of Ethnicity*. Princeton, NJ, Princeton University Press, 1999.

Manezhev, S. A. *Russian Far East*. London, Royal Institute of International Affairs, 1993.

Melvin, N. *Regional Foreign Policies in the Russian Federation*. London, Royal Institute of International Affairs, 1995.

Minakir, P. A., and Freeze, G. L., (Eds). *The Russian Far East: An Economic Handbook*. Armonk, NY, M. E. Sharpe, 1994.

Moses, J. C. *Regional Party Leadership and Policy-Making in the USSR*. London, Praeger, 1974.

Mote, V. L. *Siberia*. Boulder, CO, Westview, 1998.

Murray, W. E., and Bradshaw, M. J. *Rising Tensions in the Natural Resource Market of Pacific Asia and the Role of the Russian Far East*. Birmingham, University of Birmingham, 1997.

Orttung, R. *From Leningrad to St Petersburg: Democratization in a Russian City*. New York, NY, St Martin's Press, 1995.

Orttung, R., (Ed.). *The Republics and Regions of the Russian Federation*. Armonk, NY, M. E. Sharpe, 2000.

Rigby, T. H. *Political Elites in the USSR: Central Leaders and Local Cadres from Lenin to Gorbachev*. Aldershot, Edward Elgar, 1990.

Rorlich, A.-A. *The Volga Tatars: A Profile in National Resilience*. Stanford, CA, Hoover Institution Press, 1986.

Ross, C. *Local Government in the Soviet Union: Problems of Implementation and Control*. London, Croom Helm, 1987.

Ruble, B. *Leningrad: Shaping a City*. Berkeley, CA, University of California Press, 1990.

Rutland, P. *The Politics of Economic Stagnation in the Soviet Union: The Role of Local Party Organs in Economic Management*. Cambridge, Cambridge University Press, 1993.

Scalapino, R. A., and Akaha, T., (Ed.). *Politics and Economics in the Russian Far East*. London, Routledge, 1997.

Schiffer, J. R. *Soviet Regional Economic Policy: The East–West Debate over Pacific Siberian Development*. London, Macmillan, 1989

Seely, R. *The Russo-Chechen Conflict 1800–2000*. London, Frank Cass, 2001.

Segbers, K. *Explaining Post-Soviet Patchworks Vol. 3: The Political Economy of Regions, Regimes and Republics*. Aldershot, Ashgate, 2001.

Smith, G., (Ed.). *The Nationalities Question in the Soviet Union*, 2nd edn. London, Longman, 1996.

Smith, S. *Allah's Mountains: The Battle for Chechnya*. London, I. B. Tauris, 2000.

Stephan, J. J. *The Russian Far East: A History*. Stanford, CA, Stanford University Press, 1996.

Stavrakis, P. J., de Bardeleben, J., and Black, L., (Eds). *Beyond the Monolith: The Emergence of Regionalism in Post-Soviet Russia*. Washington, DC, Woodrow Wilson Press Centre and John Hopkins Press, 1997.

Stoner-Weiss, K. *Local Heroes: The Political Economy of Russian Regional Governance*. Princeton, NJ, Princeton University Press, 1997.

Tichotsky, J. *Russia's Diamond Colony*. Reading, Gordon & Breach, 2000.

Valencia, M. *The Russian Far East in Transition: Opportunities for Regional Economic Co-operation*. Boulder, CO, Westview, 1995.

Wallich, C. I., (Ed.). *Russia and the Challenge of Fiscal Federalism*. Washington, DC, World Bank, 1994.

Wood, A, and French, R. A., (Eds). *The Development of Siberia: People and Resources*. London, Macmillan, 1989.

Zelkina, A. *The Chechens*. London, Caucasus World, 2001.

PART FOUR
Indexes

Alphabetic List of Territories

(including a gazetteer of alternative names)

	Adygeya	*see Krasnodar*
	Aga-Buryat AOk	*see Chita*
	Alaniya	*see North Osetiya*
115	Altai	Krai
46	Altai (Republic)	Autonomous Republic
134	Amur	Oblast
137	Archangel	Oblast
283	Nenets AOk (Nenets Republic)	Autonomous Okrug
140	Astrakhan	Oblast
	Balkariya	*see Kabardino-Balkariya*
	Bashkiriya	*see Bashkortostan*
49	Bashkortostan	Autonomous Republic
143	Belgorod	Oblast
	Birobidzhan	*see Khabarovsk (Jewish AO)*
145	Bryansk	Oblast
53	Buryatiya	Autonomous Republic
	Chechen Republic	*see Chechen Republic of Ichkeriya (Chechnya)*
	Chechen-Ingush ASSR	*see Chechen Republic of Ichkeriya (Chechnya) or Ingushetiya*
56	Chechnya (Chechen Republic of Ichkeriya)	Autonomous Republic
147	Chelyabinsk	Oblast
	Cherkessiya	*see Stavropol (Karachayevo-Cherkessiya)*
150	Chita	Oblast
268	Aga-Buryat AOk	Autonomous Okrug
	Chkalov	*see Orenburg*
270	Chukchi AOk	Autonomous Okrug
	Chukot (Chukotka) AOk	*see Chukchi*
61	Chuvash Republic (Chuvashiya)	Autonomous Republic
	Circassia (Cherkessiya)	*see Stavropol (Karachayevo-Cherkessiya)*
64	Dagestan	Autonomous Republic
	Dolgan-Nenets AOk	*see Krasnoyarsk (Taimyr AOk)*
	East Vogul AOk	*see Tyumen (Khanty-Mansii AOk)*
	Evenk AOk	*see Krasnoyarsk*
	Far Eastern Republic	*see Chita Oblast, etc.*
	Gorkii	*see Nizhnii Novgorod*
	Gorno-Altai AO	*see Altai (Altai—Republic)*
	Gorskaya People's Republic	*see Kabardino-Balkariya, etc.*
	Ichkeriya	*see Chechnya*
	Ingodinskoye Zirnove	*see Chita*
68	Ingushetiya	Autonomous Republic
153	Irkutsk	Oblast
289	Ust-Orda Buryat AOk	Autonomous Okrug
156	Ivanovo	Oblast
266	Jewish AO (Birobidzhan)	Autonomous Oblast
72	Kabardino-Balkar (Kabardino-Balkariya)	Autonomous Republic
	Kabardiya	*see Kabardino-Balkariya*
	Kalinin	*see Tver*
158	Kaliningrad	Oblast
75	Kalmykiya	Autonomous Republic
161	Kaluga	Oblast
163	Kamchatka	Oblast
281	Koryak AOk	Autonomous Okrug
	Karachayevo-Cherkessiya	*see Stavropol*

Federal Okrugs

Economic Areas